Middle School 2-1
중간고사 완벽대비

적중100

영어 기출 문제집

중2

능률 | 양현권

Best Collection

구성과 특징

교과서의 주요 학습 내용을 중심으로 학습 영역별 특성에 맞춰 단계별로 다양한 학습 기회를 제공하여 단원별 학습능력 평가는 물론 중간 및 기말고사 시험 등에 완벽하게 대비할 수 있도록 내용을 구성

Words & Expressions

Step1
Key Words 단원별 핵심 단어 설명 및 풀이
Key Expression 단원별 핵심 숙어 및 관용어 설명
Word Power 반대 또는 비슷한 뜻 단어 배우기
English Dictionary 영어로 배우는 영어 단어

Step2 실력평가 단원별 수시평가 대비 주관식, 객관식 문제풀이

Step3 서술형 대비 학업성취도 및 수행능력평가 대비 서술형 문제풀이

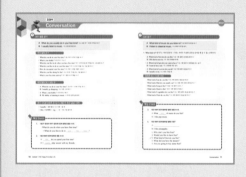

Conversation

Step1
핵심 의사소통 의사소통에 필요한 주요 표현 방법 요약
핵심 Check 기본적인 표현 방법 및 활용능력 확인

Step2 대화문 익히기 상황에 따른 대화문 활용 및 연습

Step3 기본평가 시험대비 기초 학습 능력 평가

Step4 실력평가 단원별 수시평가 대비 주관식, 객관식 문제풀이

Step5 서술형 대비 학업성취도 및 수행능력평가 대비 서술형 문제풀이

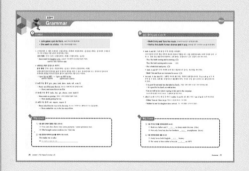

Grammar

Step1
주요 문법 단원별 주요 문법 사항과 예문을 알기 쉽게 설명
핵심 Check 기본 문법사항에 대한 이해 여부 확인

Step2 기본평가 시험대비 기초 학습 능력 평가

Step3 실력평가 단원별 수시평가 대비 주관식, 객관식 문제풀이

Step4 서술형 대비 학업성취도 및 수행능력평가 대비 서술형 문제풀이

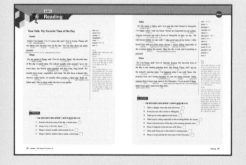

Reading

Step1
구문 분석 단원별로 제시된 문장에 대한 구문별 분석과 내용 설명
확인문제 문장에 대한 기본적인 이해와 인지능력 확인

Step2 확인학습A 빈칸 채우기를 통한 문장 완성 능력 확인

Step3 확인학습B 제시된 우리말을 영어로 완성하여 작문 능력 키우기

Step4 실력평가 단원별 수시평가 대비 주관식, 객관식 문제풀이

Step5 서술형 대비 학업성취도 및 수행능력평가 대비 서술형 문제풀이
교과서 구석구석 교과서에 나오는 기타 문장까지 완벽 학습

Composition

|영역별 핵심문제|

단어 및 어휘, 대화문, 문법, 독해 등 각 영역별 기출문제의 출제 유형을 분석하여 실전에 대비하고 연습할 수 있도록 문제를 배열

|서술형 실전 및 창의사고력 문제|

학교 시험에서 점차 늘어나는 서술형 시험에 집중 대비하고 고득점을 취득하는데 만전을 기하기 위한 학습 코너

|단원별 예상문제|

기출문제를 분석한 후 새로운 시험 출제 경향을 더하여 새롭게 출제될 수 있는 문제를 포함하여 시험에 완벽하게 대비할 수 있도록 준비

|단원별 모의고사|

영역별, 단계별 학습을 모두 마친 후 실전 연습을 위한 모의고사

on the textbook .... 교과서 파헤치기

- **단어Test1~2** 영어 단어 우리말 쓰기와 우리말을 영어 단어로 쓰기
- **대화문Test1~2** 대화문 빈칸 완성 및 전체 대화문 쓰기
- **본문Test1~5** 빈칸 완성, 우리말 쓰기, 문장 배열연습, 영어 작문하기 복습 등 단계별 반복 학습을 통해 교과서 지문에 대한 완벽한 습득
- **구석구석지문Test1~2** 지문 빈칸 완성 및 전문 영어로 쓰기

이책의 차례

Contents

Lesson **1** **What Is Your Color?** 05~56

Lesson **2** **Old Things, New Art** 57~108

Lesson **3** **Go, Team!** 109~160

〈Insight on the textbook〉 교과서 파헤치기 01~58

〈책 속의 책〉 정답 및 해설 01~40

Lesson 1

What Is Your Color?

🎤 의사소통 기능

- 진술하기
  They say that a Hamlet-type person is thoughtful.

- 선호에 대해 묻기
  Which season do you prefer?

🎤 언어 형식

- which로 시작하는 의문문
  Which activities do you enjoy?

- 재귀대명사
  Do you know **yourself**?

교과서
Words & Expressions

Key Words

- **active** [ǽktiv] 형 활기 있는
- **activity** [æktívəti] 명 활동
- **artist** [ɑ́:rtist] 명 예술가, 미술가
- **as** [əz] 전 ~으로, ~로서
- **careful** [kέərfəl] 형 신중한
- **caring** [kέəriŋ] 형 배려하는, 보살피는
- **chance** [tʃæns] 명 가능성, 기회
- **circle** [sə́:rkl] 동 동그라미 표시를 하다
- **cool** [ku:l] 형 멋진, 시원한
- **curious** [kjúəriəs] 형 호기심 많은
- **direction** [dirékʃən] 명 (복수형으로 사용되는 경우) 지시, 명령
- **energetic** [ènərdʒétik] 형 활동적인
- **energize** [énərdʒàiz] 동 활기를 북돋우다
- **energizer** [énərdʒàizər] 명 활력을 주는 사람
- **engineer** [èndʒiníər] 명 기술자
- **expect** [ikspékt] 동 기대하다
- **faithful** [féiθfəl] 형 충직한, 충성스러운, 신의가 있는
- **find** [faind] 동 찾다
- **flavor** [fléivər] 명 맛
- **follow** [fálou] 동 따르다
- **friendly** [fréndli] 형 친근한
- **honest** [ánist] 형 정직한
- **imaginative** [imǽdʒənətiv] 형 창의적인, 상상력이 풍부한
- **inventor** [invéntər] 명 발명가
- **line** [lain] 명 행, 선
- **lively** [láivli] 형 생기 넘치는
- **make** [meik] (발달 · 성장해서) ~이 되다
- **open** [óupən] 형 개방적인, 솔직한, 문을 연, 영업을 하는
- **organize** [ɔ́:rɡənàiz] 동 조직하다, 정리 정돈하다

- **pattern** [pǽtərn] 명 패턴, 정형화된 양식
- **personality** [pə̀:rsənǽləti] 명 성격, 개성
- **playful** [pléifl] 형 장난기 많은
- **please** [pli:z] 동 기쁘게 하다
- **position** [pəzíʃən] 명 위치, 자리, 자세
- **prefer** [prifə́:r] 동 선호하다
- **quiet** [kwáiət] 형 조용한
- **result** [rizʌ́lt] 명 결과
- **scientist** [sáiəntist] 명 과학자
- **season** [sí:zn] 명 계절
- **serve** [sə:rv] 동 제공하다
- **setting** [sétiŋ] 명 환경, 장소, 배경, 상황
- **side** [said] 명 옆(면), 측면
- **snack** [snæk] 명 간식
- **solve** [sɑlv] 동 해결하다
- **sound** [saund] 동 ~처럼 들리다[생각되다]
- **stage** [steidʒ] 명 무대
- **step** [step] 명 걸음, 단계, 조치
- **stomach** [stʌ́mək] 명 위(장)
- **talkative** [tɔ́:kətiv] 형 수다스러운
- **thoughtful** [θɔ́:tfəl] 형 생각이 깊은
- **tradition** [trədíʃən] 명 전통
- **type** [taip] 명 유형
- **unhealthy** [ənhélθi] 형 건강하지 못한
- **unique** [ju:ní:k] 형 독특한, 하나뿐인
- **warm** [wɔ:rm] 형 따뜻한
- **with** [wið] 전 ~을 가지고
- **witty** [wíti] 형 재치 있는
- **worst** [wə:rst] 형 가장 나쁜
- **yummy** [jʌ́mi] 형 맛있는

Key Expressions

- **ask ~ for advice** ~에게 조언[충고]을 구하다
- **be going to** 동사원형 ~할 것이다
- **be good at** ~을 잘하다
- **How did you like ~?** ~이 어땠어?
- **look at** ~을 보다
- **make the most of ~** ~을 최대한 이용하다
- **on one's own** 혼자서, 단독으로

- **plan ~ out** ~을 생각해 내다, 안을 세우다, ~을 기획하다
- **They[People] say that** 주어 동사 ~. (그들이/사람들이) ~라고 말한다.
- **What is ~ like?** ~는 어때?
- **what kind of ~** 어떤 종류의 ~
- **Why don't we ~?** ~하는 게 어때?
- **would like to** 동사원형 ~하고 싶다

Word Power

※ 서로 비슷한 뜻을 가진 단어

□ **active**(활기 있는) : **energetic**(활동적인)

□ **faithful**(충직한, 충성스러운, 신의가 있는) : **loyal**(충성스러운)

□ **find**(찾다) : **discover** (발견하다)

□ **personality**(성격, 개성) : **character**(성격, 기질)

□ **result**(결과) : **outcome**(결과), **consequence**(결과)

□ **cool**(멋진) : **good**(훌륭한), **fashionable**(멋있는)

□ **flavor**(맛) : **taste**(맛)

□ **please**(기쁘게 하다) : **delight**(아주 즐겁게 하다)

□ **tradition**(전통) : **custom**(관습, 풍습)

□ **yummy**(맛있는) : **tasty**(맛있는), **delicious**(맛있는)

※ 성격과 관련된 단어

□ **active**: 활기 있는
□ **honest**: 정직한
□ **open**: 개방적인

□ **energetic**: 활동적인
□ **quiet**: 조용한
□ **playful**: 장난기 많은

□ **faithful**: 신의가 있는
□ **talkative**: 수다스러운
□ **careful**: 신중한

□ **friendly**: 친근한
□ **thoughtful**: 생각이 깊은
□ **warm**: 따뜻한

English Dictionary

□ **activity** 활동
→ things that people do; something that you do because you enjoy it
사람들이 하는 것; 당신이 즐기기 때문에 하는 어떤 것

□ **caring** 배려하는, 보살피는
→ kind, helpful, and sympathetic towards other people
다른 사람들에게 친절하고, 도움을 주고, 공감을 나타내는

□ **chance** 기회
→ the possibility that something will happen, especially something you want
특별히 당신이 원하는 무엇인가가 발생할 수 있는 가능성

□ **circle** 동그라미 표시를 하다
→ to draw a circle around something
무엇인가의 주위에 원을 그리다

□ **engineer** 기술자
→ someone whose job is to design, build, or repair machines, roads, bridges, etc.
직업이 기계, 도로, 다리 등을 설계하거나 만들거나 고치는 사람

□ **faithful** 충직한, 충성스러운, 신의가 있는
→ continuing to support someone or be their friend, even in a difficult situation
어려운 상황에 있을 때조차 계속해서 누군가를 지지하거나 친구가 되는

□ **follow** 따르다
→ to do what someone has advised you to do
누군가가 당신에게 조언해 준 것을 하다

□ **lively** 생기 넘치는
→ full of life and spirit
생기와 활기로 가득한

□ **organize** 조직하다, 정리 정돈하다
→ to prepare or arrange an activity or event
어떤 활동이나 행사를 준비하거나 정리하다

□ **pattern** 패턴, 정형화된 양식
→ a set of lines, shapes, or colors that are repeated regularly
규칙적으로 반복되는 일련의 선, 모양, 색깔

□ **personality** 성격, 개성
→ someone's character, especially the way they behave towards other people
어떤 사람의 특성, 특히 다른 사람들을 대할 때 그들이 행동하는 방식

□ **please** 기쁘게 하다
→ to make someone feel happy and satisfied
어떤 사람을 행복하고 만족스럽게 만들다

□ **position** 자세
→ a way in which something or somebody is placed
사람이나 사물이 놓여 있는 방식

□ **prefer** 선호하다
→ to like someone or something more than another person or thing
어떤 사람이나 물건을 다른 사람이나 물건보다 더 좋아하다

□ **solve** 해결하다
→ to find a solution to something that is causing difficulties
어려움을 야기하는 것에 대한 해결책을 찾다

□ **stage** 무대
→ the part of a theater where the actors or musicians perform
극장의 배우나 음악가가 공연하는 부분

□ **stomach** 위(장)
→ a baglike organ in the body where food is broken down for use in the body after being eaten
음식이 섭취된 후 몸에서 사용되기 위해 분해되는 몸 안의 주머니 같은 기관

□ **tradition** 전통
→ a very old custom or belief
매우 오래된 관습이나 믿음

□ **type** 유형
→ a group of people or things with similar characteristics that make them different from others
그들을 다른 것들과 차이 나게 하는 비슷한 특징을 가진 한 그룹의 사람들이나 물건들

01 다음 중 성격이 다른 하나를 고르시오.

① talkative ② open
③ warm ④ yummy
⑤ witty

[02~03] 다음 빈칸에 들어갈 말로 적절한 것은?

02
• Take this _____ an example.
• I think of her _____ my best friend.

① as ② with
③ for ④ in
⑤ to

03 중요
• Does our team have a _____ of winning?
• This is your big _____.

① choice ② change
③ chance ④ condition
⑤ character

서답형
04 다음 주어진 우리말에 맞게 빈칸을 채우시오.

(1) 아이들은 동물에 대해 호기심이 많다.
➡ Children are _____ about animals.
(2) 너무 많은 것을 기대하지 마세요.
➡ Don't _____ too much.
(3) 당신은 몇 가지 지침을 따라야 합니다.
➡ You must _____ a few guidelines.
(4) 너는 그 자세로 자면 안 된다.
➡ You shouldn't sleep in that _____.

05 중요 다음 대화의 빈칸에 들어갈 말을 고르시오.

A: Which _____ do you prefer?
B: I like summer most.

① vacation ② year
③ weather ④ setting
⑤ season

[06~07] 다음 영영 풀이에 해당하는 단어를 고르시오.

06
to make someone feel happy and satisfied

① thank ② enjoy
③ accept ④ like
⑤ please

07
to find a solution to something that is causing difficulties

① save ② solve
③ spend ④ reduce
⑤ decide

[08~09] 다음 밑줄 친 부분과 의미가 가장 가까운 것을 고르시오.

08
The ice cream has an orange flavor.

① ingredient ② recipe
③ taste ④ look
⑤ shape

09 중요
You always said she was witty.

① caring ② thoughtful
③ warm ④ funny
⑤ unique

[01~02] 빈칸에 공통으로 들어갈 단어를 주어진 철자로 시작하여 쓰시오.

01
- Rome is the perfect s_____ for romance.
- The s_____ of his first novel was London.

02
- How did you l_____ the movie?
- I would l_____ to ask you a few questions.

03 주어진 단어를 이용해 빈칸을 완성하시오.

(1) She's a _____ friend. (faith)
(2) My uncle is an _____. (energize)
(3) You must be _____ to draw a nice picture. (imagine)

04 다음 빈칸에 알맞은 단어를 〈보기〉에서 골라 쓰시오. (형태 변화 가능)

┌─── 보기 ───┐
organize   prefer   sound   serve
└────────────┘

(1) I _____ reading books to playing computer games.
(2) What style of food does the restaurant _____?
(3) That story _____ true.
(4) Jack is going to _____ the party.

05 밑줄 친 부분과 의미가 가장 가까운 단어를 주어진 철자로 시작하여 쓰시오.

(1) <u>Cool</u> sunglasses, Jack!
  ➡ F_____
(2) He has a very outgoing <u>personality</u>.
  ➡ c_____

06 다음 우리말에 맞게 주어진 단어를 바르게 배열하시오.

(1) 각각의 사람의 지문은 하나뿐이다.
  (person's, unique, fingerprints, are, each)
  ➡ _____

(2) 우리는 이 동물이 매우 충직하다는 것을 알고 있다.
  (that, know, faithful, animal, we, this, is, very)
  ➡ _____

(3) 얼마나 많은 선이 책상 위에 있니?
  (are, lines, there, the table, many, how, on)
  ➡ _____

(4) 이 나라는 나이든 사람들을 존경하는 오래된 전통을 가지고 있다.
  (respecting, country, tradition, people, of, a, old, has, this, long)
  ➡ _____
  _____

(5) 너는 초콜릿 케이크를 혼자서 만들 수 있니?
  (chocolate, can, own, on, make, the, you, cake, your)
  ➡ _____
  _____

① 진술하기

> They say that a Hamlet-type person is thoughtful.
> 햄릿 유형의 사람은 생각이 깊다고들 말한다.

- 'People[They] say that ~.'은 제3자에게서 얻은 정보를 전달할 때 사용할 수 있는 표현이다. 전달자에 따라 people을 he, someone, my friend 등으로 바꿔 말할 수 있다. 여기서 that은 생략될 수 있다.
- that절을 목적어로 취할 경우 'It + be 동사 + p.p. + that ~.' 형태의 수동태가 가능하기 때문에 'People[They] say that ~.'과 'It is said that ~.'은 뜻이 비슷하다. 또한 'It is reported that ~.', 'It is believed that ~.' 등도 정보를 전달할 때 사용된다. 이때 전달되는 정보는 'that ~'에 제시된다.

진술하기

- They say (that) 주어 동사 ~.
- It is said that 주어 동사 ~.
- It is reported that 주어 동사 ~.
- It is believed that 주어 동사 ~.

핵심 Check

1. 다음 주어진 문장과 같은 의미가 되도록 빈칸을 채우시오.

   They say that he is honest.
   ➡ It is said _____.

2. 다음 우리말과 일치하도록 빈칸에 알맞은 말을 쓰시오.

   A: _____ _____ _____ a brand-new computer _____ very expensive.
   (그가 새로 나온 컴퓨터가 매우 비싸다고 그러네.)

   B: Really? How much is it?

3. 다음 문장과 같은 의미가 되도록 주어진 단어를 이용해 쓰시오.

   They say that we can't take pictures here.
   ➡ _____ (said)

② 선호에 대해 묻기

Which season do you prefer? 넌 어느 계절을 선호하니?

- 'Which ~ do you prefer?'는 주어진 대상 가운데 어느 것을 더 좋아하는지를 묻는 표현이다. prefer는 like better[more]로 바꿀 수 있으므로 'Which do you like better[more], A or B?'라고도 할 수 있다. which는 뒤에 명사를 수식하는 의문형용사로도 쓰일 수 있다.

- 더 좋아하는 것에 대해 말할 때는 'I like A better[more] than B.' 또는 'I prefer A to B.'로 표현한다. 이때 비교 대상이 되는 than B나 to B는 생략할 수 있다. prefer A to B에서 to는 전치사이므로 뒤에 명사나 동명사가 오는 것에 유의해야 한다.

  A Which color do you prefer, red or blue?
  B I prefer red (to blue). / I love[like] red more than blue.

선호 묻기

- Which (명사) do you prefer?
- Which (명사) do you prefer, A or B?
- Which do you like better[more], A or B?

선호 대답하기

- I prefer A (to B).   · I like A better[more] than B.

핵심 Check

4. 다음 우리말과 일치하도록 빈칸에 알맞은 말을 쓰시오. (철자가 주어진 것도 있음)

A: _____ do you prefer, comedies or tragedies? (너는 어느 것을 좋아하니, 희극 아니면 비극?)

B: _____ _____ _____ . (나는 희극을 더 좋아해.)

A: Which do you _____ b_____, meat or fish? (너는 고기와 생선 중에 어느 것을 더 좋아하니?)

B: I prefer meat _____ fish. (나는 생선보다 고기를 더 좋아해.)

5. 우리말과 일치하도록 주어진 단어를 배열하여 쓰시오.

A: _____ (너는 야구와 테니스 중에 어느 것을 더 좋아하니?)
   (tennis, prefer, you, which, baseball, do, or)

B: _____ (나는 테니스보다 야구가 더 좋아.)
   (prefer, tennis, I, to, baseball)

A. Listen & Speak ① A-1

G: I'm hungry.
B: ❶Me, too. ❷Why don't we go to Sweet Snack?
G: That's a good idea. But is it ❸open today?
B: Yes, it is. They say that ❹it ❺serves special pancakes ❻on Sunday.

G: 나 배고파.
B: 나도 그래. 우리 Sweet Snack에 가는 게 어때?
G: 그거 좋은 생각이야. 그런데 그곳이 오늘 문을 열었니?
B: 응, 열었어. 일요일에는 특별 팬케이크를 제공한다고 그러네.

❶ Me, too. = So am I.
❷ 상대방에게 제안이나 권유할 때에는 'Why don't we ~?'를 사용할 수 있다.
❸ open: 문을 연, 영업을 하는
❹ it = Sweet Snack
❺ serve: 제공하다
❻ 요일 앞에는 전치사 on을 사용한다.

Check(√) True or False

(1) Sweet Snack is open on Sunday.   T ☐ F ☐

(2) Not the girl but the boy is hungry.   T ☐ F ☐

(3) It is said that Sweet Snack serves special pancakes on Sunday.   T ☐ F ☐

B. Listen & Speak ② A-1

G: ❶Look at the cakes!
B: ❷They look yummy.
G: ❸Which cake do you like most?
B: ❹I like the chocolate cake most.

G: 저 케이크들을 봐!
B: 맛있어 보여.
G: 넌 어떤 케이크를 가장 좋아하니?
B: 난 초콜릿 케이크를 가장 좋아해.

❶ look at: ~을 보다
❷ They는 The cakes를 받는 대명사이다. look+형용사: ~하게 보이다 yummy: 맛있는 (= delicious)
❸ 'Which ~ do you like most?(너는 어떤 ~를 가장 좋아하니?)'는 상대방이 가장 좋아하는 것을 묻는 표현으로 'What's your favorite ~?'로 질문할 수도 있다.
❹ 'I like ~ most.(나는 ~를 가장 좋아해.)'의 의미로 가장 좋아하는 것을 묻는 말에 대한 대답이다.

Check(√) True or False

(4) They are looking at the cakes.   T ☐ F ☐

(5) The girl's favorite cake is the chocolate cake.   T ☐ F ☐

(6) The boy likes the chocolate cake most.   T ☐ F ☐

Listen & Speak ① A-2

G: ❶Are there any good programs this weekend?

B: Well, ❷they say that there's a special dance show at the Youth Center on Saturday.

G: ❸What kind of dance show is it?

B: It's an Indian dance show. ❹People say that it's really exciting.

❶ Are there ~?: ~가 있니? this weekend: 이번 주말에
❷ 'They say that ~.'은 제3자에게서 얻은 정보를 전달할 때 사용할 수 있는 표현이다. 여기서 that은 생략이 가능하다. 'There is ~'는 '~이 있다.'라는 뜻이다.
❸ What kind of ~: 어떤 종류의 ~
❹ People say that it's really exciting: 정말 흥미롭다고 그러네. (= It is said that it's really exciting.) that절에 있는 it은 an Indian dance show를 받는 대명사이다.

Listen & Speak ② A-2

B: Are they new ice cream ❶flavors?

G: Yes, they are. They ❷look delicious.

B: ❸Which flavor do you prefer?

G: I ❹prefer the strawberry flavor.

❶ flavor: 맛
❷ look+형용사: ~하게 보이다 '보이다(look), 들리다(sound), 느껴지다(feel), 맛이 나다(taste)'와 같이 감각을 나타내는 동사들을 감각동사라고 하는데, 이러한 감각동사들 뒤에는 보어로 부사가 아닌 형용사를 써야 한다.
❸ 'Which ~ do you prefer?(넌 어떤 ~을 선호하니?)'는 주어진 대상 가운데 어떤 것을 더 좋아하는지를 묻는 표현이다.
❹ prefer: 선호하다

Listen & Speak ① B-1

A: What was the ❶result?

B: I got Hamlet.

A: ❷What is a Hamlet-type person like?

B: They say that a Hamlet-type person is ❸thoughtful.

❶ result: 결과
❷ What is ~ like?: ~는 어때? 'What+주어+be동사+like?'는 모습이나 상태를 설명할 때 쓰인다.
❸ thoughtful: 생각이 깊은

Listen & Speak ② B-1

A: ❶Which season do you prefer?

B: ❷I prefer summer. What are summer people like?

A: They say that summer people are ❸quiet and thoughtful. Are you?

B: Yes, I am.

❶ Which season do you prefer?: 넌 어떤 계절을 선호하니? 계절에 대한 선호도를 묻는 표현이다.
❷ prefer: 선호하다 I prefer summer. (= My favorite season is summer. = I like summer most.)
❸ quiet: 조용한

Communication

Nara: ❶How did you like the test?

Seho: It was really fun. I learned a lot about ❷myself.

Nara: What ❸type of person are you?

Seho: I'm a da-Vinci-type person.

Nara: That sounds cool. What ❹are da-Vinci people good at?

Seho: They say that da-Vinci people ❺make good inventors and artists.

Nara: Which one do you prefer?

Seho: I'm not sure. ❻I'm going to ask my teacher for some advice.

❶ 'How did you like ~?'는 '~이 어땠어?'라는 의미로 어떤 것에 대한 상대방의 생각을 묻는 표현이다. 비슷한 표현으로 'How did you feel about ~?', 'How was ~?'가 있다
❷ 전치사(about)의 목적어가 주어와 동일인이므로 재귀대명사를 사용한다.
❸ type: 유형
❹ be good at: ~을 잘하다
❺ make: [사람이] (발달 · 성장해서) ~이 되다(= become), inventor: 발명가 artist: 예술가, 미술가
❻ be going to 동사원형: ~할 것이다, ask ~ for advice: ~에게 조언[충고]을 구하다

다음 우리말과 일치하도록 빈칸에 알맞은 말을 쓰시오.

Listen & Speak 1 A

1. G: _____ hungry.
   B: Me, _____. Why _____ _____ _____ to Sweet Snack?
   G: That's a good idea. But is it _____ today?
   B: Yes, it is. They _____ _____ it _____ special pancakes _____ Sunday.

2. G: _____ _____ any good programs _____ weekend?
   B: Well, they _____ _____ _____ a special dance show at the Youth Center on Saturday.
   G: _____ _____ _____ dance show is it?
   B: It's an Indian dance show. People _____ _____ _____ _____ _____.

Listen & Speak 1 B

1. A: What was _____ _____?
   B: I _____ Hamlet.
   A: What is a Hamlet-type person _____?
   B: They _____ that a Hamlet-type person _____ _____.

2. A: _____ was the _____?
   B: _____ _____ da Vinci.
   A: _____ is a da-Vinci-type person like?
   B: _____ _____ _____ a da-Vinci-type person is _____.

Listen & Talk 2 A

1. G: Look _____ the cakes!
   B: They look yummy.
   G: _____ cake _____ _____ _____ most?
   B: I like the chocolate cake _____.

2. B: _____ they new ice cream _____?
   G: Yes, they are. _____ _____ delicious.
   B: _____ flavor do you prefer?
   G: I _____ the strawberry flavor.

해석

1. G: 나 배고파.
   B: 나도 그래. 우리 Sweet Snack에 가는 게 어때?
   G: 그거 좋은 생각이야. 그런데 그곳이 오늘 문을 열었니?
   B: 응, 열었어. 일요일에는 특별 팬케이크를 제공한다고 그러네.

2. G: 이번 주말에 무슨 좋은 프로그램이 있니?
   B: 음, 토요일에 청소년 센터에서 특별 댄스 공연이 있다고 그러네.
   G: 어떤 종류의 댄스 공연이야?
   B: 인도의 댄스 공연이야. 정말 흥미롭다고 그러네.

1. A: (성격 검사) 결과가 뭐야?
   B: (내가 받은 결과는) 햄릿이야.
   A: 햄릿 유형의 사람은 어때?
   B: 햄릿 유형의 사람은 생각이 깊다고 그러네.

2. A: 결과가 뭐야?
   B: 다빈치야.
   A: 다빈치 유형의 사람은 어때?
   B: 다빈치 유형의 사람은 상상력이 풍부하다고 그러네.

1. G: 저 케이크들을 봐!
   B: 맛있어 보여.
   G: 넌 어떤 케이크를 가장 좋아하니?
   B: 난 초콜릿 케이크를 가장 좋아해.

2. B: 그것들이 새로 나온 아이스크림 맛이니?
   G: 응, 그래. 맛있어 보여.
   B: 넌 어떤 맛을 선호하니?
   G: 난 딸기 맛을 선호해.

Listen & Talk 2 B

1. **A:** _____ _____ do you prefer?

   B: I prefer summer. _____ are summer people like?

   A: They say that summer people are _____ _____ _____.
   Are you?

   B: Yes, I _____. / No, _____ _____.

2. **A:** _____ _____ _____?

   B: I prefer winter. What are winter people _____?

   A: They say that winter people are _____ _____ _____.
   Are you?

   B: Yes, _____ _____. / No, I'm not.

Communication

Nara: _____ did you like the test?

Seho: It was really fun. I learned a lot _____ _____.

Nara: What _____ of person are you?

Seho: I'm a da-Vinci-type person.

Nara: That _____ cool. What are da-Vinci people _____
_____?

Seho: They _____ _____ da-Vinci _____ make good
inventors and artists.

Nara: _____ _____ do you prefer?

Seho: I'm not sure. _____ _____ _____ _____ my teacher
_____ some advice.

Real-Life Task

Step 2

A: In _____ position do you sleep?

B: I sleep _____ the back _____.

A: What are back sleepers _____?

B: People _____ _____ they are _____ _____ _____.

A: _____ _____ is that position for your _____?

B: Scientists say that it's _____ _____ _____ for sleeping.

1. A: 넌 어떤 계절을 선호하니?
   B: 난 여름을 선호해. 여름 사람들은 어떻지?
   A: 여름 사람들은 조용하고 생각이 깊대. 네가 그러니?
   B: 응, 그래. / 아니, 난 그렇지 않아.

2. A: 넌 어떤 계절을 선호하니?
   B: 난 겨울을 선호해. 겨울 사람들은 어떻지?
   A: 겨울 사람들은 신의가 있고 절친하대. 네가 그러니?
   B: 응, 그래. / 아니, 난 그렇지 않아.

나라: 검사는 어땠니?
세호: 정말 재미있었어. 나 자신에 대해 많이 배웠어.
나라: 너는 어떤 유형의 사람이니?
세호: 나는 다빈치 유형의 사람이야.
나라: 멋지다. 다빈치 유형의 사람은 무엇을 잘하니?
세호: 다빈치 유형의 사람들은 훌륭한 발명가와 예술가가 된다고 해.
나라: 너는 어느 것이 더 좋으니?
세호: 잘 모르겠어. 선생님께 조언을 요청하려고 해.

A: 넌 어떤 자세로 잠을 자니?
B: 난 등을 대고 잠을 자
A: 등을 대고 자는 사람들은 어때?
B: 그들은 따뜻하고 친근하다고 하네.
A: 그 자세는 건강에 얼마나 좋아?
B: 과학자들은 그게 수면에 가장 좋은 자세라고 해.

01 다음 대화의 밑줄 친 문장과 같은 의미의 문장을 고르시오.

> G: Look at those nice suitcases!
> B: They look great.
> G: Which one do you prefer?
> B: I prefer the black one. Which one do you prefer?
> G: I prefer the white one.

① I like the black one more.
② I like the white one and the black one.
③ I like the black one more than white one.
④ I prefer the white one and the black one.
⑤ I like the white one better.

[02~03] 다음 대화를 읽고 물음에 답하시오.

> A: ___(A)___ was the result?
> B: I got Hamlet.
> A: ___(B)___ is a Hamlet-type person like?
> B: They ___(C)___ that a Hamlet-type person is thoughtful.

02 (A)와 (B)에 공통으로 들어갈 말을 쓰시오.

➡ _____

03 빈칸 (C)에 알맞은 말을 고르시오.

① are   ② say   ③ is said
④ is believed   ⑤ are reported

04 다음 대화의 빈칸에 알맞은 것은?

> G: Look at the cakes!
> B: They look yummy.
> G: _____
> B: I like the chocolate cake most.

① What is the chocolate cake like?
② Which do you prefer, milk or coke?
③ Which cake do you like most?
④ Why don't we eat some cake?
⑤ How did you like the chocolate cake?

[01~03] 다음 대화를 읽고 물음에 답하시오.

G: I'm hungry. (①)
B: Me, too. (②) Why don't we go to Sweet Snack? (③)
G: That's a good idea. (④)
B: Yes, it is. (⑤) They say that it _____(A)_____ special pancakes on Sunday.

01 위 대화의 ①~⑤ 중 다음 주어진 말이 들어갈 알맞은 곳은?

> But is it open today?

① ② ③ ④ ⑤

02 빈칸 (A)에 알맞은 말을 고르시오.

① buys ② takes ③ serves
④ prefers ⑤ requires

03 위 대화를 읽고 알 수 없는 것을 고르시오.

① The boy wants to go to Sweet Snack.
② Today is Sunday.
③ Sweet Snack is open on weekends.
④ The girl is hungry now.
⑤ They can eat special pancakes today.

[04~06] 다음 대화를 읽고, 물음에 답하시오.

G: Look _____(A)_____ the cakes!
B: They look ⓐyummy.
G: _____(B)_____ do you like most?
B: I like the chocolate cake most.

04 빈칸 (A)와 (B)에 들어갈 말로 알맞게 짝지어진 것은?

	(A)	(B)
①	at	Which chocolate cake
②	at	Which cake
③	at	What kind of chocolate
④	for	Which cake
⑤	for	What kind of cake

05 밑줄 친 ⓐ와 의미가 비슷한 것을 모두 고르시오.

① delicious ② fresh
③ popular ④ sweet
⑤ tasty

06 위 대화의 내용과 일치하지 않는 것은?

① The boy likes the chocolate cake most.
② They may be in the bakery.
③ They boy thinks the cakes look yummy.
④ The boy asks the girl which cake she likes most.
⑤ They are looking at the cakes.

07 다음 대화의 ①~⑤ 중 흐름상 어색한 것은?

G: ①Are there any good programs this weekend?
B: ②Well, they say that there's a special dance show at the Youth Center on Saturday.
G: ③What kind of dance show do you prefer?
B: ④It's an Indian dance show. ⑤People say that it's really exciting.

① ② ③ ④ ⑤

08 다음 중 짝지어진 대화가 <u>어색한</u> 것은?

① A: What is a Don-Quixote-type person like?
  B: They say that a Don-Quixote-type person is energetic.

② A: Which do you prefer, going to the mountain or going to the sea?
  B: Of course I do.

③ A: Which flavor do you prefer?
  B: I prefer the chocolate flavor.

④ A: They say that there's going to be a class party.
  B: That sounds exciting.

⑤ A: What kind of dance show is it?
  B: It's a Korean dance show.

[09~10] 다음 대화를 읽고, 물음에 답하시오.

Nara: How did you like the test?
Seho: It was really fun. I learned a lot ⓐ_____ .
Nara: ⓑ_____ person are you?
Seho: I'm a da-Vinci-type person.
Nara: That sounds cool. What are da-Vinci people ⓒ_____ ?
Seho: ⓓ_____ da-Vinci people make good inventors and artists.
Nara: <u>너는 어느 것이 더 좋으니?</u>
Seho: I'm not sure. I'm going to ⓔ_____ .

09 위 대화의 빈칸 ⓐ~ⓔ에 알맞지 <u>않은</u> 표현을 고르시오.

① What type of   ② They say that
③ about myself   ④ going to
⑤ ask my teacher for some advice

10 밑줄 친 우리말을 주어진 단어를 이용하여 영작하시오.

➡ _____ (one, prefer)

[11~12] 다음 대화를 읽고, 물음에 답하시오.

A: In which position do you sleep?
B: I sleep in the back position.
A: What are back sleepers like?
B: People say ____(A)____ they are warm and friendly.
A: How good is ____(B)____ position for your health?
B: Scientists say ____(C)____ it's the best position for sleeping.

11 위 (A)~(C)에 공통으로 들어갈 말을 쓰시오.

➡ _____

12 위 대화를 읽고 대답할 수 <u>없는</u> 질문은?

① What are they talking about?
② Which position is the best one for sleeping?
③ What are back sleepers like?
④ In which position does *B* sleep?
⑤ Is *B* warm and friendly?

13 주어진 문장에 이어질 대화의 순서를 바르게 배열하시오.

Is that a new snack shop?

(A) I'm hungry. Would you like to get some pancakes at the shop?
(B) Sure, I'd love to.
(C) Yes, it is. They say that it has delicious pancakes.

➡ _____

[01~02] 주어진 문장에 이어질 대화의 순서를 바르게 배열하시오.

01

> It's very hot.

> (A) Yeah, it really is.
> (B) I prefer the chocolate flavor.
> (C) Why don't we get some ice cream at the shop across the street?
> (D) That's a good idea. Which flavor do you prefer?

➡ _____

02

> Are there any good programs this weekend?

> (A) It's an Indian dance show. People say that it's really exciting.
> (B) Well, they say that there's a special dance show at the Youth Center on Saturday.
> (C) What kind of dance show is it?

➡ _____

[03~05] 다음 대화를 읽고, 물음에 답하시오.

A: In which position do you sleep?
B: I sleep in the ____(A)____ position.
A: ___ⓐ___ are ___(B)___ sleepers like?
B: People say that they are careful and thoughtful.
A: ___ⓑ___ good is that position for your health?
B: <u>과학자들은 등을 대고 자는 것이 수면에 가장 좋은 자세라고 말해.</u>

03 그림을 보고, (A)와 (B)에 공통으로 들어갈 단어를 쓰시오.

➡ _____

04 빈칸 ⓐ와 ⓑ에 알맞은 의문사를 쓰시오.

➡ ⓐ _____ ⓑ _____

05 밑줄 친 우리말을 영어로 옮기시오. (12단어)

➡ _____ position is the best position for sleeping.

06 다음 그림을 보고 대화의 단어를 이용해 (A)와 (B)에 공통으로 들어갈 문장을 쓰시오.

G: Look at those nice suitcases!
B: They look great.
G: _____(A)_____
B: I prefer the black one.
_____(B)_____
G: I prefer the white one.

➡ _____

07 우리말을 영어로 옮기시오. (10단어)

> 학급 파티가 있을 거라고 그러네.

➡ _____

Grammar

교과서

1 which로 시작하는 의문문

- **Which** activities do you enjoy? 너는 어떤 활동을 즐기니?
- **Which** do you like better, soccer or baseball?
  너는 축구와 야구 중에서 어느 것을 더 좋아하니?

■ 형태: Which + 명사 ~?

의미: 어떤[어느] ~인가?

■ 질문의 답이 될 만한 대상이 한정된 경우 which로 시작하는 의문문을 사용한다.

의문사 which는 what과 비슷한 의미를 지니지만, what은 전제되지 않은 대상에 대해 질문할 때 사용할 수 있는 반면에, which는 전제된 대상 가운데에서 선택하여 응답하게 한다는 차이가 있다.

- **Which** song do you like best? 너는 어떤 노래를 가장 좋아하니? 〈답을 할 대상이 몇몇 노래로 한정되어 있음〉
- **What** song do you like? 너는 무슨 노래를 좋아하니? 〈답을 할 대상이 한정되어 있지 않음〉

■ Which는 뒤에 'A or B'와 함께 전제된 대상 가운데 한 가지를 선택하여 물을 때도 사용된다. (선택의문문) 보통 답할 때는 Yes나 No로 하지 않고 그 중 하나를 선택하여 답한다.

- A: **Which** do you like better, coffee or tea? 커피와 차 중 어떤 것으로 하시겠어요?
  B: Coffee, please. 커피로 하겠습니다.

핵심 Check

1. 다음 괄호 안에서 알맞은 것을 고르시오.

(1) (Which / How) place do you want to visit?

(2) (Which / What) one do you want to have between the two?

2. 다음 문장에서 <u>틀린</u> 부분을 찾아 바르게 고쳐 쓰시오.

What sport do you like better, baseball or soccer?

_____ ➡ _____

② 재귀대명사

> • Do you know **yourself**? 당신은 당신 자신을 아는가?
>
> • Jake introduced **himself**. Jake는 자기소개를 했다.

- 형태: -self / -selves

  의미: ~ 자신
- 재귀대명사를 사용하여 '~ 자신'이라는 뜻을 나타낸다.
  - Jack told me that Tom was proud of **him**. (him = Jack)
  - Jack told me that Tom was proud of **himself**. (himself = Tom)
- **재귀 용법**

  주어와 목적어의 관계가 동일한 경우 즉 어떤 행위의 결과가 주어 자신에게 돌아갈 때 목적어로 재귀대명사를 쓴다. 재귀 용법의 재귀대명사는 생략할 수 없다.
  - He killed **himself**. 그는 자살했다. (He = himself)
  - He killed **him**. 그는 그를 죽였다. (He ≠ him)
- **강조 용법**

  '스스로', '직접'이라는 의미로 행위자 바로 뒤나 문장의 끝에 쓰여 행위자를 강조하며 생략할 수 있다.
  - He **himself** did the work. = He did the work **himself**. 그 사람 자신이 그 일을 했다.
- **재귀대명사의 관용적 표현**

  - by oneself 혼자서
  - for oneself 혼자 힘으로
  - of itself 저절로
  - enjoy oneself 즐기다
  - say to oneself 혼잣말하다

핵심 Check

3. 괄호 안에서 알맞은 것을 고르시오.

(1) Emily taught (herself / himself) English.

(2) Kay made the kite (herself / her).

(3) They enjoyed (theirselves / themselves).

01 다음 빈칸에 알맞은 것은?

> We enjoyed _____ at the party.

① we   ② our   ③ us

④ ours   ⑤ ourselves

02 다음 빈칸에 알맞은 것을 고르시오.

> _____ shoes do you like better?

① Which   ② What   ③ Where

④ Where   ⑤ That

03 다음 중 어법상 어색한 문장은?

① Melanie herself finished writing the report.
② Mary introduced herself to us.
③ The door opened of it.
④ I met her while walking down the street.
⑤ She was proud of herself.

04 다음 문장에서 어법상 어색한 부분을 바르게 고쳐 쓰시오.

(1) Who subject can I do well in?

_____ ➡ _____

(2) What do you like better, meat or vegetables?

_____ ➡ _____

(3) I enjoyed me a lot.

_____ ➡ _____

(4) Help you to the potato chips.

_____ ➡ _____

01 다음 중 밑줄 친 부분의 성격이 다른 것을 고르시오.

① She herself told me that the story was true.
② She forced herself to believe that John would be fine.
③ She did her best to justify herself.
④ She taught herself how to read and write.
⑤ She made herself known after she became forty.

02 다음 중 어법상 바른 문장은?

① She can express himself through the dress.
② How subject should I study more?
③ Jane doesn't think about her. She always thinks about others.
④ Which do you prefer, meat or fish?
⑤ I could express me in English when I was a little child.

03 다음 빈칸에 알맞은 것은?

• I met her parents and introduced _____ to them.

① I ② my ③ me
④ mine ⑤ myself

04 다음 괄호 안에서 알맞은 것을 고르시오.

(1) Jimin is a baby and cannot eat by (her / herself).
(2) Mike (him / himself) took the photos in Jejudo.
(3) I dressed (me / myself) up as a traveler.
(4) (Which / What) season do you like better, summer or winter?

05 빈칸에 들어갈 말을 순서대로 바르게 연결한 것은?

• Laura _____ came to meet me.
• _____ subject do you study harder at home?

① herself – Which ② her – Which
③ herself – How ④ her – What
⑤ himself – What

06 다음 중 어법상 어색한 문장은?

① Donald looked at oneself on the water.
② Cinderella was talking about herself at the class.
③ Terry saw her playing the violin on the stage.
④ Be careful, and take good care of yourself.
⑤ The man is carrying the table for himself.

07 다음 우리말과 의미가 같도록 괄호 안의 말을 이용하여 영작하시오. ^{서답형}

(1) 우체국은 어느 쪽입니까? (way, the post office, please)

➡ _____

(2) 내 여동생은 혼자서 걷는 연습을 한다. (my little sister, practice, by, walk)

➡ _____

(3) 하늘은 스스로 돕는 자를 돕는다. (heaven, those who)

➡ _____

08 다음 빈칸에 알맞은 것은? ^{중요}

In _____ year of 2010s, did the number of customer complaints increase?

① what
② which
③ when
④ where
⑤ how

09 그림을 보고 주어진 어휘를 이용하여 빈칸에 알맞은 말을 쓰시오. ^{서답형}

➡ They are _____ _____ at the party. (enjoy)

10 다음 중 어법상 어색한 문장은? ^{중요}

① Richard looked at himself in the mirror.
② What do you prefer, swimming or running?
③ Come in and make yourselves at home.
④ She herself taught him as much as she could.
⑤ What time does the bank close today?

11 다음 빈칸에 들어갈 알맞은 말을 고르시오.

Harry and Sharon seated _____ at a large table.

① himself
② herself
③ themselves
④ him
⑤ them

12 다음 우리말을 영어로 바르게 옮긴 것은?

우리는 자기 자신보다 국가를 더 중시합니다.

① We like to place our country above we.
② We like to place our country above our.
③ We like to place our country above us.
④ We like to place our country above ourselves.
⑤ We like to place our ourselves above country.

13 다음 그림을 보고 대화의 빈칸에 알맞은 말을 쓰시오.

| apple juice ₩1,500 | strawberry juice ₩1,200 | orange juice ₩1,000 |
| apple pie ₩1,000 | chocolate pie ₩1,500 | cream pie ₩1,300 |

A: _____ one do you want to drink?
B: I will have the cheapest one.
A: Do you mean orange juice?
B: Yes, I do.

➡ _____

14 다음 밑줄 친 부분의 쓰임이 어색한 것은?

① Every morning I wash <u>myself</u> and brush my teeth.
② Why don't you make the most of <u>them</u>?
③ Christine studied math very hard for <u>herself</u>.
④ Did Joanne meet <u>herself</u>? –No, she met Jake.
⑤ Mike always thinks about <u>himself</u> and doesn't mind others.

서답형

15 괄호 안에 주어진 어휘를 이용하여 빈칸에 알맞은 말을 쓰시오.

(1) We consider _____ unique. (we)
(2) The candle went out of _____. (it)
(3) Socrates told, "Know _____." (you)

16 다음 밑줄 친 부분 중 어법상 <u>틀린</u> 것은?

① <u>Which</u> juice do you want to have today?
② <u>How many</u> pieces do I need for six people?
③ <u>Why</u> does the man want to help the lady in a white dress?
④ To <u>whom</u> did you give the chocolate?
⑤ <u>What</u> of these issues is the most important?

중요

17 〈보기〉의 밑줄 친 부분과 쓰임이 같은 것을 고르시오.

┤ 보기 ├
I don't want to wash <u>myself</u> in cold water.

① I don't want to eat by <u>myself</u> anymore.
② I <u>myself</u> did it.
③ I find <u>myself</u> thinking about him unexpectedly.
④ I would like to solve the problem for <u>myself</u>.
⑤ I am an excellent organizer <u>myself</u>.

서답형

18 다음 문장에서 <u>틀린</u> 부분을 찾아 바르게 고쳐 다시 쓰시오.

(1) I think it's important to believe in your.
_____ ➡ _____
(2) Sometimes we need to look deep into us.
_____ ➡ _____
(3) What day in a week do you prefer?
_____ ➡ _____
(4) She had to live for oneself.
_____ ➡ _____

01 괄호 안에 주어진 어휘의 알맞은 형태를 빈칸에 쓰시오.

(1) Linda hurt _____ and is in the hospital now. (she)

(2) Be my guest and help _____ to food on the table. (you)

(3) The bridge _____ was the longest one at that time. (it)

02 다음을 재귀대명사를 이용해서 괄호 안의 지시대로 고치시오. ⭐중요

(1) We went camping last weekend. (주어를 강조하는 문장으로)
➡ _____
_____

(2) Even the best sports teams lose from time to time. (주어를 강조하는 문장으로)
➡ _____
_____

(3) Mr. Green came out to welcome us. (주어를 강조하는 문장으로)
➡ _____
_____

(4) Grace became an architect and designed the building. (목적어를 강조하는 문장으로)
➡ _____
_____

(5) Alex met the famous actress. (목적어를 강조하는 문장으로)
➡ _____
_____

03 다음 그림을 보고 대화의 빈칸에 알맞은 말을 쓰시오.

strawberry ice cream   chocolate ice cream   green tea ice cream

A: How about having an ice cream?
B: Nice idea. I will have a green tea ice cream. _____ one will you have?
A: I will have a strawberry ice cream.
B: Good.

➡ _____

04 다음 우리말을 주어진 어휘를 이용하여 문장을 완성하시오. 고난이도

(1) 그는 대회에서 우승한 후 스스로를 자랑스러워했다. (proud of, win the contest)
➡ _____
_____

(2) 그녀는 혼잣말을 중얼거리며 슬픈 미소를 지었다. (say to, as, smile, sadly)
➡ _____
_____

(3) 혼자서 일하는 걸 좋아하세요, 아니면 다른 사람들과 함께 일하는 걸 좋아하세요? (prefer, working, with other people, alone)
➡ _____
_____

(4) 어느 요일을 가장 좋아하세요? (day of the week, best)
➡ _____
_____

05 다음 문장에서 <u>어색한</u> 곳을 찾아 바르게 고쳐 전체 문장을 다시 쓰시오.

(1) Many of us do not know how to love us.

➡ _____

_____

(2) He him promised that he would stop drinking.

➡ _____

_____

(3) Evelyne was left alone. She looked at her in the mirror and said to her.

➡ _____

_____

(4) Tom spent a lot of time by oneself that year.

➡ _____

_____

(5) I taught me how to play the guitar.

➡ _____

_____

(6) The greenhouse effect in themselves is actually natural.

➡ _____

_____

06 다음 그림을 보고 대화의 빈칸에 한 단어씩 채워 문장을 완성하시오.

carrot cake
chocolate cake   green tea cake

A: _____ _____ would you like?
B: I'd like carrot cake.

➡ _____ _____ _____

07 다음 〈보기〉에 주어진 단어를 이용하여 어법에 맞게 문장을 완성하시오.

┌─ 보기 ┤

oneself

(1) History repeats _____.
(2) I _____ have a lot of questions about school life.
(3) Mary was looking at _____ in the mirror every morning.
(4) I cannot make _____ understood.
(5) I wonder why John _____ drove his car last night.

08 다음 두 문장을 해석하고 그 차이점을 설명하시오.

• Which color do you like most?
• What color do you like?

➡ 해석 (1) _____
　　　 (2) _____
　차이점(1) _____
　　　 (2) _____

09 다음 대화의 빈칸을 알맞게 채우시오.

A: Welcome home, Son. I made chocolate cake and strawberry cake. _____ cake do you want to eat?
B: I'd like chocolate cake, Mom.
A: Great. Help _____.
B: Thanks a lot, Mom.

➡ _____, _____

WHO AM I? WHAT IS YOUR COLOR?

WHAT IS YOUR COLOR?

Who am I? What type of person am I? Do you have these questions?

'어떤 유형'이라는 뜻으로, What kind와 비슷한 의미임.

Here we have an interesting personality test for you.

Here는 상대방의 주의를 끌기 위한 표현으로, '여기에' 정도의 뜻을 지님.

Step 1 Which activities do you enjoy, and which ones are you good at?

one의 복수 (= activities)

I enjoy … / I'm good at …

1. being free and having fun.

enjoy는 동명사를 목적어로 취한다. being free와 having fun이 목적어에 해당한다.

2. working with people. 3. taking chances. 4. following traditions.

5. working on my own. 6. writing stories. 7. learning new things.

나 혼자서

8. following the rules. 9. making new friends.

10. planning things out.

'생각해 내다, 안을 세우다, 기획하다' things는 plan과 out 사이에서 목적어의 역할을 한다.

11. pleasing others. 12. finding new patterns.

= other people

13. being on stage.

enjoy와 at의 목적어 역할을 함.

14. working with directions. 15. solving puzzles. 16. playing sports.

Step 2 What is your color?

Circle the numbers from Step 1, and find the line with the most

주어 you가 생략된 명령문. Circle과 find로 시작하는 동사구가 and로 대등하게 연결하는 형용사구 the line을 수식

circles.

| 확인문제

● 다음 문장이 본문의 내용과 일치하면 T, 일치하지 않으면 F를 쓰시오.

1   This is an intelligence test. □

2   There are sixteen activities in the test. □

3   We circle the numbers from Step 1. □

4   We should find the line with the fewest circles. □

---

type 유형

personality 성격, 개성

activity 활동

be good at ~을 잘하다

chance 기회

follow 따르다

tradition 전통

please 기쁘게 하다

pattern 패턴, 정형화된 양식

stage 무대

direction (복수형으로 사용되는 경우)
지시, 명령

solve 해결하다

circle 동그라미 표시를 하다

find 찾다

Step 3 What type of person are you?

If you have more circles on the orange line, you are a wonderful
_{조건을 나타내는 부사절}　_{주절}
energizer. You are witty and lively, and you work best in game settings.
_{and에 의해 대등하게 연결된 보어}　_{well의 최상급}　_{부사구}
If you have more circles on the gold line, you are an excellent
_{many의 비교급}
organizer. You are faithful and careful, and you work best with clear
_{~을 가지고}
rules.

Knowing yourself is the beginning of all wisdom. - Aristotle
_{동명사구 (주어)}

If you have more circles on the blue line, you are a great listener. You

are warm and caring, and you work best in groups.
_{등위접속사 and에 의해 연결된 보어}

If you have more circles on the green line, you are a curious thinker.

You are cool and quiet, and you work best on your own.
_{혼자서}

What is your type, and how much do you like it? Take this personality
_{= your type}
test as a first step and try to find your true color.
_{~으로}　_{~하기 위해 노력하다}
Everyone is unique and has a special color. Why don't you listen
_{단수 취급}　_{단수형 동사 is와 has 사용}　_{~하는 게 어때?}
to yourself, find special things about yourself, and make the most of
_{주어 you와 목적어가 같은 경우이므로 재귀대명사를 사용}
them?
= special things (about yourself)

witty 재치 있는
lively 생기 넘치는
setting 상황
organize 조직하다, 정리 정돈하다
faithful 충직한, 충성스러운
caring 배려하는, 보살피는
on one's own 혼자서
as ~로서
step 걸음, 단계, 조치
unique 독특한, 하나뿐인
make the most of … ~를 최대한
이용하다

확인문제

● 다음 문장이 본문의 내용과 일치하면 T, 일치하지 않으면 F를 쓰시오.

1 If you have more circles on the orange line, you are witty and lively. ☐

2 If you have more circles on the gold line, you are faithful and careful, and you work best with clear rules. ☐

3 Plato said knowing yourself is the beginning of all wisdom. ☐

4 If you have more circles on the blue line, you are cool and quiet, and you work best on your own. ☐

5 If you have more circles on the green line, you work best on your own. ☐

6 Everyone is ordinary and has a common color. ☐

● 우리말을 참고하여 빈칸에 알맞은 말을 쓰시오.

1 _____ Is Your Color?

2 _____ am I?

3 _____ _____ of person am I?

4 Do you have _____ _____?

5 Here we have an _____ _____ _____ for you.

6 Step 1 _____ _____ do you enjoy, and _____ _____ are you good at?

7 I enjoy … / I'm _____ _____ …

8 1. being _____ and _____ _____. 2. working _____ people.

9 3. _____ _____. 4. _____ traditions.

10 5. working _____ _____ _____. 6. writing stories.

11 7. _____ new things. 8. _____ the rules.

12 9. _____ new friends. 10. _____ things _____.

13 11. _____ others. 12. finding new patterns.

14 13. being _____ _____. 14. working _____ _____.

15 15. _____ puzzles. 16. playing sports.

1 당신의 색깔은 무엇입니까?

2 나는 누구인가?

3 나는 어떤 유형의 사람인가?

4 이런 질문들을 가지고 있나요?

5 여기에 당신을 위한 흥미로운 성격 검사가 있습니다.

6 [Step1] 당신은 어떤 활동을 즐겨 합니까, 그리고 어떤 활동을 잘하나요?

7 나는 ~을 즐긴다/나는 ~을 잘한다

8 1. 자유로우며 재미있게 놀기 2. 사람들과 함께 일하기

9 3. 운(運)에 맡기고 해 보기 4. 전통을 따르기

10 5. 혼자서 일하기 6. 이야기 쓰기

11 7. 새로운 것 배우기 8. 규칙을 따르기

12 9. 새로운 친구를 사귀기 10. 계획을 세우기

13 11. 다른 사람을 즐겁게 해 주기 12. 새로운 패턴을 찾기

14 13. 무대에 서기 14. 지시를 받고 일하기

15 15. 수수께끼 풀기 16. 운동 경기를 하기

16 Step 2 What is _____ _____?

17 _____ the numbers _____ Step 1, and find the line _____ the _____ circles.

18 Step 3 _____ _____ _____ _____ are you?

19 If you have more circles on the orange line, you are a _____ _____.

20 You are _____ and _____, and you work best _____ game settings.

21 If you have more circles on the gold line, you are an _____ _____.

22 You are _____ and careful, and you work _____ _____ clear rules.

23 _____ _____ is the beginning of all _____. - Aristotle

24 If you have more circles on the blue line, you are a _____ _____.

25 You are warm and _____, and you work best _____ _____.

26 If you have more circles on the green line, you are a _____ _____.

27 You are _____ and quiet, and you work best _____ _____ _____.

28 What is your type, and _____ _____ do you like it?

29 _____ this personality test _____ a first step and try to find your true color.

30 Everyone is _____ and has a _____ color.

31 _____ _____ _____ listen to yourself, find special things about yourself, and _____ _____ _____ _____ them?

16 [Step2] 당신의 색깔은 무엇입니까?

17 Step 1에서 고른 숫자에 동그라미 표시를 하고, 가장 많은 동그라미 표시가 있는 줄을 찾으세요.

18 [Step3] 당신은 어떤 유형의 사람입니까?

19 주황색 줄에 더 많은 동그라미 표시가 있다면, 당신은 놀라운 활력을 주는 사람입니다.

20 당신은 재치 있고 생기 있으며, 게임 환경에서 가장 잘 일합니다.

21 황금색 줄에 더 많은 동그라미 표시가 있다면, 당신은 뛰어난 조직가입니다.

22 당신은 충직하고 조심스러우며, 분명한 규칙이 제시된 경우에 가장 잘 일합니다.

23 스스로를 아는 것은 모든 지혜의 시작이다. - 아리스토텔레스

24 푸른색 줄에 더 많은 동그라미 표시가 있다면, 당신은 대단한 경청자입니다.

25 당신은 따뜻하고 남을 잘 돌보며, 집단과 더불어 가장 잘 일합니다.

26 초록색 줄에 더 많은 동그라미 표시가 있다면, 당신은 호기심 많은 사색가입니다.

27 당신은 멋지고 조용하며, 혼자서 (일할 때) 가장 잘 일합니다.

28 당신의 유형은 무엇이며, 그것을 얼마나 좋아합니까?

29 이 성격 검사를 첫 단계로 삼아서, 당신의 진정한 색깔을 찾아보려고 노력하세요.

30 모든 사람들은 독특하고 특별한 색깔을 지니고 있습니다.

31 스스로에게 귀를 기울이고, 스스로에 관하여 특별한 것들을 발견하며, 그것들을 최대한 이용해 보면 어떨까요?

● 우리말을 참고하여 본문을 영작하시오.

1 당신의 색깔은 무엇입니까?
➡ _____

2 나는 누구인가?
➡ _____

3 나는 어떤 유형의 사람인가?
➡ _____

4 이런 질문들을 가지고 있나요?
➡ _____

5 여기에 당신을 위한 흥미로운 성격 검사가 있습니다.
➡ _____

6 [Step1] 당신은 어떤 활동을 즐겨 합니까, 그리고 어떤 활동을 잘하나요?
➡ _____

7 나는 ~을 즐긴다/나는 ~을 잘한다
➡ _____

8 1. 자유로우며 재미있게 놀기 2. 사람들과 함께 일하기
➡ _____

9 3. 운(運)에 맡기고 해 보기 4. 전통을 따르기
➡ _____

10 5. 혼자서 일하기 6. 이야기 쓰기
➡ _____

11 7. 새로운 것 배우기 8. 규칙을 따르기
➡ _____

12 9. 새로운 친구를 사귀기 10. 계획을 세우기
➡ _____

13 11. 다른 사람을 즐겁게 해 주기 12. 새로운 패턴을 찾기
➡ _____

14 13. 무대에 서기 14. 지시를 받고 일하기
➡ _____

15 15. 수수께끼 풀기 16. 운동 경기를 하기
➡ _____

16 [Step2] 당신의 색깔은 무엇입니까?

➡ _____

17 Step 1에서 고른 숫자에 동그라미 표시를 하고, 가장 많은 동그라미 표시가 있는 줄을 찾으세요.

➡ _____

18 [Step3] 당신은 어떤 유형의 사람입니까?

➡ _____

19 주황색 줄에 더 많은 동그라미 표시가 있다면, 당신은 놀라운 활력을 주는 사람입니다.

➡ _____

20 당신은 재치 있고 생기 있으며, 게임 환경에서 가장 잘 일합니다.

➡ _____

21 황금색 줄에 더 많은 동그라미 표시가 있다면, 당신은 뛰어난 조직가입니다.

➡ _____

22 당신은 충직하고 조심스러우며, 분명한 규칙이 제시된 경우에 가장 잘 일합니다.

➡ _____

23 스스로를 아는 것은 모든 지혜의 시작이다. – 아리스토텔레스

➡ _____

24 푸른색 줄에 더 많은 동그라미 표시가 있다면, 당신은 대단한 경청자입니다.

➡ _____

25 당신은 따뜻하고 남을 잘 돌보며, 집단과 더불어 가장 잘 일합니다.

➡ _____

26 초록색 줄에 더 많은 동그라미 표시가 있다면, 당신은 호기심 많은 사색가입니다.

➡ _____

27 당신은 멋지고 조용하며, 혼자서 (일할 때) 가장 잘 일합니다.

➡ _____

28 당신의 유형은 무엇이며, 그것을 얼마나 좋아합니까?

➡ _____

29 이 성격 검사를 첫 단계로 삼아서, 당신의 진정한 색깔을 찾아보려고 노력하세요.

➡ _____

30 모든 사람들은 독특하고 특별한 색깔을 지니고 있습니다.

➡ _____

31 스스로에게 귀를 기울이고, 스스로에 관하여 특별한 것들을 발견하며, 그것들을 최대한 이용해 보면 어떨까요?

➡ _____

[01~03] 다음 글을 읽고, 물음에 답하시오.

Who am I? What type of person am I? Do you have these questions? Here we have an interesting personality test for you.

Step 1: Which activities do you enjoy, and which ones are you good at?

I enjoy … / I'm good at …
1. being free and ⓐhaving fun.
2. working with people.
3. taking chances.
4. following traditions.
5. working on my own.
6. writing stories.
7. learning new things.
8. following the rules.
9. making new friends.
10. planning things out.
11. pleasing others.
12. finding new patterns.
13. being on stage.
14. working with directions.
15. solving puzzles.
16. playing sports.

서답형

01 본문의 내용과 일치하도록 다음 빈칸 (A)와 (B)에 알맞은 단어를 쓰시오.

Here is a _____(A)_____ test to find out your _____(B)_____ .

➡ (A) _____ (B)_____

02 위 글의 밑줄 친 ⓐhaving과 문법적 쓰임이 같은 것을 모두 고르시오.

① I saw the girl having fun with friends.
② Who doesn't like having fun?
③ People are having fun on Chuseok.
④ I know the boy having fun there.
⑤ Is having fun always good for you?

중요

03 위 글의 성격 검사의 테스트 항목에 들어 있지 않은 것을 고르시오.

① Do you enjoy working with people?
② Are you good at following traditions?
③ Do you write stories well?
④ Are you good at making the rules?
⑤ Do you solve puzzles well?

[04~06] 다음 글을 읽고, 물음에 답하시오.

Who am I? What type of person am I? Do you have these questions? Here we have an interesting personality test for you.

Step 1: Which activities do you enjoy, and which ones are you good at?

I enjoy … / I'm good at …
1. being free and having fun.
2. working with people.
3. taking ⓐchances.
4. following traditions.
13. being on stage.
14. working with ____ⓑ____ .
15. solving puzzles.
16. playing sports.

04 위 글의 밑줄 친 ⓐchances와 바꿔 쓸 수 있는 말을 고르시오.

① actions   ② notes   ③ risks
④ steps   ⑤ notices

서답형

05 주어진 영영풀이를 참고하여 빈칸 ⓑ에 철자 d로 시작하는 단어를 쓰시오.

instructions that tell you what to do, how to do something, or how to get somewhere

➡ _____

06 위 글의 test에 관해 대답할 수 <u>없는</u> 질문은?

① What kind of test is it?

② What can you know through this test?

③ How many activities are there in it?

④ Which activity do they circle most?

⑤ What does the test mainly ask about?

[07~09] 다음 글을 읽고, 물음에 답하시오.

I enjoy … / I'm good at …
1. being free and having fun.
2. working with people.
3. taking chances.
4. following traditions.
5. working on my own.
6. writing stories.
7. learning new things.
8. following the rules.
9. making new friends.
10. planning things out.
11. pleasing others.
12. finding new patterns.
13. being on stage.
14. working with directions.
15. solving puzzles.
16. playing sports.

Step 2: _____(A)_____

Numbers			
1	3	13	16
④	8	⑩	14
2	⑥	9	11
⑤	⑦	⑫	⑮

*(B) <u>Circle the numbers from Step 1, and finding the line with the most circles.</u>

07 위 글의 빈칸 (A)에 들어갈 말로 알맞은 것을 고르시오.

① Do you enjoy the personality test?

② Too many items are difficult to test.

③ What is your color?

④ Are you good at following traditions?

⑤ Which color do you like most?

08 위 글의 밑줄 친 (B)에서 어법상 틀린 부분을 찾아 고치시오.

➡ _____

09 위 글의 성격 검사를 한 사람에 대한 설명으로 옳지 <u>않은</u> 것을 고르시오.

① 자유로우며 재미있게 놀기를 즐긴다.

② 혼자서 일하기를 즐긴다.

③ 새로운 것 배우기를 잘한다.

④ 새로운 패턴 찾기를 즐긴다.

⑤ 수수께끼 풀기를 잘한다.

[10~13] 다음 글을 읽고, 물음에 답하시오.

Step 3 What type of person are you?

If you have more circles on the orange line, you are a wonderful energizer. You are witty and lively, and you work best in game settings.

If you have more circles on the gold line, you are an excellent organizer. You are faithful and careful, and you work best ___ⓐ___ clear rules.

___ⓑ___ yourself is the beginning of all wisdom. - Aristotle

If you have more circles on the blue line, you are a great listener. You are warm and caring, and you work best ___ⓒ___ groups.

If you have more circles on the green line, you are a curious thinker. You are ⓓcool and quiet, and you work best on your own.

10 위 글의 빈칸 ⓐ와 ⓒ에 들어갈 전치사가 바르게 짝지어진 것은?

① with – in　　② for – by

③ for – from　　④ with – to

⑤ to – in

11 위 글의 빈칸 ⓑ에 know를 알맞은 형태로 쓰시오.

➡ _____

12 위 글의 밑줄 친 ⓓcool과 같은 의미로 쓰인 것을 고르시오.

① Let's sit in the shade and keep cool.
② She tried to remain cool.
③ The soup is getting cool.
④ You look cool with that new haircut.
⑤ I like this cool breeze.

중요
13 위 글의 내용과 일치하지 <u>않는</u> 것은?

① 주황색 줄에 더 많은 동그라미 표시가 있다면, 당신은 재치 있고 생기 있다.
② 황금색 줄에 더 많은 동그라미 표시가 있다면, 당신은 게임 환경에서 가장 잘 일한다.
③ 황금색 줄에 더 많은 동그라미 표시가 있다면, 당신은 뛰어난 조직가이다.
④ 푸른색 줄에 더 많은 동그라미 표시가 있다면, 당신은 따뜻하고 남을 잘 돌본다.
⑤ 초록색 줄에 더 많은 동그라미 표시가 있다면, 당신은 호기심 많은 사색가이다.

[14~15] 다음 글을 읽고, 물음에 답하시오.

Dear Diary

 Which subjects should I study more? Which after-school activities should I join? I have ⓐa lot of questions about school life.

 The personality test says that I am an excellent organizer. It also says that I am faithful and careful, and I work best with clear rules.

 I am going to start from my strong points. I want to make the most of them. I know that I can do really well this year.

14 위 글의 밑줄 친 ⓐa lot of questions의 예를 본문에서 찾아 쓰시오.

➡ _____
_____

15 위 일기를 쓴 사람에 대한 설명으로 옳지 <u>않은</u> 것을 고르시오.

① 뛰어난 조직가이다.
② 추진하고 조심스럽다.
③ 분명한 규칙이 제시된 경우에 가장 잘 일한다.
④ 자신의 단점에서 시작하려고 한다.
⑤ 자신이 올해 정말 잘할 수 있을 것임을 안다.

[16~18] 다음 글을 읽고, 물음에 답하시오.

Step 2: What is your color?

Numbers			
1	3	13	16
④	⑧	⑩	⑭
2	6	9	11
5	⑦	⑫	⑮

*Circle the numbers from Step 1, and find the line with the most circles.

Step 3 What type of person are you?
 ⓐ주황색 줄에 더 많은 동그라미 표시가 있다면, 당신은 훌륭한 활력소입니다. You are witty and lively, and you work best in game settings.

 If you have more circles on the gold line, you are an excellent organizer. You are faithful and careful, and you work best with clear rules.

ⓑKnowing yourself is the beginning of all wisdom. - Aristotle

16 위 글의 밑줄 친 ⓐ의 우리말에 맞게 한 단어를 보충하여, 주어진 어휘를 알맞게 배열하시오.

are / on the orange line / if / a / circles / have / you / wonderful / more / you

➡ _____
_____

서답형

17 다음 빈칸 (A)와 (B)에 알맞은 단어를 넣어 위 글의 성격 검사를 한 사람의 유형을 설명하시오.

> This person is _____(A)_____ and is faithful and careful as he (or she) has more circles on the ____(B)____ line.

➡ (A) _____

(B) _____

18 아래 보기에서 위 글의 밑줄 친 ⓑKnowing과 문법적 쓰임이 같은 것의 개수를 고르시오.

┌─ 보기 ┐

① I met the singing girl yesterday.
② He is fond of taking pictures.
③ Did you finish writing your report?
④ The boy is playing soccer on the field.
⑤ My favorite hobby is playing soccer.

① 1개 ② 2개 ③ 3개 ④ 4개 ⑤ 5개

[19~21] 다음 글을 읽고, 물음에 답하시오.

What is your type, and how much do you like it? Take this personality test ___ⓐ___ a first step and try to find your true color.

Everyone is unique and has a special color. ⓑWhy don't you listen to you, find special things about you, and ⓒmake the most of them?

19 위 글의 빈칸 ⓐ에 들어갈 알맞은 말을 고르시오.

① to ② as ③ by
④ from ⑤ in

서답형

20 위 글의 밑줄 친 ⓑ에서 어법상 틀린 부분을 찾아 고치시오. (두 군데)

➡ _____

21 위 글의 밑줄 친 ⓒmake the most of와 바꿔 쓸 수 있는 말을 고르시오.

① make up for ② make much of
③ take care of ④ care about
⑤ make the best of

[22~24] 다음 글을 읽고, 물음에 답하시오.

Which subjects can I do well in? ⓐWhich clubs should I join? I have a lot of questions about school life.

The ___ⓑ___ test says that I am a curious thinker. It also says that I am cool and quiet and I work best on my own.

I am going to start from my strong points. I want ⓒto make the most of them. I know that I can do really well this year.

서답형

22 밑줄 친 ⓐ를 다음과 같이 바꿔 쓸 때 빈칸에 들어갈 알맞은 말을 쓰시오.

➡ Which clubs should I _____ _____ _____? =Which clubs should I _____ _____?

23 위 글의 빈칸 ⓑ에 들어갈 알맞은 말을 고르시오.

① popularity ② performance
③ personality ④ intelligence
⑤ population

24 위 글의 밑줄 친 ⓒto make와 to부정사의 용법이 같은 것을 고르시오.

① I was surprised to see the sight.
② She planned to visit her aunt.
③ Show me the fastest way to go there.
④ I studied hard to pass the test.
⑤ He grew up to be a police officer.

[01~03] 다음 글을 읽고 물음에 답하시오.

Who am I? What type of person am I? Do you have these questions? Here we have an (A)[interesting / interested] personality test for you.

Step 1: Which activities do you enjoy, and (B)[which / what] ones are you good (C)[at / for]?

I enjoy … / I'm good at …
2. working with people.
3. taking chances.
4. following traditions.
5. working ⓐ나 혼자서.

Step 2: What is your color?

Numbers			
①	③	⑬	⑯
4	8	10	14
②	⑥	⑨	⑪
5	7	12	15

*Circle the numbers from Step 1, and find the line with the most circles.

Step 3 What type of person are you?

If you have more circles on the orange line, you are a wonderful energizer. You are witty and lively, and you work best in game settings.

01 위 글의 괄호 (A)~(C)에서 문맥이나 어법상 알맞은 낱말을 골라 쓰시오.

➡ (A) _____ (B) _____ (C) _____

02 위 글의 밑줄 친 ⓐ의 우리말에 맞게 괄호 안에 주어진 어휘를 이용하여 3 단어로 영작하시오. (on)

➡ _____

03 다음 빈칸 (A)에 알맞은 단어를 넣어 위 글의 Step 2처럼 동그라미 표시를 한 사람의 유형을 설명하시오.

You are ___(A)___ as there are more circles on the ___(B)___ line.

➡ (A) _____
　(B) _____

[04~06] 다음 글을 읽고, 물음에 답하시오.

Who am I? What ⓐtype of person am I? Do you have ⓑthese questions? Here we have an interesting personality test for you.

Step 1: Which activities do you enjoy, and which ones are you good at?

I enjoy … / I'm good at …
1. being free and ⓒ fun.
2. working with people.
3. taking chances.

04 위 글의 밑줄 친 ⓐtype과 바꿔 쓸 수 있도록 철자 k로 시작하는 단어를 쓰시오.

➡ _____

05 위 글의 밑줄 친 ⓑthese questions가 가리키는 것을 본문에서 찾아 쓰시오.

➡ _____

06 위 글의 빈칸 ⓒ에 have를 알맞은 형태로 쓰시오.

➡ _____

[07~09] 다음 글을 읽고, 물음에 답하시오.

Step 2: What is your color?

Numbers			
1	3	13	16
④	8	⑩	14
2	⑥	9	11
⑤	⑦	⑫	⑮

*Circle the numbers from Step 1, and find the line with the most circles.

Step 3 What type of person are you?

If you have more circles on the orange line, you are a wonderful energizer. You are witty and lively, and you work best in game settings.

If you have more circles on the gold line, you are an excellent organizer. You are faithful and careful, and you work best with clear rules.

If you have more circles on the blue line, you are a great listener. You are warm and caring, and you work best in groups.

If you have more circles on the green line, you are a curious thinker. You are cool and quiet, and you work best on your own.

07 다음 질문에 대한 알맞은 대답을 주어진 단어로 시작하여 쓰시오. (3단어)

Q: What type is the person who circled the numbers like Step 2?

A: He or she is _____.

08 If a person works best with clear rules, what is the person's color? Fill in the blank with a suitable word.

➡ It's _____.

09 본문의 내용과 일치하도록 다음 빈칸 (A)와 (B)에 알맞은 단어를 쓰시오.

> If your color is ___(A)___ , you are a great listener. You work best ___(B)___ .

➡ (A) _____ (B) _____

[10~11] 다음 글을 읽고, 물음에 답하시오.

Which subjects can I do well in? Which clubs should I join? I have a lot of questions about school life.

The personality test says ___ⓐ___ I am a curious thinker. It also says ___ⓑ___ I am cool and quiet and I work best on my own.

I am going to start from Ⓐmy strong points. I want to make the most of them. I know ___ⓒ___ I can do really well this year.

10 위 글의 밑줄 친 Ⓐmy strong points가 가리키는 것 세 가지를 우리말로 쓰시오.

➡ (1) _____
　 (2) _____
　 (3) _____

11 위 글의 빈칸 ⓐ~ⓒ에 공통으로 들어갈 알맞은 말을 쓰시오.

➡ _____

[12~13] 다음 글을 읽고, 물음에 답하시오.

What is your type, and how much do you like it? Take this personality test as a first step and try to find your true color.

Everyone is unique and has a special color. ⓐWhy don't you listen to yourself, find special things about yourself, and make the most of ⓑthem?

12 위 글의 밑줄 친 ⓐ를 다음과 같이 바꿔 쓸 때 빈칸에 들어갈 알맞은 말을 쓰시오.

➡ How about _____ to yourself

13 위 글의 밑줄 친 ⓑthem이 가리키는 것을 본문에서 찾아 쓰시오.

➡ _____

Communication Step B

My color is orange.

I'm a fall person, and I'm a stomach sleeper.
어떤 특성을 많이 가진 사람 ex) a dog person: 개를 좋아하는 사람 stomach: 위(장)

They say that I'm a Don-Quixote type person.
They say that 주어 동사 ~.: (그들이) ~라고 그러네. ~형의 뜻을 나타내는 명사를 만든다.)

I'm going to put an art board on the classroom wall.
be going to 동사원형: ~할 것이다

Why don't you show your dreams, plans, and ideas on the board?
상대방에게 어떤 것을 제안할 때는 'Why don't you ~?'의 형태로 말할 수 있다.

내 색깔은 오렌지색이야.

나는 가을 사람이고, 엎드려서 자는 사람이야.

나는 돈키호테 유형의 사람이라고 해

나는 교실 벽에 미술 게시판을 걸 거야.

게시판에 너희들의 꿈과 계획, 그리고 생각들을 보여주는 게 어때?

Look and Write

Which subjects can I do well in? Which clubs should I join?
질문의 답이 될 만한 대상이 한정된 경우 which로 시작하는 의문문을 사용한다.

I have a lot of questions about school life.
= lots of = many

The personality test says that I am a curious thinker. It also says that I am
목적어를 이끄는 접속사(생략 가능)

cool and quiet and I work best on my own.
well의 최상급   혼자서

I am going to start from my strong points. I want to make the most of them. I
want의 목적어가 되는 to부정사   = my strong points

know that I can do really well this year.
목적어를 이끄는 접속사(생략 가능)

구문해설 • subject: 과목 • personality: 성격 • curious: 호기심 많은 • cool: 멋진
• strong point: 장점 • make the most of: ~을 최대한 이용하다

나는 어떤 과목들을 잘할 수 있을까? 어떤 동아리에 가입해야 할까? 나는 학교생활에 대한 질문이 많다. 성격 검사에서는 내가 호기심 많은 사색가라고 한다. 또한 멋지고 조용하며, 혼자서 (일할 때) 가장 잘한다고 한다. 나는 나의 장점에서 시작하려 한다. 나는 그 장점들을 최대한 잘 이용하고 싶다. 나는 올해 정말 잘할 수 있을 것임을 안다.

Language Detective

I went to Mina's birthday party. I met her parents and introduced myself to
주어와 목적어의 관계가 동일하므로 재귀대명사를 써야 한다.

them. They welcomed me and said, "Would you please help yourself to the
help의 목적어로 쓰인 재귀대명사

food?" It was a great party, and my friends and I enjoyed a lot.
(동사 · 형용사 · 부사를 수식하여) 대단히, 많이

구문해설 • introduce: 소개하다 • Help yourself to ~: ~을 마음대로[양껏] 드십시오.

나는 미나의 생일 파티에 갔다. 나는 그녀의 부모님을 만났고 그분들에게 나를 소개했다. 그분들은 나를 환영해 주셨고, "음식을 마음껏 먹지 그러니?"라고 말씀하셨다. 굉장한 파티였고, 내 친구들과 나는 아주 즐거운 시간을 보냈다.

영역별 핵심문제

01 다음 짝지어진 단어의 관계가 같도록 빈칸에 알맞은 말을 쓰시오. (주어진 철자로 시작할 것)

> faithful : loyal – active : e_____

02 다음 빈칸에 들어갈 말로 적절한 것은?

> He is very _____. He always tells the truth, and do not try to deceive people or break the law.

① kind　　　　② clever
③ open　　　　④ honest
⑤ friendly

03 다음 밑줄 친 단어와 의미가 같은 단어를 고르시오.

> Can you <u>find</u> a way to solve it?

① discover　　② take
③ keep　　　　④ buy
⑤ see

04 괄호 안에 주어진 단어를 변형시켜 빈칸을 채우시오.

(1) We enjoyed lots of _____, such as swimming, surfing, and drawing pictures. (act)
(2) He is a very _____ person. He enjoys taking care of poor children and old people. (care)

05 자연스러운 대화가 되도록 가장 알맞게 배열한 것은?

> (A) I prefer the black one. Which one do you prefer?
> (D) Which one do you prefer?
> (C) Look at those nice suitcases!
> (D) They look great.
> (E) I prefer the white one.

① (A) – (E) – (B) – (D) – (C)
② (A) – (C) – (D) – (B) – (E)
③ (C) – (A) – (D) – (B) – (E)
④ (C) – (D) – (A) – (E) – (B)
⑤ (C) – (D) – (B) – (A) – (E)

06 다음 대화 중 어색한 것은?

① A: What's your favorite subject?
　B: My favorite subject is math.
② A: I'm gaining weight.
　B: Don't worry. Scientists say that gaining some weight is natural for teens.
③ A: They say that Jane broke her leg yesterday.
　B: I should call and ask why she doesn't come.
④ A: Which day do you prefer, Friday or Saturday?
　B: I prefer Friday to Saturday.
⑤ A: What is your favorite free time activity?
　B: Riding a bike.

[07~09] 다음 대화를 읽고, 물음에 답하시오.

> G: _____(A)_____
> B: Well, they say that there's a special dance show at the Youth Center on Saturday.
> G: _____(B)_____ show is it? (kind)
> B: It's an Indian dance show. 정말 흥미롭다고 그러네.
> B: That sounds nice.

07 빈칸 (A)에 알맞은 말을 고르시오.

① Are you good at making good programs?
② How did you like a special dance show at the Youth Center?
③ Why don't we make good programs this weekend?
④ Are there any good programs this weekend?
⑤ Would you like to stay home this weekend?

08 빈칸 (B)에 들어갈 말을 괄호 안의 단어를 이용하여 쓰시오. (4 단어)

➡ _____

09 밑줄 친 우리말을 주어진 단어를 이용하여 영작하시오.

(people, exciting, it, really) (6 단어)

➡ _____

[10~12] 다음 대화를 읽고, 물음에 답하시오.

> A: What was the (A)[cause / result / report]?
> B: I (B)[gave / told / said / got] da Vinci.
> A: What is a da-Vinci-type person (C)like?
> B: 다빈치 유형의 사람은 상상력이 풍부하다고 그러네.

10 (A)와 (B)에 어울리는 말을 골라 쓰시오.

➡ (A)_____ (B)_____

11 (C)의 like와 같은 의미로 쓰이지 않은 문장을 고르시오.

① I don't like to wash the dishes.
② He sometimes behaves like an idiot.
③ There's no one like you in the world.
④ I want to live in a house like that.
⑤ This cloth feels like silk.

12 밑줄 친 우리말에 맞게 주어진 단어를 배열할 때 6번째 나오는 단어를 고르시오.

> a da-Vinci-type, is, say, imaginative, person, they, that

① that   ② person
③ da-Vinci-type   ④ is
⑤ a

Grammar

13 다음 중 밑줄 친 부분을 생략할 수 있는 것을 모두 고르시오.

① Jack, it's time to wash yourself.
② He killed himself last night.
③ Henry won the contest and he was proud of himself.
④ If we heat ice, it will become water itself.
⑤ Gina herself wanted to meet William.

14 다음 중 어법상 맞는 것은?

① My grandmother lives there of herself.
② Which TV program do you like?
③ What do you like better, tea or coffee?
④ George him made the cake for his girlfriend.
⑤ Why don't you introduce you?

15 밑줄 친 부분의 쓰임이 <u>다른</u> 하나는?

① He wrote the interesting romance novel <u>himself</u>.
② Did she cook *bulgogi* <u>herself</u>?
③ Does Brian often look at <u>himself</u> in the mirror?
④ They <u>themselves</u> prepared the party for their parents.
⑤ You <u>yourself</u> have to think about it.

16 괄호 안의 말을 바르게 배열하여 문장으로 쓰시오.

(1) (Namho / the mirror / himself / looking / enjoys / in / at).

   ➡ _____

(2) (picture / you / which / more / like / do)?

   ➡ _____

(3) (please / yourself / the cake / help / to).

   ➡ _____

17 우리말과 같은 뜻이 되도록 주어진 어휘를 활용하여 문장을 완성하시오.

(1) 그녀는 혼자 힘으로 그 어려운 문제들을 풀었다. (solve, difficult, for) (7 단어)

   ➡ _____

(2) Bill 자신이 그 학교를 졸업했다. (graduate from) (6 단어)

   ➡ _____

(3) Avatar와 Alita 중 어느 것이 더 재미있었니? (interesting, or) (7 단어)

   ➡ _____

18 다음 문장에서 어법상 <u>잘못된</u> 부분을 찾아 바르게 고쳐 쓰시오.

(1) Ask you who you really are.

   _____ ➡ _____

(2) What department of the three will Robert be working in?

   _____ ➡ _____

19 다음 우리말을 영어로 바르게 옮긴 것은?

Jasmine은 혼자 그것을 물 밖으로 꺼내려고 했다.

① Jasmine tried to pull it out of the water by herself.
② Jasmine tried to pull out it of the water on herself.
③ Jasmine tried to pull out it of the water herself.
④ Jasmine tried to pull out it of the water with herself.
⑤ Jasmine tried to pull it out of the water in herself.

20 다음 문장에서 어법상 어색한 부분을 찾아 바르게 고쳐 다시 쓰시오.

(1) Don't compare you with others.

➡ _____

(2) What sport do you play, tennis or baseball?

➡ _____

(3) He him invented the machine which could cook in itself.

➡ _____

(4) Nora never tried to do anything of herself.

➡ _____

Reading

[21~23] 다음 글을 읽고, 물음에 답하시오.

Step 1: Which activities do you enjoy, and which ⓐones are you good at?

I enjoy … / I'm good at …
1. being free and ⓑhaving fun.
2. working with people.
3.   ⓒ   chances.
4. following traditions.

21 위 글의 밑줄 친 ⓐones가 가리키는 것을 본문에서 찾아 쓰시오.

➡ _____

22 위 글의 밑줄 친 ⓑhaving fun과 바꿔 쓸 수 있는 말을 모두 고르시오.

① telling jokes   ② having a good time

③ making fun   ④ causing excitement

⑤ enjoying myself

23 위 글의 빈칸 ⓒ에 들어갈 알맞은 말을 고르시오.

① giving   ② getting

③ having   ④ taking

⑤ keeping

[24~26] 다음 글을 읽고, 물음에 답하시오.

Step 2: What is your color?

Numbers			
①	③	⑬	⑯
4	8	10	14
②	⑤	⑨	⑪
5	7	12	15

*Circle the numbers from Step 1, and find the line with the most circles.

Step 3 What type of person are you?

If you have more circles on the orange line, you are a wonderful energizer. You are witty and lively, and you work best in game settings.

If you have more circles on the gold line, you are an excellent organizer. You are faithful and careful, and you work best with clear rules.

If you have more circles on the blue line, you are a great listener. You are warm and caring, and you work best in groups.

If you have more circles on the green line, you are a curious thinker. You are cool and quiet, and you work best on your own.

24 위 글의 주제로 알맞은 것을 고르시오.

① how to circle the numbers

② the kinds of activities

③ four personality types

④ the difficulty of finding your true color

⑤ the unique and special test

25 위 글의 성격 검사를 한 사람에 대한 설명으로 옳지 않은 것을 고르시오.

① 훌륭한 활력소이다.　　② 재치 있다.
③ 생기 있다.　　④ 멋지고 조용하다.
⑤ 게임 환경에서 가장 잘 일한다.

26 위 글을 읽고 대답할 수 없는 질문은?

① What type is the person who circled the numbers like Step 2?
② If you are an excellent organizer, what is your color?
③ Why does the gold type of person work best with clear rules?
④ If you have more circles on the blue line, what type of person are you?
⑤ Is the green type of person cool and quiet?

[27~28] 다음 글을 읽고, 물음에 답하시오.

What is your type, and how much do you like it? Take this personality test as a first ⓐ <u>step</u> and try to find your true color.

Everyone is unique and has a special color. Why don't you listen to yourself, find special things about yourself, and make the most of them?

27 위 글의 밑줄 친 ⓐstep과 같은 의미로 쓰인 것을 고르시오.

① If you complete the first stage, you can move on to <u>step</u> 2.
② He doesn't like to <u>step</u> across a street.
③ She was sitting on the bottom <u>step</u> of the staircase.
④ I didn't <u>step</u> foot on the ground.
⑤ Let's take a <u>step</u> to avoid troubles.

28 다음 빈칸 (A)와 (B)에 공통으로 들어갈 알맞은 단어를 본문에서 찾아 쓰시오.

Everyone has a ___(A)___ color, so how about listening to yourself, finding ___(B)___ things about yourself, and making the most of them?

➡ _____

[29~30] 다음 글을 읽고, 물음에 답하시오.

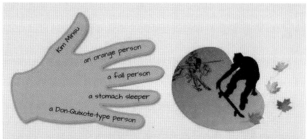

My color is orange. I'm a fall person, and I'm a stomach sleeper. They say that I'm a Don-Quixote-type person. I'm going to put an art board on the classroom wall. ⓐ<u>당신의 꿈, 계획, 그리고 생각들을 게시판에 보여주는 것이 어떨까요?</u>

29 위 글의 밑줄 친 ⓐ의 우리말에 맞게 한 단어를 보충하여, 주어진 어휘를 알맞게 배열하시오.

your / dreams / on the board / plans / why / and / you / ideas / show / ?

➡ _____

_____

30 다음 문장에서 위 글의 내용과 <u>다른</u> 부분을 찾아서 고치시오.

The writer's color is orange. He or she is a fall person, and a stomach sleeper. They say that the writer is a Hamlet-type person.

➡ _____

출제율 90%

01 다음 밑줄 친 부분과 의미가 가장 가까운 것을 주어진 철자로 시작하여 쓰시오.

> He works in productive environment.

➡ s_____

출제율 95%

02 다음 중 밑줄 친 부분의 뜻풀이가 바르지 않은 것을 고르시오.

① Circle the correct answers. (동그라미 표시를 하다)

② He is a mechanical engineer. (기술자)

③ He is a very lively child. (생기 넘치는)

④ I had a chance to hear his music once. (가능성)

⑤ The scarf had some strange patterns on it. (패턴, 무늬)

출제율 90%

03 다음 제시된 의미에 맞는 단어를 주어진 철자로 시작하여 빈칸에 쓰고, 알맞은 것을 골라 문장을 완성하시오. (형태 변화 가능)

> • f_____ : to do what someone has advised you to do
> • o_____ : to prepare or arrange an activity or event
> • p_____ : to make someone feel happy and satisfied

(1) We can't _____ everybody.

(2) You need to _____ his advice.

(3) You can _____ your messages by using folders.

출제율 85%

04 다음 우리말 해석에 맞게 빈칸을 완성하시오. (철자가 주어진 경우 그 철자로 시작할 것)

(1) Thomas Edison was a great _____.
(토마스 에디슨은 위대한 발명가였다.)

(2) His p_____ is hard to understand.
(그의 성격은 이해하기 힘들다.)

(3) What's the _____ of your exam?
(시험 결과는 어떻게 나왔어?)

(4) Summer is the best _____ for swimming. (여름은 수영하기에 가장 좋은 계절이다.)

(5) He has u_____ taste in clothes.
(그는 옷 고르는 취향이 독특하다.)

(6) People are dancing on the _____.
(사람들이 무대에서 춤을 추고 있다.)

[05~06] 다음 글을 읽고 물음에 답하시오.

> W: 여러분들은 어느 잠자는 자세를 선호합니까? Some positions are good, and some are bad. Sleep scientists say that we become healthy when we sleep in a bad position.

출제율 95%

05 밑줄 친 우리말을 영작하시오.

➡ _____

출제율 95%

06 밑줄 친 부분에서 내용상 어색한 것을 골라 고치시오.

➡ _____

07 다음 대화 중 어색한 것은?

① A: They say that you're a new class leader.

　 B: Yes, I feel so great.

② A: What's your favorite dessert?

　 B: I love strawberry ice cream.

③ A: Which bag do you prefer?

　 B: I'm not sure.

④ A: What are summer people like?

　 B: They like surfing.

⑤ A: What test is the boy taking?

　 B: He is taking a personality test.

08 다음 대화의 빈칸 ⓐ~ⓔ에 들어갈 수 없는 표현을 고르시오.

A: ___ⓐ___ do you sleep?

B: I sleep in the stomach position.

A: ___ⓑ___ stomach sleepers like?

B: People ___ⓒ___ are open and playful.

A: ___ⓓ___ is that position for your health?

B: Scientists ___ⓔ___ the worst position for sleeping.

① say that they　　② What are

③ When　　　　　 ④ say that it's

⑤ How good

[09~10] 다음 대화를 읽고, 물음에 답하시오.

G: Is that a new snack shop?

B: Yes, it is.

G: I'm hungry. ___(A)___ you like to get some pancakes at the shop?

B: Sure, I'd love to.

09 빈칸 (A)에 알맞은 말을 고르시오.

① Should　　② Could　　③ Will

④ Would　　⑤ May

10 According to the dialog, what will they do? Answer in English. (10 words)

➡ _____

[11~12] 다음 대화를 읽고, 물음에 답하시오.

G: It's very hot.

B: Yeah, it really is.

G: _____(A)_____

B: That's a good idea. Which ___(B)___ do you prefer?

G: I prefer the chocolate flavor.

11 빈칸 (A)에 어울리는 말을 고르시오.

① Why don't we get some ice cream at the shop across the street?

② Which one do you prefer?

③ What kind of ice cream do you like?

④ Are there any good ideas?

⑤ Are you going to go to Sweet Snack?

12 빈칸 (B)에 알맞은 말을 대화에서 찾아 쓰시오.

➡ _____

13 다음 중 어법상 자연스러운 문장은?

① Jane knows himself.

② I'm afraid you may cut yourself while you are cooking.

③ Socrates, do you know you?

④ Andy finished the difficult project him.

⑤ He went there in himself.

출제율 95%

14 다음 중 어법상 어색한 것은?

① Do I know myself?
② What is your type, and how much do you like it?
③ Can you go there by yourself?
④ What of these questions is the most difficult?
⑤ You'd better practice making eye contact with yourself in the mirror.

[15~16] 다음 글을 읽고, 물음에 답하시오.

Who am I? What type of person am I? Do you have these questions? Here we have an interesting personality test for you.

Step 1: Which activities do you enjoy, and which ones are you good at?

I enjoy … / I'm good at …
1. being free and having fun.
2. working ⓐ people.
3. taking chances.
13. being on stage.
14. working ⓑ directions.
15. solving puzzles.
16. playing sports.

출제율 90%

15 위 글의 빈칸 ⓐ와 ⓑ에 공통으로 들어갈 알맞은 전치사를 고르시오.

① for ② on
③ in ④ by
⑤ with

출제율 90%

16 다음 문장에서 위 글의 내용과 다른 부분을 찾아서 고치시오.

If you want to know who you are or what type of person you are, you can try to have an interesting performance test.

➡ _____

[17~18] 다음 글을 읽고, 물음에 답하시오.

What is your type, and how much do you like it? Take this personality test as a first step and try ⓐto find your true color.

Everyone is unique and has a special color. ⓑWhy don't you listen to yourself, find special things about yourself, and make the most of them?

출제율 95%

17 위 글의 밑줄 친 ⓐto find와 to부정사의 용법이 다른 것을 모두 고르시오.

① He decided to buy a new smartphone.
② She got up early to catch the train.
③ It is difficult to know yourself.
④ My hope is to go to Paris.
⑤ I want something cold to drink.

출제율 90%

18 위 글의 밑줄 친 ⓑ와 의미가 같은 말을 모두 고르시오.

① How about listening
② How do you listen
③ Why do you listen
④ What about listening
⑤ Why can't you listen

[19~21] 다음 글을 읽고, 물음에 답하시오.

Dear Diary

Which subjects should I study more? Which after-school activities should I join? I have a lot of questions about school life.

The personality test says that I am an excellent organizer. ⓐIt also says that I am faithful and careful, and I work best with clear rules.

I am going to start from ⓑmy strong points. I want to make the most of them. I know that I can do really well this year.

19 위 글의 밑줄 친 ⓐIt이 가리키는 것을 본문에서 찾아 쓰시오.

출제율 95%

➡ _____

20 위 글의 밑줄 친 ⓑmy strong points가 가리키는 것 세 가지를 우리말로 쓰시오.

출제율 90%

➡ (1) _____
(2) _____
(3) _____

21 위 글을 읽고 글쓴이에 대해 알 수 없는 것을 고르시오.

출제율 90%

① 더 열심히 공부해야 할 과목
② 어떤 유형의 사람인가?
③ 어떤 성격인가?
④ 어떤 때 일을 가장 잘하는가?
⑤ 무엇을 최대한 활용하고 싶어 하는가?

[22~24] 다음 글을 읽고, 물음에 답하시오.

Orange
I act on a moment's notice.
I consider life as a game, here and now.
I need fun and excitement.
I value skill and courage.
I am a performer.

Gold
I need to follow rules.
I have a strong sense of right and wrong in life.
I need to be useful.
I value home, family, and tradition.
I am a helper.

Blue
I need to feel unique.
I look for meaning in life.
I need to care.
I value unity in relationships.
I am a poet.

Green
I seek knowledge and understanding.
I live a life by my own standards.
I need explanations and answers.
I value fairness, and justice.
I am a problem solver.

22 위 글의 제목으로 알맞은 것을 고르시오.

출제율 95%

① What Color Do You Like Most?
② I Prefer Orange to Gold!
③ The Most Popular Color
④ Guess Who I Am by Color!
⑤ How about Choosing One Color?

23 다음 질문에 대한 알맞은 대답을 쓰시오. (3 단어)

출제율 95%

Q: What type is the person whose color is green?
A: He or she is _____.

➡ _____

24 위 글의 내용과 일치하지 않는 것은?

출제율 95%

① 주황색 유형인 사람은 재미와 흥분을 필요로 한다.
② 기술과 용기를 가치 있게 여기는 사람은 황금색 유형의 사람이다.
③ 황금색 유형인 사람은 조력자이다.
④ 푸른색 유형인 사람은 삶의 의미를 찾는다.
⑤ 설명과 대답을 필요로 하는 사람은 초록색 유형의 사람이다.

01 다음 그림을 보고 대화에서 <u>어색한</u> 부분을 찾아 고치시오. (3개)

B: Are they new ice cream flavors?
G: Yes, they do. They look deliciously.
B: What flavor do you prefer?
G: I prefer the strawberry flavor.

➡ (1) _____
　 (2) _____
　 (3) _____

[02~03] 다음 대화를 읽고, 그림을 참고하여 물음에 답하시오.

G: Look at the cakes!
B: They look yummy.
G: (A) (do, most, cake, which, like, you)?
B: (B) <u>난 초콜릿 케이크를 가장 좋아해.</u>

02 (A)에 주어진 단어를 알맞은 순서로 배열하시오.

➡ _____

03 밑줄 친 우리말 (B)에 맞게 영작하시오.

➡ _____

04 다음 우리말을 주어진 어휘를 이용하여 영작하시오.

(1) 자연 그 자체가 교사라는 말은 사실이다. (it, true, a teacher) (9 단어)

➡ _____

(2) 태권도는 스스로를 방어하기 위해 쓰일 수 있다. (one, use Taekwondo, defend) (7 단어)

➡ _____

(3) 그는 이 검은 것과 저 빨간 것 중에서 어느 책을 읽었니? (this black one, that red one) (12 단어)

➡ _____

(4) 그것을 어떤 색으로 칠하고 싶니? (want, paint, it) (8 단어)

➡ _____

(5) 들어와서 편하게 있어요. (in, make, and, at home) (7 단어)

➡ _____

05 다음 두 문장을 해석하고 그 차이점을 설명하시오.

(1) Van Gogh painted himself.
(2) Van Gogh painted him.

➡ 해석
　 (1) _____
　 (2) _____
　 차이점
　 (1) _____
　 (2) _____

[06~08] 다음 글을 읽고, 물음에 답하시오.

Who am I? What type of person am I? Do you have these questions? Here we have an interesting ⓐ test for you.

Step 1: Which activities do you enjoy, and which ones are you good at?

I enjoy ⋯ / I'm good at ⋯
1. being free and having fun.
2. working with people.
3. taking chances.
4. following traditions.
5. working on my own.
6. writing stories.
7. learning new things.
8. following the rules.
9. making new friends.
10. planning things out.
11. pleasing others.
12. finding new patterns.
13. being on stage.
14. working with directions.
15. solving puzzles.
16. playing sports.

Step 2: What is your color?

Numbers			
1	3	13	⑯
4	8	10	14
②	6	⑨	⑪
5	7	⑫	15

*Circle the numbers from Step 1, and find the line with the most circles.

Step 3 What type of person are you?

If you have more circles on the blue line, you are a great listener. You are warm and caring, and you work best in groups.

06 주어진 영영풀이를 참고하여 빈칸 ⓐ에 철자 p로 시작하는 단어를 쓰시오.

your whole character and nature

➡ _____

07 위 글의 성격 검사를 한 사람이 즐겨하거나 잘한다고 응답한 활동을 우리말로 모두 쓰시오.

➡ (1) _____
(2) _____
(3) _____
(4) _____
(5) _____

08 다음 빈칸 (A)와 (B)에 알맞은 단어를 넣어 위 글의 성격 검사를 한 사람의 유형을 설명하시오.

Because the person has more circles on the (A)_____ line, he or she is (B)_____ _____ _____ and works best in groups.

➡ (A) _____
(B) _____ _____ _____

[09~10] 다음 글을 읽고, 물음에 답하시오.

Step 3 What type of person are you?

If you have more circles on the orange line, you are a wonderful energizer. You are (A) [wit / witty] and lively, and you work best in game settings.

If you have more circles on the gold line, you are an excellent organizer. You are (B) [faith / faithful] and careful, and you work best with clear rules.

09 위 글의 괄호 (A)~(B)에서 문맥이나 어법상 알맞은 낱말을 골라 쓰시오.

➡ (A) _____ (B) _____

10 If you have more circles on the orange line, in what circumstance do you work best? Answer in English.

➡ _____

창의사고력 서술형 문제

01 그림을 보고 주어진 조건에 맞추어 빈칸을 완성하시오.

Carrot cake Green tea cake

조건
1. 대화의 흐름에 맞게 쓸 것.
2. 한 칸에 한 단어만 쓸 것.

A: Mom, do you have something to eat?

B: Yes. _____ _____ _____ , _____ _____ or _____ _____ ?

A: I prefer _____ _____ _____ _____ _____ . I don't like carrots.

B: Okay. Here you are.

A: Thank you.

02 다음 주어진 동사와 재귀대명사를 사용하여 다양한 문장을 완성하시오.

feel, introduce, walk, make

(1) _____

(2) _____

(3) _____

(4) _____

03 다음 내용을 바탕으로 새 학년을 맞이하는 마음가짐을 나타내는 글을 쓰시오.

1. Which subjects should I study more?
Which after-school activities should I join?

2. What does the personality test say about me?
It says that I am an excellent organizer.
It also says that I am faithful and careful, and I work best with clear rules.

Dear Diary

Which (A)_____ should I study more? Which after-school activities should I join?

The (B)_____ test says that I am (C)_____ _____ _____ . It also says that I am faithful and careful, and I work best (D)_____ _____ _____ .

I am going to start from my (E)_____ _____ . I want to make the most of them. I know that I can do really well this year.

단원별 모의고사

[01~02] 다음 밑줄 친 부분과 의미가 가장 가까운 것을 쓰시오. (철자가 주어진 경우 주어진 철자로 시작할 것)

01

Make sure to follow the <u>directions</u>.

➡ i_____

02

I can fix the bicycle <u>on my own</u>.

➡ _____ (2 단어)

03 빈칸을 〈보기〉에 주어진 단어를 이용해서 채우시오. (형태 변화 가능)

┌─── 보기 ├───
| ask | buy | do | make | have |
| go | prefer | like | plan |

(1) Let's _____ the most of this chance.
(2) You have to _____ out how you're going to deal with your recovery.
(3) We should _____ our parents and teachers for good advice.

04 다음 우리말 해석에 맞게 빈칸을 완성하시오. (철자가 주어진 경우 그 철자로 시작할 것)

(1) This is a new t_____ of car. (이것은 새로운 유형의 차다.)
(2) I have a pain in the s_____. (나는 배가 아프다.)

05 다음 보기 중 영영풀이가 <u>잘못된</u> 것을 고르시오.

① activity: things that people do; something that you do because you enjoy it
② stage: the part of a theater where the actors or musicians perform
③ caring: full of life and spirit
④ personality: someone's character, especially the way they behave towards other people
⑤ tradition: a very old custom or belief

[06~07] 다음 대화를 읽고, 물음에 답하시오.

A: (A) 넌 어떤 종류의 사람이 되고 싶니?
B: I want to be a Don-Quixote-type person. They say that a Don-Quixote-type person is _____ (B) _____ (energy). I want to become a famous entertainer.

06 밑줄 친 (A)의 우리말을 주어진 단어를 이용해 영작하시오.

(be, type, want)

➡ _____

07 빈칸 (B)에 주어진 단어를 문맥에 맞게 쓰시오.

➡ _____

[08~10] 다음 대화를 읽고, 물음에 답하시오.

Nara: ___(A)___ did you like the test?

Seho: It was really fun. I learned a lot ⓐ_____.

Nara: ___(B)___ of person are you?

Seho: I'm a da-Vinci-type person.

Nara: That sounds cool. ___(C)___ are da-Vinci people good ⓑ_____?

Seho: They say that da-Vinci people ⓒmake good inventors and artists.

Nara: ___(D)___ one do you prefer?

Seho: I'm not sure. I'm going to ask my teacher for some advice.

08 빈칸 (A)~(D)에 들어갈 말을 쓰시오. ((A), (C), (D)에는 한 단어, (B)에는 두 단어)

➡ (A) _____ (B) _____

(C) _____ (D) _____

09 빈칸 ⓐ와 ⓑ에 문맥이나 어법상 올바른 표현을 골라 짝지은 것은?

	ⓐ	ⓑ
①	of me	at
②	of myself	on
③	about me	on
④	about myself	on
⑤	about myself	at

10 밑줄 친 ⓒmake와 바꾸어 쓸 수 있는 것을 고르시오.

① take   ② create

③ get   ④ put

⑤ become

[11~12] 다음 대화를 읽고, 물음에 답하시오.

A: 넌 어떤 자세로 잠을 자니?

B: I sleep in the stomach position.

A: What are stomach sleepers like?

B: People say that they are open and playful.

A: How good is that position for your health?

B: Scientists say that it's the worst position for sleeping.

11 밑줄 친 우리말을 주어진 단어를 이용해 영작하시오.

➡ _____ (in)

12 다음 영영풀이에 해당하는 단어를 대화에서 찾아 쓰시오.

> a baglike organ in the body where food is broken down for use in the body after being eaten

➡ _____

13 다음 중 어법상 어색한 것은?

① Please help yourself to the cake.

② Which movie do you prefer?

③ We can express us through our fashion.

④ What type of person are you?

⑤ Harold wrote the interesting fantasy novel by himself.

14 다음 괄호 안의 단어를 알맞게 변형하여 쓰시오. (필요한 경우 단어를 추가할 것)

(1) Sophie made the beautiful dress for her daughter all by _____. (she)

(2) He was in his car alone and he hurt _____ because of the accident. (he)

(3) The window in my room closed of _____. (it)

15 〈보기〉의 밑줄 친 부분의 용법이 나머지 넷과 <u>다른</u> 하나는?

> ┌── 보기 ──┐
> You've hurt <u>yourself</u>, haven't you?

① May I introduce <u>myself</u>?
② Did you make the model plane <u>yourself</u>?
③ Mother Terasa didn't think about <u>herself</u>.
④ You have to take care of <u>yourself</u> from now on
⑤ Jack and Gill blamed <u>themselves</u> for the whole thing.

16 다음 중 어법상 <u>어색한</u> 문장은?

① Know yourself and you will win every war.
② What kind of sleeper are you?
③ I've locked myself out of my car.
④ What color do you prefer, blue or green?
⑤ This is Goethe's saying: Magic is believing in yourself.

17 다음 문장에서 어법상 <u>어색한</u> 부분을 찾아 바르게 고쳐 다시 쓰시오.

(1) We should love us.

➡ _____

(2) Don't have the whole pizza on the table by you.

➡ _____

(3) If I don't finish this work by tomorrow, I me will be angry.

➡ _____

(4) You must expect great things of you before you can do them.

➡ _____

[18~20] 다음 글을 읽고, 물음에 답하시오.

> Who am I? What type of person am I? Do you have these questions? ⓐHere we have an interesting personality test for you.
>
> **Step 1: Which activities do you enjoy, and which ones are you good at?**
>
> | I enjoy … / I'm good at … |
> | --- |
> | 1. being free and having fun. |
> | 9. making new friends. |
> | 10. ⓑto plan things out. |
> | 11. pleasing others. |

18 위 글의 제목으로 알맞은 것을 고르시오.

① How Much Do You Know about the Test?
② The Strong Point of Personality Test
③ The Weak Point of Personality Test
④ What Type of Person Am I?
⑤ How Many Activities Can You Do?

19 위 글의 밑줄 친 ⓐHere we have를 다음과 같이 바꿔 쓸 때 빈칸에 들어갈 알맞은 단어를 쓰시오.

➡ Here _____

20 위 글의 밑줄 친 ⓑ에서 어법상 틀린 부분을 찾아 고치시오.

_____ ➡ _____

[21~23] 다음 글을 읽고, 물음에 답하시오.

Step 3 What type of person are you?

If you have more circles on the orange line, you are a wonderful ___ⓐ___ . You are witty and lively, and you work best in game settings.

If you have more circles on the gold line, you are an excellent organizer. You are faithful and careful, and you work best with clear rules.

If you have more circles on the blue line, you are a great listener. You are warm and caring, and you work best in groups.

If you have more circles on the green line, you are a curious thinker. You are cool and quiet, and you work best on your own.

What is your type, and how much do you like it? Take this personality test ⓑas a first step and try to find your true color.

Everyone is unique and has a special color. Why don't you listen to yourself, find special things about yourself, and make the most of them?

21 위 글의 빈칸 ⓐ에 들어갈 알맞은 말을 고르시오.

① consumer   ② helper
③ energizer   ④ troublemaker
⑤ mentor

22 위 글의 내용과 일치하도록 다음 빈칸 (A)와 (B)에 알맞은 단어를 쓰시오.

If your color is __(A)__ , you are a curious thinker. You are cool and quiet, and you work best _____(B)_____ .

➡ (A) _____ (B) _____

23 위 글의 밑줄 친 ⓑas와 같은 의미로 쓰인 것을 고르시오.

① You're as tall as your mother.
② I sat watching her as she got ready.
③ As she was out, he left a message.
④ As you know, Tom is leaving soon.
⑤ That box can be used as a table.

[24~25] 다음 글을 읽고, 물음에 답하시오.

Dear Diary

Which subjects should I study more? Which after-school activities should I join? I have a lot of questions ___ⓐ___ school life.

The personality test says that I am an excellent organizer. It also says that I am faithful and careful, and I work best with clear rules.

I am going to start from my strong points. I want to make the most ___ⓑ___ them. I know that I can do really well this year.

24 위 글의 빈칸 ⓐ와 ⓑ에 들어갈 전치사가 바르게 짝지어진 것은?

① for – from   ② about – of
③ for – to   ④ about – for
⑤ at – of

25 위 글을 읽고 대답할 수 없는 질문은?

① Which after-school activities should the writer join?
② What type of person is the writer?
③ Is the writer a careless person?
④ When does the writer work best?
⑤ What does the writer know?

Old Things, New Art

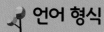 **의사소통 기능**

- 걱정 표현하기
  I'm worried about the waste problem.
- 동의하기
  You can say that again.

언어 형식

- 수동태
  It **was created by** Pablo Picasso.
- not only A but also B
  He used **not only** old things **but also** his imagination.

Words & Expressions

Key Words

- **able** [éibl] 형 ~할 수 있는
- **agree** [əgríː] 동 동의하다
- **another** [ənʌ́ðər] 형 다른, 또 하나의
- **artwork** [ɑrtwə́ːrk] 명 예술 작품
- **bit** [bit] 명 작은 조각
- **board** [bɔːrd] 명 판자
- **bottle** [bátl] 명 병
- **button** [bʌ́tən] 명 단추, 버튼
- **cloth** [klɔːθ] 명 옷감, 천
- **clothes** [klouz] 명 옷
- **collect** [kəlékt] 동 모으다, 수집하다
- **contest** [kántest] 명 대회, 시합
- **create** [kriéit] 동 창작하다, 창조하다
- **famous** [féiməs] 형 유명한
- **glue** [gluː] 동 접착제로 붙이다
- **green** [griːn] 형 환경 보호의, 친환경적인
- **handlebar** [hǽndəlbɑr] 명 (흔히 복수형으로 쓰여) 핸들
- **hurry** [hə́ːri] 동 서두르다, 급히 하다
- **imagination** [imæʤənéiʃən] 명 상상력, 상상
- **junk** [ʤʌŋk] 명 폐물, 고물
- **kind** [kaind] 명 종류
- **lamp** [læmp] 명 램프, 등
- **less** [les] 형 더 적은
- **mattress** [mǽtris] 명 매트리스
- **mess** [mes] 명 (지저분하고) 엉망인 상태
- **nail** [neil] 동 못으로 박다 명 못
- **object** [ábʤikt] 명 물건
- **often** [ɔ́ːfən] 부 흔히
- **part** [pɑrt] 명 부품, 부분, 일부

- **pass** [pæs] 동 (시험에) 통과하다
- **patch** [pæʧ] 명 부분, 조각
- **patchwork** [pǽʧwərk] 명 쪽모이 깁기, 패치워크
- **picture** [píkʧər] 명 그림
- **piece** [piːs] 명 부분, 조각
- **problem** [prábləm] 명 문제
- **quilt** [kwilt] 명 누비이불, 퀼트
- **reuse** [riːjúːz] 동 재사용하다
- **rubbish** [rʌ́biʃ] 명 쓰레기
- **sculpture** [skʌ́lpʧər] 명 조각품
- **seat** [siːt] 명 좌석, 안장
- **set** [set] 명 세트
- **slipper** [slípər] 명 슬리퍼, 실내화
- **slogan** [slóugən] 명 구호, 슬로건
- **style** [stail] 명 방식
- **such** [sʌʧi] 형 그러한
- **thread** [θred] 명 실 동 (실 등을) 꿰다
- **thrown-away** [θróunəwéi] 형 버려진
- **trash** [træʃ] 명 쓰레기
- **treasure** [tréʒər] 명 보물
- **upset** [ʌ́pset] 동 속상하게 만들다
- **used** [juːzd] 형 중고의
- **useful** [júːsfəl] 형 쓸모 있는, 유용한
- **waste** [weist] 명 쓰레기 동 낭비하다
- **woman** [wúmən] 명 여성
- **wood** [wud] 명 나무, 목재
- **worry** [wə́ːri] 동 걱정하다
- **wrap** [ræp] 동 (포장지 등으로) 싸다

Key Expressions

- **a bit** 다소, 약간
- **agree with** ~에 동의하다
- **be able to 동사원형** ~할 수 있다
- **be late for** ~에 늦다
- **be worried about** ~에 대해 걱정하다
- **clean up** 치우다, 청소하다
- **forget to 동사원형** ~할 것을 잊다
- **have a good time** 즐거운 시간을 보내다
- **hurry up** 서두르다

- **look + 형용사** ~하게 보이다
- **look at** ~을 보다
- **look like 명사** ~처럼 보이다
- **make noise** 시끄럽게 떠들다, 소란을 피우다
- **make use of** ~을 이용하다
- **not only A but also B** A뿐만 아니라 B도
- **pass the test** 시험에 합격하다
- **pick up** 줍다, 얻다

Word Power

※ 서로 비슷한 뜻을 가진 단어

□ **able**(~할 수 있는, 유능한) : **capable**(유능한, 능력 있는)

□ **contest**(대회, 시합) : **match**(경기, 시합)

□ **hurry**(서두르다, 급히 하다) : **rush**(돌진하다, 서두르다)

□ **trash**(쓰레기) : **rubbish** / **waste**(쓰레기)

□ **useful**(쓸모 있는, 유용한) : **helpful**(도움이 되는, 유용한)

□ **green**(환경 보호의, 친환경적인) : **environment-friendly**(환경 친화적인)

□ **collect**(모으다, 수집하다) : **gather**(모으다)

□ **famous**(유명한) : **well-known**(유명한)

□ **kind**(종류) : **sort**(종류), **type**(종류)

□ **used**(중고의) : **second-hand**(중고의)

□ **wrap**((포장지 등으로) 싸다) : **pack**(포장하다)

※ dis-가 붙어 반의어를 만드는 단어

□ **advantage**(유리) ↔ **disadvantage**(불리)

□ **appear**(나타나다, 출현하다) ↔ **disappear**(사라지다)

□ **agree**(동의하다) ↔ **disagree**(동의하지 않다)

□ **like**(좋아하다) ↔ **dislike**(싫어하다)

※ 접두어 re가 '다시'의 의미를 가진 단어

□ **rewrite**(다시 쓰다)   □ **reuse**(재사용하다)   □ **remake**(다시 만들다)

English Dictionary

□ **another** 다른, 또 하나의
→ being an additional thing or person of the same type
같은 종류의 사물이나 사람이 하나 더 추가되는

□ **artwork** 예술 작품
→ paintings or sculptures that are of high quality
양질의 그림이나 조각품

□ **board** 판자
→ a flat, thin, rectangular piece of wood or plastic
나무나 플라스틱의 평평하고 얇은 직사각형 모양의 조각

□ **collect** 모으다, 수집하다
→ to bring many things together from several places or people
여러 장소나 여러 사람으로부터 많은 것을 가져오다

□ **contest** 대회, 시합
→ a competition judged by a group of specially chosen judges
특별히 선정된 심판들의 모임에 의해 판정되는 경쟁

□ **create** 창조하다
→ to invent or design something
어떤 것을 발명하거나 설계하다

□ **glue** 접착제로 붙이다
→ to stick one object to another using glue
풀을 사용해서 한 물체를 다른 것과 붙이다

□ **handlebar** (흔히 복수형으로 쓰여) 핸들
→ the curved metal bar with handles for steering
조종을 위한 손잡이가 달린 곡선의 금속의 막대기

□ **junk** 폐물, 고물
→ old and used goods that have little value
거의 가치가 없는 오래되고 사용한 물건들

□ **nail** 못으로 박다
→ to attach something somewhere using one or more nails
한 개나 그 이상의 못을 사용하여 어떤 곳에 어떤 것을 붙이다

□ **problem** 문제
→ a situation that causes difficulties for people
사람들에게 어려움을 일으키는 상황

□ **reuse** 재사용하다
→ to use something again instead of throwing it away
무언가를 버리는 대신에 다시 사용하다

□ **rubbish** 쓰레기
→ unwanted things or waste materials
원하지 않는 물건이나 폐기물

□ **slogan** 구호, 슬로건
→ a short phrase expressing an advertising message
광고 메시지를 표현하는 짧은 어구

□ **trash** 쓰레기
→ waste material that will be thrown away
버려질 폐기물

□ **used** 중고의
→ no longer new
더 이상 새것이 아닌

01 다음 중 뜻이 <u>다른</u> 것을 고르시오. (2개)

① waste ② rubbish ③ litter
④ object ⑤ bit

02 다음 대화의 밑줄 친 부분과 의미가 가장 가까운 것을 고르시오.

> A: We should go green.
> B: You can say that again.

① famous
② recycled
③ valuable
④ saved
⑤ environment-friendly

03 다음 대화의 빈칸에 알맞은 단어를 고르시오.

> A: What a _____! Let's clean up your room.
> B: That's a good idea.

① mess ② difficulty ③ mattress
④ thread ⑤ part

[04~05] 다음 밑줄 친 부분과 의미가 가장 가까운 것을 고르시오.

04
> I'm looking for a <u>used</u> car.

① useful
② modern
③ safe
④ second-hand
⑤ green

05
> This city is <u>famous</u> for its fog.

① right
② common
③ special
④ well-known
⑤ several

06 주어진 단어를 이용해 빈칸을 완성하시오.

> He used his _____ to create artwork. (imagine)

[07~08] 다음 빈칸에 들어갈 말로 적절한 것은?

07
> I'm sorry, but I don't agree _____ you.

① as ② with
③ for ④ in
⑤ to

08
> There's no _____. Take your time.

① hurry ② hope
③ junk ④ reason
⑤ success

09 다음 주어진 우리말에 맞게 빈칸을 채우시오. (철자가 주어진 것이 있으면 그 철자로 시작할 것)

(1) 너 이 수학 문제를 풀 수 있니?
➡ Are you _____ _____ solve this math problem?

(2) 이 병을 어떻게 열지?
➡ _____ do I open this _____?

(3) 아빠가 옷을 세탁기에 넣고 있다.
➡ My dad is putting c_____ in the washing machine.

(4) 당신은 무엇을 모으는 것을 좋아하세요?
➡ What do you like to _____?

01 다음 짝지어진 단어의 관계가 같도록 빈칸에 알맞은 말을 쓰시오.

> happy : unhappy – agree : _____

02 주어진 단어를 이용해 우리말 해석에 맞게 빈칸을 완성하시오.

(1) Eco-friendly things are easier to _____. (use) (환경 친화적인 물건들은 더 쉽게 다시 사용된다.)

(2) How _____ are you about the waste problem? (worry) (넌 쓰레기 문제에 대해 얼마나 걱정하고 있니?)

[03~05] 빈칸에 공통으로 들어갈 단어를 쓰시오.

03
> • They say that we should _____ less trash.
> • You should _____ use of every chance of speaking English.

04
> • They need those _____s to make the engine.
> • This is the most interesting _____ in this movie.

05
> • I forgot _____ bring the camera.
> • Are you able _____ sing the song?

06 밑줄 친 부분과 의미가 가장 가까운 단어를 주어진 철자로 시작하여 쓰시오.

(1) The street is full of <u>trash</u>.

　➡ r_____

(2) He carefully <u>packed</u> the Christmas gift.

　➡ w_____

07 다음 우리말에 맞게 주어진 단어를 바르게 배열하시오.

(1) 그들이 원하는 건 오직 약간의 빵이다.
(they, bread, a, all, bit, want, of, is, little)

➡ _____

(2) 남자가 탁자를 천으로 덮었다.
(man, with, the, the, a, cloth, covered, table)

➡ _____

(3) 자전거 경기 중에 그의 핸들이 부러졌다.
(handlebars, bicycle, his, during, race, broke, a)

➡ _____

(4) 폐품 예술가는 쓰레기를 아름다운 모양으로 바꾼다.
(artists, beautiful, junk, shapes, into, trash, turn)

➡ _____

(5) 나는 표지판을 못으로 벽에 박았다.
(to, nailed, the, the, I, wall, sign)

➡ _____

Conversation

① 걱정 표현하기

I'm worried about the waste problem. 난 쓰레기 문제에 대해 걱정하고 있어.

■ 걱정 표현하기(I'm worried about the waste problem.)에서 'be worried about'은 걱정을 나타내는 표현으로, '~에 대해 걱정하다'라는 뜻을 지닌다. 걱정의 정도를 강조할 때에는, be so[very] worried about과 같이 worried 앞에 so 또는 very를 사용할 수 있다.

■ 걱정을 표현하는 다른 것으로 'I'm worried (that)+주어+동사'가 있다. 이것은 '나는 (주어)가 ~인 것이 걱정돼'라는 의미로 that절 이하에 걱정하는 내용이 온다. 그 외에 '~에 대해 걱정하다'라는 의미의 표현으로 be anxious about, be concerned about 등이 있다.

걱정 표현하기

- be worried about (동)명사 ~.
- be concerned about (동)명사 ~.
- be anxious about (동)명사 ~.
- be worried (that) 주어+동사 ~.

걱정과 관련한 표현

- I'm worried about ~. 나는 ~에 대해 걱정하고 있어.
- I'm not worried about ~. 나는 ~을 걱정하지 않아.
- I never worry about ~. 나는 ~을 전혀 걱정 안 해.

걱정 표현하기

- Don't worry. 걱정하지 마.
- Try not to get worried. you'll do fine. 걱정하지 않도록 해 봐. 넌 잘할 거야.
- I'm sure everything will be OK. 분명히 모든 것이 잘될 거야.

핵심 Check

1. 다음 우리말과 일치하도록 빈칸에 알맞은 말을 쓰시오.

   A: _____ really _____ _____ my sister. (나는 나의 여동생이 매우 걱정스러워.)

   B: Why? (왜?)

   A: She doesn't exercise at all. (그녀는 운동을 전혀 하지 않아.)

2. 다음 우리말과 일치하도록 주어진 단어를 배열하여 문장을 만드시오.

   A: You look down. Is something wrong? (너 우울해 보여. 무슨 문제가 있니?)

   B: _____ (do, the, on, I'm, test, worried, well, didn't, English, I) (영어 시험을 잘 못 봐서 걱정이야.)

② 동의하기

> **You can say that again.** 전적으로 동감이야.

- 'You can say that again.'은 상대방의 말에 동의하는 표현으로, '동감이다' 또는 '정말 그렇다'라는 뜻을 나타낸다.
- 상대방의 말이나 의견에 전적으로 동의할 때, 'You're telling me.(내 말이 바로 그 말이에요[전적으로 동의해요].)', 'That's precisely my point.(당신의 의견에 동의해요.)'라는 표현을 사용할 수 있다.

동의하기

- You can say that again.
- I'm with you.
- That makes two of us.
- You read my mind.
- I think so.

- I agree (with you).
- I'm in favor of that.
- I'm with you on that.
- You're right.
- I couldn't agree more.

동의하지 않을 때

- I don't think so.
- I'm afraid I don't think so.

- No, I don't agree.
- I'm against it.

핵심 Check

3. 다음 밑줄 친 부분과 같은 의미가 되도록 주어진 단어를 이용해 문장을 만드시오.

A: The musical is interesting. Don't you think so?

B: <u>I think so, too.</u>

➡ _____ (agree)

4. 다음 우리말과 일치하도록 빈칸에 알맞은 말을 쓰시오.

A: I can't believe that we are moving on to high school.

B: You're _____ _____. (내 말이 바로 그 말이야.)

5. 다음 우리말과 일치하도록 주어진 단어를 배열하여 쓰시오.

A: What do you think of online shopping? (너는 온라인 쇼핑에 대해 어떻게 생각하니?)

B: In my opinion, it saves time. (내 생각에 그것은 시간을 절약해 줘.)

A: _____ (that, can, you, again, say)

(나도 그렇게 생각해.)

A. Listen & Speak ① A-1

G: ❶What's wrong, Seho?

B: ❷I'm worried about my science presentation.

G: ❸Don't worry too much. ❹You'll do a good job.

G: 무슨 일이니, 세호야?
B: 내 과학 발표에 대해 걱정하고 있어.
G: 너무 걱정하지 마. 넌 잘할 거야.

❶ 상대방의 걱정에 대해 물어보는 표현으로 '무슨 일이니?'의 의미를 가진다. 비슷한 표현으로 'What's wrong with you?', 'What's the matter?', 'Is there anything wrong (with you)?', 'What happened?', 'What's the problem?' 등이 있다.

❷ be worried about: ~에 대해 걱정하다 about은 전치사이기 때문에 명사나 동명사가 나올 수 있다. 비슷한 표현으로 be anxious about, be concerned about 등이 있다.

❸ 상대방이 낙담하지 않도록 위로할 때 'Don't worry (about it)', 혹은 'Don't worry too much' 등으로 말할 수 있다.

❹ 걱정을 하는 상대방을 안심시키는 표현이다. 'Try not to get worried. You'll do fine.', 'I'm sure everything will be OK.' 등으로 바꿔 쓸 수 있다.

Check(√) True or False

(1) Seho made presentation about science. T ☐ F ☐

(2) The girl tries to cheer up Seho. T ☐ F ☐

(3) Seho is concerned about his presentation. T ☐ F ☐

B. Listen & Speak ② A-1

G: ❶Look at this mess!

B: ❷Let's clean it up. We ❸should ❹keep our classroom clean.

G: ❺You can say that again.

G: 이 엉망인 상태를 봐!
B: 청소하자. 우리는 우리 교실을 깨끗하게 유지해야 해.
G: 전적으로 동감이야.

❶ look at: ~을 보다 mess: (지저분하고) 엉망인 상태

❷ 'clean up'은 이어동사인데, 이어동사는 '타동사+부사(on, off, up, over 등)'로 이루어져 있다. '동사+부사+목적어'의 어순이나 '동사+목적어+부사'의 어순 둘 다 가능하다. 하지만 목적어 자리에 it, them 따위의 인칭대명사가 올 때는 반드시 '동사+목적어(인칭대명사)+부사'의 어순으로 써야 한다. (put off the concert (O), put the concert off (O), put off it (X), put it off (O))

❸ 'should'는 '~해야 한다'라는 뜻으로, 어떤 사람에게 그 일을 해야 한다는 의무를 강조하는 조동사로 쓰인다.

❹ keep은 5형식 구조(keep+목적어+목적격보어(형용사))로 '목적어가 ~하도록 유지하다'의 의미로 사용된다.

❺ 'You can say that again.'은 상대방의 의견에 동의하는 표현으로 '전적으로 동감이야.'의 의미이다.

Check(√) True or False

(4) The classroom is dirty now. T ☐ F ☐

(5) After the conversation, they aren't going to clean their classroom. T ☐ F ☐

(6) The girl agrees with the boy's opinion. T ☐ F ☐

Listen & Speak ① A-2

B: Oops. I ❶forgot to bring your book.

G: No, not again, Namho!

B: I'm sorry. ❷I'm really worried about forgetting things.

❶ forget은 목적어로 쓰인 동명사와 to부정사에 따라 의미가 달라진다. forget to부정사: ~할 것을 잊다 forget 동명사: ~한 것을 잊다
❷ I'm worried about ~.: 나는 ~에 대해 걱정이다.

Listen & Speak ① A-3

B: You ❶look unhappy, Sumi.

G: ❷I'm worried about the test.

B: ❸Don't worry too much. ❹You will pass.

❶ look+형용사: ~하게 보이다
❷ be worried about: ~에 대해 걱정하다
❸ Don't worry too much: 너무 걱정하지 마.
❹ You will pass 다음에 the test가 생략되어 있다. pass the test: 시험에 합격하다

Listen & Speak ① B-1

A: I'm worried about the waste problem.

B: ❶Me, too. ❷We should reuse everyday things.

A: ❸That's a good idea. We can reuse bottles ❹as flower vases.

❶ Me, too. = So am I. (나도 그래.)
❷ should+동사원형: ~해야 한다 reuse: 재사용하다
❸ 상대방의 제안에 대하여 동의할 때 'That's a good idea', 혹은 'That sounds good.' 등으로 표현할 수 있다.
❹ as: ~으로, ~로써

Listen & Speak ② A-2

G: ❶Hurry up! ❷We're going to be late.

B: ❸I think we should have longer lunch breaks.

G: Well, ❹I don't agree.

❶ hurry up: 서두르다
❷ be going to 동사원형: ~할 것이다 be late (for): (~에) 늦다
❸ 'I think we should 동사원형 ~.'은 의견을 표현할 때 사용하는 것으로 '우리는 ~해야 한다고 생각해.'의 의미이다. have a lunch break: 점심 휴식 시간을 가지다
❹ 'I don't agree.(난 동의하지 않아.)'는 상대방의 의견에 동의하지 않을 때 사용한다. 비슷한 표현으로, 'I don't think so.', 'I'm against it.'이 있다.

Listen & Speak ② A-3

B: ❶He's wearing his slippers, isn't he?

G: Yes, he is.

B: We ❷shouldn't wear slippers in the school garden.

G: ❸I agree.

❶ is wearing+옷/장신구: 옷 이외에도 안경, 신발 등 잡화 및 장신구를 착용할 때 'is wearing'을 사용한다.
❷ shouldn't 동사원형 = should not 동사원형: ~하지 말아야 한다. should는 조동사이기 때문에 부정문을 만들려면 should 뒤에 not을 붙인다.
❸ 의견에 동의할 때는 'I agree. (동의해.)'로 말할 수 있다.

Communication

Seho: Is this your poster ❶for the art contest, Nara?

Nara: Yes, it is, Seho.

Seho: I like your ❷slogan, ❸"Reuse More, Waste Less!" Where did you get that idea?

Nara: I got ❹it from junk art.

Seho: ❺Junk art uses thrown-away things, doesn't it?

Nara: Yes, it does. I'm worried about the waste problem. We ❻have to do something about it.

Seho: You can say that again.

❶ for: ~을 위한 contest: 대회
❷ slogan: 구호, 슬로건
❸ more: 더 많이 less: 더 적게 waste: 낭비하다
❹ 앞 문장의 that idea를 가리킨다.
❺ junk: 폐물, 고물 thrown-away: 버려진 (throw something away: (더 이상 필요 없는 것을) 버리다[없애다])
❻ have to 동사원형: ~해야 한다. it은 앞 문장의 the waste problem(쓰레기 문제)을 의미한다.

● 다음 우리말과 일치하도록 빈칸에 알맞은 말을 쓰시오.

Listen & Speak 1 Get Ready

1. **B:** _____ wrong?

   G: I'm worried _____ my dog. He is very sick.

B: 뭐가 문제야?
G: 난 내 개가 걱정돼. 개가 몹시 아파.

Listen & Speak 1 A

1. **G:** _____ wrong, Seho?

   B: I'm _____ _____ my science _____.

   G: _____ worry too much. You'll _____ a good job.

2. **B:** Oops. I _____ _____ bring your book.

   G: No, not again, Namho!

   B: I'm sorry. I'm really _____ _____ _____ things.

3. **B:** You look _____, Sumi.

   G: _____ _____ about the test.

   B: _____ _____ too much. You will _____.

1. **G:** 무슨 일이니, 세호야?
   B: 내 과학 발표에 대해 걱정하고 있어.
   G: 너무 걱정하지 마. 넌 잘할 거야.

2. **B:** 이런. 네 책을 가져오는 것을 잊었어.
   G: 안돼, 남호야, 또야!
   B: 미안해. 난 잊어버리는 게 정말로 걱정돼.

3. **B:** 너 안 좋아 보여, 수미야.
   G: 난 시험이 걱정돼.
   B: 너무 걱정하지 마. 넌 통과할 거야.

Listen & Speak 1 B

1. **A:** _____ _____ _____ the _____ problem.

   B: Me, too. We should _____ everyday things.

   A: That's a good idea. We _____ _____ _____ as flower vases.

2. **A:** I'm _____ _____ the waste problem.

   B: Me, _____. We _____ _____ everyday things.

   A: That's a good _____. We can _____ old paper _____ wrapping paper.

1. **A:** 난 쓰레기 문제에 대해 걱정하고 있어.
   B: 나도 그래. 우리는 일상용품들을 재사용해야 해.
   A: 그거 좋은 생각이야. 우리는 병을 꽃병으로 재사용할 수 있어.

2. **A:** 난 쓰레기 문제에 대해 걱정하고 있어.
   B: 나도 그래. 우리는 일상용품들을 재사용해야 해.
   A: 그거 좋은 생각이야. 우리는 낡은 종이를 포장지로 재사용할 수 있어.

Listen & Speak 2 Get Ready

B: We should go _____.

G: You can _____ that again.

B: 우리는 친환경적이 되어야 해.
G: 전적으로 동감이야.

Listen & Talk 2 A

1. **G:** Look at this _____!

   B: Let's _____ it _____. We should _____ our classroom _____.

   G: You _____ _____ that again.

2. **G:** _____ up! We're _____ _____ be late.

   B: _____ _____ _____ _____ have longer lunch breaks.

   G: Well, I don't _____.

3. **B:** He's _____ his slippers, isn't he?

   G: Yes, he _____.

   B: We _____ _____ slippers in the school garden.

   G: I _____.

1. G: 이 엉망인 상태를 봐!
   B: 청소하자. 우리는 우리 교실을 깨끗하게 유지해야 해.
   G: 전적으로 동감이야.

2. G: 서둘러! 우리는 지각할 거야.
   B: 우리는 보다 긴 점심 휴식 시간을 가져야 한다고 생각해.
   G: 음, 난 동의하지 않아.

3. B: 그는 슬리퍼를 신고 있어, 그렇지 않니?
   G: 응, 그래.
   B: 우리는 학교 정원에서는 슬리퍼를 신지 말아야 해.
   G: 동의해.

Conversation

Seho: Is this your _____ _____ the art _____, Nara?

Nara: Yes, it _____, Seho.

Seho: I _____ your slogan, "Reuse _____, Waste _____!" _____ did you _____ that _____?

Nara: I _____ it _____ junk art.

Seho: Junk art _____ thrown-away things, doesn't it?

Nara: Yes, it _____. I'm _____ _____ the waste problem. We _____ _____ do something about it.

Seho: You _____ _____ _____ again.

세호: 나라야, 이것이 미술 대회를 위한 너의 포스터니?
나라: 그래, 세호야.
세호: "더 재사용하고 덜 낭비하자!"라는 구호가 마음에 들어. 어디서 저런 아이디어를 얻었니?
나라: 폐품 예술에서 얻었어.
세호: 폐품 예술은 버려진 물건들을 사용하지, 그렇지 않니?
나라: 그래. 나는 쓰레기 문제에 대해 걱정하고 있어. 우리는 그것에 대해 무언가를 해야만 해.
세호: 동감이야.

Check My Progress

G: You _____ nervous, Minho. What's wrong?

B: _____ _____ about the _____ contest.

G: _____ worry too much. You're _____ a good speaker.

B: Thank you, but I feel _____.

G: _____ _____ nervous. You'll do _____.

B: Thanks.

G: 너 긴장한 것 같아, 민호야. 무슨 일이니?
B: 난 웅변 대회가 걱정돼.
G: 너무 걱정하지 마. 넌 정말 훌륭한 연설가잖아.
B: 고마워, 하지만 난 걱정이 돼.
G: 긴장하지 마. 넌 잘할 거야.
B: 고마워.

01 다음 대화에서 밑줄 친 부분의 의미로 가장 바른 것은?

> G: What's wrong, Seho?
> B: I'm worried about my science presentation.
> G: Don't worry too much. You'll do a good job.

① 걱정 표현하기 ② 확인 요청하기

③ 제안하기 ④ 능력 표현하기

⑤ 안심시키기

[02~03] 다음 대화를 읽고, 물음에 답하시오.

> B: You look unhappy, Sumi.
> G: (about, I'm, test, worried, the)
> B: Don't worry too much. You will ___(A)___.

 02 빈칸 (A)에 알맞은 말을 고르시오.

① study ② fail ③ watch ④ pass ⑤ carry

서답형

03 괄호 안에 주어진 단어를 알맞게 배열하시오.

➡ _____

04 밑줄 친 부분과 같은 의미로 쓰인 것을 모두 고르시오.

> G: Hurry up! We're going to be late.
> B: I think we should have longer lunch breaks.
> G: Well, I don't agree.

① you can say that again

② I agree with you

③ I don't think so

④ I think so

⑤ I'm against it

[01~02] 다음 대화를 읽고, 물음에 답하시오.

G: What's wrong, Seho?
B: I'm (A)worried about my science presentation.
G: _____(B)_____. You'll do a good job.

01 (A)와 바꿔 쓸 수 있는 것을 고르시오.

① excited
② bored
③ tired
④ concerned
⑤ satisfied

02 빈칸 (B)에 알맞은 말을 모두 고르시오.

① You look worried.
② You don't practice a lot.
③ Don't worry too much.
④ You can say that again.
⑤ Everything will be okay.

[03~06] 다음 대화를 읽고, 물음에 답하시오.

Seho: Is this your poster for the art contest, Nara? (①)
Nara: Yes, it is, Seho. (②)
Seho: I like your slogan, "Reuse More, Waste Less!" (③) Where did you get that idea?
Nara: I got it from junk art.
Seho: (④) Junk art uses _____(A)_____ things, doesn't it?
Nara: Yes, it does. (⑤) We have to do something about it.
Seho: (B) 동감이야.

03 빈칸 (A)에 알맞은 말을 고르시오.

① ready-made
② artistic
③ clean
④ thrown-away
⑤ special

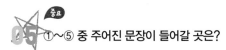
04 밑줄 친 (B)의 우리말을 주어진 단어를 이용하여 영작하시오.

➡ _____ (say, again)

05 ①~⑤ 중 주어진 문장이 들어갈 곳은?

I'm worried about the waste problem.

①　　②　　③　　④　　⑤

06 위 대화의 내용과 일치하지 않는 것은?

① Seho likes the slogan which Nara made.
② Nara is worried about the waste problem.
③ Seho agrees with Nara's opinion about the waste problem.
④ Seho made a poster for the art contest.
⑤ Junk art uses waste articles.

07 다음 대화의 ①~⑤ 중 흐름상 어색한 것은?

B: Oops. I ①forgot ②bringing your book.
G: No, not again, Namho!
B: ③I'm sorry. I'm ④really worried about ⑤forgetting things.

①　　②　　③　　④　　⑤

[08~10] 다음 대화를 읽고, 물음에 답하시오.

> G: _____(A)_____, Seho?
> B: I'm worried ___(B)___ my science presentation.
> G: Don't worry too much. You'll do a good _____(C)_____.

08 빈칸 (A)에 들어갈 수 없는 것은?

① How was your presentation
② What's wrong with you
③ What happened
④ Is there anything wrong
⑤ What's the matter

09 빈칸 (B)에 알맞은 말을 고르시오.

① in   ② with   ③ on
④ of   ⑤ about

서답형

10 빈칸 (C)에 알맞은 말을 쓰시오.

➡ _____

서답형

11 주어진 문장의 뒤에 이어질 대화의 순서를 바르게 배열하시오.

> I'm really worried about the trash problem.

> (A) That's a good idea.
> (B) So am I. We should reuse used things.
> (C) I couldn't agree more. Why don't we reuse old magazines as wrapping paper?

➡ _____

12 다음 중 짝지어진 대화가 어색한 것은?

① A: I'm worried about my dog.
   B: What's wrong?
② A: Summer vacation should be longer than it is now.
   B: In my opinion, it's not good. You can say that again.
③ A: This math test is too hard. Don't you agree?
   B: That's right. I agree with you.
④ A: I'm worried about my math test.
   B: Don't worry a lot. Everything will be okay.
⑤ A: Blue whales are in danger because of environmental changes. I'm worried about them.
   B: So am I.

13 다음 대화의 흐름상 빈칸 (A)와 (B)에 들어갈 말로 가장 적절한 것은?

> A: I'm worried about the waste problem.
> B: _____(A)_____ We should reuse everyday things.
> A: _____(B)_____ We can reuse bottles as flower vases.

          (A)   /   (B)
① Don't worry too much. / I'm sorry to hear that.
② That's a good idea. / You will pass.
③ That sounds exciting. / Don't you agree?
④ Me, too. / That's a good idea.
⑤ I'm also worried about it. / Throw away everyday things.

[01~02] 다음 글을 읽고, 물음에 답하시오.

> B: (A) <u>많은 사람들이 너무나 많은 쓰레기에 대해 걱정하고 있다.</u> (B) <u>They say that we should make more trash.</u> I couldn't agree more. Why don't we reuse used things?

01 밑줄 친 (A)의 우리말을 주어진 단어를 이용하여 영작하시오.

➡ _____

(about, too, much, trash)

02 밑줄 친 (B) 부분에서 내용상 어색한 것을 골라 고치시오.

_____ ➡ _____

03 다음 대화의 빈칸 (A)를 본문의 단어를 활용해서 채우시오.

> B: Oops. I forgot to bring your book.
> G: No, not again, Namho!
> B: I'm sorry. I'm really worried about ____(A)____ things.

➡ _____

04 다음 대화에서 문법상 어색한 부분을 찾아 고치시오.

> G: Look at this mess!
> B: Let's clean up it. We should keep our classroom clean.
> G: You can say that again.

➡ _____

05 다음 대화에서 흐름상 어색한 부분을 찾아 고치시오.

> B: You look happy, Sumi.
> G: I'm worried about the test.
> B: Don't worry too much. You will pass.

➡ _____

06 다음 대화의 밑줄 친 우리말에 맞게 영작하시오.

> A: I'm worried about the waste problem.
> B: Me, too. We should reuse everyday things.
> A: That's a good idea. <u>우리는 수저를 옷걸이로 재사용할 수 있어.</u> (as, can, hangers)

➡ _____

[07~08] 주어진 문장 앞에 올 대화의 순서를 바르게 배열하시오.

07
> Don't be nervous. You'll do fine.

> (A) Thank you, but I feel worried.
> (B) You look nervous, Minho. What's wrong?
> (C) I'm worried about the speech contest.
> (D) Don't worry too much. You're such a good speaker.

➡ _____

08
> You can say that again.

> (A) Yes, I'm afraid he is.
> (B) I think people shouldn't be late for meetings. It's not nice.
> (C) Is Tom late again?

➡ _____

Grammar

① 수동태

It **was created** by Pablo Picasso. 그것은 Pablo Picasso에 의해 만들어졌습니다.

- 형태: be동사 + 과거분사 (+ by ~)

  의미: (~에 의해) …되다

- 수동태는 '주어+be동사+동사의 과거분사+by+행위자'의 형식을 가지며 수동태 문장의 주어 자리에는 능동태 문장의 목적어가 오고, by 다음에는 능동태 문장의 주어를 쓴다. 누가 그 동작을 했는지 중요하지 않거나 잘 모를 때, 수동태 문장으로 표현한다. 수동태는 현재, 과거, 미래 시제로 쓸 수 있고, 'be동사+동사의 과거분사'에서 be동사로 시제를 표현한다.

- 4형식 문장의 수동태는 간접목적어와 직접목적어를 각각 주어로 하는 수동태가 가능하다. 직접목적어를 주어로 한 수동태에서는 간접목적어 앞에 특정한 전치사를 써야 한다.

  전치사 to를 쓰는 동사는 'give, send, tell, teach, show, bring' 등이고, 전치사 for를 쓰는 동사는 'buy, make, choose, cook, get' 등이며, 전치사 of를 쓰는 동사는 'ask'가 있다. 또한 make, buy, read, write 등은 직접목적어를 주어로 하는 수동태만 가능하다. 전치사 to를 쓰는 경우 뒤에 대명사가 올 때는 생략할 수 있다.

  - Sean **was given** a toy by Mary. Sean은 Mary에 의해 장난감 하나가 주어졌다.
  - A toy **was given** to Sean by Mary. 장난감 하나가 Mary에 의해 Sean에게 주어졌다.

- 조동사가 있는 문장의 수동태는 '조동사+be+p.p.' 형식을 갖는다.
  - The work **can be finished** by us. 그 일은 우리에 의해 끝내질 수 있다.

- 목적격보어가 원형부정사인 경우, 수동태 문장에서는 to부정사로 바뀐다.
  - Jake **was made** to finish it by Judy. Jake는 Judy에 의해 그것을 끝내도록 시켜졌다.

- by 이외의 전치사를 사용하는 수동태에 유의한다.

  - be interested in: ~에 흥미가 있다
  - be covered with: ~로 덮여 있다
  - be made of: ~로 만들어지다(물리적 변화)
  - be satisfied with: ~에 만족하다
  - be filled with: ~로 가득 차다
  - be surprised at: ~에 놀라다
  - be made from: ~로 만들어지다(화학적 변화)
  - be pleased with: ~에 기뻐하다

핵심 Check

1. 다음 우리말에 맞게 빈칸에 알맞은 말을 쓰시오.

   (1) 에펠탑은 1899년에 지어졌다.

   ➡ The Eiffel Tower _____ _____ in 1899.

   (2) 케이크가 엄마에 의해 나를 위해 만들어졌다.

   ➡ A cake _____ _____ _____ me by Mom.

2 not only A but also B

He used not only old things but also his imagination.
그는 오래된 것들뿐만 아니라 그의 상상력도 사용하였습니다.

- 형태: not only A but also B

  의미: A뿐만 아니라 B노

- '~뿐만 아니라 …도'라는 의미로, 초점이 but also 다음의 B에 놓인다.

  • He speaks **not only** English **but also** French. 그는 영어뿐만 아니라 불어도 말한다.

- 'B as well as A'도 비슷한 뜻으로 쓰이는데, 이 경우에는 앞의 B에 초점이 놓인다.

  • He needed **not only** food **but also** clothes.

  = He needed clothes **as well as** food. 그는 음식뿐만 아니라 의복도 필요했다.

- 'not only A but also B'에서 A와 B 자리에는 명사(구)와 동사(구)를 비롯하여 다양한 표현이 사용될 수 있으며, but also에서 also가 생략되기도 한다.

  • My daughter is **not only** smart **but also** kind. 내 딸은 영리할 뿐만 아니라 친절하다.

  • I **not only** love you **but also** want to say I love you. 나는 널 사랑할 뿐만 아니라 사랑한다고 말하고 싶어.

  • He plays **not only** basketball **but also** soccer. 그는 농구뿐만 아니라 축구도 한다.

    = He plays **not only** basketball **but** soccer.

    = He plays **not only** basketball **but** soccer **as well**.

    = He plays **not simply[merely, just]** basketball **but (also)** soccer.

- 'not only A but also B'와 'B as well as A'가 주어로 쓰일 경우 B에 수를 일치시킨다.

  • **Not only** I **but also** Alex **likes** science.

    = Alex **as well as** I **likes** science.

핵심 Check

2. 다음 우리말에 맞게 빈칸을 알맞게 채우시오.

(1) 그는 가난할 뿐만 아니라 아프기도 하다.

➡ He is _____ _____ poor but also sick.

(2) 나는 책에서뿐만 아니라 사람들한테서도 많은 걸 배울 수 있었다.

➡ I could learn a lot _____ _____ as well as from books.

01 다음 중 어법상 바르지 <u>않은</u> 것은?

① The window was broken by Jake.

② An e-mail was sent to Jim.

③ His brother was killed in the war.

④ The Mona Lisa was drawn by Leonardo da Vinci.

⑤ Some nice dresses are sell at the store.

02 다음 빈칸에 알맞은 것을 고르시오.

> Cinderella _____ to the party by the prince.

① invited   ② inviting

③ was inviting   ④ was invited

⑤ invites

03 주어진 문장의 빈칸에 들어갈 알맞은 말을 고르시오.

> I have not only a brother but _____ five sisters.

① very   ② too   ③ also

④ so   ⑤ as well

04 다음 괄호 안에서 알맞은 말을 고르시오.

(1) The letter was (written / write) by Gloria.

(2) Mike is not only rude but also (is cruel / cruel).

(3) The houses (was / were) built by him.

05 다음 문장에서 어법상 <u>어색한</u> 부분을 바르게 고쳐 쓰시오.

> Not only I but also Anna were enjoying riding a bike.

_____ ➡ _____

01 다음 중 수동태로의 전환이 <u>어색한</u> 것은?

① Pablo Picasso created it.
　→ It was created by Pablo Picasso.
② He used a bicycle seat and handlebars to make this sculpture!
　→ A bicycle seat and handlebars were used by him to make this sculpture!
③ Picasso couldn't stop creating artwork.
　→ Creating artwork couldn't be stopped by Picasso.
④ He picked up junk such as old bicycles and mattress springs.
　→ Junk such as old bicycles and mattress springs was picked up by him.
⑤ He used not only old things but also his imagination to create this sculpture in 1942.
　→ Not only old things but also his imagination were used by him to create this sculpture in 1942.

02 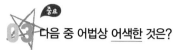 다음 중 어법상 바른 문장은?

① The desk will be made by my elder brother last weekend.
② The light bulb invented Thomas Edison in 1879.
③ By whom was the building built hundreds years ago?
④ These boxes were sent for her by Tom.
⑤ The question was asked to the teacher by students.

03 다음 중 어법상 <u>어색한</u> 것은?

① He can speak not only English but also Chinese.
② James is not only a hero but also strong.
③ Esther likes to sing not only at home but also at the park.
④ Harry will welcome your friends as well as you.
⑤ She not only wrote the poem but also composed music.

04 서답형 다음 괄호 안에서 알맞은 것을 고르시오.

(1) Foreign goods are (bringing / brought) into this country illegally.
(2) The building (had / was) built years ago.
(3) It is (supporting / supported) by many people.
(4) The book was bought (to / for) me by Ann.

05 빈칸에 들어갈 말로 적절한 것은?

I need not only a present but a card _____.

① as well　　② also
③ too　　④ so
⑤ simply

서답형

06 다음 빈칸에 들어갈 괄호 안에 주어진 동사의 형태가 <u>다른</u> 하나는?

① The houses _____. (destroy)
② His room _____ by his mom. (clean)
③ The photo _____ by Sean. (take)
④ The police _____ the thief. (catch)
⑤ The door _____ blue. (paint)

서답형

07 다음 우리말과 의미가 같도록 괄호 안의 말을 이용하여 영작하시오.

(1) 불국사는 528년에 지어졌다. (Bulguksa, build)

➡ _____

(2) 해바라기는 Vincent van Gogh에 의해 그려졌다. (*Sunflowers*, paint)

➡ _____

(3) Katherine은 똑똑할 뿐만 아니라 친절하다. (only, also, smart)

➡ _____

중요

08 두 문장의 뜻이 같도록 빈칸에 들어갈 말을 차례대로 바르게 쓴 것은?

> I want this shirt as well as that hat one.
> = I want _____ that hat but this shirt _____.

① not only – also
② not only – as well
③ not simply – also
④ not merely – much
⑤ not only – very

서답형

09 주어진 어휘를 이용하여 빈칸을 채워 다음 예술 작품을 소개하는 글을 쓰시오.

• Artist: Su Blackwell
• Title: *Treasure Island* (2013)

> This artwork _____ _____ (create) by Su Blackwell. It _____ _____ (title) *Treasure Island* and _____ _____ (make) in 2013.

10 다음 주어진 두 문장을 한 문장으로 <u>잘못</u> 바꾼 것을 고르시오.

> • Angelina has a beautiful house.
> • She has a nice car, too.

① Angelina has a beautiful house and a nice car.
② Angelina has not only a beautiful house but also a nice car.
③ Angelina has not only a beautiful house but a nice car as well.
④ Angelina has not only a beautiful house but has a nice car.
⑤ Angelina has a nice car as well as a beautiful house.

서답형

11 다음 우리말을 영어로 쓰시오.

> 네 지갑이 John에 의해 발견되었니? (wallet)

➡ _____

서답형

12 다음 두 문장을 'not only ~ but also ...' 구문을 사용하여 한 문장으로 연결하시오.

(1) • Sam understood it.
    • He remembered it, too.

➡ _____

_____

(2) • He plays soccer.
    • He plays baseball, too.

➡ _____

_____

서답형

13 다음 문장에서 틀린 것을 고쳐 다시 쓰시오.

(1) He was respected lots of people.

➡ _____

(2) The children were appeared in the park.

➡ _____

(3) This question was asked to all the students by the teacher.

➡ _____

_____

(4) The furniture was made from oak tree.

➡ _____

(5) Butterflies were seen fly from flower to flower.

➡ _____

(6) The voices of people in the next room can hear.

➡ _____

중요

14 다음 빈칸에 들어갈 말을 순서대로 바르게 짝지은 것을 고르시오.

> • Jimin is good at not only singing _____ dancing.
> • Art can _____ out of all kinds of old things around us.

① but also – make
② also – make
③ but also – be made
④ also – be made
⑤ too – be made by

15 다음 우리말을 영어로 바르게 옮긴 것은?

> 이 규칙은 자녀들뿐만 아니라 부모에게도 적용된다.

① This rule applies to children as well as parents.
② This rule applies to parents as well as children.
③ This rule applies to not only children but to parents.
④ This rule applies not only parents but also children.
⑤ This rule applies not only parents but children as well.

중요

16 다음 빈칸에 들어갈 전치사가 나머지와 다른 것은?

① The bridge was built _____ birds.
② The diary was written _____ my sister.
③ Hangeul was invented _____ King Sejong.
④ The medicine was taken _____ a patient.
⑤ The bucket is filled _____ sand and some dirty things.

01 괄호 안에 주어진 어휘의 알맞은 형태를 빈칸에 쓰시오.

(1) Hangeul _____ in 1443. (invent)

(2) *The Kiss* _____ by Gustav Klimt in 1908. (paint)

(3) A loud noise _____ from outside this morning. (hear)

02 다음 문장에서 **틀린** 것을 고쳐 다시 쓰시오.

(1) The birthday party was cancelling due to the bad weather.

➡ _____

_____

(2) David Edgar was created this artwork, *Fish Lamp*.

➡ _____

_____

(3) *Dakgalbi* was cooked to Angie by me.

➡ _____

(4) I was surprised with the speed.

➡ _____

(5) It was made teach people a foreign language.

➡ _____

_____

(6) Cecil was written a letter by Edan.

➡ _____

03 다음 문장을 as well as를 사용하여 바꾸어 쓰시오.

(1) Sumi is not only a good singer but also a good dancer.

➡ _____

(2) I watched not only *Avatar* but also *Frozen*.

➡ _____

(3) We smile not only with our mouths but also with our eyes.

➡ _____

_____

(4) I not only ate a hamburger but drank some juice.

➡ _____

(5) Not only the teacher but also her students were excited to see the films.

➡ _____

_____

04 다음 우리말을 주어진 어휘를 활용하여 문장을 완성하시오.

(1) 건강한 식사는 어른뿐만 아니라 아이들에게도 중요하다. (a healthy diet, well, adults)

➡ _____

_____

(2) 그 여자는 아름답기만 한 게 아니라 지적이기까지 하다. (the woman, only, intelligent, also)

➡ _____

_____

(3) 당신뿐만 아니라 Alex도 그것에 책임이 있습니다. (well, as, responsible)

➡ _____

(4) 누구에 의해 라디오가 발명되었니? (whom, the radio, invent)

➡ _____

(5) 그 문제는 곧 해결될 거야. (the problem, soon, solve, will)

➡ _____

05 주어진 어휘를 이용하여 빈칸을 채워 다음 예술 작품을 소개하는 글을 쓰시오.

- Artist: Louise Baldwin
- Title: *Wednesday*

This artwork _____ _____ (create) by Louise Baldwin. It _____ _____ (title) *Wednesday* and recycled materials _____ _____ (use).

06 다음 문장을 수동태로 바꿔 쓰시오.

(1) Hannah gave some presents to her mom. (두 가지로 쓸 것.)

➡ _____
_____

(2) In some areas, people used the shells of sea snails as money for a long time.

➡ _____
_____

(3) I heard him sing while he was doing the dishes.

➡ _____
_____

(4) Anna read a storybook to her daughter every night.

➡ _____
_____

(5) The services at the restaurant satisfied Dorothy.

➡ _____
_____

(6) We will finish the work by tomorrow.

➡ _____
_____

07 다음 문장을 as well as를 사용하여 바꾸시오.

(1) Mathematics has not only truth but beauty.

➡ _____

(2) She not only taught how to sing to students but wanted to be a singer as well.

➡ _____
_____

(3) Not only I but also Andrew wants to play basketball.

➡ _____

Reading

Old Things, New Art

Art can be made out of all kinds of old things around us.
수동태 → 능동태: We can make art out of all kinds of old things around us.

Famous sculptures and pictures are often made from everyday things
수동태 → 능동태: People often make famous sculptures and pictures from everyday
things such as cans, bottles, and bits of paper. 빈도부사 often은 be동사 다음에 위치
such as cans, bottles, and bits of paper.
= like: ~와 같은

Bicycle Junk and *Bull's Head*

How do you like this artwork? It was created by Pablo Picasso.
= This artwork

He used a bicycle seat and handlebars to make this sculpture!
to부정사의 부사적 용법(목적)

During World War II, there were not a lot of useful things for art. But
~ 동안   주어가 복수(a lot of useful things)이므로 was(X)

Picasso couldn't stop creating artwork, so he picked up junk such as
stop은 목적어로 동명사를 취한다. artwork은 셀 수 없는 명사로 쓰였음.   = like: ~와 같은
he = Pablo Picasso. picked와 up은 이어동사로 junk가 목적어임.
old bicycles and mattress springs. He used not only old things but also
not only A but also B: A뿐만 아니라 B도

his imagination to create this sculpture in 1942.
= Bull's Head

글로사리 (오른쪽 여백)

out of ~으로
kind 종류
famous 유명한
sculpture 조각품
picture 그림
bit 작은 조각
artwork 예술 작품
create 창작하다, 창조하다
seat 좌석, 안장
handlebar (흔히 복수형으로 쓰여) 핸들
useful 쓸모 있는, 유용한
pick up 줍다, 얻다
imagination 상상력, 상상

 확인문제

● 다음 문장이 본문의 내용과 일치하면 T, 일치하지 <u>않으면</u> F를 쓰시오.

1   Art can be made out of all kinds of new things around us. ☐

2   Picasso used a bicycle seat and handlebars to make *Bull's Head*. ☐

3   Picasso had a lot of useful things to create artwork. ☐

4   Picasso used his imagination, as well as old things to create *Bull's Head*. ☐

Thrown-away Things and New Art

object 물건
collect 모으다
glue 접착제로 붙이다
nail 못으로 박다
board 판자
style 방식
rubbish 쓰레기

This artwork was created by Kurt Schwitters. He used thrown-away

수동태 → 능동태: Kurt Schwitters created this artwork.　　= Kurt Schwitters　　버려진

objects to make artwork. He often said, "Old things are good for art."

부사적 용법(목적)　　　　빈도부사(일반동사 앞에 위치)

Schwitters walked the streets and collected not only pieces of paper

= bits of wood as well

but also bits of wood. He glued and nailed them to a board, and created

as pieces of paper

a new style of art, Rubbish.

a new style of art와 Rubbish는 동격 관계

In 1937, he moved to Norway. He was able to take his famous work

= could

out of Germany because it looked like rubbish.

~에서　　　　　　　　it = his famous artwork. looked like+명사: ~처럼 보였다.

What old things do you have around you? What new artwork can you

make out of them? Use your imagination and create something new.

~으로　　　　V1(명령문)　　　　　　　V2(명령문)　-thing으로 끝나는 부정대명사는
　　　　　　　　　　　　　　　　　　　　　　　　형용사가 뒤에서 수식

One person's trash is another's treasure!

확인문제

● 다음 문장이 본문의 내용과 일치하면 T, 일치하지 <u>않으면</u> F를 쓰시오.

1　Schwitters used thrown-away objects to make artwork.　□

2　Schwitters often said, "New and useful things are good for art."　□

3　In 1937, Schwitters moved to Germany.　□

4　If you use your imagination, you can create something new.　□

● 우리말을 참고하여 빈칸에 알맞은 말을 쓰시오.

1 _____ Things, _____ Art

2 Art can _____ _____ _____ _____ all kinds of old things around us.

3 Famous sculptures and pictures _____ _____ _____ _____ everyday things _____ _____ cans, bottles, and bits of paper.

4 Bicycle _____ and *Bull's Head*

5 _____ do you _____ this artwork?

6 It _____ _____ by Pablo Picasso.

7 He used a bicycle seat and handlebars _____ _____ this sculpture!

8 _____ World War II, _____ _____ _____ a lot of useful things for art.

9 But Picasso couldn't _____ _____ artwork, so he _____ _____ junk such as old bicycles and mattress springs.

10 He used _____ _____ old things _____ _____ his imagination _____ _____ this sculpture in 1942.

1	낡은 것들, 새로운 예술
2	예술은 우리 주변의 모든 오래된 것들로 만들어질 수 있습니다.
3	유명한 조각품들과 그림들은 종종 깡통, 병 및 종잇조각과 같은 일상 용품으로 만들어집니다.
4	자전거 고물과 *Bull's Head*
5	이 작품은 어떻습니까?
6	그것은 Pablo Picasso에 의해 만들어졌습니다.
7	그는 이 조각 작품을 만들기 위해 자전거 좌석과 핸들을 사용했습니다!
8	제2차 세계 대전 중에는 예술을 위해 쓸 수 있는 것들이 많지 않았습니다.
9	그러나 Picasso는 작품 창작을 멈출 수 없어서, 오래된 자전거나 매트리스 스프링과 같은 고물을 주웠습니다.
10	그는 오래된 것들뿐만 아니라 그의 상상력도 사용하여 1942년에 이 조각품을 창작하였습니다.

11 _____ Things and New Art

12 This artwork _____ _____ _____ Kurt Schwitters.

13 He used _____ _____ to make artwork.

14 He often said, "Old things _____ _____ _____ art."

15 Schwitters walked the streets and collected not only _____ _____ _____ but also _____ _____ _____.

16 He _____ and _____ them _____ a board, and created a new style of art, Rubbish.

17 In 1937, he _____ _____ Norway.

18 He was able to _____ his famous work _____ _____ Germany because it _____ _____ rubbish.

19 _____ _____ _____ do you have around you?

20 _____ _____ _____ can you make out of them?

21 Use your imagination and create _____ _____.

22 One person's _____ is _____ _____!

11 버려진 것들과 새로운 예술

12 이 작품은 Kurt Schwitters에 의해 창작되었습니다.

13 그는 작품을 만들기 위해 버려진 물건들을 사용했습니다.

14 그는 종종 "오래된 것들은 예술에 좋다"고 말했습니다.

15 Schwitters는 거리를 걸으면서 종잇조각뿐만 아니라 나무 조각도 모았습니다.

16 그는 그것들을 판자에 풀이나 못으로 붙여, Rubbish라는 새로운 방식의 예술을 창조했습니다.

17 1937년 그는 노르웨이로 이주했습니다.

18 쓰레기처럼 보였기 때문에 그는 그의 유명한 작품을 독일에서 가져갈 수 있었습니다.

19 당신 주변에 어떠한 오래된 것들이 있습니까?

20 당신은 그것들로 어떤 새로운 작품을 만들 수 있습니까?

21 당신의 상상력을 이용하여 새로운 것을 창작하십시오.

22 한 사람의 쓰레기가 다른 사람의 보물입니다!

● 우리말을 참고하여 본문을 영작하시오.

1 낡은 것들, 새로운 예술

➡ _____

2 예술은 우리 주변의 모든 오래된 것들로 만들어질 수 있습니다.

➡ _____

3 유명한 조각품들과 그림들은 종종 깡통, 병 및 종잇조각과 같은 일상 용품으로 만들어집니다.

➡ _____

4 자전거 고물과 *Bull's Head*

➡ _____

5 이 작품은 어떻습니까?

➡ _____

6 그것은 Pablo Picasso에 의해 만들어졌습니다.

➡ _____

7 그는 이 조각 작품을 만들기 위해 자전거 좌석과 핸들을 사용했습니다!

➡ _____

8 제2차 세계 대전 중에는 예술을 위해 쓸 수 있는 것들이 많지 않았습니다.

➡ _____

9 그러나 Picasso는 작품 창작을 멈출 수 없어서, 오래된 자전거나 매트리스 스프링과 같은 고물을 주웠습니다.

➡ _____

10 그는 오래된 것들뿐만 아니라 그의 상상력도 사용하여 1942년에 이 조각품을 창작하였습니다.

➡ _____

11 버려진 것들과 새로운 예술

➡ _____

12 이 작품은 Kurt Schwitters에 의해 창작되었습니다.

➡ _____

13 그는 작품을 만들기 위해 버려진 물건들을 사용했습니다.

➡ _____

14 그는 종종 "오래된 것들은 예술에 좋다"고 말했습니다.

➡ _____

15 Schwitters는 거리를 걸으면서 종잇조각뿐만 아니라 나무 조각도 모았습니다.

➡ _____

16 그는 그것들을 판자에 풀이나 못으로 붙여, Rubbish라는 새로운 방식의 예술을 창조했습니다.

➡ _____

17 1937년 그는 노르웨이로 이주했습니다.

➡ _____

18 쓰레기처럼 보였기 때문에 그는 그의 유명한 작품을 독일에서 가져갈 수 있었습니다.

➡ _____

19 당신 주변에 어떠한 오래된 것들이 있습니까?

➡ _____

20 당신은 그것들로 어떤 새로운 작품을 만들 수 있습니까?

➡ _____

21 당신의 상상력을 이용하여 새로운 것을 창작하십시오.

➡ _____

22 한 사람의 쓰레기가 다른 사람의 보물입니다!

➡ _____

[01~03] 다음 글을 읽고, 물음에 답하시오.

Art can be made out of all kinds of old things around us. Famous sculptures and pictures are often made from everyday things such as cans, bottles, and bits of paper.

Bicycle Junk and ①*Bull's Head*

How do you like ②this artwork? ③It was created by Pablo Picasso. He used a bicycle seat and handlebars ⓐto make this sculpture!

During World War II, there were not a lot of useful things for art. But Picasso couldn't stop creating artwork, so he picked up ④ junk such as old bicycles and mattress springs. He used not only old things but also his imagination to create ⑤this sculpture in 1942.

01 위 글의 밑줄 친 ①~⑤ 중에서 가리키는 대상이 나머지 넷과 다른 것은?

①   ②   ③   ④   ⑤

02 위 글의 밑줄 친 ⓐto make와 to부정사의 용법이 같은 것을 모두 고르시오.

① There are many things to do today.

② It's important to exercise regularly.

③ I was surprised to hear the news.

④ He decided to call her right now.

⑤ She must be a liar to say so.

03 위 글의 내용과 일치하지 않는 것은?

① 일상의 것들로 예술 작품이 만들어질 수 있다.

② 유명한 조각품들과 그림들이 매일 만들어진다.

③ Bull's Head의 재료는 자전거 좌석과 핸들이다.

④ 제2차 세계 대전 중에는 미술을 위해 쓸 수 있는 것들이 많지 않았다.

⑤ Bull's Head는 1942년에 만들어졌다.

[04~06] 다음 글을 읽고, 물음에 답하시오.

Thrown-away Things and New Art

This artwork was created by Kurt Schwitters. ⓐHe used thrown-away objects to make artwork. He often said, "Old things are good   ⓑ   art."

Schwitters walked the streets and collected not only pieces of paper but also bits of wood. He glued and nailed them   ⓒ   a board, and created a new style of art, Rubbish.

서답형

04 위 글의 밑줄 친 ⓐ를 수동태로 바꾸시오.

➡ _____

_____

05 위 글의 빈칸 ⓑ와 ⓒ에 들어갈 전치사가 바르게 짝지어진 것은?

① for – from   ② in – by

③ at – for   ④ for – to

⑤ at – to

06 위 글의 요지로 알맞은 것을 고르시오.

① Schwitters wanted to recycle many useful objects.

② Old things are not proper objects to create artwork.

③ Schwitters created artwork using old things.

④ Schwitters collected pieces of paper.

⑤ It's not easy to create a new style of art.

[07~09] 다음 글을 읽고, 물음에 답하시오.

In 1937, he moved to Norway. He was able to take his famous work out of Germany because ⓐit looked like rubbish.

What old things do you have around you? What new artwork can you make out of them? Use your imagination and create something new. ⓑ한 사람의 쓰레기가 다른 사람의 보물입니다!

<he = Schwitters>

서답형

07 위 글의 밑줄 친 ⓐit이 가리키는 것을 본문에서 찾아 영어로 쓰시오.

➡ _____

서답형

08 위 글의 밑줄 친 ⓑ의 우리말에 맞게 주어진 어휘를 이용하여 6 단어로 영작하시오.

person, trash, another's

➡ _____

09 위 글을 읽고 대답할 수 없는 질문은?

① When did Schwitters move to Norway?
② Why was it possible for Schwitters to take his famous work out of Germany?
③ Did Schwitters's famous work look valuable?
④ How many pieces of artwork did Schwitters make out of old things?
⑤ To create something new, what do you need to use?

[10~12] 다음 폐품 예술 작품을 소개하는 글을 읽고 물음에 답하시오.

Artwork: Color Fish
We used: a plastic bottle, a big white button, a small black button, and colored paper
Special ⓐFeature: Give the fish some water, and it will swim around.

(①) This is our artwork. (②) It is called *Color Fish*. (③) We used a plastic bottle, a big white button, a small black button, and colored paper. (④) Give the fish some water, and put it in the pool. (⑤) The colorful fish will swim around.

중요

10 위 글의 밑줄 친 ⓐFeature와 같은 의미로 쓰인 것을 고르시오.

① Olive oil and garlic feature in his recipes.
② An interesting feature of the city is the old market.
③ I'm reading a special feature on Korean culture on this newspaper.
④ He didn't feature in that movie.
⑤ The show will feature this famous dancer.

11 위 글의 흐름으로 보아, 주어진 문장이 들어가기에 가장 적절한 곳은?

It was created by the three of us: Minho, Changsu, and Nami.

①   ②   ③   ④   ⑤

12 위 글의 폐품 예술 작품에 대한 설명에 해당하지 <u>않는</u> 것을 고르시오.

① Color Fish라고 불린다.
② 플라스틱 병 한 개, 큰 흰색 단추, 작은 검은색 단추, 그리고 색종이를 사용해서 만들었다.
③ 플라스틱 병의 입구를 막아야 한다.
④ 민호, 창수, 그리고 나미가 만들었다.
⑤ 물고기에게 물을 약간 주고 그것을 수영장에 놓으면 알록달록한 물고기가 주변을 헤엄쳐 다닐 것이다.

[13~15] 다음 글을 읽고, 물음에 답하시오.

Art can be made out of all kinds of old things around us. Famous sculptures and pictures are often made from everyday things such as cans, bottles, and bits of paper.

Bicycle Junk and *Bull's Head*

How do you like this artwork? It was created by Pablo Picasso. He used a bicycle seat and handlebars to make this sculpture!

During World War II, there were not a lot of useful things for art. But Picasso couldn't stop creating artwork, so he picked up junk such as old bicycles and mattress springs. He used @not only old things but also his imagination to create this sculpture in 1942.

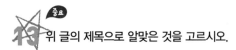

13 위 글의 제목으로 알맞은 것을 고르시오.

① How to Enjoy Famous Sculptures
② Various Everyday Things like Cans
③ Art Made of Old Things around Us
④ Creative Activities during the War
⑤ The Importance of Imagination

14 다음 문장에서 위 글의 내용과 <u>다른</u> 부분을 찾아서 고치시오. (두 군데)

Picasso stopped creating artwork during World War II because there were not a lot of useful things for art.

➡ (1) _____
  (2) _____

15 위 글의 밑줄 친 @not only와 바꿔 쓸 수 없는 말을 <u>모두</u> 고르시오.

① as well as   ② not merely
③ not simply   ④ not just
⑤ not always

[16~18] 다음 글을 읽고, 물음에 답하시오.

Thrown-away Things and New Art

This artwork was created by Kurt Schwitters. He used @thrown-away objects ⓑto make artwork. He often said, "Old things are good for art."

Schwitters walked the streets and collected not only pieces of paper but also bits of wood. ⓒHe glued and nailed them to a board, and created an old style of art, Rubbish.

16 위 글의 밑줄 친 @thrown-away objects의 구체적인 예에 해당하는 것을 본문에서 찾아 쓰시오. (두 개)

➡ (1) _____ (2) _____

17 위 글의 밑줄 친 ⓑ와 바꿔 쓸 수 <u>없는</u> 말을 고르시오.

① in order to make artwork
② enough to make artwork
③ so that he could make artwork
④ so as to make artwork
⑤ in order that he could make artwork

18 위 글의 밑줄 친 ⓒ에서 문맥상 어색한 부분을 찾아 고치시오.

➡ _____

[19~21] 다음 글을 읽고, 물음에 답하시오.

In 1937, he moved to Norway. He was able to take his famous work out of Germany because it looked ⓐlike rubbish.

What old things do you have around you? What new artwork can you make out of them? ⓑUse your imagination and create new something. One person's trash is another's treasure!

19 위 글의 제목으로 알맞은 것을 고르시오.

① How to Take Artwork out of Germany
② Do You Have Old Things around You?
③ Can You Make New Artwork?
④ Seems Valueless? No, It's Valuable!
⑤ Imagination and Creative Artists

20 위 글의 밑줄 친 ⓐlike와 같은 의미로 쓰인 것을 고르시오.

① He's very like his father.
② How did you like the movie?
③ Which bag do you like best?
④ She responded in like manner.
⑤ Do you like your new house?

21 위 글의 밑줄 친 ⓑ에서 어법상 틀린 부분을 찾아 고치시오.

➡ _____

[22~23] 다음 글을 읽고, 물음에 답하시오.

This artwork is ⓐ*Fish Lamp*. It was created by David Edgar. He used not only a plastic bottle but also his imagination to make this artwork. ⓑOne person's trash is another's treasure.

22 위 글의 밑줄 친 ⓐ*Fish Lamp*를 창작하기 위해 David Edgar가 사용했던 것이 무엇인지를 우리말로 쓰시오. (두 가지)

➡ (1) _____ (2) _____

23 다음 빈칸 (A)와 (B)에 알맞은 단어를 넣어 밑줄 친 ⓑ의 구체적인 의미를 완성하시오. (본문의 단어를 사용하시오.)

Some people considered a plastic bottle as ___(A)___, but David Edgar considered it as a valuable material to make his ___(B)___.

➡ (A) _____ (B) _____

24 다음 〈보기〉에서 알맞은 단어를 골라 폐품 예술 작품(junk artwork)의 창작 과정을 완성하시오.

┌─── 보기 ───┐
bits of wood, used, pieces of paper
└─────────────┘

(1)　　　　　　　　(2)

(1) Collect _____ things.
(2) Glue _____ to the board.

(3)

(3) Nail _____ to the board.

[01~03] 다음 글을 읽고, 물음에 답하시오.

ⓐArt can be made out of all kinds of old things around us. Famous sculptures and pictures are often made (A)[by / from] everyday things such as cans, bottles, and bits of paper.

Bicycle Junk and *Bull's Head*

(B)[How / What] do you like this artwork? It was created by Pablo Picasso. He used a bicycle seat and handlebars to make this sculpture!

(C)[During / While] World War II, there were not a lot of useful things for art. But Picasso couldn't stop creating artwork, so he picked up junk such as old bicycles and mattress springs. He used not only old things but also his imagination to create this sculpture in 1942.

01 위 글의 밑줄 친 ⓐ를 능동태로 바꾸시오.

➡ _____

_____

02 위 글의 괄호 (A)~(C)에서 어법상 알맞은 낱말을 골라 쓰시오.

➡ (A) _____ (B) _____ (C) _____

03 다음 질문에 대한 알맞은 대답을 영어로 쓰시오. (5단어)

> Q: Write the examples of old things which were used to make *Bull's Head* by Picasso.
>
> A: _____

[04~06] 다음 글을 읽고, 물음에 답하시오.

Thrown-away Things and New Art

This artwork was created by Kurt Schwitters. He used thrown-away objects to make artwork. He often said, "Old things are good for art."

Schwitters walked the streets and collected ⓐnot only pieces of paper but also bits of wood. He glued and nailed ⓑthem to a board, and ⓒRubbish라는 새로운 방식의 미술을 창조했습니다.

04 위 글의 밑줄 친 ⓐ를 as well as를 사용하여 고치시오.

➡ _____

05 위 글의 밑줄 친 ⓑthem이 가리키는 것을 영어로 쓰시오.

➡ (1) _____ (2) _____

06 위 글의 밑줄 친 ⓒ의 우리말에 맞게 한 단어를 보충하여, 주어진 어휘를 알맞게 배열하시오.

> Rubbish / style / new / created / a / art / ,

➡ _____

[07~08] 다음 글을 읽고, 물음에 답하시오.

Schwitters walked the streets and collected not only pieces of paper but also bits of wood. He glued and nailed them to a board, and created a new style of art, ⓐRubbish.

In 1937, he moved to Norway. He was able to take his famous work out of Germany because it looked like ⓑrubbish.

What old things do you have around you? What new artwork can you make out of them? Use your imagination and create something new. ©One person's trash is another's treasure!

07 위 글의 밑줄 친 ⓐRubbish와 ⓑrubbish의 차이를 쓰시오.

➡ _____

_____

08 중요 다음 문장의 (A)와 (B)에 알맞은 단어를 넣어 밑줄 친 ©의 구체적인 의미를 완성하시오. (value를 변형하시오.)

> Something that one person considers __(A)__ may be considered __(B)__ by someone else.

➡ (A) _____ (B) _____

[09~11] 다음 글을 읽고, 물음에 답하시오.

Bicycle Junk and *Bull's Head*

ⓐ이 작품은 어떻습니까? It was created by Pablo Picasso. He used a bicycle seat and handlebars to make this sculpture!

During ⓑWorld War II, ©there was not a lot of useful things for art. But Picasso couldn't stop creating artwork, so he picked up junk such as old bicycles and mattress springs. He used not only old things but also his imagination to create this sculpture in 1942.

09 위 글의 밑줄 친 ⓐ의 우리말에 맞게 주어진 어휘를 이용하여 6 단어로 영작하시오.

> like, artwork

➡ _____

10 위 글의 밑줄 친 ⓑWorld War II를 영어로 읽는 법을 쓰시오.

➡ _____

11 중요 위 글의 밑줄 친 ©에서 어법상 틀린 부분을 찾아 고치시오.

➡ _____

[12~14] 다음 글을 읽고, 물음에 답하시오.

Thrown-away Things and New Art

This artwork was created by Kurt Schwitters. He used thrown-away objects to make artwork. He often said, "Old things are good for art."

Schwitters walked the streets and collected not only ⓐpieces of paper but also bits of wood. He glued and nailed them to a board, and created a new style of art, ⓑRubbish.

12 다음 질문에 대한 알맞은 대답을 빈칸에 쓰시오.

> Q: What was used to make artwork by Schwitters?
>
> A: _____ were used.

13 위 글의 밑줄 친 ⓐpieces와 바꿔 쓸 수 있는 단어를 쓰시오.

➡ _____

14 중요 Schwitters가 ⓑRubbish라는 새로운 방식의 예술을 창조한 방법을 우리말로 설명하시오.

➡ _____

_____

Let's Write Step 1

This artwork is *Bull's Head*. It was created by Pablo Picasso.
과거시제 수동태: 주어+was/were+pp+by+행위자

He used not only old bicycle parts but also his imagination to make this
not only A but also B: A뿐만 아니라 B도 (= B as well as A)   to부정사의 부사적 용법(목적, ～하기 위해서)

artwork. One person's trash is another's treasure.
쓰레기

구문해설 · part: 부분, 부품 · imagination: 상상력, 상상 · treasure: 보물

이 미술 작품은 Bull's Head입니다. 그것은 Pablo Picasso에 의해 창작되었습니다. 그는 오래된 자전거 부품들뿐만 아니라 그의 상상력도 사용하여 이 작품을 만들었습니다. 한 사람의 쓰레기는 다른 사람의 보물입니다.

Project Across Subjects Step 3

Artwork: Color Fish

We used: a plastic bottle, a big white button, a small black button, and

colored paper
색종이

Special Feature: Give the fish some water, and it will swim around.
= If you give the fish some water. it will swim around.

This is our artwork. It is called *Color Fish*. It was created by the three of us:
→능동태: We call it *Color Fish*.

Minho, Changsu, and Nami. We used a plastic bottle, a big white button, a

small black button, and colored paper. Give the fish some water, and put it in
= Give some water to the fish(3형식)

the pool. The colorful fish will swim around.

구문해설 · button: 단추 · colored paper: 색종이 · feature: 특징 · create: 창조[창작]하다

예술 작품: Color Fish
우리는 사용했다: 플라스틱 병 한 개, 큰 흰색 단추, 작은 검은색 단추, 그리고 색종이
특징: 물고기에게 물을 약간 주면 주변을 헤엄쳐 다닐 것이다. 이것은 우리의 미술 작품이다. 그것은 Color Fish라고 불린다. 그것은 우리 세 명에 의해 창작되었다: 민호, 창수, 그리고 나미. 우리는 플라스틱 병 한 개, 큰 흰색 단추, 작은 검은색 단추, 그리고 색종이를 사용했다. 물고기에게 물을 약간 주고 그것을 수영장에 놓아라. 알록달록한 물고기가 주변을 헤엄쳐 다닐 것이다.

Check My Progress 4

Seminole Indians in the U.S. use old cloth to make clothes such as skirts.
to부정사의 부사적 용법(목적)   ～와 같은(= like)

People in Bangladesh use thread and old cloth to make flowery patchwork
to부정사의 부사적 용법(목적)

quilts.

1. Making beautiful artwork is not easy at all.
   동명사 주어   동명사 주어는 단수 취급

2. Indians love to make skirts and wrapping cloth.
   love의 목적어(= making)

3. People around the world use old cloth to make useful things.
   전 세계의   부정사의 부사적 용법(목적)

구문해설 · clothes: 옷 · flowery: 꽃무늬의 · patchwork: 쪽무늬 깁기 · quilt: 퀼트, 누비이불
· not ～ at all: 전혀 ～ 않다 · wrapping cloth: 보자기

미국의 세미놀 인디언들은 스커트와 같은 옷을 만들기 위해 오래된 천을 사용한다. 방글라데시 사람들은 꽃무늬 쪽모이 퀼트를 만들기 위해 실과 오래된 천을 사용한다.
1. 아름다운 미술 작품을 만드는 것은 전혀 쉽지 않다.
2. 인디언들은 스커트와 보자기를 만드는 것을 좋아한다.
3. 전 세계의 사람들은 유용한 것을 만들기 위해 낡은 천을 사용한다.

Words & Expressions

01 다음 짝지어진 단어의 관계가 같도록 빈칸에 알맞은 말을 쓰시오. (주어진 철자로 시작할 것)

> rubbish : trash – able : c_____

02 다음 두 문장에 공통으로 알맞은 것을 고르시오.

> • He was trying to mend the shoes with _____.
> • Let me _____ the broken pieces together.

① collect   ② thread   ③ throw
④ glue   ⑤ pass

03 다음 밑줄 친 단어와 의미가 같은 단어를 모두 고르시오.

> What <u>sort</u> of things do you have in mind?

① type   ② form   ③ class
④ shape   ⑤ kind

04 다음 영영풀이에 해당하는 단어를 고르시오.

> a flat, thin, rectangular piece of wood or plastic

① bottle   ② rubbish   ③ board
④ coin   ⑤ plate

Conversation

05 자연스러운 대화가 되도록 가장 알맞게 배열한 것은?

> (A) What's that noise, Nami?
> (B) They shouldn't make noise in the park. What do you think, Nami?
> (C) Well, they are just having a good time together.
> (D) The little boys over there, Minsu.

① (A) – (B) – (D) – (C)
② (A) – (D) – (B) – (C)
③ (C) – (A) – (D) – (B)
④ (C) – (D) – (A) – (B)
⑤ (C) – (D) – (B) – (A)

06 다음 대화 중 <u>어색한</u> 것은?

① A: This song is really good. Don't you agree?
   B: I'm not sure.
② A: He is the best singer in our class. Don't you think so?
   B: I'm afraid I don't. Why do you think so?
③ A: This chair is very comfortable. What do you think?
   B: You can't say that again. I like it very much.
④ A: Is Grandma back?
   B: No, not yet. I'm worried about her.
⑤ A: This math problem is too hard. What do you think?
   B: No, I don't agree. I solved the problem.

07 다음 대화에서 어색한 부분을 찾아 고치시오.

> B: What's wrong?
> G: I'm worried at my dog. He is very sick.

_____ ➡ _____

[08~10] 다음 대화를 읽고, 물음에 답하시오.

> B: Oops. I forgot to bring your book.
> G: No, not again, Namho!
> B: _____(A)_____ (B)난 잊어버리는 게 정말로 걱정돼.

08 빈칸 (A)에 알맞은 말을 고르시오.

① You can say that again.
② I'm sorry.
③ That's a good idea.
④ Thank you.
⑤ Don't worry.

09 밑줄 친 우리말 (B)를 주어진 단어를 이용하여 영작하시오.

(really, things, be, things)

➡ _____

10 위 대화의 내용과 일치하지 않는 것은?

① Namho borrowed the girl's book.
② Namho feels sorry for the girl.
③ This is the first time that Namho didn't bring the girl's book.
④ Namho forgot to bring the book which he had borrowed from the girl.
⑤ Namho often forgets things.

[11~12] 다음 대화를 읽고, 물음에 답하시오.

> G: Look at this ____(A)____ !
> B: Let's clean it ____(B)____ . We should keep our classroom clean.
> G: You can say that again.

11 빈칸 (A)에 어울리는 말을 고르시오.

① order   ② difficulty   ③ trouble
④ mess   ⑤ green

12 (B)에 알맞은 전치사를 쓰시오.

➡ _____

Grammar

13 다음 중 어법상 올바른 것은?

① I need not only wrapping paper also a ribbon.
② John played only the flute but also the trumpet.
③ Tom not only drives a car well but also fix a car well.
④ Chuck likes not only soccer and also tennis.
⑤ He is not only a painter but a sculptor.

14 다음 중 어법상 어색한 것은?

① The Great Sphinx was built about 4,500 years ago.
② The movie was directed by Bong Junha.
③ Harold was written a long e-mail by Jessy.
④ The picture was painted by a famous artist.
⑤ The pizza was cooked for my sister by Jake.

15 다음 빈칸에 들어갈 전치사가 나머지와 <u>다른</u> 것은?

① The drums are played _____ him.
② *Romeo and Juliet* was written _____ Shakespeare.
③ They were chosen _____ the coach.
④ The mountain is covered _____ snow.
⑤ The baby was taken care of _____ her sister.

16 다음 문장의 빈칸에 들어갈 알맞은 말을 고르시오.

> Sangmin is not only handsome but _____ gentle.

① very　　② also　　③ so
④ as　　⑤ too

17 주어진 어휘를 이용하여 빈칸을 채워 다음 예술 작품을 소개하는 글을 쓰시오.

• Artist: Kyle Bean
• Title: *What Came First* (2013)

> This artwork _____ _____ (create) by Kyle Bean. It _____ _____ (title) *What Came First* and _____ _____ (make) from eggshells.

18 우리말과 같은 뜻이 되도록 주어진 어휘를 이용하여 문장을 완성하시오.

(1) 그녀는 그 파티에 초대받지 못했다. (invite) (7 단어)

　➡ _____

(2) America는 Columbus에 의해 발견되었다. (discover) (5 단어)

　➡ _____

(3) Mariel은 그녀의 딸에게 사전을 사주었다. (dictionary) (9 단어로 수동태로 쓸 것.)

　➡ _____

(4) 그녀는 테니스뿐만 아니라 골프도 친다. (play, only, also, golf) (8 단어)

　➡ _____

(5) 그는 학자일 뿐만 아니라 시인이기도 하다. (a poet, a scholar, well) (9 단어)

　➡ _____

(6) 이것은 맛있을 뿐 아니라 영양분도 많습니다. (it, nutrients, only, but, taste, good, full, well) (12 단어)

　➡ _____

19 다음 문장에서 틀린 것을 고쳐 다시 쓰시오.

(1) He can not only read English but also speaks.

　➡ _____

(2) Amy as well as I like to enjoy a cup of coffee after dinner.

　➡ _____

20 능동태는 수동태로, 수동태는 능동태로 바꾸어 쓰시오.

(1) My famous artwork was taken out of Germany by me.

➡ _____

(2) Harry Potter was written by J. K. Rowling.

➡ _____

(3) The Eiffel Tower was built in 1889.

➡ _____

(4) What new artwork can you make out of old things?

➡ _____

_____

(5) He used not only a plastic bottle but also his imagination to make this artwork.

➡ _____

_____

Reading

[21~23] 다음 글을 읽고, 물음에 답하시오.

Art can be made out of all kinds of old things around us. Famous sculptures and pictures are often made from everyday things such as cans, bottles, and bits of paper.

Bicycle Junk and *Bull's Head*

How do you like this artwork? It was created by Pablo Picasso. He used a bicycle seat and handlebars to make this sculpture!

During World War II, there were not a lot of useful things for art. But Picasso couldn't stop creating artwork, so he picked up ⓐ _____ such as old bicycles and mattress springs. He used not only old things but also his imagination ⓑto create this sculpture in 1942.

21 위 글의 주제로 알맞은 것을 고르시오.

① how to produce creative artwork
② the kinds of sculptures and pictures
③ the standard of creative artwork
④ the artwork made out of old things
⑤ the imagination of Pablo Picasso

22 주어진 영영풀이를 참고하여 빈칸 ⓐ에 철자 j로 시작하는 단어를 쓰시오.

> old and used goods that have little value and that you do not want any more

➡ _____

23 아래 〈보기〉에서 위 글의 밑줄 친 ⓑto create와 to부정사의 용법이 다른 것의 개수를 고르시오.

┌─── 보기 ───┐
① He is studying English to get a good job.
② I have a lot of work to do.
③ She promised me to come back by noon.
④ To write English well is difficult.
⑤ He read the book again to understand it.
└─────────┘

① 1개　② 2개　③ 3개　④ 4개　⑤ 5개

[24~25] 다음 글을 읽고, 물음에 답하시오.

Thrown-away Things and New Art

This artwork was created by Kurt Schwitters. He used thrown-away ⓐobjects to make artwork. He often said, "Old things are good for art."

Schwitters walked the streets and collected not only pieces of paper but also bits of wood. He glued and nailed them to a board, and created a new style of art, Rubbish.

24 위 글의 밑줄 친 @objects와 같은 의미로 쓰인 것을 고르시오.

① Their objects in life is to succeed and to live happily.
② Put the round objects in the box.
③ The objects of my study are the cultures of various countries.
④ There are two objects in this sentence.
⑤ The weather conditions are the objects of consideration when we travel.

25 위 글의 내용과 일치하지 <u>않는</u> 것은?

① Schwitters는 작품을 만들기 위해 버려진 물건들을 사용했다.
② Schwitters는 종종 "오래된 것들은 미술에 좋다."라고 말했다.
③ Schwitters는 거리를 걸으면서 종잇조각뿐만 아니라 나무 조각도 모았다.
④ Schwitters는 모은 물건들을 상자에 풀이나 못으로 붙였다.
⑤ Schwitters는 Rubbish라는 새로운 방식의 미술을 창조했다.

[26~28] 다음 글을 읽고, 물음에 답하시오.

In 1937, he moved to Norway. He was able to take his famous work ⓐ Germany (A) [because / because of] it looked (B)[at / like] rubbish.

What old things do you have around you? (C)[How / What] new artwork can you make ⓑ them? Use your imagination and create something new. One person's trash is another's treasure!

26 위 글의 괄호 (A)~(C)에서 어법상 알맞은 낱말을 골라 쓰시오.

➡ (A) _____ (B) _____ (C) _____

27 위 글의 빈칸 ⓐ와 ⓑ에 공통으로 들어갈 알맞은 말을 고르시오.

① at   ② of
③ on   ④ into
⑤ out of

28 위 글에서 필자가 주장하는 바로 가장 적절한 것은?

① 쓰레기처럼 보이는 예술 작품은 해외로 가지고 가기 쉽다.
② 한 사람의 쓰레기가 다른 사람에게는 보물이 된다.
③ 우리 주변에는 오래된 것들이 많이 있다.
④ 새로운 미술 작품을 만들기 위해 재활용을 해야 한다.
⑤ 상상력이 없으면 새로운 미술 작품을 만들기 어렵다.

[29~30] 다음 글을 읽고, 물음에 답하시오.

This artwork is Fish Lamp. It was created by David Edgar. ⓐHe used not only a plastic bottle but also his imagination to make ⓑthis artwork. One person's trash is another's treasure.

29 위 글의 밑줄 친 ⓐ를 다음과 같이 바꿔 쓸 때 빈칸에 들어갈 알맞은 말을 쓰시오.

➡ (1) He used his imagination _____ _____ _____ a plastic bottle
(2) He used not only a plastic bottle but his imagination _____ _____ _____

30 위 글의 밑줄 친 ⓑthis artwork이 가리키는 것을 본문에서 찾아 쓰시오.

➡ _____

01 출제율 90%

다음 중 밑줄 친 부분의 뜻풀이가 바르지 <u>않은</u> 것은?

① The man is hammering a <u>nail</u> into the board. (못)

② A <u>quilt</u> is made of pieces of cloth. (누비이불)

③ That store sells new and <u>used</u> books. (사용했다)

④ Would you like <u>another</u> slice of cake? (또 다른)

⑤ Dad put a <u>piece</u> of pizza on the table. (조각)

[02~03] 다음 빈칸에 공통으로 들어갈 말을 쓰시오.

02 출제율 95%

- It's hard work but it's _____ a lot of fun.
- His job is not only interesting but _____ very well-paid.

03 출제율 90%

- Some artists _____ old computer parts to make the artwork.
- Why don't we make _____ of online newspapers?

04 출제율 95%

다음 영영풀이에 해당하는 단어를 주어진 철자로 시작하여 쓰시오.

the curved metal bar with handles for steering

➡ h_____

[05~08] 다음 대화를 읽고, 물음에 답하시오.

Seho: Is this your poster for the art contest, Nara? (①)

Nara: Yes, it is, Seho.

Seho: I like your slogan, "더 재사용하고 덜 낭비하라!" (②)

Nara: I got it from junk art.

Seho: Junk art uses thrown-away things, doesn't it? (③)

Nara: Yes, it does. I'm worried about the waste problem. (④) We have to do something about (A)it. (⑤)

Seho: You can say that again.

05 출제율 100%

①~⑤ 중 주어진 문장이 들어갈 곳은?

Where did you get that idea?

①　　②　　③　　④　　⑤

06 출제율 85%

다음 조건에 맞춰 밑줄 친 우리말을 영작하시오.

┌─ 조건 ─┐
1. 두 단어는 위의 대화의 단어를 이용하거나 변형하여 사용할 것.
2. 두 단어는 비교급을 사용할 것.
3. 4단어로 쓸 것.

➡ _____

07 출제율 95%

다음 영영풀이에 해당하는 단어를 대화에서 찾아 쓰시오.

a competition judged by a group of specially chosen judges

➡ _____

08 밑줄 친 (A)it이 가리키는 것을 대화에서 찾아 쓰시오.

➡ _____

09 다음 대화의 빈칸 ⓐ~ⓔ에 들어갈 수 없는 표현을 고르시오.

> G: You look ⓐ , Minho. What's wrong?
> B: I'm worried ⓑ the speech contest.
> G: Don't worry ⓒ . You're ⓓ a good speaker.
> B: Thank you, but I feel worried.
> G: Don't be nervous. You'll do ⓔ .
> B: Thanks.

① too much   ② so
③ about   ④ fine
⑤ nervous

[10~12] 다음 대화를 읽고, 물음에 답하시오.

> B: What's that noise, Nami?
> G1: The little boys over there, Minsu.
> B: ⓐ그들은 공원에서 시끄럽게 굴면 안 돼. (A) do you think, Nami?
> G1: Well, they are just ⓑ a good time together. (B) do you think, Sumi?
> G2: I agree with you, Nami. A little bit of noise is no problem.

10 빈칸 (A)와 (B)에 공통으로 들어갈 의문사를 쓰시오.

① How   ② Where
③ Which   ④ What
⑤ Why

11 밑줄 친 ⓐ의 우리말을 주어진 단어를 이용해 영작하시오. (7 words)

(should, in, noise)

➡ _____

12 빈칸 ⓑ에 알맞은 말을 쓰시오.

➡ _____

13 다음 문장을 괄호 안에 지시한 대로 바꾸어 쓰시오.

(1) This artwork was created by Kurt Schwitters. (능동태로)
➡ _____

(2) He created a new style of art, Rubbish. (수동태로)
➡ _____

(3) This flower is not only pretty but also fragrant. (as well as를 써서)
➡ _____

14 다음 중 어법상 올바른 것은?

① This book was writing by a famous writer.
② He was heard open the door.
③ Lots of Christmas presents were given for the children.
④ The air conditioner was turned on by Emily.
⑤ Jack was written an e-mail by Amanda yesterday.

[15~17] 다음 글을 읽고, 물음에 답하시오.

Art can be made ___ⓐ___ all kinds of old things around us. Famous sculptures and pictures are often made from everyday things such as cans, bottles, and bits of paper.

Bicycle Junk and _Bull's Head_

How do you like this artwork? It was created by Pablo Picasso. He used a bicycle seat and handlebars to make this sculpture!

During World War II, there were not a lot of useful things for art. But Picasso couldn't stop ⓑcreating artwork, so he picked up junk such as old bicycles and mattress springs. ⓒ그는 오래된 것들 뿐만 아니라 그의 상상력도 사용하여 1942년에 이 조각품을 창작하였습니다.

📝 출제율 90%

15 위 글의 빈칸 ⓐ에 들어갈 알맞은 말을 고르시오.

① into
② by
③ at
④ out of
⑤ in

📝 출제율 95%

16 위 글의 밑줄 친 ⓑcreating과 문법적 쓰임이 같은 것을 모두 고르시오.

① She is making a model airplane.
② He finished doing his homework.
③ My hobby is cooking for my friends.
④ The boy running on a treadmill is Ted.
⑤ I heard her yelling with excitement.

📝 출제율 85%

17 위 글의 밑줄 친 ⓒ의 우리말에 맞게 (1) not only ~ but also, (2) as well as, (3) as well을 사용하여 영작하시오.

➡ (1) _____

_____

(2) _____

_____

(3) _____

[18~20] 다음 글을 읽고, 물음에 답하시오.

Thrown-away Things and New Art

This artwork was created by Kurt Schwitters. He used thrown-away objects to make artwork. He often said, "Old things are good for art."

ⓐSchwitters walked the streets and collecting not only pieces of paper but also bits of wood. He glued and nailed them to a board, and created a new style of art, ___ⓑ___.

In 1937, he moved to Norway. He was able to take his famous work out of Germany because it looked like rubbish.

📝 출제율 100%

18 위 글의 밑줄 친 ⓐ에서 어법상 틀린 부분을 찾아 고치시오.

_____ ➡ _____

📝 출제율 90%

19 위 글의 빈칸 ⓑ에 들어갈 알맞은 말을 본문에서 찾아 쓰시오. (대문자로 쓰시오.)

➡ _____

✏️ 출제율 90%

20 위 글을 읽고 대답할 수 <u>없는</u> 질문은?

① Did Schwitters use new objects to make artwork?

② What did Schwitters often say?

③ What did Schwitters collect?

④ Where did Schwitters glue and nail the objects that he collected?

⑤ Why did Schwitters create a new style of art?

[21~22] 다음 글을 읽고, 물음에 답하시오.

> **Artwork: Color Fish**
>
> **We used:** a plastic bottle, a big white button, a small black button, and colored paper
>
> **Special Feature:** ⓐ<u>Give the fish some water, and it will swim around.</u>
>
> This is our artwork. It is called Color Fish. It was created by the three of us: Minho, Changsu, and Nami. We used a plastic bottle, a big white button, a small black button, and colored paper. Give the fish some water, and put it in the pool. The colorful fish will swim around.

✏️ 출제율 95%

21 위 글의 밑줄 친 ⓐ를 다음과 같이 바꿔 쓸 때 빈칸에 들어갈 알맞은 말을 쓰시오.

➡ _____ you give the fish some water, it will swim around.

✏️ 출제율 100%

22 위 글의 Color Fish를 만들 때 필요한 재료가 <u>아닌</u> 것을 고르시오.

① 플라스틱 병 한 개　　② 큰 흰색 단추

③ 작은 검은색 단추　　④ 화려한 천

⑤ 색종이

[23~25] 다음 글을 읽고, 물음에 답하시오.

> Schwitters walked the streets and collected ①<u>not only pieces of paper but also bits of wood.</u> He glued and nailed them to a board, and created ②a new style of art, Rubbish.
>
> In 1937, he moved to Norway. He was able to take ③<u>his famous work</u> out of Germany because it looked like rubbish.
>
> What ④<u>old things</u> do you have around you? What ⑤<u>new artwork</u> can you make out of them? Use your imagination and create something new. ⓐ<u>One person's trash is another's treasure!</u>

✏️ 출제율 95%

23 다음 문장에서 위 글의 내용과 다른 부분을 찾아서 고치시오.

> In 1937, when he moved to Norway, he could take his famous work out of Germany because it looked wonderful.

➡ _____

✏️ 출제율 90%

24 위 글의 밑줄 친 ①~⑤에서 ⓐ에 해당하는 것을 <u>모두</u> 찾아 쓰시오.

➡ _____

✏️ 출제율 85%

25 위 글의 내용과 일치하지 <u>않는</u> 것은?

① Schwitters는 종잇조각뿐만 아니라 나무 조각도 창조했다.

② Schwitters는 1937년에 노르웨이로 이주했다.

③ Schwitters는 자신의 유명한 작품을 독일에서 가져갈 수 있었다.

④ 새로운 것을 창작할 때 당신의 상상력을 이용하여야 한다.

⑤ 한 사람의 쓰레기가 다른 사람의 보물이다.

[01~02] 다음 대화를 읽고, 물음에 답하시오.

> B: He's wearing his slippers, isn't he?
> G: Yes, he is.
> B: (A)우리는 학교 정원에서는 슬리퍼를 신지 말아야 해.
> G: (B)I agree.

01 밑줄 친 (A)의 우리말에 맞게 주어진 단어를 이용해 영작하시오. (8 words)

(should, garden, in)

➡ _____

02 밑줄 친 (B)와 바꿔 쓸 수 있는 말을 주어진 단어와 조건에 맞춰 쓰시오.

➡ _____ (with, that, 5 단어)
_____ (again, that, 5 단어)
_____ (agree, 4 단어)

03 다음 대화에서 내용상 어색한 부분을 찾아 고치시오.

> B: What's that noise, Nami?
> G1: The little boys over there, Minsu.
> B: They shouldn't make noise in the park. What do you think, Nami?
> G1: Well, they are just having a good time together. What do you think, Sumi?
> G2: I don't think so. A little bit of noise is no problem.

➡ _____
_____

04 능동태는 수동태로, 수동태는 능동태로 바꾸어 쓰시오.

(1) The Great Wall of China was built about 2,200 years ago.

➡ _____
_____

(2) Many great sculptures were created by Picasso.

➡ _____

(3) She sings the song very beautifully.

➡ _____

(4) Melanie read her daughter *Harry Potter*.

➡ _____

(5) Snow covered the house.

➡ _____

(6) They put off the game because of the rain.

➡ _____

05 두 문장을 'not only ~ but also ...' 구문을 사용하여 한 문장으로 연결하시오.

(1) This dress is cheap.
It is beautiful, too.

➡ _____

(2) Willy writes French well.
He speaks French well, too.

➡ _____

06 다음 문장을 as well as를 이용하여 바꿔 쓰시오.

(1) Schwitters collected not only pieces of paper but also bits of wood.

➡ _____

_____

(2) The artist used not only toilet paper rolls but his imagination as well to make this artwork.

➡ _____

_____

(3) Aaron is not only poor but lazy.

➡ _____

[07~09] 다음 글을 읽고, 물음에 답하시오.

Art can be made out of all kinds of old things around us. ⓐFamous sculptures and pictures are often made from everyday things such as cans, bottles, and bits of paper.

Bicycle Junk and *Bull's Head*

ⓑHow do you like this artwork? It was created by Pablo Picasso. He used a bicycle seat and handlebars to make this sculpture!

During World War II, there were not a lot of useful things for art. But Picasso couldn't stop creating artwork, so he picked up junk such as old bicycles and mattress springs. He used not only old things but also his imagination to create this sculpture in 1942.

07 위 글의 밑줄 친 ⓐ에서 문맥상 낱말의 쓰임이 적절하지 않은 것을 찾아 알맞게 고치시오.

_____ ➡ _____

08 위 글의 밑줄 친 ⓑ를 What을 사용하여 바꿔 쓰시오.

➡ _____

09 다음 빈칸 (A)와 (B)에 알맞은 단어를 넣어 질문에 대한 알맞은 대답을 완성하시오.

> Q: Why did Picasso pick up junk such as old bicycles and mattress springs during World War II?

A: During World War II, there were not a lot of (A)_____ _____ for art, but he couldn't (B)_____ _____ artwork.

➡ (A) _____ _____

(B) _____ _____

[10~12] 다음 글을 읽고, 물음에 답하시오.

Thrown-away Things and New Art

ⓐThis artwork created by Kurt Schwitters. He used (A)[throwing-away / thrown-away] objects to make artwork. He often said, "ⓑ오래된 것들은 예술에 좋다."

Schwitters walked the streets and (B)[collected / corrected] not only pieces of paper but also bits of wood. He glued and nailed them to a board, and created a new style of art, Rubbish.

10 위 글의 밑줄 친 ⓐ에서 어법상 틀린 부분을 찾아 고치시오.

_____ ➡ _____

11 위 글의 괄호 (A)~(B)에서 문맥이나 어법상 알맞은 낱말을 골라 쓰시오.

➡ (A) _____ (B) _____

12 위 글의 밑줄 친 ⓑ의 우리말에 맞게 주어진 어휘를 이용하여 6 단어로 영작하시오.

> things

➡ _____

창의사고력 서술형 문제

01 다음 그림을 보고 빈칸에 알맞은 말을 쓰시오.

A: Oops, I am sorry I'm _____.

B: You _____ _____ _____ _____ again.

A: I'm sorry. I was _____ _____ the test, so I couldn't fall asleep.

B: _____ _____ too much. You'll do a good job.

02 다음 주어진 동사와 재귀대명사를 사용하여 다양한 문장을 완성하시오.

produce	sing	laugh at	make	create

(1) _____

(2) _____

(3) _____

(4) _____

(5) _____

03 다음 내용을 바탕으로 폐품 예술 작품을 소개하는 글을 쓰시오.

What is the artwork? It is *Fish Lamp*.

By whom was it create? It was created by David Edgar.

What did the artist use? He used not only a plastic bottle but also his imagination

This artwork is *Fish Lamp*. It (A)_____ by David Edgar. He used (B)_____ a plastic bottle (C)_____ his imagination to make this artwork. One person's (D)_____ is another's (E)_____.

단원별 모의고사

01 다음 밑줄 친 부분과 의미가 가까운 것을 주어진 철자로 시작하여 쓰시오.

> We have plenty of time. There's no need to <u>rush</u>.

➡ h_____

02 다음 빈칸에 들어갈 말로 적절한 것은?

> It's _____ a beautiful day!

① very　② too　③ such　④ so　⑤ lot

03 다음 〈보기〉에 주어진 단어를 이용해서 빈칸을 채우시오. (같은 단어를 다른 문장에 사용하지 말 것)

> ┤ 보기 ├
>
> slogan　　part　　seat　　object

(1) There are no more chairs. You have to use this box as a _____.

(2) What is that _____ over there?

(3) That _____ belongs to the engine.

(4) We need a better campaign _____.

04 다음 우리말 해석에 맞게 빈칸을 완성하시오. (철자가 주어진 경우 그 철자로 시작할 것)

(1) The whole house is a m_____. (온 집 안이 난장판이다.)

(2) I sewed p_____ on my jeans. (나는 청바지에 헝겊 조각들을 덧대어 기웠다.)

(3) There are beautiful ice _____ in the hotel. (호텔 안에는 아름다운 얼음 조각상들이 있다.)

(4) Children are the _____ of our country. (어린이는 우리나라의 보물이다.)

(5) I didn't mean to u_____ you. (당신의 기분을 나쁘게 할 생각은 아니었다.)

05 주어진 우리말에 맞게 단어를 배열하여 문장을 완성하시오.

(1) 걱정할 것이 없다. (about, is, there, to, nothing, worry)

➡ _____

(2) 모든 유리잔을 신문지로 싸라. (in, the, newspaper, wrap, glasses, all)

➡ _____

(3) 그녀가 양손에 물건을 들고 있다. (her, she, hands, an, in, is, holding, object)

➡ _____

[06~08] 다음 대화를 읽고, 물음에 답하시오.

> A: I'm really worried about the trash problem.
> B: So am I. We should ___(A)___ ___(B)___ things.
> A: I couldn't agree (C)[more / less]. (D)[How / Why] don't we reuse paper bags as waste bags?
> B: That's a good idea.

06 다음 영영풀이에 해당하는 단어를 위 대화에서 찾아 쓰시오.

> a situation that causes difficulties for people

➡ _____

07 빈칸 (A)와 (B)에 use를 사용하여 문맥에 맞게 채우시오.

➡ (A) _____ (B) _____

08 (C)와 (D)에 알맞은 단어를 골라 쓰시오.

➡ (C) _____ (D) _____

[09~10] 다음 대화를 읽고, 물음에 답하시오.

> G: You look nervous, Minho. What's wrong?
> B: I'm worried about the speech contest.
> G: Don't worry too much. You're such a good speaker.
> B: Thank you, but I feel ____(A)____.
> G: Don't be nervous. You'll do fine.
> B: Thanks.

09 빈칸 (A)에 알맞은 단어를 대화에서 찾아 쓰시오. (nervous 제외)

➡ _____

10 위 대화의 내용과 일치하지 <u>않는</u> 것은?

① Minho is going to take part in the speech contest.
② Minho is good at speech.
③ Minho is worried about the speech contest.
④ Minho is cheering up the girl.
⑤ Minho looks nervous.

[11~14] 다음 대화를 읽고, 물음에 답하시오.

> Seho: Is this your poster ___ⓐ___ the art contest, Nara?
> Nara: Yes, it is, Seho.
> Seho: I like your slogan, "Reuse More, ____(A)____ Less!" Where did you get that idea?
> Nara: I got it ___ⓑ___ junk art.
> Seho: Junk art uses thrown-away things, doesn't it?
> Nara: Yes, it does. I'm worried ___ⓒ___ the waste problem. We ___(B)___ do something ___ⓓ___ it.
> Seho: You ___(C)___ say that again.

11 빈칸 (A)에 들어가 말을 위의 대화에서 찾아 쓰시오.

➡ _____

12 빈칸 (B)와 (C)에 알맞은 것으로 짝지어진 것은?

	(B)	(C)
①	have to	can
②	shouldn't	have to
③	have to	should
④	can't	can
⑤	shouldn't	have to

13 ⓐ~ⓓ에 알맞은 말을 〈보기〉에서 골라 쓰시오.

> ┤ 보기 ├
>
> as   about   for   from   with

➡ ⓐ _____ ⓑ _____ ⓒ _____

　ⓓ _____

14 다음 영영풀이에 해당하는 단어를 대화에서 찾아 쓰시오.

> a short phrase expressing an advertising message

➡ _____

15 다음 우리말과 일치하도록 주어진 단어를 활용하여 영어로 옮기시오.

> 나는 그 책을 읽었을 뿐만 아니라 그것에 대한 에세이도 썼다.
> (only, also, write, it, an essay)

➡ _____

16 능동태는 수동태로, 수동태는 능동태로 바꾸어 쓰시오.

(1) By whom is the artwork going to be created?

➡ _____

(2) Zootopia was watched by about 4.7 million Korean people.

➡ _____

_____

(3) Matilda made Tom a bowl of chicken soup.

➡ _____

_____

(4) People laughed at many of his discoveries at first.

➡ _____

_____

17 다음 문장과 같은 뜻을 가진 문장은?

Jerry asked Vivian not only her address but also her phone number.

① Jerry asked Vivian not her phone number but her address.

② Jerry asked Vivian her address as well as her phone number.

③ Jerry asked Vivian neither her phone number nor her address.

④ Jerry asked Vivian not only her address as well as her phone number.

⑤ Jerry asked Vivian her phone number as well as her address.

18 다음 문장에서 어법상 어색한 부분을 찾아 바르게 고쳐 다시 쓰시오.

(1) I as well as my sisters are learning English.

➡ _____

(2) Chris likes not only playing the piano but also the guitar.

➡ _____

_____

(3) The bulgogi had made last night.

➡ _____

(4) Didn't the house painted by Dan?

➡ _____

[19~21] 다음 글을 읽고, 물음에 답하시오.

Art can be made out of all kinds of old things around us. Famous sculptures and pictures are often made from everyday things ⓐsuch as cans, bottles, and bits of paper.

Bicycle Junk and *Bull's Head*

How do you like this artwork? ⓑIt was created by Pablo Picasso. He used a bicycle seat and handlebars to make this sculpture!

During World War II, there were not a lot of useful things for art. ⓒBut Picasso couldn't stop to create artwork, so he picked up junk such as old bicycles and mattress springs. He used not only old things but also his imagination to create this sculpture in 1942.

19 위 글의 밑줄 친 ⓐsuch as와 바꿔 쓸 수 있는 한 단어를 쓰시오.

➡ _____

20 위 글의 밑줄 친 ⓑ를 능동태로 바꾸시오.

➡ _____

21 위 글의 밑줄 친 ⓒ에서 어법상 <u>틀린</u> 부분을 찾아 고치시오.

_____ ➡ _____

[22~23] 다음 글을 읽고, 물음에 답하시오.

_____ⓐ_____

This artwork ①was created by Kurt Schwitters. He used thrown-away objects ②to make artwork. He often said, "Old things are good for art."

Schwitters walked the streets and collected not only pieces of paper but also bits of wood. He glued and nailed ③it to a board, and created a new style of art, Rubbish.

In 1937, he moved to Norway. He was able to take his famous work ④out of Germany because it looked ⑤like rubbish.

22 위 글의 빈칸 ⓐ에 들어갈 제목으로 알맞은 것을 고르시오.

① Schwitters Used Thrown-away Objects
② Thrown-away Things and New Art
③ What Schwitters Often Said
④ Where Did Schwitters Move?
⑤ Where to Glue and Nail the Objects?

23 위 글의 밑줄 친 ①~⑤에서 어법상 낱말의 쓰임이 적절하지 <u>않은</u> 것을 찾아 알맞게 고치시오.

➡ _____

[24~26] 다음 글을 읽고, 물음에 답하시오.

In 1937, he moved to Norway. He was able to take his famous work out of Germany because it looked like rubbish.

What old things do you have around you? What new artwork can you make out of ⓐ them? Use your imagination and create something new. One person's ⓑtrash is another's treasure!

24 다음 빈칸에 알맞은 단어를 <u>모두</u> 고르시오.

He was able to take his famous work out of Germany because it looked _____.

① valuable
② worthless
③ priceless
④ precious
⑤ valueless

25 위 글의 밑줄 친 ⓐthem이 가리키는 것을 본문의 단어를 사용하여 쓰시오.

➡ _____

26 위 글의 밑줄 친 ⓑ와 바꿔 쓸 수 있는 단어를 본문에서 찾아 쓰시오.

➡ _____

Lesson 3

Go, Team!

의사소통 기능

- 바람, 소원 표현하기
  I'm looking forward to doing a group dance.
- 강조하기
  It's important to hit the ball hard.

언어 형식

- 형식 주어 It
  It's important **to play** for the team.
- 형용사를 수식하는 enough
  Michael was **good enough** for the senior team.

Words & Expressions

Key Words

- **as**[əz] 쩝 ~와 같이
- **ball**[bɔːl] 명 공
- **basket**[bǽskit] 명 바구니, (농구의) 바스켓, 득점
- **believe**[bilíːv] 동 믿다
- **call**[kɔːl] 동 전화하다, 부르다
- **chance**[tʃæns] 명 기회
- **coach**[koutʃ] 명 코치, 감독
- **congratulation**[kəngrætʃuléiʃən] 명 축하
- **deny**[dinái] 동 부인하다
- **ever**[évər] 부 어느 때고, 한 번이라도
- **festival**[féstəvəl] 명 축제
- **first**[fəːrst] 부 먼저, 우선
- **guess**[ges] 동 추측하다
- **hand**[hænd] 동 건네주다
- **hang**[hæŋ] 동 매달리다
- **hard**[hɑːrd] 부 세게, 열심히
- **heart**[hɑːrt] 명 가슴, 심장
- **important**[impɔ́rtənt] 형 중요한
- **junior**[dʒúːnjər] 형 (스포츠에서) 주니어의
  명 (스포츠 팀의) 주니어 선수
- **kick**[kik] 명 발길질, 차기 동 발로 차다
- **kicker**[kíkər] 명 (축구에서 공을) 차는 사람
- **leap**[liːp] 동 뛰다, 빠르게 움직이다
- **like**[laik] 전 ~처럼
- **list**[list] 명 목록, 명단
- **locker room** 로커 룸

- **opening**[óupəniŋ] 명 기회, 자리, 개막식
- **penalty kick** 페널티 킥
- **pick**[pik] 동 뽑다, 선발하다
- **popular**[pápjulər] 형 인기 있는, 유명한
- **position**[pəzíʃən] 명 위치
- **pull**[pul] 동 당기다
- **quickly**[kwíkli] 부 빨리, 빠르게
- **quite**[kwait] 부 아주, 매우
- **rope**[roup] 명 줄, 로프
- **safety**[séifti] 명 안전
- **same**[seim] 형 같은, 동일한
- **save**[seiv] 동 아끼다, 절약하다
- **score**[skɔːr] 동 득점하다 명 득점
- **senior**[síːnjər] 형 (스포츠에서) 시니어의
  명 (스포츠 팀의) 고급 실력자
- **shoot**[ʃuːt] 동 슛을 쏘다
- **shot**[ʃɑt] 명 슛을 쏘는 사람
- **shout**[ʃaut] 동 소리 지르다
- **sigh**[sai] 동 한숨 쉬다
- **team player** 팀플레이어, 단체에서 협력 작업을 잘하는 사람
- **teamwork**[tíːmwərk] 명 팀워크, 협력
- **three-legged race** 2인 3각 경주
- **tie**[tai] 명 동점 동 동점을 이루다
- **whether**[hwéðər] 접 ~이든 아니든
- **while**[hwail] 접 ~하는 동안
- **yeah**[jɛə] 감 (질문에 대한 답으로) 응, 그래

Key Expressions

- **at the same time** 동시에
- **be going to** 동사원형 ~할 것이다
- **be ready for** ~할 준비가 되다
- **be ready to** 동사원형 ~할 준비가 되다
- **congratulations** 축하합니다
- **do one's best** 최선을 다하다
- **feel like + 동명사** ~하고 싶다
- **It's important to + 동사원형 ~** ~하는 것은 중요하다
- **look for** ~을 바라다[기대하다]

- **look forward to (동)명사** ~을 기대하다, ~을 고대하다
- **make a basket** (농구 경기에서) 득점하다
- **need to** 동사원형 ~할 필요가 있다
- **next to** ~ 옆에
- **take part in** ~에 참여[참가]하다
- **turn off** [불 · 라디오 · 텔레비전 등을] 끄다
- **want to** 동사원형 ~하기를 원하다
- **whether ~ or not** ~이든 아니든
- **형용사 + enough** 충분히 ~한

Word Power

※ 서로 비슷한 뜻을 가진 단어

☐ **chance**(기회) : **opportunity**(기회)

☐ **hand**(건네주다) : **give**(건네다, 주다)

☐ **pick**(뽑다, 선발하다) : **select**(선발[선정/선택]하다)

☐ **same**(같은, 동일한) : **identical**(동일한, 꼭 같은)

☐ **tie**(동점을 이루다, 동점) : **draw**(비기다, 무승부)

☐ **guess**(추측하다) : **infer**(추측하다)

☐ **important**(중요한) : **significant, crucial, critical**(중요한)

☐ **safety**(안전) : **security**(안전, 무사)

☐ **save**(아끼다, 절약하다) : **cut down**(절약하다)

※ 서로 반대의 뜻을 가진 단어

☐ **deny**(부인하다) ↔ **admit**(인정하다)

☐ **quickly**(빨리, 빠르게) ↔ **slowly**(천천히, 느리게)

☐ **pull**(당기다) ↔ **push**(밀다)

☐ **same**(같은) ↔ **different**(다른)

English Dictionary

☐ **chance** 기회
→ a possibility of something happening
무언가가 발생할 가능성

☐ **coach** 코치, 감독
→ someone training a person or team of people
개인이나 사람들의 팀을 훈련시키는 사람

☐ **deny** 부인하다
→ to say that something is not true
어떤 것이 사실이 아니라고 말하다

☐ **guess** 추측하다
→ to try to give an answer or make a judgement about something without being sure of all the facts
모든 사실에 대한 확신이 없이 무언가에 대해 답을 하거나 판단을 하려고 노력하다

☐ **hand** 건네주다
→ to pass or give something to somebody
어떤 것을 누군가에게 전달하거나 주다

☐ **hang** 매달리다
→ to attach something, or to be attached
어떤 것에 붙거나 붙여지다

☐ **leap** 뛰다, 빠르게 움직이다
→ to move or act quickly or suddenly
빠르게 또는 갑작스럽게 움직이거나 행동하다

☐ **opening** 기회, 자리
→ an available job or position
이용할 수 있는 일자리나 직책

☐ **pick** 뽑다, 선발하다
→ to choose or select from among a group
그룹 가운데서 고르거나 뽑다

☐ **save** 아끼다, 절약하다
→ to keep something to use or enjoy in the future
나중에 사용하거나 즐기기 위해 무언가를 남겨놓다

☐ **score** 득점하다
→ to gain points in a game
경기에서 점수를 얻다

☐ **shoot** 슛을 쏘다
→ to try to kick, hit, or throw the ball into a goal
골대 안으로 공을 차거나 때리거나 던지려고 하다

☐ **shot** 슛을 쏘는 사람
→ a person who shoots
슛을 쏘는 사람

☐ **shout** 외침, 고함
→ a loud call or cry
큰 소리의 부름 또는 고함

☐ **sigh** 한숨 쉬다
→ to let out one's breath with sound, as from sorrow, weariness, or relief
슬프거나 피로하거나 또는 안도하여 소리와 함께 숨을 내뱉다

☐ **tie** 동점을 이루다
→ to have the same number of points
같은 숫자의 점수를 갖다

☐ **yeah** (질문에 대한 답으로) 응, 그래
→ another way of saying yes
'네'라고 말하는 또 다른 방법

01 다음 중 'as'의 뜻이 〈보기〉와 같은 것을 고르시오.

> ┌─ 보기 ─┐
> Do in Rome as the Romans do.

① As I said, this is an important fact.
② As Mom was cooking, I did my homework.
③ Treat me as a friend.
④ As I had to wait for him for a long time, I was annoyed.
⑤ She was known as a famous star.

[02~04] 다음 빈칸에 들어갈 말로 적절한 것은?

02

> This penalty kick is a great _____ to win the match.

① accident   ② position
③ job   ④ chance
⑤ activity

03

> A lot of pretty leaves are _____ on the tree.

① flying   ② hanging
③ falling   ④ drawing
⑤ losing

04

> Turn off the light to _____ energy.

① use   ② need
③ spend   ④ store
⑤ save

[05~06] 밑줄 친 부분과 의미가 가장 가까운 것을 고르시오.

05

> We will select the next manager from among the qualified applicants.

① require   ② pick
③ pull   ④ save
⑤ collect

06

> You will be able to cut down your expenses in that way.

① raise   ② recycle
③ prevent   ④ save
⑤ require

서답형

07 다음 주어진 우리말에 맞게 빈칸을 채우시오. (철자가 주어진 것이 있으면 그 철자로 시작할 것)

(1) 소년은 창문을 깬 것을 부인했다.
➡ The boy _____ breaking the window.

(2) 가족은 내게 가장 중요한 것이다.
➡ Family is the most _____ thing to me.

(3) 첫 번째 선수는 페널티 킥을 놓쳤다.
➡ The first player missed the _____ _____.

(4) 나는 학교 소풍을 고대하고 있다.
➡ I'm _____ _____ _____ the school picnic.

(5) 나미는 반에서 가장 인기 있는 학생이다.
➡ Nami is the most p_____ student in the class.

01 다음 짝지어진 단어의 관계가 같도록 빈칸에 알맞은 말을 쓰시오.

> kick : kicker – speak : _____

02 주어진 두 문장이 비슷한 의미가 되도록 빈칸을 알맞게 채우시오.

> The player scored a goal in the basketball for two points.

➡ The player _____ _____ _____ for two points.

03 다음 빈칸에 들어갈 말을 〈보기〉에서 찾아 쓰시오.

> ┤ 보기 ├
> coach / list / opening / penalty kick

(1) Jina scored a goal on a(n) _____.
(2) The soccer team has a(n) _____ for a new coach.
(3) The new _____ trained the soccer players.
(4) I made a _____ of things to do.

[04~05] 빈칸에 공통으로 들어갈 단어를 쓰시오.

04
> • Many people look _____ a change now.
> • I don't think I'll ever be ready _____ the exam tomorrow!

05
> • I really don't feel _____ working anymore.
> • I can dance _____ that.

[06~07] 다음 영영풀이에 해당하는 말을 주어진 철자로 시작하여 쓰시오.

06
> to have the same number of point

➡ t_____

07
> to try to give an answer or make a judgement about something without being sure of all the facts

➡ g_____

08 다음 우리말에 맞게 주어진 단어를 바르게 배열하시오.

(1) 남자는 그에 대한 소문을 부인했다.
   (the, the, about, man, him, denied, rumor)
   ➡ _____
(2) 그는 주니어 축구 클럽에 속해 있다.
   (in, club, he, the, soccer, is, junior)
   ➡ _____
(3) 나는 그녀가 오든지 말든지 상관없다.
   (whether, comes, I, not, or, don't, she, care)
   ➡ _____
(4) 그는 페널티 킥으로 득점을 올렸다.
   (penalty, on, kick, a, he, scored)
   ➡ _____

Conversation

1 바람, 소원 표현하기

> **I'm looking forward to doing a group dance.** 난 단체 춤을 추는 것을 고대하고 있어.

- 앞으로 하고 싶은 일에 대한 기대를 표현할 때 'I'm looking forward to ~.'나 'I look forward to ~.'의 표현을 사용한다. 여기서 to는 전치사이므로 뒤에 명사나 동명사가 와야 한다. 바람, 소원을 표현하기 위해 want to도 사용할 수 있다.
  - I'm looking forward to traveling to Korea. 나는 한국에 여행가는 것을 고대하고 있어.
  - I look forward to my birthday party this weekend. 나는 이번 주말의 내 생일을 고대하고 있어.

바람, 소원 표현하기

- I'm looking forward to (동)명사 ~.
- I look forward to (동)명사 ~.
- I can't wait to 동사원형 ~.
- I can't wait for (동)명사 ~.
- I want to 동사원형 ~.

- I'm looking forward to (doing) a group dance.

  = I look forward to (doing) a group dance.

  = I can't wait to do a group dance.

  = I can't wait for a group dance.

  = I want to do a group dance.

핵심 Check

1. 다음 우리말과 일치하도록 빈칸에 알맞은 말을 쓰시오.

   A: I heard that you are going on a trip. (나는 네가 여행 간다고 들었어.)

   B: Yeah. I'm _____ forward _____ the _____. (응. 난 여행을 고대하고 있어.)

2. 주어진 문장 이후에 이어질 대화의 순서를 바르게 배열하시오.

   What are you going to do next Saturday?

   (A) Yeah, I am really looking forward to visiting her.

   (B) I'm going to go to my grandmother's house.

   (C) That's great. You must be excited.

   ➡ _____

② 강조하기

It's important to hit the ball hard. 공을 세게 치는 것이 중요해.

■ 'It's important to + 동사원형 ～.'은 '～하는 것은 중요하다'라는 의미이고, 가주어 it과 진주어 to부정사를 이용하여 강조하는 표현이다.

■ 어떤 일에 있어서 중요한 사항, 항목 및 정보 등을 나타낼 때 'It's important to + 동사원형 ～.'을 사용한다. 강조하는 표현은 다양하나 to부정사 부분을 강조하는 'It's important to 동사원형 ～.' 구문이 자주 쓰인다. 절을 강조할 때에는 'It's important that 주어 + 동사 ～.'의 형태를 취하게 된다. 다음과 같은 표현으로도 강조하기를 나타낼 수 있다.

- I want to stress that we hit the ball hard.
- It's important that we hit the ball hard.

강조하기

- It's important to 동사원형 ～.
- It's important that 주어 + 동사 ～.
- It's crucial[critical] to 동사원형 ～.
- It's significant to 동사원형 ～.
- I want to stress that 주어 + 동사 ～.

핵심 Check

3. 다음 문장과 같은 의미가 되도록 주어진 단어를 이용하여 영어로 쓰시오.

A: What should we do to keep the air clean?

B: First of all, it's important to use public transportation.

➡ _____ (significant)

_____ (want, stress)

4. 우리말과 일치하도록 주어진 단어를 배열하시오.

A: I'm sorry, Ms. Song. (송선생님, 죄송해요.)

B: You're late again. _____

(time, to, it's, important, on, be) (또 늦었구나. 시간을 지키는 것은 중요하단다.)

A. Listen & Speak ① A-1

G: ❶You know what, Minho? We ❷are going to go to Jeju for our school trip.

B: Yes, I know. ❸I'm really looking forward to it!

G: 그거 아니, 민호야? 우리는 학교 여행으로 제주도를 갈 거야.
B: 응, 나도 알아. 난 그걸 정말 고대하고 있어!

❶ 상대방의 주의를 끌 때 'You know what?' 혹은 'Guess what?' 등의 표현을 쓸 수 있다.
❷ be going to 동사원형: ~할 거야 'be going to 동사원형' 대신에 'will 동사원형'을 사용할 수도 있다. go to 장소: ~에 가다
❸ 앞으로 하고 싶은 일에 대한 기대를 표현할 때 'I'm looking forward to ~.'의 표현을 사용한다. to는 전치사이므로 뒤에 명사나 동명사가 와야 한다.

Check(√) True or False

(1) They are going to Japan for their school trip.   T ☐ F ☐

(2) They are the students of the same school.   T ☐ F ☐

(3) The boy looks forward to going to Jeju for their school trip.   T ☐ F ☐

B. Conversation

Junha: Namho, ❶I think you should take the penalty kick.

Namho: No way! You are the penalty taker, not me!

Junha: But you ❷are looking for a chance to join the All-Star Team, ❸aren't you?

Namho: Yes, I am. But ❹we are looking forward to winning the match, and you are the best kicker.

Junha: All right. ❺It's more important to win it, and I'll go for it.
(Junha scores on the penalty kick.)

Namho: ❻What a shot! You did it, Junha!

Junha: No, WE did it!

준하: 남호야, 나는 네가 페널티 킥을 차야 한다고 생각해.
남호: 무슨 소리야! 내가 아니라 네가 페널티 킥 전담이잖니!
준하: 그런데 너는 올스타 팀에 선발될 기회를 바라고 있지, 그렇지 않니?
남호: 맞아. 그러나 우리는 시합을 이기는 것을 고대하고 있고, 네가 공을 가장 잘 차는 선수야.
준하: 알았어. 시합을 이기는 것이 더 중요하니, 내가 페널티 킥을 찰게. (준하가 페널티 킥으로 점수를 얻는다.)
남호: 놀라운 슛이야! 너 해냈구나, 준하야!
준하: 아니야, 우리가 해낸 거지!

❶ 충고할 때, 'I think you should+동사원형 ~.'의 표현을 쓸 수 있다. 그 외에 'You'd better ~.', 'Why don't you ~?' 'What[How] about ~?', 'I advise you to ~' 등을 쓸 수 있다.
❷ look for: ~을 바라다[기대하다] chance to 동사원형: ~할 기회 to부정사가 명사 chance를 꾸며주는 형용사 역할을 한다.
❸ 어떤 말을 하고 그에 대해서 상대방에게 확인을 요청할 때는 짧은 의문문을 문장 뒤에 붙여 말할 수 있다. 이때 긍정문 뒤에는 부정의 부가의문문이, 부정문 뒤에는 긍정의 부가의문문이 온다. 부가의문문의 주어는 앞의 주어에 맞는 인칭대명사를 쓴다.
❹ 앞으로 하고 싶은 일에 대한 기대를 표현할 때 'I'm looking forward to ~.'나 'I look forward to ~.'의 표현을 사용한다. (= We look forward to winning the match.)
❺ 어떤 일에 있어서 중요한 사항, 항목 및 정보 등을 나타낼 때 'It's important to+동사원형 ~.'을 사용한다. 여기서 it은 앞 문장에 있는 the match를 받는 대명사이다.
❻ What a shot!은 감탄문으로 'What+a+(형용사)+명사+(주어+동사)!'의 어순이다.

Check(√) True or False

(4) Junha is the penalty taker.   T ☐ F ☐

(5) Namho wants to join the All-Star Team.   T ☐ F ☐

(6) They don't want to win the match.   T ☐ F ☐

📌 Listen & Speak ① A-2

B: Are the N-Boys coming to the school ❶ festival, Jimin?

G: Yes, they are. ❷I'm really looking forward to seeing them!

B: Me, too. ❸I can't believe it!

❶ festival: 축제
❷ to는 전치사이므로 뒤에 명사나 동명사가 와야 한다. be looking forward to (동)명사: ~하는 것을 고대하고 있다 I'm really looking forward to seeing them! = I look forward to seeing them! = I can't wait to see them! = I can't wait for seeing them! = I want to see them!
❸ I can't believe it!: 믿을 수 없는 일이야! 어떤 상황에 대하여 놀람을 표현할 때 'It's surprising!' 혹은 'I can't believe it!' 등을 쓸 수 있다.

📌 Listen & Speak ② A-1

B: I ❶want to be a good English speaker ❷like you. ❸What do I need to do?

G: Well, ❹it's important to use English every day.

❶ want to 동사원형: ~하기를 원하다 want 동사 뒤에는 'to+동사원형'이 와야 하며 이는 잇에 뉴ㅋ빈나.
❷ 여기서 like는 전치사이다. like: ~처럼
❸ 어떤 목표나 하고 싶은 일을 달성하기 위해서 무엇을 해야 할지 물을 때 'What do I need to do ~?'를 사용한다. need to 대신 should, have to를 쓸 수도 있다.
❹ 어떤 일에 있어서 중요한 사항, 항목 및 정보 등을 나타낼 때 'It's important to + 동사원형 ~.'을 사용한다.

📌 Listen & Speak ① A-3

B: Sumi, ❶we are going to have an English speech contest next Friday.

G: Wow, we are ❷finally having it. ❸I am looking forward to winning a prize!

❶ have a contest: 대회를 열다 next Friday: 다음 주 금요일
❷ finally: 드디어, 마침내
❸ be looking forward to (동)명사: ~하는 것을 고대하고 있다 win a prize: 상을 타다

📌 Listen & Speak ② A-2

B: I ❶am ready to go bike riding.

G: Wait, ❷safety first. ❸It's important to wear gloves.

❶ be ready to 동사원형: ~할 준비가 되다
❷ safety: 안전
❸ It's important to+동사원형 ~: ~하는 것이 중요하다 wear: 입다, 착용하다

📌 Listen & Speak ① B-1

A: ❶School Sports Day ❷is coming soon! ❸I can't wait.

B: ❹Same here. What are you looking forward to doing?

A: I'm looking forward to doing a group dance.

❶ school sports: 학교 체육대회, 운동회
❷ 현재 진행되고 있는 일을 말할 때 'be 동사의 현재형+일반 동사의 ~ing형'을 사용한다.
❸ I can't wait: 정말 기다려져. 희망이나 기대를 나타내는 표현이다.
❹ Same here.: 나도 마찬가지야.

📌 Listen & Speak ② A-3

B: What are you ❶still doing in the classroom? Hurry up!

G: ❷Just a minute. ❸Let me ❹turn off the lights. ❺It's important to save energy.

❶ still: 아직 Hurry up!: 서둘러!
❷ Just a minute.: 잠깐만. (= Just a moment.)
❸ make, have, let과 같은 사역동사는 목적격보어로 동사원형을 취하여 '사역동사+목적어+동사원형'의 어순으로 쓰며 '(목적어)가 ~하게 하다'라는 의미를 나타낸다.
❹ turn off: (전등 · 라디오 · 텔레비전 등을) 끄다
❺ It's important to+동사원형 ~: ~하는 것은 중요하다 save: 아끼다, 절약하다

● 다음 우리말과 일치하도록 빈칸에 알맞은 말을 쓰시오.

Listen & Speak 1 Get Ready

W: Grandpa is _____ _____ this Friday.

G: Great! I'm looking _____ _____ _____ him!

Listen & Speak 1 A

1. G: You _____ what, Minho? We _____ _____ _____ _____ _____ Jeju for our school trip.

   B: Yes, I know. _____ really looking _____ to it!

2. B: Are the N-Boys _____ to the school festival, Jimin?

   G: Yes, they _____. I'm really _____ _____ _____ _____ them!

   B: Me, too. I can't _____ it!

3. B: Sumi, we _____ _____ _____ _____ an English speech contest _____ Friday.

   G: Wow, we are _____ having it. I _____ looking forward to _____ a prize!

Listen & Speak 1 B

1. A: School Sports Day _____ _____ soon! I _____ _____.

   B: Same here. What are you _____ forward to _____?

   A: I'm _____ forward to doing a group _____.

2. A: School Sports Day is coming soon! _____ _____ _____.

   B: Same here. _____ _____ _____ _____ _____ _____?

   A: I'm _____ _____ to _____ in the _____ race.

Listen & Speak 2 Get Ready

M: When there's a fire, _____ important to _____ 119 first.

W: 할아버지께서 이번 금요일에 우리를 방문하실 거야.

G: 좋아요! 나는 할아버지를 뵙기를 고대해요!.

1. G: 그거 아니, 민호야? 우리는 학교 여행으로 제주도에 갈 거야.

   B: 응, 나도 알아. 난 그걸 정말 고대하고 있어!

2. B: N-Boys가 학교 축제에 오니, 지민아?

   G: 응, 와. 난 그들을 보기를 정말로 고대하고 있어!

   B: 나도 그래. 믿을 수 없는 일이야!

3. B: 수미야, 우리는 다음 주 금요일에 영어 웅변 대회를 열게 될 거야.

   G: 와, 드디어 하는구나. 난 상을 타기를 고대하고 있어!

1. A: 학교 체육대회가 곧 있을 거야! 정말 기다려져.

   B: 나도 그래. 넌 뭘 하기를 고대하고 있니?

   A: 난 단체 춤을 추는 것을 고대하고 있어.

2. A: 학교 체육대회가 곧 있을 거야! 정말 기다려져.

   B: 나도 그래. 넌 뭘 하기를 고대하고 있니?

   A: 난 이인삼각 경주를 하는 것을 고대하고 있어.

M: 불이 났을 때는 먼저 119에 전화하는 것이 중요해요.

Listen & Talk 2 A

1. **B:** I _____ _____ _____ a good English speaker _____
   you. What do I need to do?

   G: Well, _____ _____ _____ _____ English every day.

2. **B:** I am _____ _____ _____ bike riding.

   G: Wait, _____ first. _____ important to _____ gloves.

3. **B:** _____ are you still _____ in the classroom? Hurry up!

   G: Just a minute. Let me _____ _____ the lights. _____
   important _____ _____ _____.

Listen & Talk 2 B

1. **A:** Are you _____ _____ the baseball game?

   B: Yes, I _____. _____ _____ forward to _____ it.

   A: Me, too. What should we do to _____ it?

   B: _____ _____ _____ hit the ball _____.

2. **A:** _____ _____ _____ for the soccer match?

   B: Yes, I am. I'm looking _____ _____ _____ it.

   A: Me, too. _____ _____ _____ _____ to win it?

   B: _____ _____ _____ _____ the ball quickly.

Real-Life Task

Step 2

A: _____ team sport are you _____ _____ join on School
Sports Day?

B: I'm _____ _____ _____ the group jump rope
game. How _____ you?

A: I'm _____ looking forward to it. _____ _____ _____
_____ _____ _____ the game?

B: I think _____ important _____ _____ together _____ the
same time.

해석

1. **B:** 난 너처럼 영어를 잘하는 사람이
   되고 싶어. 내가 뭘 할 필요가 있
   니?
   G: 음, 매일 영어를 사용하는 것이
   중요해.

2. **B:** 난 자전거 타러 갈 준비가 다 됐
   어.
   G: 기다려, 안전이 먼저야. 장갑을
   착용하는 것이 중요해.

3. **B:** 교실에서 아직 뭘 하고 있니? 서
   둘러!
   G: 잠깐만. 불을 끌게. 에너지를 절
   약하는 것이 중요해.

1. **A:** 야구 시합 준비는 됐니?
   B: 응, 됐어. 난 시합에서 이기기를
   고대하고 있어.
   A: 나도 그래. 시합에서 이기려면 우
   리가 뭘 해야 할까?
   B: 공을 세게 치는 것이 중요해.

2. **A:** 축구 시합 준비는 됐니?
   B: 응, 됐어. 난 시합에서 이기기를
   고대하고 있어.
   A: 나도 그래. 시합에서 이기려면 우
   리가 뭘 해야 할까?
   B: 공을 빠르게 패스하는 것이 중요
   해.

A: 넌 학교 체육 대회에서 어떤 단체 운
동 경기에 참여할 거니?
B: 난 단체 줄넘기 경기에 참여하는 것
을 고대하고 있어. 너는?
A: 나도 그걸 고대하고 있어. 우리가 경
기에서 이기려면 뭘 해야 할까?
B: 동시에 함께 점프하는 것이 중요하다
고 생각해.

01 다음 대화에서 밑줄 친 부분의 목적으로 가장 알맞은 것은?

> B: I am ready to go bike riding.
> G: Wait, safety first. It's important to wear gloves.

① 소원 표현하기　　② 보고하기　　③ 강조하기
④ 경고하기　　⑤ 비교하기

02 밑줄 친 부분을 알맞은 형으로 고치시오.

> W: Grandpa is visiting us this Friday.
> G: Great! I'm looking forward to see him!

➡ _____

03 대화의 순서를 바르게 배열한 것을 고르시오.

> (A) Yes, I am. I'm looking forward to winning it.
> (B) Are you ready for the baseball game?
> (C) It's important to hit the ball hard.
> (D) Me, too. What should we do to win it?

① (B) – (A) – (C) – (D)　　② (B) – (A) – (D) – (C)
③ (B) – (C) – (A) – (D)　　④ (C) – (A) – (B) – (D)
⑤ (C) – (B) – (A) – (D)

04 빈칸에 알맞은 말을 고르시오.

> G: You know what, Minho? We are going to go to Jeju for our school trip.
> B: Yes, I know. _____

① I look forward to School Sports Day.
② It's important to study hard.
③ I want to be a tourist like you.
④ We'll not go to Jeju for our trip.
⑤ I'm really looking forward to it!

01 빈칸에 알맞은 말을 고르시오.

> W: Grandpa is visiting us this Friday.
> G: Great! I'm looking forward _____!

① to see him   ② to seeing him
③ seeing him   ④ for seeing him
⑤ at seeing him

02 다음 대화의 빈칸에 들어갈 말을 〈보기〉에서 골라 순서대로 옳게 배열한 것은?

> Junha: Namho, I think you should take the penalty kick.
> Namho: No way! You are the penalty taker, not me!
> Junha: _____
> Namho: _____
> Junha: _____
> Namho: _____
> Junha: No, WE did it!

┤ 보기 ├

(A) All right. It's more important to win it, and I'll go for it. (Junha scores on the penalty kick.)
(B) Yes, I am. But we are looking forward to winning the match, and you are the best kicker.
(C) But you are looking for a chance to join the All-Star Team, aren't you?
(D) What a shot! You did it, Junha!

① (B) – (A) – (C) – (D)
② (B) – (C) – (D) – (A)
③ (C) – (A) – (B) – (D)
④ (C) – (B) – (A) – (D)
⑤ (C) – (D) – (B) – (A)

[03~05] 다음 대화를 읽고, 물음에 답하시오.

> G: You know __(A)__, Minho? We are going to go __(B)__ Jeju for our school trip.
> B: Yes, I know. I'm really looking forward __(C)__ it!

서답형

03 빈칸 (A)에 알맞은 말을 쓰시오.

➡ _____

서답형

04 (B)와 (C)에 공통으로 들어갈 말을 쓰시오.

➡ _____

서답형

05 위 대화를 읽고 주어진 질문에 대한 대답을 영어로 쓰시오.

> What does the boy look forward to?

➡ _____
_____

[06~07] 다음 대화를 읽고, 물음에 답하시오.

> B: I am ready __(A)__ (go) bike riding.
> G: Wait, __(B)__ first. It's important to wear gloves.

서답형

06 빈칸 (A)를 주어진 단어를 이용해 채우시오.

➡ _____

07 빈칸 (B)에 알맞은 말을 고르시오.

① equipment   ② accident
③ exam   ④ safety
⑤ performance

[08~09] 다음 대화를 읽고, 물음에 답하시오.

> A: Are you ready ____(A)____ the soccer match?
> B: Yes, I am. I'm looking forward to winning it.
> A: Me, too. What should we do to win it?
> B: _____(B)_____

08 빈칸 (A)에 가장 알맞은 말을 고르시오.

① for   ② to   ③ forward
④ at   ⑤ in

09 빈칸 (B)에 가장 어울리는 말을 고르시오.

① I think it's important to call a teacher.
② It's important to wear gloves to catch the ball.
③ It's important to save energy to win the match.
④ It's important to pass the ball quickly.
⑤ I think it's important to join a soccer team.

10 중요 다음 중 짝지어진 대화가 어색한 것은?

① A: Are you looking forward to hearing from her?
   B: Yes, I am.
② A: What is important in making a lot of friends?
   B: I think it's important to be active in group work.
③ A: What are you looking forward to?
   B: Me, too. I look forward to doing a group dance.

④ A: Are you looking forward to getting good grades in school?
   B: Yes. I want to get good grades in school.
⑤ A: What is important when there is a fire?
   B: It's important to call 119 first.

11 다음 대화의 밑줄 친 ①~⑤ 중 흐름상 어색한 것은?

> B: What are you ①still doing in the classroom? ②Hurry up!
> G: ③Just a minute. ④Let me ⑤turn on the lights. It's important to save energy.

①   ②   ③   ④   ⑤

12 다음 대화의 흐름상 빈칸 (A)와 (B)에 공통으로 들어갈 말로 가장 적절한 것은?

> W: Wait, ____(A)____ today. Let me get you a mask.
> B: Thanks, Mom.
> W: Here you go. It's important to wear a mask when ____(B)____ enough.

① the air is heavy with moisture.
② the air is not clean
③ the air is mild
④ the air is dry
⑤ the air is extremely thin

서답형
13 다음 대화의 흐름상 어색한 것을 골라 고치시오.

> B: ①Are the N-Boys coming to the school festival, Jimin?
> G: ②Yes, they are. ③I'm really looking forward to seeing them!
> B: ④Me, too. ⑤I can believe it!

➡ _____

[01~02] 다음 대화에서 문법상 또는 흐름상 어색한 부분을 찾아 고치시오. (01은 2개, 02는 1개)

01

> B: Sumi, we are going having an English speech contest next Friday.
> G: Wow, we are finally having it. I am looking forward to win a prize!

➡ (1) _____
   (2) _____

02 중요

> B: What are you still doing in the classroom? Hurry up!
> G: Just a minute. Let me turn off the lights. It's important to saving energy.

➡ _____
   _____

03 다음 밑줄 친 부분과 같은 뜻이 되도록 주어진 단어를 이용해 영작하시오.

> M: When there's a fire, it's important to call 119 first.

(want, stress, must)

➡ _____

[04~05] 다음 대화를 읽고, 물음에 답하시오.

> B: I want ___(A)___ (be) a good English speaker like you. What do I need ___(B)___ (do)?
> G: Well, 매일 영어를 사용하는 것이 중요해.

04 중요 빈칸 (A)와 (B)에 주어진 단어를 활용하여 채우시오.

➡ (A) _____ (B) _____

05 밑줄 친 우리말에 맞게 주어진 단어를 이용해 영작하시오.
(important)

➡ _____

[06~07] 대화의 순서를 바르게 배열하시오.

06

> (A) I'm looking forward to taking part in the parade.
> (B) School Sports Day is coming soon! I can't wait.
> (C) Same here. What are you looking forward to doing?

➡ _____

07 고난이도

> (A) Yes, I know. I'm looking forward to it!
> (B) Sounds great!
> (C) Look at this. There is a robot festival this weekend!
> (D) So am I. Why don't we go there together?

➡ _____

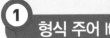

Grammar

① 형식 주어 It

> - **It** is easy **to solve** the problem. 그 문제를 푸는 것은 쉽다.
> - **It** is important **to keep** a secret. 비밀을 지키는 것은 중요하다.

- 가주어 It이라고도 부르는 형식주어 It은 진주어인 to부정사의 길이가 길어서 문장의 뒷부분으로 배치하고 주어 자리에 쓰인 것이다. 가주어 it, 진주어 to부정사 구문이라고도 한다.

  - **It** is hard **to make** a decision. 결정을 내리는 것은 힘들다.

    = **To make** a decision is hard.

  - **It** is easy **to make** friends. 친구를 사귀는 것은 쉽다.

    = **To make** friends is easy.

- 가주어 It은 따로 해석하지 않으며 to부정사구를 주어로 해석해야 한다.

  - **It** is fun **to learn** Yoga. 요가를 배우는 것은 재미있다.

  - **It** is not difficult **to go** green. 환경 보호 활동을 하는 일은 어렵지 않다.

- to부정사의 의미상의 주어를 나타내기 위해서는 to부정사 앞에 for A(명사 또는 목적격대명사)를 붙인다.

  - **It** is natural **for a baby** to cry. 아기가 우는 것은 당연하다.

  - **It** is impossible **for her** to finish the work in a day. 그녀가 그 일을 하루에 끝내는 것은 불가능하다.

- 'It is … of A to ~'의 형태를 취할 때가 있다. 이때는 It is의 뒤에 다음과 같이 사람의 성격을 나타내는 형용사가 온다.

  > kind, thoughtful, clever, wise, foolish, brave, careful, careless, polite, rude, honest

  - **It** was stupid **of you** to agree to the proposal. 그 제안에 동의했다니 너는 어리석었다.

핵심 Check

1. 다음 우리말과 같도록 빈칸에 알맞은 말을 쓰시오.

(1) 헬멧을 쓰는 것은 안전하다.

➡ It is _____ _____ _____ a helmet.

(2) 좋은 친구를 고르는 것은 중요하다.

➡ It is important _____ _____ good friends.

(3) 네가 지금 당장 가는 것이 현명하다.

➡ It is wise _____ _____ _____ _____ right now.

② 형용사를 수식하는 enough

> • My pie is not big **enough**. 나의 파이는 충분히 크지 않다.
>
> • Tom is not tall **enough** to play basketball. Tom은 농구를 할 만큼 충분히 크지 않다.

- enough가 부사로 쓰인 경우 형용사나 부사 뒤에서 수식한다. '형용사/부사+enough'의 어순임에 유의하자.

  - He is brave **enough** to protect us. 그는 우리를 보호할 만큼 용감해.

  - We are not old **enough** to see the movie. 우리는 그 영화를 볼 만큼 나이 들지 않았어.

  - They have been waiting long **enough** already. 그들은 이미 충분히 오래 기다리고 있는 중입니다.

  - The sofa is wide **enough** to accommodate all of us. 이 소파는 우리 모두 앉을 수 있을 만큼 넓다.

- enough가 형용사로 쓰인 경우, 명사 앞에서 명사를 수식하는 경우가 많다. 'enough+명사'의 어순이므로 enough가 부사로 쓰인 경우와 혼동하지 않도록 한다.

  - There are **enough** books to read. 읽을 충분한 책이 있다.

  - Two weeks is **enough** time for you to finish. 2주는 네가 끝낼 수 있는 충분한 시간이다.

  - I had **enough** cash for a one-way ticket. 나에게는 편도 승차권을 한 장 살 수 있는 충분한 현금이 있었다.

핵심 Check

2. 다음 우리말과 같도록 빈칸에 알맞은 말을 쓰시오.

(1) 그녀는 가족들과 함께 충분한 시간을 보내지 않는다.

➡ She doesn't spend _____ _____ with her family.

(2) 이 방은 충분히 따뜻하지 않다.

➡ This room is not _____ _____.

(3) 아마도 너는 충분히 멀리 보지 못한 거야.

➡ Maybe you haven't looked _____ _____.

(4) 입을 충분히 넓게 벌리세요.

➡ Open your mouth _____ _____.

01 다음 문장에서 어법상 <u>어색한</u> 부분을 바르게 고쳐 쓰시오.

(1) It is important exercise regularly.

_____ ➡ _____

(2) The soup is not enough warm.

_____ ➡ _____

(3) It is not common to attending the meeting.

_____ ➡ _____

(4) We certainly were enough close.

_____ ➡ _____

02 다음 괄호 안에서 어법에 맞는 것을 고르시오.

(1) This room is not (enough clean / clean enough).

(2) It is important (to listen carefully / listen carefully).

(3) You are (enough cute / cute enough).

(4) It is necessary (for us / of us) to pay attention.

(5) It is thoughtful (for him / of him) to help her.

03 주어진 단어를 바르게 배열하여 다음 우리말을 영어로 쓰시오. 필요하다면 단어를 추가하시오.

(1) 걷는 동안 휴대 전화기를 사용하는 것은 위험하다.
   (it / while / your phone / walking / dangerous / is / use)

   ➡ _____

(2) 네가 나에게 거짓말 하는 것은 옳지 않아.
   (tell / wrong / to me / it / for / a lie / is / you)

   ➡ _____

(3) 그 자전거는 네가 사기에 충분히 저렴해.
   (to buy / the bike / you / cheap / is / for / enough)

   ➡ _____

(4) 그 내용이 충분히 익숙하니? (enough / the content / is / familiar)

   ➡ _____

01 다음 중 밑줄 친 부분의 쓰임이 <u>다른</u> 하나는?

① <u>It</u> is good to see you clean your room.
② <u>It</u> is possible to meet early in the morning.
③ <u>It</u> is on the table in your room.
④ <u>It</u> is common to think no news is good news.
⑤ <u>It</u> is dangerous to wander around alone at night.

02 다음 빈칸에 들어갈 말로 가장 적절한 것은?

Can you hear the radio? Is it _____ for you?

① enough quiet   ② quiet enough
③ enough loud   ④ loud enough
⑤ enough loudly

03 다음 우리말을 영어로 바르게 옮긴 것은?

충분한 에너지를 갖는 것은 중요하다.

① It is not good to have energy enough.
② It is important to have energy.
③ It is important to have enough energy.
④ It is important to having energy enough.
⑤ It is not good have enough energy.

서답형

04 주어진 단어를 활용하여 다음 우리말을 영어로 쓰시오.

미래에 관하여 이야기하는 것은 흥미롭다.
(it / interesting)

➡ _____

05 다음 중 어법상 바르지 <u>않은</u> 문장의 개수는?

ⓐ It is silly of her believe what he said.
ⓑ I am not fit enough to run very far.
ⓒ He is enough old to ride the bike.
ⓓ It is essential for you having conversation with your family.
ⓔ The boxes were light enough to carry.

① 1개   ② 2개   ③ 3개   ④ 4개   ⑤ 5개

06 다음 중 빈칸에 들어갈 말이 바르게 짝지어진 것은?

• Your furniture is _____. You don't have to buy another one.
• Julian is short and thin. He is _____ to pass through the hole.

① enough good – small enough
② enough good – too small
③ good enough – too small
④ good enough – enough small
⑤ good enough – small enough

07 다음 중 어법상 바르지 <u>않은</u> 것은?

①It is ②impolite ③to leaving ④without ⑤saying a word.

①   ②   ③   ④   ⑤

서답형

08 주어진 단어를 바르게 배열하여 다음 우리말을 영어로 쓰시오. 필요하다면 단어를 추가하시오.

최선을 다하는 것은 중요하다.
(do / is / best / our / important / it)

➡ _____

09 다음 중 빈칸에 들어갈 말이 다른 하나는?

① _____ is easy to make a pie.

② _____ is necessary to remember her students' names.

③ _____ is important to try again and again.

④ _____ is impossible to solve this problem.

⑤ _____ English well is not difficult.

10 다음 ①~②에서 어법상 옳은 것을 골라 쓰시오.

A: Joe is ①[enough experienced / experienced enough] to do the job.

B: Really? Does he have enough experience?

A: Yes. I think it is a good idea ②[ask / to ask] him to do the job.

➡ ① _____ ② _____

11 서답형 다음 우리말을 영어로 쓰시오.

바깥은 충분히 따뜻하지 않아.

➡ It _____

12 다음 중 빈칸에 들어갈 말로 가장 적절한 것은?

You are lazy. _____

① You work too hard.

② You work hard enough.

③ You don't work enough hard.

④ You don't work hard enough.

⑤ You work too much.

13 다음 중 주어진 문장의 밑줄 친 It과 쓰임이 같은 것은?

It is important to take advanced math courses.

① It makes me upset.

② It is kind of you to help your friends.

③ It is found in all the world's major oceans.

④ It was cloudy and windy yesterday.

⑤ It is time to say goodbye to your family.

14 서답형 다음 대화의 빈칸에 알맞은 말을 쓰시오.

A: Mom, the soup is not _____.

B: Wait a minute. It will become cool soon.

➡ _____

15 다음 중 밑줄 친 부분의 쓰임이 다른 하나는?

① Jacob went to the market to buy some food.

② I am so happy to hear you won the prize.

③ He must be foolish to say such a thing.

④ They went abroad to study music.

⑤ It is a good idea to learn Spanish.

16 서답형 주어진 단어를 바르게 배열하여 다음 우리말을 영어로 쓰시오.

이 자동차는 경주용으로는 충분히 빠르지 않다.
(racing / this / for / fast / car / enough / not / is)

➡ _____

17 다음 중 어법상 바르지 <u>않은</u> 것은?

① It is my right to say "No."

② Is your brother strong enough?

③ Jason is enough handsome to be a model.

④ It is good to renew the water filter as often as possible.

⑤ There are enough people here to vote.

18 다음 중 우리말을 영어로 바르게 옮기지 <u>않은</u> 것은?

① 이 칼은 충분히 날카로워.

➡ This knife is sharp enough.

② 약속을 지키는 것은 중요하다.

➡ It is important to keep a promise.

③ 그 산은 충분히 가파르다.

➡ The mountain is steep enough.

④ 나는 이미 충분히 기분이 나빠.

➡ I feel enough bad already.

⑤ Jim은 그녀를 돕기로 마음먹었다.

➡ Jim decided to help her.

19 상황에 맞게 빈칸에 알맞은 말을 두 단어로 쓰시오.

> **A:** Is the coat _____?
> **B:** Yes, it is. It is so thick that it makes me stay warm.

➡ _____

20 다음 중 어법상 바르지 <u>않은</u> 것은?

> I think ①it is natural ②to vote ③for Jake. He is ④enough talented ⑤to be the president.

①   ②   ③   ④   ⑤

21 다음 중 의미가 <u>다른</u> 하나는?

① It is not easy to take care of babies.

② Taking care of babies is not easy.

③ It is not easy taking care of babies.

④ It is easy not to take care of babies.

⑤ To take care of babies is not easy.

22 다음 우리말을 영어로 바르게 옮긴 것은?

> 충분히 가벼운 것이 중요하다.

① It is important to being light enough.

② It is important to be light enough.

③ It is important be light enough.

④ It is important to be enough light.

⑤ It is important be enough light.

23 다음 빈칸에 들어갈 말로 적절한 것은?

> 너는 충분히 빨리 뛰어.
> You _____.

① are running fast

② run enough fast

③ run fastly enough

④ run fast enough

⑤ run enough fastly

24 주어진 단어를 활용하여 다음 우리말을 영어로 쓰시오.

> 그 수프를 만드는 것은 쉽습니다.
> (It / the soup)

➡ _____

01 다음 우리말을 영어로 쓸 때 빈칸에 알맞은 말을 쓰시오.

> 이 책을 읽는 것은 흥미롭다.

➡ To _____ .

➡ It _____ .

02 주어진 단어를 어법에 맞게 빈칸에 쓰시오.

> short / sweet / warm / long / close

(1) The coffee is _____ . Don't put more sugar in the coffee.

(2) Are you _____ ? Or shall I switch on the heater?

(3) The special event was _____ to see. Be prepared to see the event.

(4) Your hair is _____ . I don't want you to cut it.

(5) The pants are not _____ for him. He is very tall and has long legs.

03 (중요) 빈칸에 알맞은 말을 두 단어로 쓰시오.

> A: Is the room _____ for the group?
> B: No, it is not. It is a little small for them.

➡ _____

04 다음 우리말에 맞게 빈칸에 알맞은 말을 다섯 단어로 쓰시오.

> 당신과 다시 함께 일하게 되어 기쁩니다.
> It is a pleasure _____ .

➡ _____

05 주어진 단어를 바르게 배열하여 답변을 완성하시오.

> A: Did you hear what he was saying?
> B: Yes. I was (enough / hear / to / close) what he was saying.

➡ _____

06 (중요) 주어진 어구를 바르게 배열하여 다음 우리말을 영어로 쓰시오. 필요한 경우 단어를 추가하시오.

> 그 일을 내일까지 끝내는 것이 필요합니다.
> (by tomorrow / it / the work / is / finish / necessary)

➡ _____

07 다음 대화의 빈칸에 알맞은 말을 쓰시오.

> A: I want to fly a kite.
> B: I think it is not possible _____ today. If you want to fly a kite, the weather should be windy enough. However, there isn't _____ today.

➡ _____ , _____

08 (중요) 주어진 단어를 활용하여 다음 우리말을 영어로 쓰시오.

> 다른 사람을 이해하는 것은 쉽지 않습니다.
> (it / other)

➡ _____

09 다음 대화의 빈칸에 알맞은 말을 네 단어로 쓰시오.

A: Is _____ for swimming?
B: Yes, it is. This lake is so clean that it is famous for a safe lake to swim in.

➡ _____

10 다음 우리말을 영어로 옮길 때 빈칸에 알맞은 말을 쓰시오.

신문을 읽는 것은 필수적입니다. 하지만 나에게는 신문을 읽을 충분한 시간이 없습니다.
It is necessary _____ _____ a newspaper. But I don't have enough _____ _____ _____ a newspaper.

➡ _____, _____

11 주어진 단어를 활용하여 다음 우리말을 영어로 쓰시오.

그녀의 사과를 받아주는 것은 당연했어.
(natural / accept)

➡ _____

12 다음 빈칸에 알맞은 말을 쓰시오.

I bought a sweater yesterday. But it was not _____ for me. So I have to exchange it for a bigger one.

➡ _____

13 주어진 단어를 바르게 배열하여 문장을 완성하시오.

Put it down! (a knife / it / dangerous / is / with / play / to)

➡ _____

14 주어진 어구를 활용하여 다음 밑줄 친 우리말을 영어로 쓰시오.

A: It's late, but I don't want to go to bed now.
B: Why?
A: 충분히 피곤하지 않기 때문이야. (It's because)

➡ _____

15 다음 밑줄 친 말을 대신할 수 있는 말을 다섯 단어로 이루어진 한 문장으로 쓰시오.

Don't buy that coat. It's nice, but it's a little short.

➡ _____

16 다음 우리말을 영어로 쓸 때, 빈칸에 알맞은 말을 쓰시오.

그 계획을 바꾸는 것은 불가능하다.
It is impossible _____.

➡ _____

17 주어진 단어를 활용하여 다음 우리말을 영어로 쓰시오.

(1) 수영장 근처에서 뛰는 것은 위험하다.
   (it / run / near / pool)
   ➡ _____

(2) 그곳에 제시간에 가는 것은 중요하다.
   (it / in time)
   ➡ _____

(3) 목욕물이 충분히 따뜻하지 않아요. (the bath)
   ➡ _____

Reading

Go, Team!

The game was over. The junior team won it, and all the players were
~이 끝난(= finished. done)   = the game

happy. While they were in the locker room, the coach handed every
접속사(~하는 동안)   4형식 동사(hand+간접목적어+직접목적어)

boy a card. It had a list of the players on the junior team.
= A card

"As you all know, we have an opening for a player on the senior
~인 것처럼

team," said the coach. "Why don't you pick a player for the team?
Why don't you+동사원형 ~?: ~하는 게 어때?

Check one name on the list."

Scottie looked at the list and saw his name. Then he sighed and put
looked와 saw가 등위접속사 and로 연결 됨

a check next to Michael's name. He couldn't deny that Michael was
장소를 나타내는 부사구(~ 옆에)   명사절을 이끄는 접속사

good enough for the senior team.
enough가 형용사를 수식할 경우 형용사 뒤에서 수식

The coach collected every card from the boys. Everyone's hopes
every+단수 명사

were high. They all wanted to be on the senior team. The coach looked
to부정사를 목적어로 취하는 동사

up and said, "Well, it's a tie between Michael and Scottie."
(보통 둘 사이에서) ~ 사이에

Scottie's heart leaped. He was surprised that he was tied with
감정을 느낄 때 쓰는 과거분사형 형용사

Michael.

be over: 끝나다
locker room: 로커 룸
coach: 코치, 감독
hand: 건네주다
opening: 기회, 자리
pick: 뽑다, 선발하다
list: 목록
sigh: 한숨 쉬다
deny: 부인하다
tie: 동점을 이루다
leap: 뛰다, 빠르게 움직이다

확인문제

● 다음 문장이 본문의 내용과 일치하면 T, 일치하지 않으면 F를 쓰시오.

1 Scottie was disappointed when he heard that he was tied with Michael. ☐

2 Only one player was able to join the senior team. ☐

3 Scottie wasn't interested in being on the senior team. ☐

4 Michael was good enough to be on the senior team. ☐

"Well," said the coach, "both are wonderful enough for the senior
둘 다
team, and it's hard to pick just one player. But I have to, so I'll
형식 주어 it   진주어 to부정사구   그래서
pick Scottie." Then the coach walked over to Scottie and said,
~에게 걸어갔다
"Congratulations!"
"축하해!"라고 표현할 때는 복수형을 사용

"Thank you, but Michael is such a good shot. He makes the most
'such+a+형용사+명사' 어순에 유의   가장 많은 득점을 하다
baskets," said Scottie.

"Of course, he does," said the coach. "But he shoots whether there's
= makes the most baskets   문장 뒤의 or not과 함께 '~이든 아니든'이란 의미로 쓰임
a player in a better position or not. It's important to play for the team!
형식주어 it   진주어 to부정사구
Don't worry. I know a good player when I see one."
= a good player

Scottie walked out of the room. He felt like giving a loud and happy
~에서
shout. Then he saw Michael.
부사(그때)

Suddenly Scottie felt sorry for him. "I guess you don't care, but I
guess 다음에 접속사 that이 생략됨
picked you for the senior team," said Scottie.

Michael smiled. "You know what? I picked YOU."
상대방의 주의를 끌기 위해 많이 쓰이는 표현
Scottie was surprised. "You did?"
= You picked me?
"Yeah. You always do your best, and you're a team player. Today you
do one's best: 최선을 다하다
played for the team, and we won the game. Congratulations!"

확인문제

● 다음 문장이 본문의 내용과 일치하면 T, 일치하지 않으면 F를 쓰시오.

1 The coach thought Michael and Scottie were equally wonderful players. ☐
2 Michael was poor at shooting. ☐
3 Michael didn't care whether there was a player in a better position or not when he shot. ☐
4 Scottie was sad to be selected on the senior team. ☐
5 Michael didn't think Scottie did his best. ☐

shot: 슛을 쏘는 사람
make a basket: 농구 경기에서 득점하다
shoot: 슛을 쏘다
whether: ~이든 아니든
better: 더 나은
feel like Ving: ~하고 싶다
shout: 소리 지름, 외침
guess: 추측하다
yeah: (질문에 대한 답으로) 응, 그래
team player: 팀플레이어, 단체에서 협력 작업을 잘하는 사람

● 우리말을 참고하여 빈칸에 알맞은 말을 쓰시오.

1 The game was _____.

2 The junior team won _____, and all the players _____ happy.

3 _____ they _____ _____ the locker room, the coach _____ every boy _____ _____.

4 It had _____ _____ _____ the players _____ the junior team.

5 "_____ _____ _____ _____, we have _____ _____ for a player on the senior team," said the coach.

6 "_____ _____ _____ _____ a player for the team?

7 _____ one name on the list."

8 Scottie _____ _____ the list and _____ his name.

9 Then he _____ and _____ a check _____ _____ Michael's name.

10 He couldn't _____ _____ Michael was _____ _____ for the senior team.

11 The coach _____ _____ _____ from the boys.

12 Everyone's hopes _____ _____.

13 They all _____ _____ _____ on the senior team.

14 The coach _____ _____ and said, "Well, it's _____ _____ _____ Michael and Scottie."

15 Scottie's heart _____.

16 He _____ _____ _____ he was tied with Michael.

17 "Well," said the coach, "both are _____ _____ for the senior team, and it's _____ _____ _____ just one player.

18 But I _____ _____, so I'll _____ Scottie."

19 Then the coach _____ _____ to Scottie and said, "Congratulations!"

20 "Thank you, but Michael is _____ _____ _____ _____.

21 He makes _____ _____ _____," said Scottie.

22 "Of course, he _____," said the coach.

23 "But he shoots _____ _____ _____ _____ in a better position _____ _____.

24 It's important _____ _____ _____ the team!

25 _____ worry. I know a good player _____ I _____ _____."

26 Scottie _____ _____ _____ the room.

27 He _____ _____ _____ a loud and happy shout.

28 _____ he _____ Michael.

29 _____ Scottie felt _____ _____ him.

30 "I guess you _____ _____, but I picked you _____ the senior team," said Scottie.

31 Michael _____. "You know _____? I picked YOU."

32 Scottie _____ _____. "You _____?"

33 "Yeah. You always _____ _____ _____, and you're a team player.

34 Today you _____ _____ the team, and we _____ the game.

35 _____!"

---

17 "흠." 코치가 말했다. "둘 다 시니어 팀에 들어가기에 충분히 훌륭하고, 단 한 명의 선수를 선정하는 것은 어려운 일이야.

18 그러나 나는 선정해야 하기에, Scottie를 뽑겠어."

19 그리고 코치가 Scottie에게 걸어와서 말했다. "축하해!"

20 "감사합니다. 그러나 Michael은 훌륭한 골잡이에요.

21 Michael이 득점을 가장 많이 하고 있어요." Scottie가 말했다.

22 "물론, Michael이 그렇지." 코치가 말했다.

23 "그러나 Michael은 더 나은 위치에 선수가 있든 없든, 슛을 쏴.

24 팀을 위해 경기하는 것이 중요해!

25 걱정 마. 나는 보면 좋은 선수인지 안단다."

26 Scottie는 방에서 걸어 나갔다.

27 그는 크고 기쁜 소리를 지르고 싶은 마음이었다.

28 그때 그는 Michael을 보았다.

29 갑자기 Scottie는 그에게 미안한 감정이 들었다.

30 "나는 네가 신경 쓰지 않으리라고 추측하지만, 시니어 팀에 너를 뽑았어."라고 Scottie가 말했다.

31 Michael이 미소 지었다. "너 그거 아니? 나도 너를 뽑았어."

32 Scottie가 놀랐다. "네가 그랬어?"

33 "응. 너는 항상 최선을 다 해. 그리고 너는 팀플레이어야.

34 오늘 너는 팀을 위해 경기했고, 우리는 게임에서 이겼는걸.

35 축하해!"

● 우리말을 참고하여 본문을 영작하시오.

1 경기는 끝났다.

➡ _____

2 주니어 팀은 경기에서 승리했고, 모든 선수들이 행복했다.

➡ _____

3 그들이 로커 룸에 있는 동안, 코치가 모든 소년들에게 카드 한 장씩을 건네주었다.

➡ _____

4 그 카드는 주니어 팀의 모든 선수들의 명단을 담고 있었다.

➡ _____

5 "모두 알고 있듯이, 우리는 시니어 팀에 한 자리가 비어 있어." 코치가 말했다.

➡ _____

6 "여러분들이 시니어 팀에 들어갈 선수를 뽑아 보는 것이 어떨까?

➡ _____

7 명단 위의 이름 하나에 체크 표시를 해 주게."

➡ _____

8 Scottie는 명단을 보았고 자신의 이름을 보았다.

➡ _____

9 그러고는 한숨을 쉰 후 Michael의 이름 옆에 체크 표시를 하였다.

➡ _____

10 그는 Michael이 시니어 팀에 충분히 훌륭하다는 것을 부인할 수 없었다.

➡ _____

11 코치가 소년들로부터 모든 카드를 거두었다.

➡ _____

12 모든 선수들의 바람은 높았다.

➡ _____

13 그들은 모두 시니어 팀에 들어가기를 원했다.

➡ _____

14 코치가 올려다보고 말했다. "흠, Michael과 Scottie가 동점이구나."

➡ _____

15 Scottie의 심장이 뛰었다.

➡ _____

16 그는 자기가 Michael과 동점이 되어서 놀라웠다.

➡ _____

17 "흠." 코치가 말했다. "둘 다 시니어 팀에 들어가기에 충분히 훌륭하고, 단 한 명의 선수를 선정하는 것은 어려운 일이야.

➡ _____

18 그러나 나는 선정해야 하기에, Scottie를 뽑겠어."

➡ _____

19 그리고 코치가 Scottie에게 걸어와서 말했다. "축하해!"

➡ _____

20 "감사합니다, 그러나 Michael은 훌륭한 골잡이에요.

➡ _____

21 Michael이 득점을 가장 많이 하고 있어요." Scottie가 말했다.

➡ _____

22 "물론, Michael이 그렇지." 코치가 말했다.

➡ _____

23 "그러나 Michael은 더 나은 위치에 선수가 있든 없든, 슛을 쏴.

➡ _____

24 팀을 위해 경기하는 것이 중요해!

➡ _____

25 걱정 마. 나는 보면 좋은 선수인지 안단다."

➡ _____

26 Scottie는 방에서 걸어 나갔다.

➡ _____

27 그는 크고 기쁜 소리를 지르고 싶은 마음이었다.

➡ _____

28 그때 그는 Michael을 보았다.

➡ _____

29 갑자기 Scottie는 그에게 미안한 감정이 들었다.

➡ _____

30 "나는 네가 신경 쓰지 않으리라고 추측하지만, 시니어 팀에 너를 뽑았어."라고 Scottie가 말했다.

➡ _____

31 Michael이 미소 지었다. "너 그거 아니? 나도 너를 뽑았어."

➡ _____

32 Scottie가 놀랐다. "네가 그랬어?"

➡ _____

33 "응. 너는 항상 최선을 다 해, 그리고 너는 팀플레이어야.

➡ _____

34 오늘 너는 팀을 위해 경기했고, 우리는 게임에서 이겼는걸.

➡ _____

35 축하해!"

➡ _____

[01~03] 다음 글을 읽고, 물음에 답하시오.

The game was over. The junior team won it, and all the players were happy. __(A)__ they were in the locker room, the coach handed every boy a card. It had a list of the players on the junior team.

"As you all know, we have an opening for a player on the senior team," said the coach. "Why don't you __(B)__ a player for the team? Check one name on the list."

01 다음 중 빈칸 (A)에 들어갈 말과 같은 말이 들어가는 것은?

① _____ he is young, he can't see the movie.

② _____ you arrive at the airport, please tell me.

③ Tom's parents died _____ he was still at school.

④ I will go out _____ it's fine tomorrow.

⑤ Take a taxi, _____ you will be late.

 서답형

02 다음과 같이 풀이되는 말을 빈칸 (B)에 쓰시오.

choose or select from among a group

➡ _____

중요

03 다음 중 위 글을 읽고 답할 수 없는 것은?

① How did all the players feel after the game?

② Where were they after the game?

③ What was on the list?

④ How many openings are there on the senior team?

⑤ How many names are there on the list?

[04~07] 다음 글을 읽고, 물음에 답하시오.

"Well," said the coach, "both are wonderful enough for the senior team, and it's hard to pick just one player. But I have to, so I'll pick Scottie." Then the coach walked over to Scottie and said, "Congratulations!"

"Thank you, but Michael is ____(A)____. He makes the most baskets," said Scottie.

"Of course, he does," said the coach. "But he shoots whether there's a player in a better position or not. (B)It's important to play for the team! Don't worry. I know a good player when I see one."

04 다음 중 빈칸 (A)에 들어갈 말로 적절한 것은?

① so good a shot　　② good so a shot

③ such a good shot　④ good such a shot

⑤ such shot a good

중요

05 다음 중 밑줄 친 (B)와 쓰임이 같은 것은?

① It is not your problem.

② It was sunny and warm yesterday.

③ It made me really nervous.

④ It is not your fault to forget about it.

⑤ It is very far from my house to the park.

06 위 글의 내용과 일치하지 <u>않는</u> 것은?

① The coach thought Michael and Scottie were both wonderful.

② The coach picked Scottie for the senior team.

③ Michael makes the most baskets.

④ The coach has an eye for a good player.

⑤ The coach thought it is important to play for oneself.

서답형

07 위 글의 표현을 이용하여 다음 우리말을 영어로 쓰시오.

> 단 한 명의 선수를 선정하는 것은 쉽지 않았다.

➡ _____

[08~10] 다음 글을 읽고, 물음에 답하시오.

Scottie walked out of the room. ① He felt like giving a loud and happy shout. ② Suddenly Scottie felt sorry for him. "I guess you don't care, but I picked you for the senior team," said Scottie. ③ Michael smiled. "You know what? I picked YOU." Scottie was surprised. "You (A)did?" ④ "Yeah. You always do your best, and you're a team player. ⑤ Today you played for the team, and we won the game. Congratulations!"

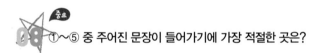

08 ①~⑤ 중 주어진 문장이 들어가기에 가장 적절한 곳은?

> Then he saw Michael.

①　　　　②　　　　③　　　　④　　　　⑤

서답형

09 밑줄 친 (A)가 의미하는 것을 어법에 맞게 쓰시오.

➡ _____

10 다음 중 위 글을 읽고 답할 수 없는 것은?

① How did Scottie feel when he walked out of the room?
② Whom did Scottie pick for the senior team?
③ Who is a team player?
④ What is Michael good at?
⑤ Whom did Michael pick for the senior team?

[11~13] 다음 글을 읽고, 물음에 답하시오.

Scottie looked at the list and saw his name. Then he sighed and put a check next to Michael's name. He couldn't deny that Michael was good enough for the senior team.

The coach collected every card from the boys. Everyone's hopes were high. They all wanted to be on the senior team. The coach looked up and said, "Well, it's a tie between Michael and Scottie." Scottie's heart leaped. He was surprised that he was tied ___(A)___ Michael.

11 다음 중 빈칸 (A)에 들어갈 말과 같은 것은?

① Please take good care _____ the dog.
② Helen isn't satisfied _____ the result.
③ Did you turn _____ the light?
④ Did you make _____ your mind?
⑤ The glass is full _____ milk.

12 다음 중 위 글의 내용과 일치하는 것은?

① Scottie couldn't find his name on the list.
② Scottie didn't think Michael was good for the senior team.
③ The coach ordered one of the boys to collect cards.
④ Scottie and Michael got the same number of votes.
⑤ Scottie didn't want Michael to go to the senior team.

서답형

13 Why did Scottie pick Michael for the senior team?

➡ It was because _____

_____.

[14~17] 다음 글을 읽고, 물음에 답하시오.

The game was over. The junior team won it, and all the players were happy. (A)[While / During] they were in the locker room, the coach handed every boy a card. (B)[It / They] had a list of the players on the junior team.

"ⓐ여러분 모두 알고 있듯이, we have an opening for a player on the senior team," said the coach. "Why don't you (C)[pick / picking] a player for the team? Check one name on the list."

서답형

14 밑줄 친 우리말 ⓐ를 영어로 쓰시오.

➡ _____

중요

15 (A)~(C)에서 어법상 옳은 것끼리 바르게 묶은 것은?

① While – It – pick
② During – It – pick
③ While – It – picking
④ During – They – picking
⑤ While – They – pick

16 다음 중 위 글의 내용과 일치하는 문장의 개수는?

ⓐ The junior team felt happy because they won the game.
ⓑ The coach didn't meet the players after the game.
ⓒ There was an opening for a player on the senior team.
ⓓ The coach wanted the players to pick one player for the senior team.
ⓔ There was only one name on the list.

① 1개　② 2개　③ 3개　④ 4개　⑤ 5개

서답형

17 According to the passage, where did the coach hand cards to the boys? Answer in English with a full sentence.

➡ _____

[18~21] 다음 글을 읽고, 물음에 답하시오.

Scottie looked at the list and saw his name. Then he sighed and put a check (A)next to Michael's name. He couldn't deny that Michaels was good enough for the senior team.

The coach collected every card from the boys. Everyone's hopes were high. They all wanted to be on the senior team. The coach looked up and said, "Well, it's a tie between Michael and Scottie." Scottie's heart leaped. He was surprised that he was tied with Michael.

중요

18 다음 중 밑줄 친 (A)를 대신하여 쓰일 수 있는 것은?

① between　② beside　③ among
④ in front of　⑤ side by side

19 다음 중 위 글의 내용과 일치하지 <u>않는</u> 것은?

① Scottie's name was on the list.
② Scottie didn't put a check next to his name.
③ Not all the players wanted to be on the senior team.
④ The coach collected all the cards from the boys.
⑤ Scottie didn't expect he would be tied with Michael.

서답형

20 How did Scottie feel when he heard he was tied with Michael? Answer in English with a full sentence.

➡ _____

서답형

21 위 글의 내용에 맞게 빈칸에 알맞은 말을 쓰시오.

> It is all the players' hope _____ .

➡ _____

[22~25] 다음 글을 읽고, 물음에 답하시오.

"Well," said the coach, "(A)both are wonderful enough for the senior team, and it's hard to pick just one player. But I have to,   (B)   I'll pick Scottie." Then the coach walked over to Scottie and said, "Congratulations!"

"Thank you, but Michael is such a good shot. He makes the most baskets," said Scottie.

"Of course, he does," said the coach. "But he shoots whether there's a player in a better position or not. It's important to play for the team! Don't worry. I know a good player when I see one."

서답형

22 밑줄 친 (A)가 의미하는 것을 영어로 쓰시오.

➡ _____

23 다음 중 빈칸 (B)에 들어갈 말로 가장 적절한 것은?

① although   ② because   ③ so

④ if   ⑤ unless

24 다음 중 위 글을 읽고 답할 수 <u>없는</u> 것은?

① How did the coach feel about the both players?

② Whom did the coach pick for the senior team?

③ Who makes the most baskets in the team?

④ How many people does the coach have to pick?

⑤ How many baskets did Michael make?

서답형

25 Write the reason why it was hard to pick just one player. Answer in English.

➡ _____

_____

[26~28] 다음 글을 읽고, 물음에 답하시오.

Scottie walked out of the room. He felt like giving a loud and happy shout. Then he saw Michael.

Suddenly Scottie felt sorry for him. "I guess you don't care, but I picked you for the senior team," said Scottie.

Michael smiled. "You know what? I picked YOU."

Scottie was surprised. "You did?"

"Yeah. (A)너는 항상 최선을 다해, and you're (B)a team player. Today you played for the team, and we won the game. Congratulations!"

서답형

26 밑줄 친 우리말 (A)를 영어로 쓰시오.

➡ _____

서답형

27 다음은 밑줄 친 (B)를 설명하는 말이다. 빈칸에 알맞은 말을 위 글에서 찾아 어법에 맞게 쓰시오.

> A team player means a person who ____ .

➡ _____

28 다음 중 Scottie의 심경 변화로 올바른 것은?

① annoyed → happy → upset

② depressed → annoyed → upset

③ upset → sorry → surprised

④ happy → surprised → sorry

⑤ happy → sorry → surprised

[01~04] 다음 글을 읽고, 물음에 답하시오.

The game was over. The junior team won it, and all the players were happy. While they were in the locker room, (A)the coach handed every boy a card. It had a list of the players on the junior team.

"As you all know, we have an opening for a player on the senior team," said the coach. "Why don't you pick a player for the team? Check one name on the list."

01 According to the passage, how did the game turn out? Answer in English.

➡ _____

02 알맞은 전치사를 이용하여 밑줄 친 문장 (A)와 같은 의미의 문장을 쓰시오.

➡ _____

03 What was on the card? Use the phrase "there was/ were."

➡ _____

_____

04 글의 내용에 맞게 빈칸에 알맞은 말을 쓰시오.

The coach suggested that the players _____ for the senior team by _____ on the list.

➡ _____, _____

[05~08] 다음 글을 읽고, 물음에 답하시오.

Scottie looked at the list and saw his name. Then he sighed and put a check next to Michael's name. He couldn't deny that Michael was good enough for the senior team.

The coach collected every card from the boys. (A)Everyone's hopes were high. They all wanted to be on the senior team. The coach looked up and said, "Well, _____(B)_____." Scottie's heart leaped. He was surprised that he was tied with Michael.

05 밑줄 친 (A)가 의미하는 것을 위 글에서 찾아 영어로 쓰시오.

➡ _____

06 다음 문장과 같은 의미의 문장을 빈칸 (B)에 쓰시오. 주어진 단어를 활용하시오.

Michael has the same number of votes as Scottie. (it / between)

➡ _____

07 According to the passage, why did Scottie feel surprised? Fill in the blank with a right sentence.

➡ It was because _____

08 다음과 같이 풀이되는 단어를 위 글에서 찾아 쓰시오.

to move or act quickly or suddenly

➡ _____

[09~15] 다음 글을 읽고, 물음에 답하시오.

"Well," said the coach, "both are wonderful enough for the senior team, and it's hard to pick just one player. But (A)I have to, so I'll pick Scottie." Then the coach walked over to Scottie and said, "Congratulations!"

"Thank you, but Michael is such a good shot. He makes the most baskets," said Scottie.

"Of course, he does," said the coach. "But he shoots _____(B)_____. It's important to play for the team! Don't worry. I know a good player when I see one."

Scottie walked out of the room. He felt like giving a loud and happy shout. Then he saw Michael.

Suddenly Scottie felt sorry for him. "I guess you don't care, but I picked you for _____(C)_____," said Scottie.

Michael smiled. "You know what? I picked YOU."

Scottie was surprised. "You did?"

"Yeah. You always do your best, and you're a team player. Today you played for the team, and we won the game. Congratulations!"

09 밑줄 친 (A)를 생략되지 않은 문장으로 쓰시오.

➡ _____

10 주어진 어구를 바르게 배열하여 빈칸 (B)에 들어갈 말을 완성하시오.

(or not / in / whether / better / there's / a / a / player / position)

➡ _____

11 According to the passage, what does the coach think important?

➡ _____

12 글의 흐름상 빈칸 (C)에 알맞은 말을 쓰시오.

➡ _____

13 위 글의 내용에 맞게 빈칸에 알맞은 말을 쓰시오.

As soon as Scottie saw Michael, he _____.

➡ _____

14 According to the passage, who plays for the team? Answer in English with a full sentence.

➡ _____

15 위 글의 표현을 이용하여 다음 우리말을 영어로 쓰시오. 주어진 단어를 활용하시오.

득점을 가장 많이 하는 것은 중요하다.
(it / important / to / make)

➡ _____

[16~17] 다음 글을 읽고, 물음에 답하시오.

Hello, everyone,

We play soccer after school. We practice (A)(pass and shoot) because it is important to pass and shoot well in soccer. It is also important to have good teamwork. Without _____(B)_____, it's hard to win the match.

Do you want to be a team player? Come, join us and enjoy team play.

16 괄호 (A)의 단어를 어법에 맞게 쓰시오.

➡ _____

17 글의 흐름상 빈칸 (B)에 알맞은 말을 위 글에서 찾아 쓰시오.

➡ _____

After I Read B

'나는 ~라고 확신해.'라는 뜻으로 어떤 일에 대한 확신을 표현할 때 사용하는
표현으로 that은 생략할 수 있다. (= I'm certain (that) ~.)

Coach: Congratulations! I am sure that you will do well on the senior team.
'축하해!'(~s를 붙여 Congratulations!라고 표현한다.)   잘하다

Good for you!

Scottie: Thanks a lot! I'll do my best!
최선을 다하다

Coach: I know that you are wonderful enough. Don't feel so down, and
형용사 뒤에 enough가 오면 '충분히'의 의미가
추가되어 형용사의 의미를 강조하는 역할을 한다.

keep going!
keep은 동명사를 목적어로 갖는다.

Michael: Thank you so much! I'll work harder.

구문해설 · feel down: 마음이 울적하다

해석

Coach: 축하해! 난 네가 시니어 팀에서 잘할 거라고 확신한다. 잘됐구나!

Scottie: 정말 고맙습니다. 최선을 다할게요!

Coach: 너도 충분히 훌륭하다는 것을 안다. 너무 낙담하지 말고 계속 정진하거라.

Michael: 정말 고맙습니다. 더 열심히 할게요.

Before I read

My heart leaps when I think about these two players. Michael was such a good
~할 때   such+a(n)+형용사+명사

shot. No one can deny that he was a great player. Michael could make lots of
명사절을 이끄는 접속사(deny의 목적어)   = many

baskets because Scottie helped him a lot.
이유를 나타내는 접속사(~이기 때문에)   많이(부사구)

구문해설 · leap: 뛰다 · deny: 부인하다 · make baskets: 득점하다

이 두 선수들을 생각할 때면 내 심장이 뛴다. Michael은 정말 훌륭한 골잡이었다. 그가 위대한 선수였다는 것은 누구도 부인할 수 없을 것이다. Michael은 Scottie가 그를 많이 도와주었기 때문에 많은 골을 넣을 수 있었다.

Let's Write

Hello, everyone,

We play soccer after school. We practice passing and shooting because it is
방과 후에   동명사를 목적어로 취하는 동사   형식 주어

important to pass and shoot well in soccer. It is also important to have good
진주어   형식주어   진주어

teamwork. Without good teamwork, it's hard to win the match. Do you want
전치사(~가 없는)   형식주어   진주어   to부정사를 목적어로 취하는 동사

to be a team player?

Come, join us and enjoy team play.

구문해설 · practice: 연습하다 · important: 중요한 · join: 함께 하다

안녕, 모두들,
우리는 방과 후에 축구를 해. 축구에서는 패스와 슛을 잘하는 것이 중요하기 때문에 우리는 패스와 슛을 연습해. 좋은 팀워크를 갖는 것도 또한 중요해. 좋은 팀워크 없이는 시합을 이기는 것이 어려워. 너도 팀플레이어가 되고 싶니? 와서 우리와 함께 해서 팀플레이를 즐기자.

01 다음 중 밑줄 친 부분의 뜻풀이가 바르지 <u>않은</u> 것은?

① He walks very <u>quickly</u>. (빠르게)
② The small village is <u>quite</u> poor and has many problems. (조용한)
③ Have you <u>ever</u> been to New York? (한 번이라도)
④ They look the <u>same</u>. (같은)
⑤ Kick this ball as <u>hard</u> as you can. (세게)

02 다음 그림을 보고 대화의 빈칸을 채우시오.

> A: What are you looking forward to doing?
> B: I'm looking _____ _____ running in the _____ race.

03 우리말 해석에 맞게 주어진 단어를 알맞게 배열하시오.

> 여러분은 여러 사람들과 동시에 연락을 할 수 있습니다. (communicate, same, the, you, with, can, people, at, many, time)

➡ _____
_____

04 밑줄 친 단어와 의미가 가장 가까운 것을 고르시오.

> Can you <u>pass</u> me the salt?

① watch   ② carry   ③ face
④ hand   ⑤ point

05 다음 영영 풀이에 해당하는 단어를 고르시오.

> to try to kick, hit, or throw the ball into a goal

① shot   ② shoot   ③ get
④ join   ⑤ hold

[06~07] 다음 대화를 읽고, 물음에 답하시오.

> B: I want to be a good English speaker (A)[as / of / like] you. (B)[How / What / When] do I need to do?
> G: Well, <u>it's important to use English every day.</u>

06 문맥상 (A)와 (B)에 알맞은 것을 고르시오.

➡ (A) _____ (B) _____

07 밑줄 친 문장과 같은 의미가 되도록 빈칸을 채우시오.

➡ it's important that _____.

[08~09] 다음 대화를 읽고, 물음에 답하시오.

> B: Look at this. (①) There is a robot festival this weekend! (②)
> G: Yes, I know. (③) I'm looking forward to it! (④)
> B: So am I. (⑤)
> G: Sounds great!

08 ①~⑤ 중 주어진 문장이 들어갈 곳은?

> Why don't we go there together?

①   ②   ③   ④   ⑤

09 위 대화의 내용과 일치하지 않는 것은?

① The boy wants to go to a robot festival with the girl.
② The girl is looking forward to a robot festival.
③ The girl is going to go to a robot festival.
④ The robot festival will be held next weekend.
⑤ The boy is looking at something which is about a robot festival.

[10~11] 대화의 빈칸 ⓐ~ⓔ에 들어갈 수 없는 표현을 고르시오.

10

> B: Are the N-Boys _____ⓐ_____ the school festival, Jimin?
> G: Yes, ___ⓑ___. I'm really ___ⓒ___ seeing them!
> B: Me, ___ⓓ___. I ___ⓔ___ it!

① they are   ② can't believe
③ too   ④ looking at
⑤ coming to

11

> A: What team sport are you ___ⓐ___ to join on School Sports Day?
> B: I'm looking forward to ___ⓑ___ the group jump rope game. How about you?
> A: I'm also ___ⓒ___ forward to it. What should we do ___ⓓ___ the game?
> B: I think it's important ___ⓔ___ together at the same time.

① joining   ② winning   ③ going
④ to jump   ⑤ looking

[12~13] 다음 글을 읽고, 물음에 답하시오.

> M: 여러분은 이 경기에서 승리하고 싶지요, 그렇지 않아요? Well, ⓐin this match, it's important ⓑto have good teamwork. ⓒWhen the team leader shouts "hang," stay in your position and ⓓsaves your energy. When the leader shouts "pull," then pull the rope together ⓔat the same time.

12 밑줄 친 우리말을 주어진 단어를 써서 영작하시오.

➡ _____

_____ (looking, match)

13 ⓐ~ⓔ 중 문법상 어색한 곳은?

① ⓐ   ② ⓑ   ③ ⓒ   ④ ⓓ   ⑤ ⓔ

14 밑줄 친 우리말 (A)와 (B)를 주어진 단어를 이용해 영작하시오.

> A: (A)넌 이인삼각 경주 준비가 됐니? (for)
> B: Yes, I am. I'm really looking forward to winning it!
> A: Me, too. (B)우리가 경주에서 이기려면 무엇을 해야 할까? (it, should)
> B: It's important to run fast together.

➡ (A) _____
  (B) _____

15
①~⑤ 중 문법상 또는 흐름상 어색한 곳을 고르고 바르게 고치시오. (2개)

> B: Mom, I'm ready. Let's ①go.
> W: Wait, the air is ②not clean today. Let me ③to get you a mask.
> B: Thanks, Mom.
> W: Here you go. It's important to wear a mask ④when the air is not ⑤enough clean.

➡ _____ ,

_____

16
다음 우리말을 영어로 바르게 옮긴 것은?

> 이 집은 대가족에게 충분히 크지 않다.

① This house is not small enough for a large family.
② This house is small enough for a large family.
③ This house is enough large for a large family.
④ This house is not big enough for a large family.
⑤ This house is not enough big for a large family.

17
다음 중 빈칸에 들어갈 'get'의 형태가 다른 하나는?

① It is possible _____ tickets.
② _____ there on time will be difficult.
③ I want you _____ me to the airport.
④ Are there enough windows _____ sunshine?
⑤ The road traffic showed no sign of _____ better.

18
주어진 단어를 활용하여 다음 우리말을 영어로 쓰시오.

> 밤을 새는 것은 좋은 생각이 아니다.
> (it / idea / stay up)

➡ _____

19
다음 빈칸에 들어갈 말이 바르게 짝지어진 것은?

> I know you are weak. But this laptop is _____ for you _____ around.

① heavy enough – carrying
② enough good – to carry
③ light enough – to carry
④ expensive enough – carrying
⑤ enough size – carrying

20
다음 중 어법상 바르지 않은 것은?

① I hope the sofa is comfortable enough.
② It is safe to say that Michael Jackson was the king of pop.
③ Is the distance short enough to walk?
④ Is there a table big enough for 10 people?
⑤ Linda is not a good player because she doesn't enough practice.

21
다음 중 주어진 문장의 밑줄 친 부분과 쓰임이 같은 것을 모두 고르시오.

> It is not easy to read 100 books for a year.

① It is raining outside.
② It is necessary to book the ticket in advance.
③ It is over there in the bathroom.
④ It gave me the meaning of life.
⑤ It was hard for me to break bad habits.

22 주어진 단어를 활용하여 다음 빈칸에 알맞은 말을 쓰시오.

> A: Would you like to be a teacher?
> B: Yes. I _____ to be a teacher.
> 나는 선생님이 되기에 충분히 열정적입니다.
> (passionate)

➡ _____

23 다음 우리말을 영어로 쓸 때 다섯 번째로 오는 단어는?

> 말을 타는 것은 충분히 흥미롭다.

① enough   ② to   ③ ride
④ a   ⑤ horse

24 다음 빈칸에 들어갈 말로 가장 적절한 것은?

> It is easy for him _____ in front of many people.

① to speaking   ② speak
③ to speak   ④ speaks
⑤ spoke

25 주어진 단어를 활용하여 다음 우리말을 영어로 쓰시오.

> 이 안전벨트는 충분히 튼튼하다. (this safety belt)

➡ _____

26 다음 빈칸에 들어갈 말로 적절한 것을 고르시오.

> It is wrong _____ lies to your parents.

① to telling   ② tells   ③ to tell
④ tell   ⑤ told

27 주어진 단어를 바르게 배열하여 문장을 완성하시오.

> Is your English (enough / a conversation / good / have / to)?

➡ _____

Reading

[28~30] 다음 글을 읽고, 물음에 답하시오.

> The game was over. The junior team won it, and all the players were happy.
> [A] Then he sighed and ①put a check next to Michael's name. He couldn't deny that Michael was ②good enough for the senior team.
> [B] It had a list of the players on the junior team. "As you all know, we have ③an opening for a player on the senior team," said the coach.
> [C] "Why don't you pick a player for the team? Check one name on the list." Scottie looked at the list and saw his name.
> [D] ④While they were in the locker room, the coach handed ⑤every boys a card.

28 자연스러운 내용이 되도록 [A]~[D]를 바르게 나열한 것은?

① [B] – [D] – [A] – [C]
② [C] – [D] – [B] – [A]
③ [B] – [C] – [A] – [D]
④ [D] – [A] – [B] – [C]
⑤ [D] – [B] – [C] – [A]

29 다음 중 위 글의 내용과 일치하지 <u>않는</u> 것은?

① Scottie was in the junior team.

② All the players were happy because they won the game.

③ Michael's name was on the list.

④ A list of the players on the senior team was on the card.

⑤ All the players were handed cards in the locker room.

30 ①~⑤ 중 어법상 <u>틀린</u> 것을 골라 바르게 고쳐 쓰시오.

⟶ _____ ➡ _____

[31~33] 다음 글을 읽고, 물음에 답하시오.

The coach collected every card from the boys. Everyone's hopes were high. They all wanted to be on the senior team. The coach looked up and said, "Well, it's a tie between Michael and Scottie." Scottie's heart leaped. He was surprised that he was tied with Michael.

"Well," said the coach, "_____(A)_____, and it's hard to pick just one player. But I have to, so I'll pick Scottie." Then the coach walked over to Scottie and said, "Congratulations!"

"Thank you, but Michael is such a good shot. He makes the most baskets," said Scottie.

"Of course, he does," said the coach. "But he shoots whether there's a player in a better position or not. It's important to play for the team! Don't worry. I know a good player when I see one."

31 주어진 단어를 바르게 배열하여 빈칸 (A)에 들어갈 말을 완성하시오.

(for / both / enough / the senior team / are / wonderful)

➡ _____

32 다음 중 위 글을 읽고 답할 수 <u>없는</u> 것은?

① What did the coach collect from the boys?

② What did all the players want?

③ Who was tied with Michael?

④ Who picked a player for the senior team?

⑤ How did Michael feel about Scottie?

33 다음 조건에 맞게 우리말을 영어로 쓰시오.

┤ 조건 ├
• 가주어 It, 진주어 to부정사를 쓸 것.
• hard를 사용할 것.

Michael은 팀플레이어라고 말하기 힘들다.

➡ _____

[34~35] 다음 글을 읽고, 물음에 답하시오.

Hello, everyone,

We play soccer after school. We practice passing and shooting because it is important to pass and shoot well in soccer. (A)좋은 팀워크를 갖는 것 또한 중요해. Without good teamwork, it's hard to win the match.

Do you want to be a team player? Come, join us and enjoy team play.

34 밑줄 친 우리말 (A)를 영어로 쓰시오.

➡ _____

35 다음 중 위 글의 내용과 일치하는 것은?

① They play soccer on weekends.

② They practice only shooting.

③ Passing and shooting well are not so important in soccer.

④ They want someone to join them.

⑤ To have good teamwork is very difficult.

01 내용상 빈칸에 알맞은 말을 고르시오. 출제율90%

> When there's a fire, it's important to _____ 119 first.

① see   ② cry   ③ buy
④ need   ⑤ call

02 다음 빈칸에 공통으로 들어갈 말을 쓰시오. 출제율100%

> • He didn't spend _____ time to prepare a test.
> • The girl was wise _____ to solve the problem.

03 다음 영영풀이에 해당하는 단어를 주어진 철자로 시작하여 쓰시오. 출제율90%

> to move or act quickly or suddenly

➡ l_____

[04~06] 다음 글을 읽고, 물음에 답하시오.

M: You are looking forward to winning this match, aren't you? Well, in this match, it's important to have good teamwork. When the team leader shouts "hang," ___(A)___ in your position and ___(B)___ your energy. When the leader shouts "pull," then ___(C)___ the rope together at the same time.

04 위의 글은 무슨 경기에 대한 것인가? 출제율95%

① 줄다리기   ② 단체 줄넘기   ③ 축구
④ 배구   ⑤ 농구

05 〈보기〉에서 주어진 단어를 골라 빈칸 (A)~(C)를 채우시오. 출제율95%

> ┤ 보기 ├
> shout   call   pull   stay   save

➡ (A)_____ (B)_____ (C)_____

06 위 글에서 다음 영영풀이에 해당하는 단어를 찾아 쓰시오. 출제율90%

> a loud call or cry

➡ _____

07 다음 중 밑줄 친 부분의 뜻풀이가 바르지 않은 것은? 출제율90%

① Park Jisung is a wonderful team player. (단체에서 협력 작업을 잘하는 사람)
② Pick a number between 1 and 10. (뽑다)
③ The soccer team has an opening for a new coach. (자리)
④ My English teachers say my English is quite good. (조용한)
⑤ I feel like watching TV. (~처럼)

[08~10] 다음 대화를 읽고, 물음에 답하시오.

Junha: Namho, I think you should take the penalty kick.
Namho: No way! You are the penalty taker, not me!
Junha: But you are ___(A)___ for a chance to join the All-Star Team, aren't you?
Namho: Yes, I am. But we are ___(B)___ forward to winning the match, and you are the best kicker.
Junha: All right. (it, go, more, win, for, to, I'll, and, important, it, it's) (Junha ___(C)___ on the penalty kick.)
Namho: What a shot! You did it, Junha!
Junha: No, WE did it!

08 빈칸 (A)와 (B)에 공통으로 들어갈 말을 쓰시오.

➡ _____

09 빈칸 (C)에 어울리는 말을 고르시오.

① scores   ② throws   ③ gives
④ wins   ⑤ does

10 괄호 안의 주어진 단어를 알맞게 배열하시오.

➡ _____

11 다음 중 밑줄 친 부분의 쓰임이 어법상 바르지 <u>않은</u> 것은?

① It is easy <u>to speak</u> Spanish fluently.
② Is your brother <u>tall enough</u> to hang the picture?
③ It is difficult <u>to say</u> how many people use the machine.
④ Laura is <u>enough cute</u> to be loved by everyone.
⑤ The house has a garage <u>big enough</u> for 10 cars.

12 주어진 단어를 활용하여 다음 우리말을 영어로 쓰시오.

너에게 전화하는 것은 힘들었어. 나는 충분히 용기가 있지 않거든. (it / hard / call / because)

➡ _____
_____

13 다음 우리말을 영어로 바르게 옮긴 것을 <u>모두</u> 고르시오.

물 없이 살아가는 것은 불가능하다.

① It is impossible to live with water.
② It is impossible to live without water.
③ It is impossible live without water.
④ It is not possible to live without water.
⑤ It is not possible to living without water.

14 다음 빈칸에 들어갈 말로 가장 적절한 것은?

We played well, but not _____ the game.

① enough good to win
② good enough to lose
③ enough well to lose
④ well enough to win
⑤ well to winning

15 다음 우리말을 영어로 쓸 때 빈칸에 알맞은 말을 쓰시오.

The land is _____ a house.
그 땅은 집을 짓기에 충분히 단단하다.

① enough hard to build
② hard enough to build
③ enough hard building
④ hard enough build
⑤ hardly enough to build

16 주어진 단어와 enough를 사용하여 말풍선에 들어갈 말을 완성하시오.

_____. It can help me to meet you. (tall)

➡ _____

17 주어진 단어를 활용하여 다음 우리말을 영어로 쓰시오.

정각에 그곳에 도착하는 것은 불가능하다.
(it / get / on time)

➡ _____

[18~22] 다음 글을 읽고, 물음에 답하시오.

Scottie looked at the list and saw his name. Then ①he sighed and ___(A)___ a check next to Michael's name. ②He couldn't deny that Michael was good enough for the senior team.

The coach collected every card from the boys. Everyone's hopes were high. They all wanted to be on the senior team. The coach looked up and said, "Well, it's a tie between Michael and Scottie." Scottie's heart leaped. ③He was surprised that ④he was tied with Michael.

"Well," said the coach, "both are wonderful enough for the senior team, and it's hard (B)to pick just one player. But I have to, so I'll pick Scottie." Then ⑤he walked over to Scottie and said, "Congratulations!"

"Thank you, but Michael is such a good shot. He makes the most baskets," said Scottie. "Of course, he does," said the coach.

18 밑줄 친 ①~⑤가 지칭하는 것이 다른 하나는?

①   ②   ③   ④   ⑤

19 위 글의 빈칸 (A)에 알맞은 것은?

① put   ② took   ③ left
④ fixed   ⑤ gave

20 위 글의 밑줄 친 (B)와 쓰임이 다른 것은?

① It is fun to hang out with the boys.
② It is dangerous to be alone at the park.
③ It enabled her to live a comfortable life.
④ It is rude of you to ignore her efforts.
⑤ It is interesting to see you sing on stage.

21 다음 중 글의 내용과 일치하지 않는 것은?

① Scottie didn't check his name.
② Scottie thought Michael was good for the senior team.
③ Scottie didn't expect that he would be tied with Michael.
④ The coach thought Michael as well as Scottie was good enough for the senior team.
⑤ The coach didn't know Michael made lots of baskets.

22 다음은 Scottie와 Michael의 코치가 쓴 글이다. 빈칸에 알맞은 말을 위 글에서 찾아 쓰시오.

출제율 95%

> My heart _____(A)_____ when I think about these two players. Michael was _____(B)_____ . No one can _____(C)_____ that he was a great player.

➡ (A) _____ (B) _____
　 (C) _____

[23~25] 다음 글을 읽고, 물음에 답하시오.

"But he shoots ①whether there's a player in a better position or not. It's important to play for the team! Don't worry. I know a good player when I see ②one."
[A] Scottie was ③surprising. "You did?"
"Yeah. You always do your best, and you're a team player. Today you played for the team, and we won the game. ④Congratulations!"
[B] Suddenly Scottie felt sorry ⑤for him. "I guess you don't care, but I picked you for the senior team," said Scottie. Michael smiled. "You know what? I picked YOU."
[C] Scottie walked out of the room. He felt like giving a loud and happy shout. Then he saw Michael.

출제율 95%

23 자연스러운 내용이 되도록 [A]~[C]를 바르게 나열하시오.

➡ _____

출제율 100%

24 ①~⑤ 중 어법상 틀린 것은?

①　　　②　　　③　　　④　　　⑤

출제율 90%

25 According to the passage, whom did Michael pick for the senior team? Answer in English with a full sentence.

➡ _____

[26~27] 다음 글을 읽고, 물음에 답하시오.

Hello, everyone,
We play soccer after school. We practice passing and shooting _____ it is important to pass and shoot well in soccer. It is also important to have good teamwork. Without good teamwork, it's hard to win the match.
Do you want to be a team player? Come, join us and enjoy team play.

출제율 90%

26 위 글의 빈칸에 알맞은 것은? (2개)

① as　　　② if　　　③ that
④ though　　⑤ because

출제율 95%

27 위 글의 내용으로 보아 대답할 수 <u>없는</u> 질문은?

① When do they play soccer?
② What do they practice?
③ What is important in soccer?
④ Why is good teamwork important?
⑤ How long do they practice?

[01~02] 다음 글을 읽고, 물음에 답하시오.

> B: Sumi, (next, English, we, speech, Friday, going, are, contest, an, have, to)
> G: Wow, we are finally having it. <u>I am looking forward to winning a prize!</u>

01 괄호 안의 주어진 단어를 배열하여 영작하시오.

➡ _____

_____

02 밑줄 친 문장과 같은 의미가 되도록 빈칸을 채우시오. (주어진 단어로 시작할 것)

➡ _____! (want)

03 다음 대화의 어색한 부분을 찾아 고치시오. (2개)

> A: Are you ready to the baseball game?
> B: Yes, I am. I'm looking forward to winning it.
> A: Me, too. What should we do to win it?
> B: It's important to hitting the ball hard.

➡ _____

_____

04 빈칸에 들어갈 말을 두 단어로 쓰시오.

> He worked _____ to succeed.
> 그는 성공할 만큼 충분히 열심히 일했습니다.

➡ _____

05 주어진 단어를 활용하여 다음 우리말을 여덟 단어로 이루어진 문장으로 쓰시오.

> 수영하기 전에 준비 운동을 하는 것은 중요하다.
> (warm up)

➡ _____

06 다음 우리말을 영어로 옮길 때 빈칸에 알맞은 말을 쓰시오.

> 이 침대는 잠들기에 충분히 편안해요.
> This bed is _____ to fall asleep.

➡ _____

07 주어진 단어를 바르게 배열하여 다음 우리말을 영어로 쓰시오.

> 영어를 충분히 유창하게 말하는 데에는 많은 시간이 걸려. (enough / it / English / takes / speak / a lot of / to / time / fluently)

➡ _____

_____

08 주어진 단어를 활용하여 다음 우리말을 영어로 쓰시오.

> 그 둘을 비교하는 것은 어렵다.
> (difficult / the two)

➡ _____

주어진 단어를 바르게 나열하여 밑줄 친 우리말 (C)를 영어로 쓰시오. 필요하다면 단어를 변형하시오.

[09~14] 다음 글을 읽고, 물음에 답하시오.

"Well," said the coach, "both are wonderful enough for the senior team, and it's hard to pick just one player. But I have to, so I'll pick Scottie." Then the coach walked over to Scottie and said, "Congratulations!"

"Thank you, but Michael is such a good shot. He makes the most baskets," said Scottie.

"Of course, he does," said the coach. "(A) But he shoots that there's a player in a better position or not. It's important to play for the team! Don't worry. I know a good player when I see (B)one."

Scottie walked out of the room. (C)그는 크고 기쁜 소리를 지르고 싶은 마음이었다. Then he saw Michael.

Suddenly Scottie felt sorry for him. "I guess you don't care, but I picked you for the senior team," said Scottie.

Michael smiled. "You know what? I picked YOU."

Scottie was surprised. "You did?"

"Yeah. You always do your best, and you're a team player. Today you played for the team, and we won the game. Congratulations!"

09 밑줄 친 문장 (A)를 어법에 맞게 고쳐 쓰시오.

➡ _____

_____

10 밑줄 친 (B)가 의미하는 것을 위 글에서 찾아 쓰시오.

➡ _____

11 주어진 단어를 바르게 나열하여 밑줄 친 우리말 (C)를 영어로 쓰시오. 필요하다면 단어를 변형하시오.

(happy / he / shout / and / give / like / feel / a / loud)

➡ _____

12 Why was Scottie surprised? Fill in the blank with an appropriate sentence.

It was because he came to know that _____.

➡ _____

13 위 글의 표현을 이용하여 다음 코치의 말을 영어로 쓰시오. 주어진 단어를 활용하시오.

단 한 명의 선수를 뽑는 것은 나의 의무였다. (it, duty)

➡ _____

14 위 글의 내용에 맞게 빈칸에 알맞은 말을 쓰시오.

코치의 말에 따르면, 득점을 가장 많이 하는 것보다 팀을 위해 경기하는 것이 더 중요하다.
According to the coach, it is more important to _____ than to _____.

➡ _____,

_____

01 주어진 정보를 이용해 빈칸에 알맞은 말을 쓰시오.

> go to a musical with my family / my birthday

> A: I'm _____ my _____ next Sunday.
> B: What _____ do then?
> A: I _____ _____ my family.
> B: That sounds great!

02 주어진 어구를 활용하여 팀 경기에서 중요한 것들에 대해 쓰시오.

> It is a good idea ... / It is important ... / It is rude ... / It is necessary ... / It is essential ...

(1) _____

(2) _____

(3) _____

(4) _____

(5) _____

03 enough와 주어진 단어를 활용하여 여러 가지 문장을 쓰시오.

> big / large / room / flower / confident

(1) _____

(2) _____

(3) _____

(4) _____

(5) _____

단원별 모의고사

01 다음 짝지어진 단어의 관계가 같도록 빈칸에 알맞은 말을 쓰시오. (주어진 철자로 시작할 것)

> chance : opportunity – g_____ : infer

02 다음 대화의 빈칸에 들어갈 말을 주어진 철자로 시작하여 쓰시오.

> A: I won the prize!
> B: C_____!

03 빈칸을 〈보기〉에 주어진 단어를 이용해서 채우시오. (한 단어를 한 번씩만 사용할 것)

> ┌─ 보기 ┐
> believe   kick   leap   tie

(1) The fish _____ed out of the water.
(2) The soccer match ended in a _____.
(3) The boy _____ed the ball hard.
(4) I can't _____ his words.

04 다음 우리말 해석에 맞게 빈칸을 완성하시오. (철자가 주어진 경우 그 철자로 시작할 것)

(1) He tied a _____ around his body. (그는 자신의 몸에 줄을 묶었다.)
(2) The news spread _____ through the town. (그 소식은 마을에 금새 퍼졌다.)
(3) The program was q_____ fun. (그 프로그램은 매우 재미있었다.)
(4) For your _____, do not swim at night. (당신의 안전을 위해 밤에는 수영을 하지 마세요.)

[05~06] 다음 대화를 읽고, 물음에 답하시오.

> A: School Sports Day is coming soon! I can't wait.
> B: _____(A)_____ What are you looking forward to doing?
> A: 나는 퍼레이드에 참여하기를 고대하고 있어.

05 빈칸 (A)에 가장 알맞은 말을 고르시오.

① I have to.
② So do I.
③ Me, too. I can't believe it!
④ Just a minute. Let me wait for a while.
⑤ Same here.

06 밑줄 친 우리말을 주어진 단어를 이용해 영작하시오.

➡ _____

(take)

07 다음 대화의 빈칸 ⓐ~ⓔ에 들어갈 수 없는 표현을 고르시오.

> A: Are you _____ⓐ_____ the three-legged race?
> B: _____ⓑ_____. I'm looking forward _____ⓒ_____ it.
> A: Me, too. What should we do _____ⓓ_____ it?
> B: _____ⓔ_____ important to run quickly together.

① Yes, I am
② They're
③ ready for
④ to win
⑤ to winning

[08~10] 다음 대화를 읽고, 물음에 답하시오.

Junha: Namho, (①) I think you should take the penalty kick.

Namho: No way! (②)

Junha: But you are looking for a chance to join the All-Star Team, aren't you? (③)

Namho: Yes, I am. But we are looking forward to ___(A)___ the match, and you are the best ___(B)___ .

Junha: All right. (④) It's more important to win it, and I'll go for it. (⑤) (Junha scores on the penalty kick.)

Namho: What a shot! You did it, Junha!

Junha: No, WE did it!

08 ①~⑤ 중 주어진 문장이 들어갈 곳은?

> You are the penalty taker, not me!

①   ②   ③   ④   ⑤

09 빈칸 (A)와 (B)를 대화에 나온 단어를 활용하여 채우시오.

➡ (A) _____ (B) _____

10 위 대화를 읽고 대답할 수 없는 질문은?

① Who is better at kicking a ball?

② Who is the penalty taker?

③ Who is looking for a chance to join the All-Star Team?

④ What is the score now?

⑤ Where they are?

[11~12] 다음 대화의 ①~⑤ 중 문법상 또는 흐름상 어색한 곳을 고르고 바르게 고치시오.

11

B: Mom, ①I'm ready. Let's go.

W: Wait, ②the air is clean today. ③Let me get you a mask.

B: Thanks, Mom.

W: ④Here you go. ⑤It's important to wear a mask when the air is not clean enough.

➡ _____

12

B: Look at this. ①There is a robot festival this weekend!

G: ②Yes, I know. ③I'm looking forward it!

B: ④So am I. ⑤Why don't we go there together?

G: Sounds great!

➡ _____

13 다음 우리말을 영어로 바르게 옮긴 것은?

> 그는 그 문제를 풀기에 충분히 영리하다.

① He is too smart to solve the problem.

② He is enough smart to solve the problem.

③ He is smart enough to solve the problem.

④ He is so smart that he can't solve the problem.

⑤ He must be very smart to solve the problem.

14 다음 중 빈칸에 들어갈 'make'의 형태가 다른 하나는?

① It is my job _____ her laugh.
② It was difficult _____ her healthy enough to go to a regular school.
③ It was hard not _____ a noise.
④ We want you _____ something different.
⑤ Sandra kept _____ the same mistakes.

15 다음 중 어법상 바르지 않은 것은?

① Her face is not beautiful enough to be an actress.
② It is easy to get a visa.
③ These shoes are not big enough for him.
④ The book was not enough easy to read.
⑤ It was exciting to see her dance on the stage.

16 주어진 단어를 활용하여 다음 우리말을 영어로 쓰시오.

수영장에서 수영 모자를 쓰는 것은 필수적이다. (necessary)

➡ _____

17 다음 빈칸에 알맞은 말을 다섯 단어로 쓰시오.

A: What do you think about building a new airport? B: I think it is a bad idea _____.

➡ _____

[18~23] 다음 글을 읽고, 물음에 답하시오.

The game was over. The junior team won ⓐit, and all the players were happy. ① While ⓑthey were in the locker room, the coach handed every boy a card. ② "As you all know, we have an opening for a player on the senior team," said the coach. ③ "Why don't you pick a player for the team? Check one name on the list." ④

Scottie looked at the list and saw his name. ⑤ Then he sighed and put a check next to Michael's name. He couldn't deny (A)that Michael was ⓒgood enough for the senior team.

The coach collected every card from the boys. Everyone's hopes were high. They all wanted ⓓto be on the senior team. The coach looked up and said, "Well, it's a tie ⓔamong Michael and Scottie." Scottie's heart leaped. He was surprised that he was tied with Michael.

18 ①~⑤ 중 주어진 문장이 들어가기에 가장 적절한 곳은?

It had a list of the players on the junior team.

①　　②　　③　　④　　⑤

19 다음 중 위 글을 읽고 답할 수 없는 것은?

① Where did the coach give the cards to the players?
② Why were all the players happy?
③ How many players could be picked for the senior team?
④ Why was Scottie surprised?
⑤ Whom did the coach pick?

20 다음 중 밑줄 친 (A)와 쓰임이 다른 하나는?

① Did you hear that Owen didn't show up?

② I don't think that you lied to Ann.

③ Mr. Delffino is the man that we respect.

④ Jason thought that he should have accepted the job.

⑤ I knew that the thief was arrested.

21 ⓐ~ⓔ에서 어법상 바르지 않은 것은?

① ⓐ   ② ⓑ   ③ ⓒ

④ ⓓ   ⑤ ⓔ

22 According to the passage, what did the coach give to every boy? Answer in English with a full sentence.

➡ _____

23 다음은 Scottie가 쓴 글이다. 빈칸에 알맞은 말을 어법에 맞게 쓰시오.

> It was surprising to hear that _____.

➡ _____

[24~25] 다음 글을 읽고, 물음에 답하시오.

"Well," said the coach, "both are wonderful enough for the senior team, and it's hard to pick just one player. But I have to, so I'll pick Scottie." Then the coach walked over to Scottie and said, "Congratulations!"

"Thank you, but Michael is such a good shot. He makes the most baskets," said Scottie.

"Of course, he does," said the coach. "But he shoots whether there's a player in a better position or not. It's important to play for the team! Don't worry. I know a good player when I see one."

Scottie walked out of the room. He felt like giving a loud and happy shout.

24 위 글의 마지막에서 느낀 Scottie의 심경으로 가장 적절한 것은?

① lonely   ② sad

③ nervous   ④ delighted

⑤ annoyed

25 위 글의 표현을 이용하여 다음 우리말을 영어로 쓰시오.

> 이 방은 너희 둘 다에게 충분히 훌륭해.

➡ _____

INSIGHT
on the textbook

교과서 파헤치기

Lesson **1** What Is Your Color?

Lesson **2** Old Things, New Art

Lesson **3** Go, Team!

※ 다음 영어를 우리말로 쓰시오.

01 scientist _____

02 direction _____

03 stage _____

04 artist _____

05 faithful _____

06 season _____

07 friendly _____

08 honest _____

09 caring _____

10 flavor _____

11 pattern _____

12 expect _____

13 serve _____

14 playful _____

15 thoughtful _____

16 prefer _____

17 inventor _____

18 witty _____

19 worst _____

20 organize _____

21 result _____

22 talkative _____

23 yummy _____

24 line _____

25 tradition _____

26 imaginative _____

27 curious _____

28 energetic _____

29 personality _____

30 chance _____

31 solve _____

32 lively _____

33 unhealthy _____

34 careful _____

35 make the most of ~ _____

36 plan ~ out _____

37 on one's own _____

38 be good at _____

39 would like to 동사원형 _____

40 How did you like ~? _____

41 Why don't we ~? _____

42 ask ~ for advice _____

43 What is ~ like? _____

※ 다음 우리말을 영어로 쓰시오.

01 신중한 _____

02 활동적인 _____

03 위(장) _____

04 활기를 북돋우다 _____

05 맛 _____

06 따르다 _____

07 위치, 자리, 자세 _____

08 전통 _____

09 가능성, 기회 _____

10 상상력이 풍부한 _____

11 호기심 많은 _____

12 생기 넘치는 _____

13 건강하지 못한 _____

14 활기 있는 _____

15 기쁘게 하다 _____

16 기술자 _____

17 독특한, 하나뿐인 _____

18 성격, 개성 _____

19 활력을 주는 사람 _____

20 활동 _____

21 해결하다 _____

22 유형 _____

23 친근한 _____

24 수다스러운 _____

25 가장 나쁜 _____

26 배려하는, 보살피는 _____

27 충직한, 충성스러운 _____

28 재치 있는 _____

29 생각이 깊은 _____

30 조직하다, 정리 정돈하다 _____

31 제공하다 _____

32 기대하다 _____

33 결과 _____

34 장난기 많은 _____

35 ~하는 게 어때? _____

36 ~을 보다 _____

37 ~하고 싶다 _____

38 혼자서, 단독으로 _____

39 ~할 것이다 _____

40 ~에게 조언[충고]을 구하다 _____

41 어떤 종류의 ~ _____

42 ~을 잘하다 _____

43 ~는 어때? _____

※ 다음 영영풀이에 알맞은 단어를 <보기>에서 골라 쓴 후, 우리말 뜻을 쓰시오.

1 _____ : full of life and spirit: _____

2 _____ : a very old custom or belief: _____

3 _____ : kind, helpful, and sympathetic towards other people: _____

4 _____ : to do what someone has advised you to do: _____

5 _____ : things that people do; something that you do because you enjoy it:

   _____

6 _____ : to make someone feel happy and satisfied: _____

7 _____ : the possibility that something will happen, especially something you

   want: _____

8 _____ : to like someone or something more than another person or thing:

   _____

9 _____ : to find a solution to something that is causing difficulties: _____

10 _____ : someone's character, especially the way they behave towards other

   people: _____

11 _____ : the part of a theater where the actors or musicians perform: _____

12 _____ : to prepare or arrange an activity or event: _____

13 _____ : a set of lines, shapes, or colors that are repeated regularly: _____

14 _____ : someone whose job is to design, build, or repair machines, roads, bridges,

   etc.: _____

15 _____ : continuing to support someone or be their friend, even in a difficult

   situation: _____

16 _____ : a baglike organ in the body where food is broken down for use in the

   body after being eaten: _____

보기	organize	pattern	caring	stomach
	tradition	please	chance	engineer
	personality	activity	solve	prefer
	lively	stage	faithful	follow

※ 다음 우리말과 일치하도록 빈칸에 알맞은 말을 쓰시오.

Listen & Speak 1 A

1. **G:** _____ hungry.

   B: Me, _____. Why _____ _____ _____ to Sweet Snack?

   G: That's a good _____. But is it _____ today?

   B: Yes, it is. They _____ _____ it _____ _____ pancakes _____ _____.

2. **G:** _____ _____ any good programs _____ _____?

   B: Well, they _____ _____ _____ a special dance show at the Youth Center _____ _____.

   G: _____ _____ _____ dance show is it?

   B: It's an Indian dance show. People _____ _____ _____ _____ _____.

Listen & Speak 1 B

1. **A:** What was _____ _____?

   B: I _____ Hamlet.

   A: _____ is a Hamlet-type person _____?

   B: They _____ that a Hamlet-type person _____ _____.

2. **A:** _____ was the _____?

   B: _____ _____ da Vinci.

   A: _____ _____ a da-Vinci-type person _____?

   B: _____ _____ _____ a da-Vinci-type person is _____.

Listen & Speak 2 A

1. **G:** _____ _____ the cakes!

   B: They _____ _____.

   G: _____ cake _____ _____ _____ most?

   B: I _____ the chocolate cake _____.

2. **B:** _____ they new ice cream _____?

   G: Yes, _____ are. They _____.

   B: _____ _____ do you _____?

   G: I _____ the strawberry _____.

Listen & Speak 2 B

1. A: _____ _____ do you _____?

   B: I prefer summer. _____ are summer people _____?

   A: They _____ _____ summer people are _____ _____ _____. Are you?

   B: Yes, I _____. / No, _____ _____.

2. A: _____ _____ _____ _____ _____ _____ _____?

   B: I _____ winter. What are winter people _____?

   A: They say that winter people are _____ _____ _____. Are you?

   B: Yes, _____ _____. / No, _____ _____.

1. A: 넌 어떤 계절을 선호하니?
   B: 난 여름을 선호해. 여름 사람들은 어떻지?
   A: 여름 사람들은 조용하고 생각이 깊대. 네가 그러니?
   B: 응, 그래. / 아니, 난 그렇지 않아.

2. A: 넌 어떤 계절을 선호하니?
   B: 난 겨울을 선호해. 겨울 사람들은 어떻지?
   A: 겨울 사람들은 신의가 있고 정직하대. 네가 그러니?
   B: 응, 그래. / 아니, 난 그렇지 않아.

Communication

Nara: _____ _____ you _____ the test?

Seho: It was _____ _____. I learned a lot _____ _____.

Nara: _____ _____ _____ person are you?

Seho: I'm a _____ person.

Nara: That _____ cool. What _____ da-Vinci people _____ _____?

Seho: They _____ _____ da-Vinci _____ make good _____ and artists.

Nara: _____ _____ do you _____?

Seho: I'm _____ _____. _____ _____ _____ _____ my teacher _____ some _____.

나라: 검사는 어땠니?
세호: 정말 재미있었어. 나 자신에 대해 많이 배웠어.
나라: 너는 어떤 유형의 사람이니?
세호: 나는 다빈치 유형의 사람이야.
나라: 멋지다. 다빈치 유형의 사람은 무엇을 잘하니?
세호: 다빈치 유형의 사람들은 훌륭한 발명가와 예술가가 된다고 해.
나라: 너는 어느 것이 더 좋으니?
세호: 잘 모르겠어. 선생님께 조언을 요청하려고 해.

Real-Life Task

Step 2

A: _____ _____ _____ do you sleep?

B: I sleep _____ the back _____.

A: _____ are back sleepers _____?

B: People _____ _____ they are _____ _____ _____.

A: _____ _____ is that position for your _____?

B: Scientists say that it's _____ _____ _____ for sleeping.

A: 넌 어떤 자세로 잠을 자니?
B: 난 등을 대고 잠을 자.
A: 등을 대고 자는 사람들은 어때?
B: 그들은 따뜻하고 친근하다고 하네.
A: 그 자세는 건강에 얼마나 좋아?
B: 과학자들은 그게 수면에 가장 좋은 자세라고 해.

※ 다음 우리말에 맞도록 대화를 영어로 쓰시오.

Listen & Speak 1 A

1. **G:** _____

   B: _____

   G: _____

   B: _____

2. **G:** _____

   B: _____

   G: _____

   B: _____

Listen & Speak 1 B

1. **A:** _____

   B: _____

   A: _____

   B: _____

2. **A:** _____

   B: _____

   A: _____

   B: _____

Listen & Speak 2 A

1. **G:** _____

   B: _____

   G: _____

   B: _____

2. **B:** _____

   G: _____

   B: _____

   G: _____

1. **G:** 나 배고파.
   B: 나도 그래. 우리 Sweet Snack에 가는 게 어때?
   G: 그거 좋은 생각이야. 그런데 그곳이 오늘 문을 열었니?
   B: 응, 열었어. 일요일에는 특별 팬케이크를 제공한다고 그러네.

2. **G:** 이번 주말에 무슨 좋은 프로그램이 있니?
   B: 음, 토요일에 청소년 센터에서 특별 댄스 공연이 있다고 그러네.
   G: 어떤 종류의 댄스 공연이야?
   B: 인도의 댄스 공연이야. 정말 흥미롭다고 그러네.

1. **A:** (성격 검사) 결과가 뭐야?
   B: (내가 받은 결과는) 햄릿이야.
   A: 햄릿 유형의 사람은 어때?
   B: 햄릿 유형의 사람은 생각이 깊다고 그러네.

2. **A:** 결과가 뭐야?
   B: 다빈치야.
   A: 다빈치 유형의 사람은 어때?
   B: 다빈치 유형의 사람은 상상력이 풍부하다고 그러네.

1. **G:** 저 케이크들을 봐!
   B: 맛있어 보여.
   G: 넌 어떤 케이크를 가장 좋아하니?
   B: 난 초콜릿 케이크를 가장 좋아해.

2. **B:** 그것들이 새로 나온 아이스크림 맛이니?
   G: 응, 그래. 맛있어 보여.
   B: 넌 어떤 맛을 선호하니?
   G: 난 딸기 맛을 선호해.

Listen & Speak 2 B

1. A: _____

   B: _____

   A: _____

   B: _____

2. A: _____

   B: _____

   A: _____

   B: _____

Communication

Nara: _____

Seho: _____

Nara: _____

Seho: _____

Nara: _____

Seho: _____

Nara: _____

Seho: _____

Real-Life Task

Step 2

A: _____

B: _____

A: _____

B: _____

A: _____

B: _____

1. A: 넌 어떤 계절을 선호하니?
   B: 난 여름을 선호해. 여름 사람들은 어떻지?
   A: 여름 사람들은 조용하고 생각이 깊대. 네가 그러니?
   B: 응, 그래. / 아니, 난 그렇지 않아.

2. A: 넌 어떤 계절을 선호하니?
   B: 난 겨울을 선호해. 겨울 사람들은 어떻지?
   A: 겨울 사람들은 신의가 있고 정직하대. 네가 그러니?
   B: 응, 그래. / 아니, 난 그렇지 않아.

나라: 검사는 어땠니?
세호: 정말 재미있었어. 나 자신에 대해 많이 배웠어.
나라: 너는 어떤 유형의 사람이니?
세호: 나는 다빈치 유형의 사람이야.
나라: 멋지다. 다빈치 유형의 사람은 무엇을 잘하니?
세호: 다빈치 유형의 사람들은 훌륭한 발명가와 예술가가 된다고 해.
나라: 너는 어느 것이 더 좋으니?
세호: 잘 모르겠어. 선생님께 조언을 요청하려고 해.

A: 넌 어떤 자세로 잠을 자니?
B: 난 등을 대고 잠을 자
A: 등을 대고 자는 사람들은 어때?
B: 그들은 따뜻하고 친근하다고 하네.
A: 그 자세는 건강에 얼마나 좋아?
B: 과학자들은 그게 수면에 가장 좋은 자세라고 해.

※ 다음 우리말과 일치하도록 빈칸에 알맞은 것을 골라 쓰시오.

1 _____ Is _____ _____?
A. Color   B. Your   C. What

2 _____ _____ I?
A. am   B. who

3 _____ _____ of _____ am I?
A. type   B. what   C. person

4 _____ you have _____ _____?
A. questions   B. these   C. do

5 _____ we have an _____ _____ test for you.
A. personality   B. interesting   C. here

6 Step 1 _____ _____ do you enjoy, and which _____ are you good _____?
A. at   B. ones   C. which   D. activities

7 I _____ … / I'm _____ _____ …
A. enjoy   B. good   C. at

8 1. being _____ and _____ fun. 2. working _____ people.
A. with   B. free   C. having

9 3. _____ _____. 4. _____ traditions.
A. chances   B. following   C. taking

10 5. _____ on my _____. 6. _____ stories.
A. own   B. writing   C. working

11 7. _____ new things. 8. _____ the _____.
A. rules   B. learning   C. following

12 9. _____ new friends. 10. _____ things _____.
A. out   B. planning   C. making

13 11. _____ others. 12. _____ new _____.
A. patterns   B. finding   C. pleasing

14 13. being on _____. 14. working _____ _____.
A. directions   B. with   C. stage

15 15. _____ puzzles. 16. _____ sports.
A. playing   B. solving

1 당신의 색깔은 무엇입니까?

2 나는 누구인가?

3 나는 어떤 유형의 사람인가?

4 이런 질문들을 가지고 있나요?

5 여기에 당신을 위한 흥미로운 성격 검사가 있습니다.

6 [Step1] 당신은 어떤 활동을 즐겨 합니까, 그리고 어떤 활동을 잘하나요?

7 나는 ~을 즐긴다/나는 ~을 잘한다

8 1. 자유로우며 재미있게 놀기 2. 사람들과 함께 일하기

9 3. 운(運)에 맡기고 해 보기 4. 전통을 따르기

10 5. 혼자서 일하기 6. 이야기 쓰기

11 7. 새로운 것 배우기 8. 규칙을 따르기

12 9. 새로운 친구를 사귀기 10. 계획을 세우기

13 11. 다른 사람을 즐겁게 해 주기 12. 새로운 패턴을 찾기

14 13. 무대에 서기 14. 지시를 받고 일하기

15 15. 수수께끼 풀기 16. 운동 경기를 하기

16 Step 2 What is _____ _____?

A. color　　　　　B. your

17 _____ the numbers _____ Step 1, and find the line _____ the _____ circles.

A. most　　　B. circle　　　C. from　　　D. with

18 Step 3 _____ _____ _____ person are you?

A. type　　　B. of　　　C. what

19 If you have _____ _____ on the orange _____, you are a wonderful _____.

A. energizer　　B. more　　C. circles　　D. line

20 You are _____ and _____, and you work best _____ game _____.

A. lively　　　B. in　　　C. settings　　　D. witty

21 If you have more circles on the _____ _____, you are an _____ _____.

A. organizer　　B. excellent　　C. line　　D. gold

22 You are _____ and _____, and you _____ best with clear _____.

A. faithful　　B. work　　C. careful　　D. rules

23 _____ _____ is the beginning of all _____. - Aristotle

A. yourself　　B. wisdom　　C. knowing

24 If you have more _____ on the blue _____, you are a _____ _____.

A. listener　　B. great　　C. line　　D. circles

25 You are _____ and _____, and you work best _____ _____.

A. groups　　B. caring　　C. in　　D. warm

26 If you have more circles _____ the _____ line, you are a _____ _____.

A. thinker　　B. on　　C. green　　D. curious

27 You are _____ and quiet, and you _____ best on your _____.

A. work　　B. own　　C. cool

28 What is your _____, and _____ _____ do you _____ it?

A. like　　B. much　　C. how　　D. type

29 _____ this personality test _____ a first _____ and try to find your _____ color.

A. true　　B. as　　C. step　　D. take

30 Everyone is _____ and has a _____ color.

A. special　　　B. unique

31 _____ _____ you listen to yourself, find special things about yourself, and _____ the _____ of them?

A. most　　B. why　　C. don't　　D. make

16 [Step2] 당신의 색깔은 무엇입니까?

17 Step 1에서 고른 숫자에 동그라미 표시를 하고, 가장 많은 동그라미 표시가 있는 줄을 찾으세요.

18 [Step3] 당신은 어떤 유형의 사람입니까?

19 주황색 줄에 더 많은 동그라미 표시가 있다면, 당신은 놀라운 활력을 주는 사람입니다.

20 당신은 재치 있고 생기 있으며, 게임 환경에서 가장 잘 일합니다.

21 황금색 줄에 더 많은 동그라미 표시가 있다면, 당신은 뛰어난 조직가입니다.

22 당신은 충직하고 조심스러우며, 분명한 규칙이 제시된 경우에 가장 잘 일합니다.

23 스스로를 아는 것은 모든 지혜의 시작이다. – 아리스토텔레스

24 푸른색 줄에 더 많은 동그라미 표시가 있다면, 당신은 대단한 경청자입니다.

25 당신은 따뜻하고 남을 잘 돌보며, 집단과 더불어 가장 잘 일합니다.

26 초록색 줄에 더 많은 동그라미 표시가 있다면, 당신은 호기심 많은 사색가입니다.

27 당신은 멋지고 조용하며, 혼자서 (일할 때) 가장 잘 일합니다.

28 당신의 유형은 무엇이며, 그것을 얼마나 좋아합니까?

29 이 성격 검사를 첫 단계로 삼아서, 당신의 진정한 색깔을 찾아보려고 노력하세요.

30 모든 사람들은 독특하고 특별한 색깔을 지니고 있습니다.

31 스스로에게 귀를 기울이고, 스스로에 관하여 특별한 것들을 발견하며, 그것들을 최대한 이용해 보면 어떨까요?

※ 다음 우리말과 일치하도록 빈칸에 알맞은 말을 쓰시오.

1 _____ Is _____ _____?

2 _____ _____ I?

3 _____ _____ _____ person am I?

4 Do you have _____ _____?

5 Here we have _____ _____ _____ _____ for you.

6 Step 1 _____ _____ do you enjoy, and _____ _____
_____ you _____ _____?

7 I enjoy … / I'm _____ _____ …

8 1. being _____ and _____ _____. 2. _____ _____
people.

9 3. _____ _____. 4. _____ traditions.

10 5. working _____ _____ _____. 6. _____ stories.

11 7. _____ new _____. 8. _____ the _____.

12 9. _____ _____. 10. _____ things _____.

13 11. _____ others. 12. finding _____ _____.

14 13. being _____ _____. 14. working _____.

15 15. _____ puzzles. 16. _____ sports.

1 당신의 색깔은 무엇입니까?

2 나는 누구인가?

3 나는 어떤 유형의 사람인가?

4 이런 질문들을 가지고 있나요?

5 여기에 당신을 위한 흥미로운 성격 검사가 있습니다.

6 [Step1] 당신은 어떤 활동을 즐겨 합니까, 그리고 어떤 활동을 잘하나요?

7 나는 ~을 즐긴다/나는 ~을 잘한다

8 1. 자유로우며 재미있게 놀기 2. 사람들과 함께 일하기

9 3. 운(運)에 맡기고 해 보기 4. 전통을 따르기

10 5. 혼자서 일하기 6. 이야기 쓰기

11 7. 새로운 것 배우기 8. 규칙을 따르기

12 9. 새로운 친구를 사귀기 10. 계획을 세우기

13 11. 다른 사람을 즐겁게 해 주기 12. 새로운 패턴을 찾기

14 13. 무대에 서기 14. 지시를 받고 일하기

15 15. 수수께끼 풀기 16. 운동 경기를 하기

16 Step 2 What is _____ _____?

17 _____ the numbers _____ Step 1, and find the line _____ the _____ _____.

18 Step 3 _____ _____ _____ _____ are you?

19 If you have more circles on the _____ _____, you are a _____ _____.

20 You are _____ and _____, and you _____ _____ _____ game settings.

21 If you have _____ _____ on the gold line, you are an _____ _____.

22 You are _____ and _____, and you work _____ _____ clear rules.

23 _____ _____ is the beginning of all _____. - Aristotle

24 If you have more circles on the _____ _____, you are a _____ _____.

25 You are warm and _____, and you work best _____ _____.

26 If you have more circles on the green line, you are a _____ _____.

27 You are _____ and quiet, and you _____ _____ _____ _____ _____.

28 What is your _____, and _____ _____ do you like it?

29 _____ this personality test _____ a first step and _____ _____ _____ your true color.

30 Everyone is _____ and _____ a _____ color.

31 _____ _____ _____ listen to yourself, find special things about yourself, and _____ _____ _____ _____ _____ them?

16 [Step2] 당신의 색깔은 무엇입니까?

17 Step 1에서 고른 숫자에 동그라미 표시를 하고, 가장 많은 동그라미 표시가 있는 줄을 찾으세요.

18 [Step3] 당신은 어떤 유형의 사람입니까?

19 주황색 줄에 더 많은 동그라미 표시가 있다면, 당신은 놀라운 활력을 주는 사람입니다.

20 당신은 재치 있고 생기 있으며, 게임 환경에서 가장 잘 일합니다.

21 황금색 줄에 더 많은 동그라미 표시가 있다면, 당신은 뛰어난 조직가입니다.

22 당신은 충직하고 조심스러우며, 분명한 규칙이 제시된 경우에 가장 잘 일합니다.

23 스스로를 아는 것은 모든 지혜의 시작이다. – 아리스토텔레스

24 푸른색 줄에 더 많은 동그라미 표시가 있다면, 당신은 대단한 경청자입니다.

25 당신은 따뜻하고 남을 잘 돌보며, 집단과 더불어 가장 잘 일합니다.

26 초록색 줄에 더 많은 동그라미 표시가 있다면, 당신은 호기심 많은 사색가입니다.

27 당신은 멋지고 조용하며, 혼자서 (일할 때) 가장 잘 일합니다.

28 당신의 유형은 무엇이며, 그것을 얼마나 좋아합니까?

29 이 성격 검사를 첫 단계로 삼아서, 당신의 진정한 색깔을 찾아보려고 노력하세요.

30 모든 사람들은 독특하고 특별한 색깔을 지니고 있습니다.

31 스스로에게 귀를 기울이고, 스스로에 관하여 특별한 것들을 발견하며, 그것들을 최대한 이용해 보면 어떨까요?

※ 다음 문장을 우리말로 쓰시오.

1 What Is Your Color?
➡ _____

2 Who am I?
➡ _____

3 What type of person am I?
➡ _____

4 Do you have these questions?
➡ _____

5 Here we have an interesting personality test for you.
➡ _____

6 Step 1 Which activities do you enjoy, and which ones are you good at?
➡ _____

7 I enjoy … / I'm good at …
➡ _____

8 1. being free and having fun. 2. working with people.
➡ _____

9 3. taking chances. 4. following traditions.
➡ _____

10 5. working on my own. 6. writing stories.
➡ _____

11 7. learning new things. 8. following the rules.
➡ _____

12 9. making new friends. 10. planning things out.
➡ _____

13 11. pleasing others. 12. finding new patterns.
➡ _____

14 13. being on stage. 14. working with directions.
➡ _____

15 15. solving puzzles. 16. playing sports.
➡ _____

16 Step 2 What is your color?
➡ _____

17 Circle the numbers from Step 1, and find the line with the most circles.
➡ _____

18 Step 3 What type of person are you?

➡ _____

19 If you have more circles on the orange line, you are a wonderful energizer.

➡ _____

20 You are witty and lively, and you work best in game settings.

➡ _____

21 If you have more circles on the gold line, you are an excellent organizer.

➡ _____

22 You are faithful and careful, and you work best with clear rules.

➡ _____

23 Knowing yourself is the beginning of all wisdom. - Aristotle

➡ _____

24 If you have more circles on the blue line, you are a great listener.

➡ _____

25 You are warm and caring, and you work best in groups.

➡ _____

26 If you have more circles on the green line, you are a curious thinker.

➡ _____

27 You are cool and quiet, and you work best on your own.

➡ _____

28 What is your type, and how much do you like it?

➡ _____

29 Take this personality test as a first step and try to find your true color.

➡ _____

30 Everyone is unique and has a special color.

➡ _____

31 Why don't you listen to yourself, find special things about yourself, and make the most of them?

➡ _____

※ 다음 괄호 안의 단어들을 우리말에 맞도록 바르게 배열하시오.

1 (Is / Color? / Your / What)
➡ _____

2 (I? / am / who)
➡ _____

3 (type / what / of / I? / am / person)
➡ _____

4 (you / do / questions? / these / have)
➡ _____

5 (we / here / have / interesting / an / personality / you. / for / test)
➡ _____

6 (Step 1 / activities / which / you / do / enjoy, / and / ones / which / you / at? / good / are)
➡ _____

7 (enjoy / I / ... // at / good / ... / I'm)
➡ _____

8 (1. / free / and / being / fun. / having // 2. / people. / with / working)
➡ _____

9 (3. / chances. / taking / 4. / traditions. / following)
➡ _____

10 (5. / on / working / own. / my // 6. stories. / writing)
➡ _____

11 (7. / new / learning / things. // 8. / rules. / the / following)
➡ _____

12 (9. / friends. / new / making // 10. / out. / things / planning)
➡ _____

13 (11. / others. / pleasing // 12. / patterns. / new / finding)
➡ _____

14 (13. / stage. / on / being // 14. / directions. / with / working)
➡ _____

15 (15. / puzzles. / solving // 16. / sports. / playing)
➡ _____

16 (step 2 / is / color? / your / what)
➡ _____

17 (the / circle / from / numbers / Step 1, / and / line / the / find / with / circles. / most / the)
➡ _____

1 당신의 색깔은 무엇입니까?

2 나는 누구인가?

3 나는 어떤 유형의 사람인가?

4 이런 질문들을 가지고 있나요?

5 여기에 당신을 위한 흥미로운 성격 검사가 있습니다.

6 [Step1] 당신은 어떤 활동을 즐겨 합니까, 그리고 어떤 활동을 잘하나요?

7 나는 ~을 즐긴다/나는 ~을 잘한다

8 1. 자유로우며 재미있게 놀기 2. 사람들과 함께 일하기

9 3. 운(運)에 맡기고 해 보기 4. 전통을 따르기

10 5. 혼자서 일하기 6. 이야기 쓰기

11 7. 새로운 것 배우기 8. 규칙을 따르기

12 9. 새로운 친구를 사귀기 10. 계획을 세우기

13 11. 다른 사람을 즐겁게 해 주기 12. 새로운 패턴을 찾기

14 13. 무대에 서기 14. 지시를 받고 일하기

15 15. 수수께끼 풀기 16. 운동 경기를 하기

16 [Step2] 당신의 색깔은 무엇입니까?

17 Step 1에서 고른 숫자에 동그라미 표시를 하고, 가장 많은 동그라미 표시가 있는 줄을 찾으세요.

18 (Step 3 / type / what / person / of / you? / are)

➡ _____

19 (you / if / have / circles / more / the / on / line, / orange / are / you / wonderful / a / energizer.)

➡ _____

20 (are / you / and / lively, / witty / and / work / you / best / settings. / game / in)

➡ _____

21 (you / if / more / have / circles / the / line, / gold / on / are / you / organizer. / excellent / an)

➡ _____

22 (are / you / careful, / and / faithful / you / and / best / work / rules. / clear / with)

➡ _____

23 (yourself / knowing / is / beginning / the / of / wisdom. / all / - / Aristotle)

➡ _____

24 (you / if / have / circles / more / the / on / line, / blue / are / you / listener. / great / a)

➡ _____

25 (are / you / caring, / and / warm / you / and / best / work / groups. / in)

➡ _____

26 (have / you / if / circles / more / on / green / the / line, / are / you / thinker. / curious / a)

➡ _____

27 (are / you / cool / quiet, / and / you / and / best / work / own. / your / on)

➡ _____

28 (is / what / type, / your / and / much / how / like / do / it? / you)

➡ _____

29 (this / take / test / personality / as / first / a / and / step / try / find / to / color. / true / your)

➡ _____

30 (is / everyone / unique / and / a / has / color. / special)

➡ _____

31 (don't / why / listen / you / yourself, / to / special / find / about / things / yourself, / and / the / them? / of / most / make)

➡ _____

18 [Step3] 당신은 어떤 유형의 사람입니까?

19 주황색 줄에 더 많은 동그라미 표시가 있다면, 당신은 놀라운 활력을 주는 사람입니다.

20 당신은 재치 있고 생기 있으며, 게임 환경에서 가장 잘 일합니다.

21 황금색 줄에 더 많은 동그라미 표시가 있다면, 당신은 뛰어난 조직가입니다.

22 당신은 충직하고 조심스러우며, 분명한 규칙이 제시된 경우에 가장 잘 일합니다.

23 스스로를 아는 것은 모든 지혜의 시작이다. – 아리스토텔레스

24 푸른색 줄에 더 많은 동그라미 표시가 있다면, 당신은 대단한 경청자입니다.

25 당신은 따뜻하고 남을 잘 돌보며, 집단과 더불어 가장 잘 일합니다.

26 초록색 줄에 더 많은 동그라미 표시가 있다면, 당신은 호기심 많은 사색가입니다.

27 당신은 멋지고 조용하며, 혼자서 (일할 때) 가장 잘 일합니다.

28 당신의 유형은 무엇이며, 그것을 얼마나 좋아합니까?

29 이 성격 검사를 첫 단계로 삼아서, 당신의 진정한 색깔을 찾아보려고 노력하세요.

30 모든 사람들은 독특하고 특별한 색깔을 지니고 있습니다.

31 스스로에게 귀를 기울이고, 스스로에 관하여 특별한 것들을 발견하며, 그것들을 최대한 이용해 보면 어떨까요?

※ 다음 우리말을 영어로 쓰시오.

1 당신의 색깔은 무엇입니까?
➡ _____

2 나는 누구인가?
➡ _____

3 나는 어떤 유형의 사람인가?
➡ _____

4 이런 질문들을 가지고 있나요?
➡ _____

5 여기에 당신을 위한 흥미로운 성격 검사가 있습니다.
➡ _____

6 [Step1] 당신은 어떤 활동을 즐겨 합니까, 그리고 어떤 활동을 잘하나요?
➡ _____

7 나는 ~을 즐긴다/나는 ~을 잘한다
➡ _____

8 1. 자유로우며 재미있게 놀기 2. 사람들과 함께 일하기
➡ _____

9 3. 운(運)에 맡기고 해 보기 4. 전통을 따르기
➡ _____

10 5. 혼자서 일하기 6. 이야기 쓰기
➡ _____

11 7. 새로운 것 배우기 8. 규칙을 따르기
➡ _____

12 9. 새로운 친구를 사귀기 10. 계획을 세우기
➡ _____

13 11. 다른 사람을 즐겁게 해 주기 12. 새로운 패턴을 찾기
➡ _____

14 13. 무대에 서기 14. 지시를 받고 일하기
➡ _____

15 15. 수수께끼 풀기 16. 운동 경기를 하기
➡ _____

16 [Step2] 당신의 색깔은 무엇입니까?
➡ _____

17 Step 1에서 고른 숫자에 동그라미 표시를 하고, 가장 많은 동그라미 표시가 있는 줄을 찾으세요.
➡ _____

18 [Step3] 당신은 어떤 유형의 사람입니까?

➡ _____

19 주황색 줄에 더 많은 동그라미 표시가 있다면, 당신은 놀라운 활력을 주는 사람입니다.

➡ _____

20 당신은 재치 있고 생기 있으며, 게임 환경에서 가장 잘 일합니다.

➡ _____

21 황금색 줄에 더 많은 동그라미 표시가 있다면, 당신은 뛰어난 조직가입니다.

➡ _____

22 당신은 충직하고 조심스러우며, 분명한 규칙이 제시된 경우에 가장 잘 일합니다.

➡ _____

23 스스로를 아는 것은 모든 지혜의 시작이다. – 아리스토텔레스

➡ _____

24 푸른색 줄에 더 많은 동그라미 표시가 있다면, 당신은 대단한 경청자입니다.

➡ _____

25 당신은 따뜻하고 남을 잘 돌보며, 집단과 더불어 가장 잘 일합니다.

➡ _____

26 초록색 줄에 더 많은 동그라미 표시가 있다면, 당신은 호기심 많은 사색가입니다.

➡ _____

27 당신은 멋지고 조용하며, 혼자서 (일할 때) 가장 잘 일합니다.

➡ _____

28 당신의 유형은 무엇이며, 그것을 얼마나 좋아합니까?

➡ _____

29 이 성격 검사를 첫 단계로 삼아서, 당신의 진정한 색깔을 찾아보려고 노력하세요.

➡ _____

30 모든 사람들은 독특하고 특별한 색깔을 지니고 있습니다.

➡ _____

31 스스로에게 귀를 기울이고, 스스로에 관하여 특별한 것들을 발견하며, 그것들을 최대한 이용해 보면 어떨까요?

➡ _____

※ 다음 우리말과 일치하도록 빈칸에 알맞은 말을 쓰시오.

Communication Step B

1. _____ _____ is orange.

2. I'm a _____ _____, and I'm a _____ _____.

3. _____ _____ _____ I'm a Don-Quixote-_____ person.

4. _____ _____ _____ _____ an art board on the classroom wall.

5. _____ _____ _____ _____ your dreams, plans, and ideas on the board?

1. 내 색깔은 오렌지색이야.
2. 나는 가을 사람이고, 엎드려서 자는 사람이야.
3. 나는 돈키호테 유형의 사람이라고 해.
4. 나는 교실 벽에 미술 게시판을 걸 거야.
5. 게시판에 너희들의 꿈과 계획, 그리고 생각들을 보여주는 게 어때?

Look and Write

1. _____ subjects can I _____ _____ _____? _____ clubs _____ _____ join?

2. I have _____ _____ _____ questions about school life.

3. The _____ _____ says _____ I am a curious thinker.

4. It _____ _____ that I am cool and quiet and I work _____ _____ _____ _____.

5. I am _____ _____ _____ from my _____ _____.

6. I want _____ _____ the _____ _____ them.

7. I know _____ I can do really well _____ _____.

1. 나는 어떤 과목을 잘할 수 있을까? 어떤 동아리에 가입해야 할까?
2. 나는 학교생활에 대한 질문이 많다.
3. 성격 검사에서는 내가 호기심 많은 사색가라고 한다.
4. 또한 멋지고 조용하며, 혼자서 (일할 때) 가장 잘한다고 한다.
5. 나는 나의 장점에서 시작하려 한다.
6. 나는 그 장점들을 최대한 잘 활용하고 싶다.
7. 나는 올해 정말 잘할 수 있을 것임을 안다.

Language Detective

1. I _____ _____ Mina's birthday party.

2. I _____ her parents and _____ _____ to them.

3. They _____ _____ and said, "Would you please _____ _____ _____ the food?"

4. It was a _____ _____, and my friends and I enjoyed _____ _____.

1. 나는 미나의 생일 파티에 갔다.
2. 나는 그녀의 부모님을 만났고 그분들에게 나를 소개했다.
3. 그분들은 나를 환영해 주셨고, "음식을 마음껏 먹지 그러니?"라고 말씀하셨다.
4. 굉장한 파티였고, 내 친구들과 나는 아주 즐거운 시간을 보냈다.

※ 다음 우리말을 영어로 쓰시오.

Communication Step B

1. 내 색깔은 오렌지색이야.
   ➡ _____

2. 나는 가을 사람이고, 엎드려서 자는 사람이야.
   ➡ _____

3. 나는 돈키호테 유형의 사람이라고 해.
   ➡ _____

4. 나는 교실 벽에 미술 게시판을 걸 거야.
   ➡ _____

5. 게시판에 너희들의 꿈과 계획, 그리고 생각들을 보여주는 게 어때?
   ➡ _____

Look and Write

1. 나는 어떤 과목을 잘할 수 있을까? 어떤 동아리에 가입해야 할까?
   ➡ _____

2. 나는 학교생활에 대한 질문이 많다.
   ➡ _____

3. 성격 검사에서는 내가 호기심 많은 사색가라고 한다.
   ➡ _____

4. 또한 멋지고 조용하며, 혼자서 (일할 때) 가장 잘한다고 한다.
   ➡ _____

5. 나는 나의 장점에서 시작하려 한다.
   ➡ _____

6. 나는 그 장점들을 최대한 잘 활용하고 싶다.
   ➡ _____

7. 나는 올해 정말 잘할 수 있을 것임을 안다.
   ➡ _____

Language Detective

1. 나는 미나의 생일 파티에 갔다.
   ➡ _____

2. 나는 그녀의 부모님을 만났고 그분들에게 나를 소개했다.
   ➡ _____

3. 그분들은 나를 환영해 주셨고, "음식을 마음껏 먹지 그러니?"라고 말씀하셨다.
   ➡ _____

4. 굉장한 파티였고, 내 친구들과 나는 아주 즐거운 시간을 보냈다.
   ➡ _____

※ 다음 영어를 우리말로 쓰시오.

01 famous		22 seat
02 trash		23 object
03 nail		24 woman
04 cloth		25 rubbish
05 slogan		26 sculpture
06 collect		27 set
07 thrown-away		28 such
08 upset		29 useful
09 handlebar		30 junk
10 artwork		31 reuse
11 used		32 thread
12 hurry		33 waste
13 imagination		34 create
14 wood		35 be able to 동사원형
15 worry		36 hurry up
16 treasure		37 be late for
17 wrap		38 not only A but also B
18 often		39 make use of
19 patch		40 be worried about
20 problem		41 a bit
21 less		42 pick up
		43 look like+명사

※ 다음 우리말을 영어로 쓰시오.

01 판자 _____

02 (지저분하고) 엉망인 상태 _____

03 단추, 버튼 _____

04 (시험에) 통과하다 _____

05 창작하다 _____

06 보물 _____

07 접착제로 붙이다 _____

08 옷감, 천 _____

09 다른, 또 하나의 _____

10 걱정하다 _____

11 나무, 목재 _____

12 작은 조각 _____

13 폐물, 고물 _____

14 상상력, 상상 _____

15 옷 _____

16 슬리퍼, 실내화 _____

17 재사용하다 _____

18 ～할 수 있는 _____

19 버려진 _____

20 중고의 _____

21 못으로 박다; 못 _____

22 매트리스 _____

23 부품, 부분, 일부 _____

24 누비이불 _____

25 동의하다 _____

26 쓰레기; 낭비하다 _____

27 부분, 조각 _____

28 실; (실 등을) 꿰다 _____

29 모으다, 수집하다 _____

30 예술 작품 _____

31 조각품 _____

32 (포장지 등으로) 싸다 _____

33 쓸모 있는, 유용한 _____

34 유명한 _____

35 다소, 약간 _____

36 줍다, 얻다 _____

37 ～에 대해 걱정하다 _____

38 ～에 동의하다 _____

39 ～을 이용하다 _____

40 치우다, 청소하다 _____

41 ～에 늦다 _____

42 서두르다 _____

43 시끄럽게 떠들다 _____

※ 다음 영영풀이에 알맞은 단어를 <보기>에서 골라 쓴 후, 우리말 뜻을 쓰시오.

1 _____ : no longer new: _____

2 _____ : to complete a test, class, etc. successfully: _____

3 _____ : paintings or sculptures that are of high quality: _____

4 _____ : a smaller amount, not so much: _____

5 _____ : to invent or design something: _____

6 _____ : a flat, thin, rectangular piece of wood or plastic: _____

7 _____ : a competition judged by a group of specially chosen judges: _____

8 _____ : unwanted things or waste materials: _____

9 _____ : to stick one object to another using glue: _____

10 _____ : old and used goods that have little value: _____

11 _____ : a situation that causes difficulties for people: _____

12 _____ : to use something again instead of throwing it away: _____

13 _____ : a short phrase expressing an advertising message: _____

14 _____ : being an additional thing or person of the same type: _____

15 _____ : to attach something somewhere using one or more nails: _____

16 _____ : to bring many things together from several places or people:

_____

보기			
reuse	pass	used	slogan
create	contest	collect	problem
board	another	junk	less
glue	rubbish	nail	artwork

※ 다음 우리말과 일치하도록 빈칸에 알맞은 말을 쓰시오.

Listen & Speak 1 Get Ready

B: _____ wrong?

G: I'm _____ _____ my dog. He is very _____.

B: 뭐가 문제야?
G: 난 내 개가 걱정돼. 개가 몹시 아파.

Listen & Speak 1 A

1. G: _____ wrong, Seho?

   B: I'm _____ _____ my science _____.

   G: _____ _____ too much. You'll _____ a good job.

2. B: Oops. I _____ _____ _____ your book.

   G: No, _____ _____, Namho!

   B: I'm sorry. I'm really _____ _____ _____ things.

3. B: You _____ _____, Sumi.

   G: _____ _____ _____ the test.

   B: _____ _____ too much. You _____ _____.

1. G: 무슨 일이니, 세호야?
   B: 내 과학 발표에 대해 걱정하고 있어.
   G: 너무 걱정하지 마. 넌 잘할 거야.

2. B: 이런. 네 책을 가져오는 것을 잊었어.
   G: 안돼, 남호야, 또야!
   B: 미안해. 난 잊어버리는 게 정말로 걱정돼.

3. B: 너 안 좋아 보여, 수미야.
   G: 난 시험이 걱정돼.
   B: 너무 걱정하지 마. 넌 통과할 거야.

Listen & Speak 1 B

1. A: _____ _____ _____ the _____ problem.

   B: Me, too. We _____ _____ everyday things.

   A: That's a good idea. We _____ _____ _____ _____
   flower vases.

2. A: I'm _____ _____ the _____ _____.

   B: Me, _____. We _____ _____ everyday things.

   A: That's a good _____. We can _____ old paper _____
   _____ _____.

1. A: 난 쓰레기 문제에 대해 걱정하고 있어.
   B: 나도 그래. 우리는 일상용품들을 재사용해야 해.
   A: 그거 좋은 생각이야. 우리는 병을 꽃병으로 재사용할 수 있어.

2. A: 난 쓰레기 문제에 대해 걱정하고 있어.
   B: 나도 그래. 우리는 일상용품들을 재사용해야 해.
   A: 그거 좋은 생각이야. 우리는 낡은 종이를 포장지로 재사용할 수 있어.

Listen & Speak 2 Get Ready

B: We should go _____.

G: You _____ _____ that _____.

B: 우리는 친환경적이 되어야 해.
G: 전적으로 동감이야.

Listen & Speak 2 A

1. **G:** _____ _____ this _____!

   B: Let's _____ it _____. We should _____ our classroom _____.

   G: You _____ _____ _____ _____.

2. **G:** _____ _____! We're _____ _____ be late.

   B: _____ _____ _____ _____ have longer lunch breaks.

   G: Well, I _____ _____.

3. **B:** He's _____ his slippers, _____ _____?

   G: Yes, he _____.

   B: We _____ _____ _____ in the school garden.

   G: I _____.

Conversation

Seho: Is this your _____ _____ the art _____, Nara?

Nara: Yes, it _____, Seho.

Seho: I _____ your slogan, "Reuse _____, Waste _____!" _____ did you _____ that _____?

Nara: I _____ it _____ _____.

Seho: Junk art _____ thrown-away things, _____ _____?

Nara: Yes, it _____. I'm _____ _____ the waste problem. We _____ _____ _____ _____ about it.

Seho: You _____ _____ _____ again.

Check My Progress

G: You _____ nervous, Minho. _____ _____?

B: _____ _____ _____ the _____ contest.

G: _____ _____ too much. You're _____ a good speaker.

B: Thank you, but I _____ _____.

G: _____ _____ _____. You'll do _____.

B: Thanks.

1. G: 이 엉망인 상태를 봐!
   B: 청소하자. 우리는 우리 교실을 깨끗하게 유지해야 해.
   G: 전적으로 동감이야.

2. G: 서둘러! 우리는 지각할 거야.
   B: 우리는 보다 긴 점심 휴식 시간을 가져야 한다고 생각해.
   G: 음, 난 동의하지 않아.

3. B: 그는 슬리퍼를 신고 있어, 그렇지 않니?
   G: 응, 그래.
   B: 우리는 학교 정원에서는 슬리퍼를 신지 말아야 해.
   G: 동의해.

세호: 나라야, 이것이 미술 대회를 위한 너의 포스터니?
나라: 그래, 세호야.
세호: "더 재사용하고 덜 낭비하자!"라는 구호가 마음에 들어. 어디서 저런 아이디어를 얻었니?
나라: 폐품 예술에서 얻었어.
세호: 폐품 예술은 버려진 물건들을 사용하지, 그렇지 않니?
나라: 그래. 나는 쓰레기 문제에 대해 걱정하고 있어. 우리는 그것에 대해 무언가를 해야만 해.
세호: 동감이야.

G: 너 긴장한 것 같아, 민호야. 무슨 일이니?
B: 난 웅변 대회가 걱정돼.
G: 너무 걱정하지 마. 넌 정말 훌륭한 연설가잖아.
B: 고마워, 하지만 난 걱정이 돼.
G: 긴장하지 마. 넌 잘할 거야.
B: 고마워.

대화문 Test

※ 다음 우리말에 맞도록 대화를 영어로 쓰시오.

Listen & Speak 1 Get Ready

B: _____

G: _____

B: 뭐가 문제야?
G: 난 내 개가 걱정돼. 개가 몹시 아파.

Listen & Speak 1 A

1. G: _____

   B: _____

   G: _____

2. B: _____

   G: _____

   B: _____

3. B: _____

   G: _____

   B: _____

1. G: 무슨 일이니, 세호야?
   B: 내 과학 발표에 대해 걱정하고 있어.
   G: 너무 걱정하지 마. 넌 잘할 거야.

2. B: 이런. 네 책을 가져오는 것을 잊었어.
   G: 안돼, 남호야, 또야!
   B: 미안해. 난 잊어버리는 게 정말로 걱정돼.

3. B: 너 안 좋아 보여, 수미야.
   G: 난 시험이 걱정돼.
   B: 너무 걱정하지 마. 넌 통과할 거야.

Listen & Speak 1 B

1. A: _____

   B: _____

   A: _____

2. A: _____

   B: _____

   A: _____

1. A: 난 쓰레기 문제에 대해 걱정하고 있어.
   B: 나도 그래. 우리는 일상용품들을 재사용해야 해.
   A: 그거 좋은 생각이야. 우리는 병을 꽃병으로 재사용할 수 있어.

2. A: 난 쓰레기 문제에 대해 걱정하고 있어.
   B: 나도 그래. 우리는 일상용품들을 재사용해야 해.
   A: 그거 좋은 생각이야. 우리는 낡은 종이를 포장지로 재사용할 수 있어.

Listen & Speak 2 Get Ready

B: _____

G: _____

B: 우리는 친환경적이 되어야 해.
G: 전적으로 동감이야.

26 Lesson 2. Old Things, New Art

Listen & Speak 2 A

1. G: _____

   B: _____

   G: _____

2. G: _____

   B: _____

   G: _____

3. B: _____

   G: _____

   B: _____

   G: _____

1. G: 이 엉망인 상태를 봐!
   B: 청소하자. 우리는 우리 교실을 깨끗하게 유지해야 해.
   G: 전적으로 동감이야.

2. G: 서둘러! 우리는 지각할 거야.
   B: 우리는 보다 긴 점심 휴식 시간을 가져야 한다고 생각해.
   G: 음, 난 동의하지 않아.

3. B: 그는 슬리퍼를 신고 있어, 그렇지 않니?
   G: 응, 그래.
   B: 우리는 학교 정원에서는 슬리퍼를 신지 말아야 해.
   G: 동의해.

Conversation

Seho: _____

Nara: _____

Seho: _____

Nara: _____

Seho: _____

Nara: _____

Seho: _____

세호: 나라야, 이것이 미술 대회를 위한 너의 포스터니?
나라: 그래, 세호야.
세호: "더 재사용하고 덜 낭비하자!"라는 구호가 마음에 들어. 어디서 저런 아이디어를 얻었니?
나라: 폐품 예술에서 얻었어.
세호: 폐품 예술은 버려진 물건들을 사용하지, 그렇지 않니?
나라: 그래. 나는 쓰레기 문제에 대해 걱정하고 있어. 우리는 그것에 대해 무언가를 해야만 해.
세호: 동감이야.

Check My Progress

G: _____

B: _____

G: _____

B: _____

G: _____

B: _____

G: 너 긴장한 것 같아, 민호야. 무슨 일이니?
B: 난 웅변 대회가 걱정돼.
G: 너무 걱정하지 마. 넌 정말 훌륭한 연설가잖아.
B: 고마워, 하지만 난 걱정이 돼.
G: 긴장하지 마. 넌 잘할 거야.
B: 고마워.

※ 다음 우리말과 일치하도록 빈칸에 알맞은 것을 골라 쓰시오.

1 _____ Things, _____ Art

A. new   B. old

2 Art can be _____ _____ of all _____ of old things _____ us.

A. around   B. out   C. kinds   D. made

3 Famous sculptures and pictures are often _____ from everyday things _____ _____ cans, bottles, and _____ of paper.

A. bits   B. as   C. such   D. made

4 Bicycle _____ and *Bull's* _____

A. Head   B. Junk

5 _____ do you _____ this _____?

A. artwork   B. how   C. like

6 It _____ _____ _____ Pablo Picasso.

A. by   B. was   C. created

7 He _____ a bicycle _____ and handlebars _____ _____ this sculpture!

A. make   B. to   C. seat   D. used

8 _____ World War II, _____ were not a lot of _____ things for art.

A. useful   B. there   C. during

9 But Picasso couldn't stop _____ artwork, so he _____ _____ junk _____ as old bicycles and mattress springs.

A. such   B. up   C. picked   D. creating

10 He used _____ _____ old things _____ _____ his imagination to create this sculpture in 1942.

A. also   B. but   C. only   D. not

1 낡은 것들, 새로운 예술

2 예술은 우리 주변의 모든 오래된 것들로 만들어질 수 있습니다.

3 유명한 조각품들과 그림들은 종종 깡통, 병 및 종잇조각과 같은 일상 용품으로 만들어집니다.

4 자전거 고물과 *Bull's Head*

5 이 작품은 어떻습니까?

6 그것은 Pablo Picasso에 의해 만들어졌습니다.

7 그는 이 조각 작품을 만들기 위해 자전거 좌석과 핸들을 사용했습니다!

8 제2차 세계 대전 중에는 예술을 위해 쓸 수 있는 것들이 많지 않았습니다.

9 그러나 Picasso는 작품 창작을 멈출 수 없어서, 오래된 자전거나 매트리스 스프링과 같은 고물을 주웠습니다.

10 그는 오래된 것들뿐만 아니라 그의 상상력도 사용하여 1942년에 이 조각품을 창작하였습니다.

11 _____ Things and _____ Art
A. New   B. Thrown-away

12 This artwork _____ _____ _____ Kurt Schwitters.
A. by   B. created   C. was

13 He used _____ _____ to make _____.
A. artwork   B. objects   C. thrown-away

14 He _____ said, "Old _____ are _____ for art."
A. good   B. things   C. often

15 Schwitters walked the streets and collected _____ only _____ of paper but _____ _____ of wood.
A. bits   B. also   C. pieces   D. not

16 He _____ and _____ them to a board, and _____ a new _____ of art, Rubbish.
A. style   B. glued   C. nailed   D. created

17 _____ 1937, he _____ _____ Norway.
A. to   B. moved   C. in

18 He was _____ to take his famous work _____ of Germany because it _____ _____ rubbish.
A. like   B. looked   C. out   D. able

19 _____ old _____ do you have _____ you?
A. around   B. things   C. what

20 _____ new _____ can you make _____ _____ them?
A. of   B. what   C. artwork   D. out

21 Use your _____ and create _____ _____.
A. new   B. imagination   C. something

22 _____ person's _____ is _____ treasure!
A. trash   B. another's   C. one

11 버려진 것들과 새로운 예술

12 이 작품은 Kurt Schwitters에 의해 창작되었습니다.

13 그는 작품을 만들기 위해 버려진 물건들을 사용했습니다.

14 그는 종종 "오래된 것들은 예술에 좋다"고 말했습니다.

15 Schwitters는 거리를 걸으면서 종잇조각뿐만 아니라 나무 조각도 모았습니다.

16 그는 그것들을 판자에 풀이나 못으로 붙여, Rubbish라는 새로운 방식의 예술을 창조했습니다.

17 1937년 그는 노르웨이로 이주했습니다.

18 쓰레기처럼 보였기 때문에 그는 그의 유명한 작품을 독일에서 가져갈 수 있었습니다.

19 당신 주변에 어떠한 오래된 것들이 있습니까?

20 당신은 그것들로 어떤 새로운 작품을 만들 수 있습니까?

21 당신의 상상력을 이용하여 새로운 것을 창작하십시오.

22 한 사람의 쓰레기가 다른 사람의 보물입니다!

※ 다음 우리말과 일치하도록 빈칸에 알맞은 말을 쓰시오.

1 _____ Things, _____ _____

2 Art can _____ _____ _____ _____ all kinds of old things _____ _____.

3 Famous sculptures and pictures _____ _____ _____ _____ everyday things _____ _____ cans, bottles, and _____ _____ _____.

4 Bicycle _____ and *Bull's Head*

5 _____ do you _____ this artwork?

6 It _____ _____ _____ Pablo Picasso.

7 He _____ a bicycle _____ and handlebars _____ _____ this sculpture!

8 _____ World War II, _____ _____ _____ a lot of _____ _____ for art.

9 But Picasso _____ _____ _____ artwork, so he _____ _____ junk _____ _____ old bicycles and mattress springs.

10 He used _____ _____ old things _____ _____ his imagination _____ _____ this sculpture in 1942.

1	낡은 것들, 새로운 예술
2	예술은 우리 주변의 모든 오래된 것들로 만들어질 수 있습니다.
3	유명한 조각품들과 그림들은 종종 깡통, 병 및 종잇조각과 같은 일상 용품으로 만들어집니다.
4	자전거 고물과 *Bull's Head*
5	이 작품은 어떻습니까?
6	그것은 Pablo Picasso에 의해 만들어졌습니다.
7	그는 이 조각 작품을 만들기 위해 자전거 좌석과 핸들을 사용했습니다!
8	제2차 세계 대전 중에는 예술을 위해 쓸 수 있는 것들이 많지 않았습니다.
9	그러나 Picasso는 작품 창작을 멈출 수 없어서, 오래된 자전거나 매트리스 스프링과 같은 고물을 주웠습니다.
10	그는 오래된 것들뿐만 아니라 그의 상상력도 사용하여 1942년에 이 조각품을 창작하였습니다.

11 _____ Things and _____ _____

12 This artwork _____ _____ _____ Kurt Schwitters.

13 He used _____ _____ _____ _____ artwork.

14 He often said, "Old things _____ _____ _____ art."

15 Schwitters walked the streets and _____ not only _____ _____ _____ but also _____ _____ _____.

16 He _____ and _____ them _____ a board, and created a new _____ _____ _____, Rubbish.

17 In 1937, he _____ _____ Norway.

18 He _____ _____ _____ _____ his famous work _____ _____ Germany because it _____ _____ rubbish.

19 _____ _____ _____ do you have _____ you?

20 _____ _____ _____ can you make out of them?

21 Use your imagination and _____ _____ _____.

22 One person's _____ is _____ _____!

11 버려진 것들과 새로운 예술

12 이 작품은 Kurt Schwitters에 의해 창작되었습니다.

13 그는 작품을 만들기 위해 버려진 물건들을 사용했습니다.

14 그는 종종 "오래된 것들은 예술에 좋다"고 말했습니다.

15 Schwitters는 거리를 걸으면서 종잇조각뿐만 아니라 나무 조각도 모았습니다.

16 그는 그것들을 판자에 풀이나 못으로 붙여, Rubbish라는 새로운 방식의 예술을 창조했습니다.

17 1937년 그는 노르웨이로 이주했습니다.

18 쓰레기처럼 보였기 때문에 그는 그의 유명한 작품을 독일에서 가져갈 수 있었습니다.

19 당신 주변에 어떠한 오래된 것들이 있습니까?

20 당신은 그것들로 어떤 새로운 작품을 만들 수 있습니까?

21 당신의 상상력을 이용하여 새로운 것을 창작하십시오.

22 한 사람의 쓰레기가 다른 사람의 보물입니다!

※ 다음 문장을 우리말로 쓰시오.

1 Old Things, New Art

➡ _____

2 Art can be made out of all kinds of old things around us.

➡ _____

3 Famous sculptures and pictures are often made from everyday things such as cans, bottles, and bits of paper.

➡ _____

4 Bicycle Junk and *Bull's Head*

➡ _____

5 How do you like this artwork?

➡ _____

6 It was created by Pablo Picasso.

➡ _____

7 He used a bicycle seat and handlebars to make this sculpture!

➡ _____

8 During World War II, there were not a lot of useful things for art.

➡ _____

9 But Picasso couldn't stop creating artwork, so he picked up junk such as old bicycles and mattress springs.

➡ _____

10 He used not only old things but also his imagination to create this sculpture in 1942.

➡ _____

11 Thrown-away Things and New Art

➡ _____

12 ▷ This artwork was created by Kurt Schwitters.

➡ _____

13 ▷ He used thrown-away objects to make artwork.

➡ _____

14 ▷ He often said, "Old things are good for art."

➡ _____

15 ▷ Schwitters walked the streets and collected not only pieces of paper but also bits of wood.

➡ _____

16 ▷ He glued and nailed them to a board, and created a new style of art, Rubbish.

➡ _____

17 ▷ In 1937, he moved to Norway.

➡ _____

18 ▷ He was able to take his famous work out of Germany because it looked like rubbish.

➡ _____

19 ▷ What old things do you have around you?

➡ _____

20 ▷ What new artwork can you make out of them?

➡ _____

21 ▷ Use your imagination and create something new.

➡ _____

22 ▷ One person's trash is another's treasure!

➡ _____

※ 다음 괄호 안의 단어들을 우리말에 맞도록 바르게 배열하시오.

1 (Things, / Art / New / Old)

➡ _____

2 (can / art / made / be / of / out / all / of / kinds / things / old / us. / around)

➡ _____

3 (sculptures / famous / and / pictures / often / are / from / made / things / everyday / as / cans, / such / bottles, / of / and / paper. / bits)

➡ _____

➡ _____

4 (Junk / Bicycle / *Head* / *Bull's* / and)

➡ _____

5 (do / how / like / you / artwork? / this)

➡ _____

6 (was / created / it / Picasso. / Pablo / by)

➡ _____

7 (used / he / bicycle / a / and / seat / handlebars / make / sculpture! / this / to)

➡ _____

8 (World / II, / War / during / were / there / not / lot / a / of / things / useful / art. / for)

➡ _____

9 (Picasso / but / stop / couldn't / artwork, / creating / so / he / up / picked / junk / as / such / old / bicycles / and / springs. / mattress)

➡ _____

➡ _____

10 (used / he / only / not / things / old / also / but / imagination / his / create / to / sculpture / this / 1942. / in)

➡ _____

➡ _____

11 (Things / and / Thrown-away / Art / New)

➡ _____

---

1 낡은 것들, 새로운 예술

2 예술은 우리 주변의 모든 오래된 것들로 만들어질 수 있습니다.

3 유명한 조각품들과 그림들은 종 종 깡통, 병 및 종잇조각과 같은 일상 용품으로 만들어집니다.

4 자전거 고물과 *Bull's Head*

5 이 작품은 어떻습니까?

6 그것은 Pablo Picasso에 의해 만들어졌습니다.

7 그는 이 조각 작품을 만들기 위 해 자전거 좌석과 핸들을 사용 했습니다!

8 제2차 세계 대전 중에는 예술을 위해 쓸 수 있는 것들이 많지 않 았습니다.

9 그러나 Picasso는 작품 창작을 멈출 수 없어서, 오래된 자전거 나 매트리스 스프링과 같은 고 물을 주웠습니다.

10 그는 오래된 것들뿐만 아니라 그의 상상력도 사용하여 1942년 에 이 조각품을 창작하였습니다.

11 버려진 것들과 새로운 예술

12 (artwork / this / created / was / by / Schwitters. / Kurt)

➡ _____

13 (used / he / thrown-away / to / artwork. / make / objects)

➡ _____

14 (often / he / said, / "old / are / things / art." / for / good)

➡ _____

15 (walked / Schwitters / streets / the / collected / and / only / not / of / pieces / paper / also / but / wood. / of / bits)

➡ _____

_____

16 (glued / he / and / them / nailed / a / to / board, / and / a / created / new / of / style / Rubbish. / art,)

➡ _____

_____

17 (1937, / in / moved / he / Norway. / to)

➡ _____

18 (was / he / to / able / take / famous / his / out / work / of / Germany / it / because / like / rubbish. / looked)

➡ _____

_____

19 (old / what / things / you / do / around / have / you?)

➡ _____

20 (new / what / can / artwork / you / out / make / them? / of)

➡ _____

21 (your / use / and / imagination / create / new. / something)

➡ _____

22 (person's / one / is / trash / treasure! / another's)

➡ _____

12 이 작품은 Kurt Schwitters에 의해 창작되었습니다.

13 그는 작품을 만들기 위해 버려진 물건들을 사용했습니다.

14 그는 종종 "오래된 것들은 예술에 좋다"고 말했습니다.

15 Schwitters는 거리를 걸으면서 종잇조각뿐만 아니라 나무 조각도 모았습니다.

16 그는 그것들을 판자에 풀이나 못으로 붙여, Rubbish라는 새로운 방식의 예술을 창조했습니다.

17 1937년 그는 노르웨이로 이주했습니다.

18 쓰레기처럼 보였기 때문에 그는 그의 유명한 작품을 독일에서 가져갈 수 있었습니다.

19 당신 주변에 어떠한 오래된 것들이 있습니까?

20 당신은 그것들로 어떤 새로운 작품을 만들 수 있습니까?

21 당신의 상상력을 이용하여 새로운 것을 창작하십시오.

22 한 사람의 쓰레기가 다른 사람의 보물입니다!

※ 다음 우리말을 영어로 쓰시오.

1 낡은 것들, 새로운 예술

➡ _____

2 예술은 우리 주변의 모든 오래된 것들로 만들어질 수 있습니다.

➡ _____

3 유명한 조각품들과 그림들은 종종 깡통, 병 및 종잇조각과 같은 일상 용품으로 만들어집니다.

➡ _____

_____

4 자전거 고물과 *Bull's Head*

➡ _____

5 이 작품은 어떻습니까?

➡ _____

6 그것은 Pablo Picasso에 의해 만들어졌습니다.

➡ _____

7 그는 이 조각 작품을 만들기 위해 자전거 좌석과 핸들을 사용했습니다!

➡ _____

8 제2차 세계 대전 중에는 예술을 위해 쓸 수 있는 것들이 많지 않았습니다.

➡ _____

9 그러나 Picasso는 작품 창작을 멈출 수 없어서, 오래된 자전거나 매트리스 스프링과 같은 고물을 주웠습니다.

➡ _____

_____

10 그는 오래된 것들뿐만 아니라 그의 상상력도 사용하여 1942년에 이 조각품을 창작하였습니다.

➡ _____

11 버려진 것들과 새로운 예술

➡ _____

12 이 작품은 Kurt Schwitters에 의해 창작되었습니다.

➡ _____

13 그는 작품을 만들기 위해 버려진 물건들을 사용했습니다.

➡ _____

14 그는 종종 "오래된 것들은 예술에 좋다"고 말했습니다.

➡ _____

15 Schwitters는 거리를 걸으면서 종잇조각뿐만 아니라 나무 조각도 모았습니다.

➡ _____

16 그는 그것들을 판자에 풀이나 못으로 붙여, Rubbish라는 새로운 방식의 예술을 창조했습니다.

➡ _____

17 1937년 그는 노르웨이로 이주했습니다.

➡ _____

18 쓰레기처럼 보였기 때문에 그는 그의 유명한 작품을 독일에서 가져갈 수 있었습니다.

➡ _____

19 당신 주변에 어떠한 오래된 것들이 있습니까?

➡ _____

20 당신은 그것들로 어떤 새로운 작품을 만들 수 있습니까?

➡ _____

21 당신의 상상력을 이용하여 새로운 것을 창작하십시오.

➡ _____

22 한 사람의 쓰레기가 다른 사람의 보물입니다!

➡ _____

※ 다음 우리말과 일치하도록 빈칸에 알맞은 말을 쓰시오.

Let's Write Step 1

1. This _____ is *Bull's Head*.

2. It _____ _____ _____ Pablo Picasso.

3. He used _____ _____ old bicycle parts _____ _____ his imagination _____ _____ this artwork.

4. One person's _____ is _____ _____ .

1. 이 미술 작품은 Bull's Head입니다.
2. 그것은 Pablo Picasso에 의해 창작되었습니다.
3. 그는 오래된 자전거 부품들뿐만 아니라 그의 상상력도 사용하여 이 작품을 만들었습니다.
4. 한 사람의 쓰레기는 다른 사람의 보물입니다.

Project Across Subjects Step 3

1. _____: Color Fish

2. We _____: a _____ bottle, a big _____ button, a small black button, and _____ _____

3. _____ _____: Give the fish some water, and it will _____ _____ .

4. This is our _____. It is _____ *Color Fish*.

5. It _____ _____ _____ the three _____ us: Minho, Changsu, and Nami.

6. We _____ a plastic bottle, a big white button, a small black button, and colored paper.

7. _____ the fish some _____, and _____ it _____ the pool.

8. The colorful fish will _____ _____ .

1. 예술 작품: Color Fish
2. 우리는 사용했다: 플라스틱 병 한 개, 큰 흰색 단추, 작은 검은색 단추, 그리고 색종이
3. 특징: 물고기에게 물을 약간 주면 주변을 헤엄쳐 다닐 것이다.
4. 이것이 우리의 미술 작품이다. Color Fish라고 불린다.
5. 그것은 우리 세 명에 의해 창작되었다.: 민호, 창수, 그리고 나미.
6. 우리는 플라스틱 병 한 개, 큰 흰색 단추, 작은 검은색 단추, 그리고 색종이를 사용했다.
7. 물고기에게 물을 약간 주고 그것을 수영장에 놓아라.
8. 알록달록한 물고기가 주변을 헤엄쳐 다닐 것이다.

Check My Progress 4

1. Seminole Indians in the U.S. use old _____ _____ _____ clothes _____ _____ skirt.

2. People in Bangladesh use _____ and old cloth _____ _____ flowery _____ _____ .

3. 1. _____ beautiful artwork is not easy _____ _____ .

4. 2. Indians love _____ _____ skirts and _____ _____ .

5. 3. People _____ the world use _____ _____ to make _____ _____ .

1. 미국의 세미놀 인디언들은 스커트와 같은 옷을 만들기 위해 오래된 천을 사용한다.
2. 방글라데시 사람들은 꽃무늬 쪽모이 퀼트를 만들기 위해 실과 오래된 천을 사용한다.
3. 1. 아름다운 예술 작품을 만드는 것은 전혀 쉽지 않다.
4. 2. 인디언들은 스커트와 보자기를 만드는 것을 좋아한다.
5. 3. 전 세계의 사람들은 유용한 것을 만들기 위해 낡은 천을 사용한다.

※ 다음 우리말을 영어로 쓰시오.

Let's Write Step 1

1. 이 미술 작품은 Bull's Head입니다.
   ➡ _____

2. 그것은 Pablo Picasso에 의해 창작되었습니다.
   ➡ _____

3. 그는 오래된 자전거 부품들뿐만 아니라 그의 상상력도 사용하여 이 작품을 만들었습니다.
   ➡ _____

4. 한 사람의 쓰레기는 다른 사람의 보물입니다.
   ➡ _____

Project Across Subjects Step 3

1. 예술 작품: Color Fish
   ➡ _____

2. 우리는 사용했다: 플라스틱 병 한 개, 큰 흰색 단추, 작은 검은색 단추, 그리고 색종이
   ➡ _____

3. 특징: 물고기에게 물을 약간 주면 주변을 헤엄쳐 다닐 것이다.
   ➡ _____

4. 이것이 우리의 미술 작품이다. Color Fish라고 불린다.
   ➡ _____

5. 그것은 우리 세 명에 의해 창작되었다.: 민호, 창수, 그리고 나미.
   ➡ _____

6. 우리는 플라스틱 병 한 개, 큰 흰색 단추, 작은 검은색 단추, 그리고 색종이를 사용했다.
   ➡ _____

7. 물고기에게 물을 약간 주고 그것을 수영장에 놓아라.
   ➡ _____

8. 알록달록한 물고기가 주변을 헤엄쳐 다닐 것이다.
   ➡ _____

Check My Progress 4

1. 미국의 세미놀 인디언들은 스커트와 같은 옷을 만들기 위해 오래된 천을 사용한다.
   ➡ _____

2. 방글라데시 사람들은 꽃무늬 쪽모이 퀼트를 만들기 위해 실과 오래된 천을 사용한다.
   ➡ _____

3. 1. 아름다운 예술 작품을 만드는 것은 전혀 쉽지 않다.
   ➡ _____

4. 2. 인디언들은 스커트와 보자기를 만드는 것을 좋아한다.
   ➡ _____

5. 3. 전 세계의 사람들은 유용한 것을 만들기 위해 낡은 천을 사용한다.
   ➡ _____

※ 다음 영어를 우리말로 쓰시오.

01 popular		22 hand
02 congratulation		23 tie
03 ever		24 hang
04 pull		25 save
05 shoot		26 opening
06 safety		27 shout
07 first		28 pick
08 whether		29 guess
09 same		30 quickly
10 important		31 chance
11 score		32 sigh
12 believe		33 while
13 quite		34 rope
14 teamwork		35 take part in
15 heart		36 It's important to+동사원형 ~
16 shot		37 be ready for
17 three-legged race		38 at the same time
18 leap		39 be ready to+동사원형
19 kicker		40 make a basket
20 position		41 look forward to+(동)명사
21 coach		42 whether ~ or not
		43 look for

※ 다음 우리말을 영어로 쓰시오.

01 (농구의) 바스켓, 득점

02 부인하다

03 코치, 감독

04 (스포츠 팀의) 고급 실력자

05 추측하다

06 건네주다

07 소리 지르다

08 위치

09 매달리다

10 (스포츠 팀의) 주니어 선수

11 발길질, 차기

12 ~이든 아니든

13 세게, 열심히

14 팀워크, 협력

15 아주, 매우

16 전화하다

17 ~하는 동안

18 슛을 쏘다

19 기회

20 믿다

21 뛰다, 빠르게 움직이다

22 안전

23 줄, 로프

24 아끼다, 절약하다

25 기회, 자리, 개막식

26 목록, 명단

27 당기다

28 로커 룸

29 동점; 동점을 이루다

30 가슴, 심장

31 슛을 쏘는 사람

32 페널티 킥

33 중요한

34 득점하다

35 동시에

36 최선을 다하다

37 ~에 참여[참가]하다

38 ~이든 아니든

39 [불·라디오 등을] 끄다

40 ~하고 싶다

41 ~할 준비가 되다

42 ~ 옆에

43 농구 경기에서 득점하다

※ 다음 영영풀이에 알맞은 단어를 <보기>에서 골라 쓴 후, 우리말 뜻을 쓰시오.

1 _____ : a loud call or cry: _____

2 _____ : an available job or position: _____

3 _____ : a person who shoots: _____

4 _____ : to pass or give something to somebody: _____

5 _____ : a possibility of something happening: _____

6 _____ : to gain points in a game: _____

7 _____ : to have the same number of points: _____

8 _____ : to let out one's breath with sound, as from sorrow, weariness, or relief: _____

9 _____ : someone training a person or team of people: _____

10 _____ : to say that something is not true: _____

11 _____ : to try to kick, hit, or throw the ball into a goal: _____

12 _____ : to attach something, or to be attached: _____

13 _____ : to move or act quickly or suddenly: _____

14 _____ : to choose or select from among a group: _____

15 _____ : to keep something to use or enjoy in the future: _____

16 _____ : to try to give an answer or make a judgement about something without being sure of all the facts: _____

보기			
opening	shoot	guess	save
shot	chance	shout	tie
pick	hand	leap	coach
hang	deny	sigh	score

※ 다음 우리말과 일치하도록 빈칸에 알맞은 말을 쓰시오.

Listen & Speak 1 Get Ready

W: Grandpa is _____ _____ this Friday.

G: Great! I'm _____ _____ _____ _____ him!

해석

W: 할아버지께서 이번 금요일에 우리를 방문하실 거야.

G: 좋아요! 나는 할아버지를 뵙기를 고대해요!.

Listen & Speak 1 A

1. G: You _____ _____, Minho? We _____ _____ _____ _____ _____ Jeju for our school trip.

   B: Yes, I know. _____ really _____ _____ _____ it!

2. B: _____ the N-Boys _____ _____ the school festival, Jimin?

   G: Yes, they _____. I'm really _____ _____ _____ _____ them!

   B: Me, _____. I _____ _____ it!

3. B: Sumi, we _____ _____ _____ _____ an English speech contest _____ Friday.

   G: Wow, we are _____ _____ it. I _____ looking forward to _____ _____ _____!

1. G: 그거 아니, 민호야? 우리는 학교 여행으로 제주도에 갈 거야.

   B: 응, 나도 알아. 난 그걸 정말 고대하고 있어!

2. B: N-Boys가 학교 축제에 오니, 지민아?

   G: 응, 와. 난 그들을 보기를 정말로 고대하고 있어!

   B: 나도 그래. 믿을 수 없는 일이야!

3. B: 수미야, 우리는 다음 주 금요일에 영어 웅변 대회를 열게 될 거야.

   G: 와, 드디어 하는구나. 난 상을 타기를 고대하고 있어!

Listen & Speak 1 B

1. A: School Sports Day _____ _____ soon! I _____ _____.

   B: _____ here. What are you _____ forward to _____?

   A: I'm _____ forward to _____ a group _____.

2. A: School Sports Day is coming soon! _____ _____ _____.

   B: Same here. _____ _____ _____ _____ _____ _____ _____?

   A: I'm _____ _____ to _____ in the _____ race.

1. A: 학교 체육대회가 곧 있을 거야! 정말 기다려져.

   B: 나도 그래. 넌 뭘 하기를 고대하고 있니?

   A: 난 단체 춤을 추는 것을 고대하고 있어.

2. A: 학교 체육대회가 곧 있을 거야! 정말 기다려져.

   B: 나도 그래. 넌 뭘 하기를 고대하고 있니?

   A: 난 이인삼각 경주를 하는 것을 고대하고 있어.

Listen & Speak 2 Get Ready

M: When there's a fire, _____ important _____ _____ 119 first.

M: 불이 났을 때는 먼저 119에 전화하는 것이 중요해요.

Listen & Talk 2 A

1. **B:** I _____ _____ _____ a good English speaker _____ you. What do I _____ _____ do?

   G: Well, _____ _____ _____ _____ English every day.

2. **B:** I am _____ _____ _____ bike riding.

   G: Wait, _____ first. _____ important _____ _____ gloves.

3. **B:** _____ are you still _____ in the classroom? Hurry up!

   G: Just a minute. _____ _____ _____ _____ the lights. _____ important _____ _____ _____.

Listen & Talk 2 B

1. **A:** _____ you _____ _____ the baseball game?

   B: Yes, I _____. _____ _____ forward to _____ it.

   A: Me, too. What _____ we do to _____ it?

   B: _____ _____ _____ _____ the ball _____.

2. **A:** _____ _____ _____ for the soccer match?

   B: Yes, I am. I'm _____ _____ _____ _____ _____ it.

   A: Me, too. _____ _____ _____ _____ _____ to win it?

   B: _____ _____ _____ _____ the ball quickly.

Real-Life Task

Step 2

A: _____ team sport are you _____ _____ _____ on School Sports Day?

B: I'm _____ _____ _____ _____ the group jump rope game. _____ _____ you?

A: I'm _____ _____ _____ to it. _____ _____ _____ _____ _____ _____ the game?

B: I think _____ important _____ _____ together _____ _____ _____ _____.

※ 다음 우리말에 맞도록 대화를 영어로 쓰시오.

Listen & Speak 1 Get Ready

W: _____

G: _____

Listen & Speak 1 A

1. G: _____

   B: _____

2. B: _____

   G: _____

   B: _____

3. B: _____

   G: _____

Listen & Speak 1 B

1. A: _____

   B: _____

   A: _____

2. A: _____

   B: _____

   A: _____

Listen & Speak 2 Get Ready

M: _____

Listen & Talk 2 A

1. B: _____

   G: _____

2. B: _____

   G: _____

3. B: _____

   G: _____

Listen & Talk 2 B

1. A: _____

   B: _____

   A: _____

   B: _____

2. A: _____

   B: _____

   A: _____

   B: _____

Real-Life Task

Step 2

A: _____

B: _____

A: _____

B: _____

1. B: 난 너처럼 영어를 잘하는 사람이 되고 싶어. 내가 뭘 할 필요가 있니?
   G: 음, 매일 영어를 사용하는 것이 중요해.

2. B: 난 자전거 타러 갈 준비가 다 됐어.
   G: 기다려, 안전이 먼저야. 장갑을 착용하는 것이 중요해.

3. B: 교실에서 아직 뭘 하고 있니? 서둘러!
   G: 잠깐만. 불을 끌게. 에너지를 절약하는 것이 중요해.

1. A: 야구 시합 준비는 됐니?
   B: 응, 됐어, 난 시합에서 이기기를 고대하고 있어.
   A: 나도 그래. 시합에서 이기려면 우리가 뭘 해야 할까?
   B: 공을 세게 치는 것이 중요해.

2. A: 축구 시합 준비는 됐니?
   B: 응, 됐어, 난 시합에서 이기기를 고대하고 있어.
   A: 나도 그래. 시합에서 이기려면 우리가 뭘 해야 할까?
   B: 공을 빠르게 패스하는 것이 중요해.

A: 넌 학교 체육 대회에서 어떤 단체 운동 경기에 참여할 거니?
B: 난 단체 줄넘기 경기에 참여하는 것을 고대하고 있어. 너는?
A: 나도 그걸 고대하고 있어. 우리가 경기에서 이기려면 뭘 해야 할까?
B: 동시에 함께 점프하는 것이 중요하다고 생각해.

※ 다음 우리말과 일치하도록 빈칸에 알맞은 것을 골라 쓰시오.

1 The _____ was _____ .
A. over   B. game

2 The _____ team _____ it, and all the players _____ happy.
A. won   B. junior   C. were

3 _____ they _____ in the locker room, the coach _____
_____ boy a card.
A. every   B. were   C. while   D. handed

4 It had a _____ _____ the players _____ the junior team.
A. list   B. on   C. of

5 "_____ you _____ _____ , we have an _____ for a
player on the senior team," said the coach.
A. opening   B. as   C. know   D. all

6 "_____ _____ you _____ a player for the team?
A. why   B. pick   C. don't

7 _____ one name _____ the list."
A. on   B. check

8 Scottie _____ _____ the list and _____ his name.
A. at   B. saw   C. looked

9 Then he _____ and _____ a check _____ _____
Michael's name.
A. to   B. put   C. next   D. sighed

10 He couldn't _____ _____ _____ Michael was _____ _____ for
the senior team.
A. enough   B. that   C. good   D. deny

11 The coach _____ _____ card _____ the boys.
A. every   B. from   C. collected

12 _____ hopes _____ _____ .
A. were   B. everyone's   C. high

13 They _____ _____ _____ be on the senior team.
A. be   B. wanted   C. all

14 The coach _____ _____ and said, "Well, it's a _____
_____ Michael and Scottie."
A. between   B. up   C. tie   D. looked

15 Scottie's _____ _____ .
A. leaped   B. heart

16 He _____ _____ that he was _____ with Michael.
A. tied   B. surprised   C. was

1 경기는 끝났다.

2 주니어 팀은 경기에서 승리했고, 모든 선수들이 행복했다.

3 그들이 로커 룸에 있는 동안, 코치가 모든 소년들에게 카드 한 장씩을 건네주었다.

4 그 카드는 주니어 팀의 모든 선수들의 명단을 담고 있었다.

5 "모두 알고 있듯이, 우리는 시니어 팀에 한 자리가 비어 있어." 코치가 말했다.

6 "여러분들이 시니어 팀에 들어갈 선수를 뽑아 보는 것이 어떨까?

7 명단 위의 이름 하나에 체크 표시를 해 주게."

8 Scottie는 명단을 보았고 자신의 이름을 보았다.

9 그러고는 한숨을 쉰 후 Michael의 이름 옆에 체크 표시를 하였다.

10 그는 Michael이 시니어 팀에 충분히 훌륭하다는 것을 부인할 수 없었다.

11 코치가 소년들로부터 모든 카드를 거두었다.

12 모든 선수들의 바람은 높았다.

13 그들은 모두 시니어 팀에 들어가기를 원했다.

14 코치가 올려다보고 말했다. "흠, Michael과 Scottie가 동점이구나."

15 Scottie의 심장이 뛰었다.

16 그는 자기가 Michael과 동점이 되어서 놀라웠다.

17 "Well," said the coach, "_____ are wonderful _____ for the senior team, and it's _____ to _____ just one player.
    A. pick   B. enough   C. hard   D. both

18 But I _____ _____, so I'll _____ Scottie."
    A. have   B. pick   C. to

19 _____ the coach _____ _____ to Scottie and said, "Congratulations!"
    A. then   B. over   C. walked

20 "Thank you, _____ Michael is _____ _____ good _____.
    A. shot   B. a   C. but   D. such

21 He _____ the _____ _____," said Scottie.
    A. baskets   B. makes   C. most

22 "_____ course, he _____," said the coach.
    A. does   B. of

23 "But he shoots _____ _____ a player in a better position _____ _____.
    A. not   B. there's   C. or   D. whether

24 It's _____ _____ _____ for the team!
    A. play   B. to   C. important

25 _____ worry. I know a good player _____ I _____ one."
    A. see   B. when   C. don't

26 Scottie _____ _____ _____ the room.
    A. out   B. of   C. walked

27 He felt _____ giving a _____ and happy _____.
    A. loud   B. shout   C. like

28 _____ he _____ Michael.
    A. saw   B. then

29 _____ Scottie felt _____ _____ him.
    A. sorry   B. for   C. suddenly

30 "I guess you _____ _____, but I _____ you _____ the senior team," said Scottie.
    A. care   B. picked   C. for   D. don't

31 Michael _____. "You know _____? I _____ YOU."
    A. what   B. smiled   C. picked

32 Scottie _____ _____. "You _____?"
    A. was   B. surprised   C. did

33 "Yeah. You _____ _____ your _____, and you're a team player.
    A. best   B. always   C. do

34 Today you _____ _____ the team, and we _____ the game. Congratulations!"
    A. for   B. won   C. played

---

17 "흠." 코치가 말했다. "둘 다 시니어 팀에 들어가기에 충분히 훌륭하고, 단 한 명의 선수를 선정하는 것은 어려운 일이야.

18 그러나 나는 선정해야 하기에, Scottie를 뽑겠어."

19 그리고 코치가 Scottie에게 걸어와서 말했다. "축하해!"

20 "감사합니다, 그러나 Michael은 훌륭한 골잡이에요.

21 Michael이 득점을 가장 많이 하고 있어요." Scottie가 말했다.

22 "물론, Michael이 그렇지." 코치가 말했다.

23 "그러나 Michael은 더 나은 위치에 선수가 있든 없든, 슛을 쏴.

24 팀을 위해 경기하는 것이 중요해!

25 걱정 마. 나는 보면 좋은 선수인지 안단다."

26 Scottie는 방에서 걸어 나갔다.

27 그는 크고 기쁜 소리를 지르고 싶은 마음이었다.

28 그때 그는 Michael을 보았다.

29 갑자기 Scottie는 그에게 미안한 감정이 들었다.

30 "나는 네가 신경 쓰지 않으리라고 추측하지만, 시니어 팀에 너를 뽑았어."라고 Scottie가 말했다.

31 Michael이 미소 지었다. "너 그거 아니? 나도 너를 뽑았어."

32 Scottie가 놀랐다. "네가 그랬어?"

33 "응. 너는 항상 최선을 다 해, 그리고 너는 팀플레이어야.

34 오늘 너는 팀을 위해 경기했고, 우리는 게임에서 이겼는걸. 축하해!"

※ 다음 우리말과 일치하도록 빈칸에 알맞은 말을 쓰시오.

1 The game _____ _____.

2 The junior team _____ it, and all the players _____ happy.

3 _____ they _____ _____ the locker room, the coach _____ _____ boy _____ _____.

4 It had _____ _____ _____ the players _____ the junior team.

5 "_____ _____ _____ _____, we have _____ _____ for a player on the _____ team," said the coach.

6 "_____ _____ _____ a player for the team?

7 _____ one name _____ _____ _____."

8 Scottie _____ _____ the list and _____ his name.

9 Then he _____ and _____ a check _____ _____ Michael's name.

10 He _____ _____ _____ Michael was _____ _____ for the senior team.

11 The coach _____ _____ _____ _____ the boys.

12 _____ hopes _____ _____.

13 They all _____ _____ _____ on the senior team.

14 The coach _____ _____ and said, "Well, it's _____ _____ Michael and Scottie."

15 Scottie's _____ _____.

16 He _____ _____ _____ he was _____ with Michael.

1 경기는 끝났다.

2 주니어 팀은 경기에서 승리했고, 모든 선수들이 행복했다.

3 그들이 로커 룸에 있는 동안, 코치가 모든 소년들에게 카드 한 장씩을 건네주었다.

4 그 카드는 주니어 팀의 모든 선수들의 명단을 담고 있었다.

5 "모두 알고 있듯이, 우리는 시니어 팀에 한 자리가 비어 있어." 코치가 말했다.

6 "여러분들이 시니어 팀에 들어갈 선수를 뽑아 보는 것이 어떨까?

7 명단 위의 이름 하나에 체크 표시를 해 주게."

8 Scottie는 명단을 보았고 자신의 이름을 보았다.

9 그러고는 한숨을 쉰 후 Michael의 이름 옆에 체크 표시를 하였다.

10 그는 Michael이 시니어 팀에 충분히 훌륭하다는 것을 부인할 수 없었다.

11 코치가 소년들로부터 모든 카드를 거두었다.

12 모든 선수들의 바람은 높았다.

13 그들은 모두 시니어 팀에 들어가기를 원했다.

14 코치가 올려다보고 말했다. "흠, Michael과 Scottie가 동점이구나."

15 Scottie의 심장이 뛰었다.

16 그는 자기가 Michael과 동점이 되어서 놀라웠다.

17 "Well," said the coach, "both are _____ _____ for the senior team, and it's _____ _____ _____ just one player.

18 But I _____ _____, _____ I'll _____ Scottie."

19 Then the coach _____ _____ to Scottie and said, "Congratulations!"

20 "Thank you, but Michael is _____ _____ _____ _____.

21 He _____ _____ _____ _____," said Scottie.

22 "_____ _____, he _____," said the coach.

23 "But he _____ _____ _____ _____ _____ in a better position _____ _____.

24 _____ important _____ _____ _____ the team!

25 _____ _____. I know a good player _____ I _____ _____."

26 Scottie _____ _____ the room.

27 He _____ _____ _____ a _____ and happy shout.

28 _____ he _____ Michael.

29 _____ Scottie _____ _____ _____ him.

30 "I guess you _____ _____, but I _____ you _____ the senior team," said Scottie.

31 Michael _____. "You know _____? I _____ YOU."

32 Scottie _____ _____. "You _____?"

33 "Yeah. You _____ _____ _____ _____, and you're a team player.

34 Today you _____ _____ the team, and we _____ the game. _____!"

---

17 "흠." 코치가 말했다. "둘 다 시니어 팀에 들어가기에 충분히 훌륭하고, 단 한 명의 선수를 선정하는 것은 어려운 일이야.

18 그러나 나는 선정해야 하기에, Scottie를 뽑겠어."

19 그리고 코치가 Scottie에게 걸어와서 말했다. "축하해!"

20 "감사합니다. 그러나 Michael은 훌륭한 골잡이에요.

21 Michael이 득점을 가장 많이 하고 있어요." Scottie가 말했다.

22 "물론, Michael이 그렇지." 코치가 말했다.

23 "그러나 Michael은 더 나은 위치에 선수가 있든 없든, 슛을 쏴.

24 팀을 위해 경기하는 것이 중요해!

25 걱정 마. 나는 보면 좋은 선수인지 안단다."

26 Scottie는 방에서 걸어 나갔다.

27 그는 크고 기쁜 소리를 지르고 싶은 마음이었다.

28 그때 그는 Michael을 보았다.

29 갑자기 Scottie는 그에게 미안한 감정이 들었다.

30 "나는 네가 신경 쓰지 않으리라고 추측하지만, 시니어 팀에 너를 뽑았어."라고 Scottie가 말했다.

31 Michael이 미소 지었다. "너 그거 아니? 나도 너를 뽑았어."

32 Scottie가 놀랐다. "네가 그랬어?"

33 "응. 너는 항상 최선을 다 해, 그리고 너는 팀플레이어야.

34 오늘 너는 팀을 위해 경기했고, 우리는 게임에서 이겼는걸. 축하해!"

※ 다음 문장을 우리말로 쓰시오.

1 The game was over.
➡ _____

2 The junior team won it, and all the players were happy.
➡ _____

3 While they were in the locker room, the coach handed every boy a card.
➡ _____

4 It had a list of the players on the junior team.
➡ _____

5 "As you all know, we have an opening for a player on the senior team," said the coach.
➡ _____

6 "Why don't you pick a player for the team?
➡ _____

7 Check one name on the list."
➡ _____

8 Scottie looked at the list and saw his name.
➡ _____

9 Then he sighed and put a check next to Michael's name.
➡ _____

10 He couldn't deny that Michael was good enough for the senior team.
➡ _____

11 The coach collected every card from the boys.
➡ _____

12 Everyone's hopes were high.
➡ _____

13 They all wanted to be on the senior team.
➡ _____

14 The coach looked up and said, "Well, it's a tie between Michael and Scottie."
➡ _____

15 Scottie's heart leaped.
➡ _____

16 He was surprised that he was tied with Michael.
➡ _____

17 "Well," said the coach, "both are wonderful enough for the senior team, and it's hard to pick just one player.
➡ _____

18 But I have to, so I'll pick Scottie."
➡ _____

19 Then the coach walked over to Scottie and said, "Congratulations!"
➡ _____

20 "Thank you, but Michael is such a good shot.
➡ _____

21 He makes the most baskets," said Scottie.
➡ _____

22 "Of course, he does," said the coach.
➡ _____

23 "But he shoots whether there's a player in a better position or not.
➡ _____

24 It's important to play for the team!
➡ _____

25 Don't worry. I know a good player when I see one."
➡ _____

26 Scottie walked out of the room.
➡ _____

27 He felt like giving a loud and happy shout.
➡ _____

28 Then he saw Michael.
➡ _____

29 Suddenly Scottie felt sorry for him.
➡ _____

30 "I guess you don't care, but I picked you for the senior team," said Scottie.
➡ _____

31 Michael smiled. "You know what? I picked YOU."
➡ _____

32 Scottie was surprised. "You did?"
➡ _____

33 "Yeah. You always do your best, and you're a team player.
➡ _____

34 Today you played for the team, and we won the game.
➡ _____

35 Congratulations!"
➡ _____

※ 다음 괄호 안의 단어들을 우리말에 맞도록 바르게 배열하시오.

1 (game / the / over. / was)
➡ _____

2 (junior / team / the / it, / won / and / the / all / happy. / were / players)
➡ _____

3 (they / while / in / were / locker / the / room, / coach / the / every / handed / card. / boy / a)
➡ _____

4 (a / had / list / it / of / players / the / on / team. / junior / the)
➡ _____

5 (you / know, / "as / all / have / we / opening / an / player / for / a / the / on / team," / senior / coach. / the / said)
➡ _____

6 (don't / "why / pick / you / player / a / team? / the / for)
➡ _____

7 (one / check / on / name / list." / the)
➡ _____

8 (looked / Scottie / the / at / and / list / name. / his / saw)
➡ _____

9 (he / then / sighed / and / a / put / check / to / next / name. / Michael's)
➡ _____

10 (couldn't / he / that / deny / Michael / good / was / for / enough / team. / senior / the)
➡ _____

11 (coach / the / collected / card / every / boys. / the / from)
➡ _____

12 (hopes / everyone's / high. / were)
➡ _____

13 (all / they / wanted / be / to / the / on / team. / senior)
➡ _____

14 (coach / the / up / looked / said, / and / "well, / a / it's / tie / Michael / between / Scottie." / and)
➡ _____

15 (leaped. / heart / Scottie's)
➡ _____

16 (was / he / surprised / he / that / tied / was / Michael. / with)
➡ _____

1 경기는 끝났다.

2 주니어 팀은 경기에서 승리했고, 모든 선수들이 행복했다.

3 그들이 로커 룸에 있는 동안, 코치가 모든 소년들에게 카드 한 장씩을 건네주었다.

4 그 카드는 주니어 팀의 모든 선수들의 명단을 담고 있었다.

5 "모두 알고 있듯이, 우리는 시니어 팀에 한 자리가 비어 있어." 코치가 말했다.

6 "여러분들이 시니어 팀에 들어갈 선수를 뽑아 보는 것이 어떨까?

7 명단 위의 이름 하나에 체크 표시를 해 주게."

8 Scottie는 명단을 보았고 자신의 이름을 보았다.

9 그러고는 한숨을 쉰 후 Michael의 이름 옆에 체크 표시를 하였다.

10 그는 Michael이 시니어 팀에 충분히 훌륭하다는 것을 부인할 수 없었다.

11 코치가 소년들로부터 모든 카드를 거두었다.

12 모든 선수들의 바람은 높았다.

13 그들은 모두 시니어 팀에 들어가기를 원했다.

14 코치가 올려다보고 말했다. "흠, Michael과 Scottie가 동점이구나."

15 Scottie의 심장이 뛰었다.

16 그는 자기가 Michael과 동점이 되어서 놀라웠다.

17 ("well," / the / said / coach, / "both / wonderful / are / enough / for / senior / the / team, / and / hard / it's / pick / to / player. / one / just)
➡ _____

18 (I / but / to, / have / so / Scottie." / pick / I'll)
➡ _____

19 (the / then / coach / over / walked / to / Scottie / "congratulations!" / said, / and)
➡ _____

20 (you, / "thank / but / is / Michael / a / shot. / such / good)
➡ _____

21 (makes / he / most / the / baskets," / Scottie. / said)
➡ _____

22 (course, / of / does," / he / coach. / the / said)
➡ _____

23 (he / "but / shoots / there's / whether / player / a / in / a / position / better / not. / or)
➡ _____

24 (important / it's / play / to / for / team! / the)
➡ _____

25 (worry. / don't // know / I / good / a / player / when / one." / see / I)
➡ _____

26 (walked / Scottie / of / out / room. / the)
➡ _____

27 (felt / he / giving / like / loud / a / and / shout. / happy)
➡ _____

28 (he / then / Michael. / saw)
➡ _____

29 (Scottie / suddenly / sorry / felt / him. / for)
➡ _____

30 (guess / "I / you / care, / don't / but / picked / I / for / you / the / team," / senior / Scottie. / said)
➡ _____

31 (smiled. / Michael // / what? / know / "you // YOU." / picked / I)
➡ _____

32 (was / Scottie / surprised. // did?" / "you)
➡ _____

33 ("yeah. // always / you / do / best, / your / and / player. / team / a / you're)
➡ _____

34 (you / today / for / played / team, / the / and / won / we / game. / the // congratulations!")
➡ _____

---

17 "흠." 코치가 말했다. "둘 다 시니어 팀에 들어가기에 충분히 훌륭하고, 단 한 명의 선수를 선정하는 것은 어려운 일이야.

18 그러나 나는 선정해야 하기에, Scottie를 뽑겠어."

19 그리고 코치가 Scottie에게 걸어와서 말했다. "축하해!"

20 "감사합니다. 그러나 Michael은 훌륭한 골잡이에요.

21 Michael이 득점을 가장 많이 하고 있어요." Scottie가 말했다.

22 "물론, Michael이 그렇지." 코치가 말했다.

23 "그러나 Michael은 더 나은 위치에 선수가 있든 없든, 숫을 쏴.

24 팀을 위해 경기하는 것이 중요해!

25 걱정 마. 나는 보면 좋은 선수인지 안단다."

26 Scottie는 방에서 걸어 나갔다.

27 그는 크고 기쁜 소리를 지르고 싶은 마음이었다.

28 그때 그는 Michael을 보았다.

29 갑자기 Scottie는 그에게 미안한 감정이 들었다.

30 "나는 네가 신경 쓰지 않으리라고 추측하지만, 시니어 팀에 너를 뽑았어."라고 Scottie가 말했다.

31 Michael이 미소 지었다. "너 그거 아니? 나도 너를 뽑았어."

32 Scottie가 놀랐다. "네가 그랬어?"

33 "응. 너는 항상 최선을 다 해, 그리고 너는 팀플레이어야.

34 오늘 너는 팀을 위해 경기했고, 우리는 게임에서 이겼는걸. 축하해!"

※ 다음 우리말을 영어로 쓰시오.

1 경기는 끝났다.
➡ _____

2 주니어 팀은 경기에서 승리했고, 모든 선수들이 행복했다.
➡ _____

3 그들이 로커 룸에 있는 동안, 코치가 모든 소년들에게 카드 한 장씩을 건네주었다.
➡ _____

4 그 카드는 주니어 팀의 모든 선수들의 명단을 담고 있었다.
➡ _____

5 "모두 알고 있듯이, 우리는 시니어 팀에 한 자리가 비어 있어." 코치가 말했다.
➡ _____

6 "여러분들이 시니어 팀에 들어갈 선수를 뽑아 보는 것이 어떨까?
➡ _____

7 명단 위의 이름 하나에 체크 표시를 해 주게."
➡ _____

8 Scottie는 명단을 보았고 자신의 이름을 보았다.
➡ _____

9 그러고는 한숨을 쉰 후 Michael의 이름 옆에 체크 표시를 하였다.
➡ _____

10 그는 Michael이 시니어 팀에 충분히 훌륭하다는 것을 부인할 수 없었다.
➡ _____

11 코치가 소년들로부터 모든 카드를 거두었다.
➡ _____

12 모든 선수들의 바람은 높았다.
➡ _____

13 그들은 모두 시니어 팀에 들어가기를 원했다.
➡ _____

14 코치가 올려다보고 말했다. "흠, Michael과 Scottie가 동점이구나."
➡ _____

15 Scottie의 심장이 뛰었다.
➡ _____

16 그는 자기가 Michael과 동점이 되어서 놀라웠다.
➡ _____

17 "흠." 코치가 말했다. "둘 다 시니어 팀에 들어가기에 충분히 훌륭하고, 단 한 명의 선수를 선정하는 것은 어려운 일이야.
➡ _____
_____

18 그러나 나는 선정해야 하기에, Scottie를 뽑겠어."

➡ _____

19 그리고 코치가 Scottie에게 걸어와서 말했다. "축하해!"

➡ _____

20 "감사합니다, 그러나 Michael은 훌륭한 골잡이에요.

➡ _____

21 Michael이 득점을 가장 많이 하고 있어요." Scottie가 말했다.

➡ _____

22 "물론, Michael이 그렇지." 코치가 말했다.

➡ _____

23 "그러나 Michael은 더 나은 위치에 선수가 있든 없든, 슛을 쏴.

➡ _____

24 팀을 위해 경기하는 것이 중요해!

➡ _____

25 걱정 마. 나는 보면 좋은 선수인지 안단다."

➡ _____

26 Scottie는 방에서 걸어 나갔다.

➡ _____

27 그는 크고 기쁜 소리를 지르고 싶은 마음이었다.

➡ _____

28 그때 그는 Michael을 보았다.

➡ _____

29 갑자기 Scottie는 그에게 미안한 감정이 들었다.

➡ _____

30 "나는 네가 신경 쓰지 않으리라고 추측하지만, 시니어 팀에 너를 뽑았어."라고 Scottie가 말했다.

➡ _____

31 Michael이 미소 지었다. "너 그거 아니? 나도 너를 뽑았어."

➡ _____

32 Scottie가 놀랐다. "네가 그랬어?"

➡ _____

33 "응. 너는 항상 최선을 다 해, 그리고 너는 팀플레이어야.

➡ _____

34 오늘 너는 팀을 위해 경기했고, 우리는 게임에서 이겼는걸. 축하해!"

➡ _____

※ 다음 우리말과 일치하도록 빈칸에 알맞은 말을 쓰시오.

After I Read B

1. Coach: _____!
2. I _____ _____ _____ you will _____ _____ on the senior team.
3. _____ _____ you!
4. Scottie: Thanks _____ _____! I'll _____ _____ _____!
5. Coach: I know that you are _____ _____.
6. Don't _____ so _____, and _____ _____!
7. Michael: Thank you so much! I'll _____ _____.

1. Coach: 축하해!
2. 난 네가 시니어 팀에서 잘할 거라고 확신한다.
3. 잘됐구나!
4. Scottie: 정말 고맙습니다. 최선을 다할게요!
5. Coach: 너도 충분히 훌륭하다는 것을 안다.
6. 너무 낙담하지 말고 계속 정진하거라.
7. Michael: 정말 고맙습니다. 더 열심히 할게요.

Before I Read

1. My heart _____ when I _____ _____ these two players.
2. Michael was _____ a _____ _____.
3. _____ _____ can _____ that he was a great player.
4. Michael could make _____ _____ baskets _____ Scottie helped him _____ _____.

1. 이 두 선수들을 생각할 때면 내 심장이 뛴다.
2. Michael은 정말 훌륭한 골잡이였다.
3. 그가 위대한 선수였다는 것은 누구도 부인할 수 없을 것이다.
4. Michael은 Scottie가 그를 많이 도와주었기 때문에 많은 골을 넣을 수 있었다.

Let's Write

1. Hello, _____,
2. We play soccer _____ _____.`
3. We _____ passing and _____ _____ it is important _____ _____ and shoot well in soccer.
4. _____ is also important _____ _____ good teamwork.
5. _____ good teamwork, _____ hard _____ _____ the match.
6. Do you _____ _____ _____ a team player?
7. Come, _____ _____ and _____ team play.

1. 안녕, 모두들,
2. 우리는 방과 후에 축구를 해.
3. 축구에서는 패스와 슛을 잘하는 것이 중요하기 때문에 우리는 패스와 슛을 연습해.
4. 좋은 팀워크를 갖는 것도 또한 중요해.
5. 좋은 팀워크 없이는 시합을 이기는 것이 어려워.
6. 너도 팀플레이어가 되고 싶니?
7. 와서 우리와 함께 해서 팀플레이를 즐기자.

※ 다음 우리말을 영어로 쓰시오.

After I Read B

1. Coach: 축하해!
   ➡ _____

2. 난 네가 시니어 팀에서 잘할 거라고 확신한다.
   ➡ _____

3. 잘됐구나!
   ➡ _____

4. Scottie: 정말 고맙습니다. 최선을 다할게요!
   ➡ _____

5. Coach: 너도 충분히 훌륭하다는 것을 안다.
   ➡ _____

6. 너무 낙담하지 말고 계속 정진하거라.
   ➡ _____

7. Michael: 정말 고맙습니다. 더 열심히 할게요.
   ➡ _____

Before I Read

1. 이 두 선수들을 생각할 때면 내 심장이 뛴다.
   ➡ _____

2. Michael은 정말 훌륭한 골잡이였다.
   ➡ _____

3. 그가 위대한 선수였다는 것은 누구도 부인할 수 없을 것이다.
   ➡ _____

4. Michael은 Scottie가 그를 많이 도와주었기 때문에 많은 골을 넣을 수 있었다.
   ➡ _____

Let's Write

1. 안녕, 모두들.
   ➡ _____

2. 우리는 방과 후에 축구를 해.
   ➡ _____

3. 축구에서는 패스와 슛을 잘하는 것이 중요하기 때문에 우리는 패스와 슛을 연습해.
   ➡ _____

4. 좋은 팀워크를 갖는 것도 또한 중요해.
   ➡ _____

5. 좋은 팀워크 없이는 시합을 이기는 것이 어려워.
   ➡ _____

6. 너도 팀플레이어가 되고 싶니?
   ➡ _____

7. 와서 우리와 함께 해서 팀플레이를 즐기자.
   ➡ _____

MEMO

MEMO

영어 문제집

1학기

정답 및 해설

능률 | 양현권

중 2

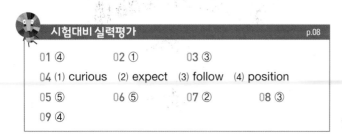

What Is Your Color?

시험대비 실력평가
p.08

01 ④　　　02 ①　　　03 ③
04 (1) curious　(2) expect　(3) follow　(4) position
05 ⑤　　　06 ⑤　　　07 ②　　　08 ③
09 ④

01 ④ 이외의 단어는 성격과 관련이 있는 단어이다. talkative: 수다스러운 open: 개방적인 warm: 따뜻한 witty: 재치 있는 yummy: 맛있는

02 as: ~으로 / 이것을 예로 들어보자. / 나는 그녀를 나의 가장 친한 친구로 생각한다.

03 chance: 가능성, 기회 / 우리 팀이 이길 가능성이 있니? 이것은 당신에게 큰 기회입니다.

04 (1) curious: 호기심 많은 (2) expect: 기대하다 (3) follow: 따르다 (4) position: 위치, 자리, 자세

05 season: 계절

06 please: 기쁘게 하다 / 어떤 사람을 행복하고 만족스럽게 만들다

07 solve: 해결하다 / 어려움을 야기하는 것에 대한 해결책을 찾다

08 flavor: 맛, 풍미 taste: 맛 / 그 아이스크림은 오렌지 맛이다.

09 witty: 재치 있는 funny: 우스운, 재미있는 / 너는 항상 그녀가 재치 있다고 말했어.

서술형 시험대비
p.09

01 (s)etting　　02 (l)ike
03 (1) faithful　(2) energizer　(3) imaginative
04 (1) prefer　(2) serve　(3) sounds　(4) organize
05 (1) (F)ashionable　(2) (C)haracter
06 (1) Each person's fingerprints are unique.
　　(2) We know that this animal is very faithful.
　　(3) How many lines are there on the table?
　　(4) This country has a long tradition of respecting old people.
　　(5) Can you make the chocolate cake on your own?

01 setting: 환경, 장소, 배경 / 로마는 연애를 하기에 완벽한 장소이다. / 그의 첫 번째 소설의 배경은 런던이었다.

02 How did you like ~?: ~는 어땠니? would like to 동사원형: ~하고 싶다 / 영화는 어땠어? / 당신에게 몇 가지 질문을 하고 싶군요.

03 (1) faithful: 충직한, 충성스러운, 신의가 있는 / 그녀는 충실한 친구입니다. (2) energizer: 활력을 주는 사람 / 나의 삼촌은 활력을 주는 사람이다. (3) imaginative: 창의적인, 상상력이 풍부한 / 멋진 그림을 그리기 위해서는 창의적이어야 한다.

04 (1) prefer: 선호하다 / 나는 컴퓨터 게임을 하는 것보다 책을 읽는 것을 선호한다. (2) serve: 제공하다 / 그 식당은 어떤 음식을 제공하니? (3) sound: ~처럼 들리다[생각되다] / 그 이야기는 사실처럼 들린다. (4) organize: 조직하다, 정리 정돈하다 / Jack은 파티를 준비할 것이다.

05 (1) cool: 멋진 fashionable: 멋있는 (2) personality: 성격, 개성 character: 성격, 기질

06 (1) unique: 독특한, 하나뿐인 (2) faithful: 충직한, 충성스러운, 신의가 있는 (3) line: 행, 선 (4) tradition: 전통 (5) on one's own: 혼자서, 단독으로

교과서
Conversation

핵심 Check
p.10~11

1 that he is honest　　　2 He, says, that, is
3 It is said that we can't take pictures here.
4 Which, I, prefer, comedies / like, (b)etter, to
5 Which do you prefer, baseball or tennis? / I prefer baseball to tennis.

교과서 대화문 익히기

Check(√) True or False
p.12

1 T　2 F　3 T　4 T　5 F　6 T

교과서 확인학습
p.14~15

Listen & Speak 1 A

1 I'm / too, don't we go / open / say that, serves, on
2 Are there, this / say that there's / What kind of / say that it's really exciting

시험대비 기본평가   p.16

01 ⑤   02 What   03 ②   04 ③

02 What: 무엇 What is ~ like?: ~는 어때?(성격을 묻는 표현)

03 They say that 주어 동사 ~.: ~라고 그래(제3자에게서 얻은 정보를 전달할 때 사용할 수 있는 표현)

04 'Which ~ do you like most?'는 상대방이 가장 좋아하는 것을 묻는 표현이다.

시험대비 실력평가   p.17~18

01 ④   02 ③   03 ③   04 ②
05 ①, ⑤   06 ④   07 ③   08 ②
09 ④   10 Which one do you prefer?
11 that   12 ⑤   13 (C) – (A) – (B)

01 Sweet Snack에 가자고 제안한 것에 동의하며, 오늘 문을 열었는지 질문할 수 있다.

02 serve: 제공하다

03 일요일에 문을 열었다고 했지만, 토요일에 여는지에 대한 정보는 언급되어 있지 않다. on weekends: 주말마다

04 look at: ~을 보다 Which ~: 어떤 ~

05 yummy: 맛있는 delicious: 맛있는, 맛좋은 tasty: 맛있는

06 ④ 소녀가 소년에게 묻고 있다.

07 What kind of dance show do you prefer? → What kind of dance show is it? 청소년 센터에서 하는 특별 댄스 공연에 대한 정보가 나와 있으므로, 댄스 공연에 대한 선호를 묻는 질문은 어울리지 않는다.

08 선호에 대해 묻고 있는 질문에, 무엇을 더 좋아한다는 답이 아닌 'Of course I do.(물론 나도 그래.)'는 어울리지 않는다.

09 ⓐ about myself ⓑ What type of ⓒ good at ⓓ They say that ⓔ ask my teacher for some advice

10 prefer: 선호하다

11 (A)와 (C)는 say의 목적어가 되는 명사절을 연결하는 접속사로 사용되었다. (B) 여기서 that은 position을 수식하는 지시 형용사로 사용되었다.

12 ① 어떤 자세로 잠을 자는지 이야기하고 있다. ② 등을 대고 자는 자세가 수면에 가장 좋은 자세라고 과학자들이 말했다. ③ 등을 대고 자는 사람들은 따뜻하고 친근하다고 한다. ④ B는 등을 대고 잠을 잔다. ⑤ B가 실제로 따뜻하고 친근한지에 대한 내용은 나와 있지 않다.

13 저것이 새로운 간식 가게인지 물어보는 질문에 (C) 그렇다고 대답하여, 맛있는 팬케이크 있다고 다른 사람들에게서 들은 사실에 대해 말하자, (A) 배가 고프다고 팬케이크를 먹자고 제안한다. (B) 상대방이 그 제안에 동의한다.

서술형 시험대비   p.19

01 (A) → (C) → (D) → (B)   02 (B) → (C) → (A)
03 side   04 What, How
05 Scientists say that the back
06 Which one do you prefer?
07 They say that there's going to be a class party.

01 매우 덥다는 말에 (A) 덥다고 동의한다. (C) 아이스크림 먹자고 제안하자 (D) 좋은 생각이라고 말하며, 어떤 맛을 선호하는지 질문하자 (B) 초콜릿 맛을 좋아한다고 대답한다.

02 주말에 좋은 프로그램이 있는지 묻자 (B) 토요일에 청소년 센터에서 댄스 공연이 있다고 말한 사실을 전해주자 (C) 어떤 종류의 댄스 공연인지 질문하고 (A) 인도의 댄스 공연이라고 대답한다.

03 side: 옆(면), 측면

04 What is ~ like?: ~는 어때?(성격을 묻는 표현) How good: 얼마나 좋은

05 Scientists say that ~: 과학자들이 ~이라고 해.

06 Which ~: 어떤 ~ prefer: 선호하다

07 there is ~.: ~가 있다. They say that 주어 동사 ~.: 그들이/사람들이 ~라고 그러네

Grammar

핵심 Check   p.20~21

1 (1) Which (2) Which   **2** What → Which

3 (1) herself (2) herself (3) themselves

시험대비 기본평가   p.22

01 ⑤   02 ①   03 ③

04 (1) Who → Which (2) What → Which

   (3) me → myself (4) you → yourself

---

01 주어와 목적어가 동일인이므로 재귀대명사가 적절하다.

02 둘 사이를 비교하는 better가 있으므로 한정된 대상 중에서 답하는 질문을 이끄는 which가 적절하다.

03 ③ of itself: 저절로

04 (1) 형용사로 쓰여서 '어떤'을 뜻하는 which가 적절하다. (2) 한정된 대상으로 질문하고 있으므로 which가 적절하다. (3) 주어와 목적어의 관계가 동일하므로 재귀대명사가 적절하다. (4) help oneself to: [음식물 따위]를 마음대로 집어먹다, 자유로이 먹다

시험대비 실력평가   p.23~25

01 ①   02 ④   03 ⑤

04 (1) herself (2) himself (3) myself (4) Which

05 ①   06 ①

07 (1) Which way is the post office, please?

   (2) My little sister practices walking by herself.

   (3) Heaven helps those who help themselves.

08 ②   09 enjoying / themselves   10 ②

11 ③   12 ④   13 Which   14 ④

15 (1) ourselves (2) itself (3) yourself   16 ⑤

17 ③

18 (1) your → yourself (2) us → ourselves

   (3) What → Which (4) oneself → herself

---

01 ①번은 강조 용법으로 쓰인 재귀대명사이고 나머지는 모두 재귀 용법의 재귀대명사이다.

02 ① She can express herself through the dress. ② Which subject should I study more? ③ Jane doesn't think about herself. She always thinks about others. ⑤ I could express myself in English when I was a little child.

03 주어와 목적어의 관계가 동일하므로 재귀대명사가 적절하다.

04 (1) by oneself: 혼자서 (2) 강조 용법으로 쓰인 재귀대명사이다. (3) 주어와 목적어가 같은 재귀 용법으로 쓰인 재귀대명사이다. (4) 둘 중에서 선택을 나타내므로 Which가 적절하다.

05 첫 번째 문장에서는 주어를 강조하는 herself가, 두 번째 문장에서는 비교급 harder로 보아 한정된 대상으로 질문하고 있으므로 (비교급은 두 개를 비교하는 것임에 유의) Which가 적절하다.

06 ① Donald looked at himself on the water. Donald와 목적어가 같은 경우 목적어로 oneself가 아니라 himself로 쓰는 것이 적절하다.

07 (1) 길을 물을 때 정해진 길 중에서 어느 길인지를 묻는 것이므로 which가 적절하다. (2) practice는 동명사를 목적어로 받으므로 walking으로 써야 한다. by oneself: 혼자서, 스스로 (3) 주어와 목적어가 동일하므로 재귀대명사 themselves를 쓴다. those who: ~하는 사람들

08 뒤에 나오는 year를 수식하면서 '2010년대에서'라고 한정되고 있으므로 which가 나와야 한다. customer complaint: 고객들의 불만

09 enjoy oneself: 즐기다, 즐겁게 보내다

10 ② Which do you prefer, swimming or running? 뒤에서 swimming or running으로 선택을 묻고 있으므로 Which가 적절하다.

11 목적어가 주어와 같은 대상이며 주어가 Harry and Sharon이므로 themselves가 적절하다.

12 place의 목적어가 주어와 같은 대상이므로 재귀대명사가 적절하다. place A above B: A를 B 위에 두다, B보다 A를 더 중시하다

13 그림에 3 종류의 주스가 있고 가장 싼 것을 마시겠다고 답하고 있으므로 한정된 대상의 경우에 쓰이는 which가 적절하다.

14 ④ Jake를 만났다고 답하고 있으므로 herself가 아니라 her가 적절하다.

15 (1) 주어와 목적어의 관계가 동일하므로 재귀대명사가 적절하다. (2) of itself: 저절로 (3) 명령문으로 주어와 목적어가 같은 대상이므로 yourself가 알맞다.

16 of these issues로 한정되고 있으므로 Which가 나와야 한다.

17 <보기>와 ③번은 재귀 용법의 재귀대명사이다. ① by oneself: 혼자서 ②, ⑤ 강조 용법으로 쓰인 재귀대명사 ④ for oneself: 혼자 힘으로, 자신을 위해서

18 (1) 전치사 in의 목적어로 재귀대명사 yourself가 적절하다. (2) 주어와 목적어의 관계가 동일하므로 재귀대명사가 적절하다. (3) 일주일의 7개 요일로 한정되고 있으므로 which가 적절하다. (4) 주어가 she이므로 herself가 적절하다.

01 (1) herself   (2) yourself   (3) itself

02 (1) We ourselves went camping last weekend.

   (2) Even the best sports teams themselves lose from time to time.

   (3) Mr. Green himself came out to welcome us.

   (4) Grace became an architect and designed the building itself.

   (5) Alex met the famous actress herself.

03 Which

04 (1) He was proud of himself after he won the contest.

   (2) She said to herself as she smiled sadly.

   (3) Which do you prefer, working with other people or alone?

   (4) Which day of the week do you like best?

05 (1) Many of us do not know how to love ourselves.

   (2) He himself promised that he would stop drinking.

   (3) Evelyne was left alone. She looked at herself in the mirror and said to herself.

   (4) Tom spent a lot of time by himself that year.

   (5) I taught myself how to play the guitar.

   (6) The greenhouse effect in itself is actually natural.

06 Which / cake

07 (1) itself   (2) myself   (3) herself   (4) myself

   (5) himself

08 (1) 어떤 색을 가장 좋아하니?   (2) 무슨 색을 좋아하니?

   (1) 답을 할 대상이 몇몇 색으로 한정되어 있음.

   (2) 답을 할 대상이 한정되어 있지 않음.

09 Which, yourself

01 (1) 주어와 목적어의 관계가 동일하므로 재귀대명사가 적절하다. (2) help yourself to ~: ~을 마음대로[양껏] 드세요 (3) 주어를 강조하는 강조 용법으로 쓰인 재귀대명사가 적절하다.

02 재귀대명사가 '스스로', '직접'이라는 의미로 주어나 목적어를 강조할 수 있으며 강조 용법으로 쓰인 재귀대명사는 생략할 수 있다. architect: 건축가

03 그림에 3 종류의 아이스크림이 있으므로 답이 될 만한 대상이 한정된 경우에 쓰이는 which가 적절하다.

04 (1) be proud of: ~을 자랑으로 여기다 (2) say to oneself: 혼잣말하다 (3) Which ~, A or B?: A 아니면 B, 어느 것을 ~하는지? (4) 정해진 요일 중에서 답해야 하는 것이므로 which를 쓴다.

05 (1) 주어와 목적어의 관계가 동일하므로 재귀대명사를 써야 한다. (2) 강조 용법의 재귀대명사가 적절하다. (3) 자기 자신을

보고 자기 자신에게 말하는 것이므로 재귀대명사가 적절하다. (4) by oneself가 '혼자서'라는 뜻이지만 주어가 Tom이므로 by himself로 써야 한다. (5) 스스로를 가르쳐 독학한 것으로 주어와 목적어가 동일하므로 재귀대명사를 써야 한다. (6) 주어가 단수이므로 itself로 써야 한다. in itself: 본질적으로

06 3개의 케이크 중에서 말하는 것이므로 which를 이용해야 한다.

07 (1) 주어가 History이므로 itself (2) 주어가 I이므로 주어를 강조하는 myself (3) 주어가 Mary이므로 herself (4) 주어가 I이므로 myself (5) 주어가 John이므로 himself가 적절하다.

08 which는 what과 비슷한 의미를 지니지만, what은 전제되지 않은 대상에 대해 질문할 때 사용할 수 있는 반면, which는 전제된 대상 가운데에서 선택하여 응답하게 한다는 차이가 있다.

09 둘 중에서 선택하는 것이므로 which가 적절하고 마음껏 먹으라는 help yourself가 적절하다.

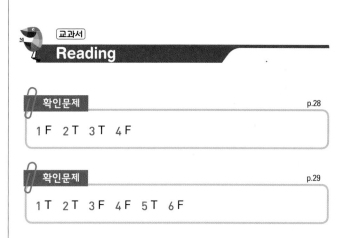

교과서
Reading

1 F   2 T   3 T   4 F

1 T   2 T   3 F   4 F   5 T   6 F

01 What   02 Who   03 What, type

04 these, questions

05 interesting, personality, test

06 Which, activities, which, ones   07 good, at

08 free, having, fun, with

09 taking, chances, following   10 on, my, own

11 learning, following

12 making, planning, out   13 pleasing

14 on, stage, with, directions   15 solving

16 your, color   17 Circle, from, with, most

18 What, type, of, person

19 wonderful, energizer

20 witty, lively, in 21 excellent, organizer

22 faithful, best, with

23 Knowing, yourself, wisdom   24 great, listener

25 caring, in, groups   26 curious, thinker

27 cool, on, your, own　　　　28 how, much

29 Take, as　　30 unique, special

31 Why, don't, you, make, the, most, of

1 What Is Your Color?

2 Who am I?

3 What type of person am I?

4 Do you have these questions?

5 Here we have an interesting personality test for you.

6 Step 1 Which activities do you enjoy, and which ones are you good at?

7 I enjoy … / I'm good at …

8 1. being free and having fun. 2. working with people.

9 3. taking chances. 4. following traditions.

10 5. working on my own. 6. writing stories.

11 7. learning new things. 8. following the rules.

12 9. making new friends. 10. planning things out.

13 11. pleasing others. 12. finding new patterns.

14 13. being on stage. 14. working with directions.

15 15. solving puzzles. 16. playing sports.

16 Step 2 What is your color?

17 Circle the numbers from Step 1, and find the line with the most circles.

18 Step 3 What type of person are you?

19 If you have more circles on the orange line, you are a wonderful energizer.

20 You are witty and lively, and you work best in game settings.

21 If you have more circles on the gold line, you are an excellent organizer.

22 You are faithful and careful, and you work best with clear rules.

23 Knowing yourself is the beginning of all wisdom. – Aristotle

24 If you have more circles on the blue line, you are a great listener.

25 You are warm and caring, and you work best in groups.

26 If you have more circles on the green line, you are a curious thinker.

27 You are cool and quiet, and you work best on your own.

28 What is your type, and how much do you like it?

29 Take this personality test as a first step and try to find your true color.

30 Everyone is unique and has a special color.

31 Why don't you listen to yourself, find special things about yourself, and make the most of them?

01 personality, type	02 ②, ⑤	03 ④
04 ③	05 directions	06 ④	07 ③
08 finding → find	09 ①	10 ①
11 Knowing [To know]	12 ④	13 ②

14 Which subjects should I study more? Which after-school activities should I join?

15 ④　　　　16 If you have more circles on the orange line, you are a wonderful energizer.

17 (A) an excellent organizer　(B) gold　　18 ③

19 ②　　　　20 to you → to yourself, about you → about yourself　　21 ⑤　　22 take, part, in, participate, in　　23 ③　　24 ②

01 여기에 당신의 '유형'을 알아내기 위한 '성격' 검사가 있습니다.

02 ⓐ와 ②번, ⑤번은 동명사, 나머지는 다 현재분사

03 테스트 항목에는 'making' the rules가 아니라 'following' the rules라고 되어 있다.

04 ③ take a chance = take a risk: 잘 되든 안 되든 해보다, 모험을 하다

05 directions: 지시(무엇을 할지, 무언가를 어떻게 할지, 어딘가에 어떻게 도착할지를 말해주는 지시)

06 ④ 사람들이 어떤 활동에 가장 많이 동그라미 표시를 하는지는 대답할 수 없다. ① It's a personality test. ② The things such as 'who I am' and 'what type of person I am.' ③ There are 16 activities. ⑤ It mainly asks about 'what I enjoy' and 'what I'm good at.'

07 이 글은 즐겨하는 활동에 동그라미 표시를 하고, 가장 많은 표시가 있는 줄을 찾는 내용인데, 줄에 색깔 표시가 있으므로 빈칸에 들어갈 말로는 '당신의 색깔은 무엇입니까?'가 적절하다.

08 주어 you가 생략된 명령문이다. circle과 find로 시작하는 동사구가 and로 대등하게 연결되도록 하는 것이 적절하다.

09 ① 이 사람은 4, 5, 6, 7, 10, 12, 15번에 동그라미 표시를 했고, 1번 항목인 자유로우며 재미있게 놀기에는 동그라미 표시를 하지 않았다.

10 ⓐ with clear rules: 분명한 규칙이 제시된 경우에, ⓒ in groups: 떼를 지어, 집단과 더불어

11 주어 자리이므로 동명사나 to부정사로 써야 한다.

12 ⓓ와 ④번은 '멋진', ①과 ⑤ '시원한', ② '차분한', '침착한', ③ '(요리 따위가) 식은

13 ② 게임 환경에서 가장 잘 일하는 사람은 '주황색' 줄에 더 많은 동그라미 표시가 있는 사람이다.

14 '어떤 과목을 더 공부해야 할까?' '어떤 방과 후 활동에 가입해야 할까?'를 가리킨다.

15 ④ 자신의 '장점'에서 시작하려고 한다.

16 'energizer'를 보충하면 된다.

17 '황금색' 줄에 더 많은 동그라미 표시가 있기 때문에 이 사람은 '뛰어난 조직가'이고 충직하고 조심스럽다.

18 ⓑ와 ②번, ③번, ⑤번은 동명사, ①번, ④번은 현재분사

19 as: (자격·기능 등이) ~으로, ~로서

20 주어와 목적어가 같으므로 재귀대명사로 쓰는 것이 적절하다.

21 ⑤ make the most of = make the best of: ~을 최대한 이용하다, ① 벌충[만회]하다, ② ~을 중시하다, ③ ~을 돌보다, ④ ~에 마음을 쓰다, ~에 관심을 가지다

22 join = take part in = participate in: ~에 가입하다

23 내가 호기심 많은 사색가이고 멋지고 조용하며, 혼자서 (일할 때) 가장 잘한다고 말해주는 것은 '성격' 검사라고 하는 것이 적절하다. ① 인기, ② 수행, ④ 지능, ⑤ 인구

24 ⓒ와 ②는 명사적 용법, ①, ④, ⑤ 부사적 용법, ③ 형용사적 용법

서술형 시험대비 p.38~39

01 (A) interesting (B) which (C) at
02 on my own
03 (A) a wonderful energizer (B) orange 04 kind
05 Who am I?, What type of person am I? 06 having
07 a curious thinker 08 gold
09 (A) blue (B) in groups 10 (1) 나는 호기심 많은 사색가이다. (2) 나는 멋지고 조용하다. (3) 나는 혼자서 (일할 때) 가장 잘한다. 11 that
12 listening 13 special things (about yourself)

01 (A) '흥미로운' 성격 검사가 있다고 해야 하므로 interesting이 적절하다. interested: 관심[흥미] 있어 하는, (B) 질문의 답이 될 만한 대상이 한정된 경우 which로 시작하는 의문문이 적절하다. (C) 어떤 활동을 '잘하나요?'라고 해야 하므로 at이 적절하다. be good at: ~에 능숙하다, ~을 잘하다, be good for: ~에 좋다

02 on one's own: 혼자서, 단독으로(alone)

03 '주황색' 줄에 더 많은 동그라미 표시가 있기 때문에 당신은 '훌륭한 활력소 (역할을 하는 사람)'입니다.

04 what type은 '어떤 유형'이라는 뜻으로, what kind와 비슷한 의미를 나타낸다.

05 '나는 누구인가?' '나는 어떤 유형의 사람인가?'를 가리킨다.

06 enjoy와 at의 목적어에 해당하므로 동명사로 쓰는 것이 적절하다.

07 초록색 줄에 더 많은 동그라미 표시가 있기 때문에, 위의 사람은 '호기심 많은 사색가'이다.

08 만약 어떤 사람이 분명한 규칙이 제시된 경우에 가장 일을 잘하면, 그 사람의 색깔은 '황금색'이다.

09 '푸른색'이 경청자이고 '집단과 더불어' 가장 잘 일한다.

10 성격 검사에서 말한 것을 쓰면 된다.

11 목적어를 이끄는 접속사 'that'이 적절하다.

12 Why don't you 동사원형? = How about ~ing? = What about ~ing?: ~하는 게 어때?

13 '(자기 자신에 관한) 특별한 것들'을 가리킨다.

영역별 핵심문제 p.41~45

01 (e)nergetic 02 ④ 03 ①
04 (1) activities (2) caring 05 ⑤ 06 ③
07 ④ 08 What kind of dance
09 People say that it's really exciting.
10 (A) result (B) got 11 ① 12 ②
13 ④, ⑤ 14 ② 15 ③
16 (1) Namho enjoys looking at himself in the mirror.
   (2) Which picture do you like more?
   (3) Please help yourself to the cake.
17 (1) She solved the difficult problems for herself.
   (2) Bill graduated from the school himself.
      또는 Bill himself graduated from the school.
   (3) Which was more interesting, Avatar or Alita?
18 (1) 앞에 you → yourselves (2) What → Which
19 ①
20 (1) Don't compare yourself with others.
   (2) Which sport do you play, tennis or baseball?
   (3) He himself invented the machine which could cook in itself.
   (4) Nora never tried to do anything for(또는 by) herself.
21 activities 22 ②, ⑤ 23 ④ 24 ③
25 ④ 26 ③ 27 ① 28 special
29 Why don't you show your dreams, plans, and ideas on the board?
30 Hamlet–type → Don–Quixote–type

01 주어진 단어는 동의어 관계이다. faithful: 충직한, 충성스러운, 신의가 있는 loyal: 충성스러운 active: 활기 있는 energetic: 활동적인

02 truth: 사실 deceive: 속이다, break the law: 법을 어기다

honest: 정직한

03 find: 찾다 discover: 찾다, 알아내다 / 그것의 해결책을 찾아낼 수 있겠니?

04 (1) activity: 활동 / 우리는 수영, 서핑, 그림 그리는 것 같은 많은 활동을 즐겼다. (2) caring: 배려하는, 보살피는 / 그는 배려하는 사람이다. 그는 가난한 아이들과 나이든 사람들을 돌보기를 즐긴다.

05 (C) 저 멋진 여행 가방들을 보라는 말에 (D) 좋아 보인다고 대답한다. (B) 어떤 것을 선호지 질문하자 (A) 검은색 여행 가방을 선호한다고 대답하고, 상대방의 선호에 대해서 묻자 (E) 상대방은 흰색 가방을 선호한다고 대답한다.

06 ③ 어제 Jane의 다리가 부러졌다는 말에, 전화를 해서 왜 안 오는지 묻겠다는 말을 어색하다.

07 주말에 무슨 좋은 프로그램이 있는지 묻는 질문에, 토요일에 청소년 센터에서 특별 댄스 공연이 있다고 대답한다. Are there ~?: ~가 있니?

08 what kind of ~: 어떤 종류의 ~

09 People say that 주어 동사 ~.: (사람들이) ~라고 그러네. exciting: 흥미로운

10 result: 결과 get: 얻다, 가지다

11 ① like: (동사)좋아하다 / 이외의 보기는 전치사로서 '~ 같은, ~처럼'의 의미로 사용되었다.

12 They say that a da-Vinci-type person is imaginative. They say that 주어 동사 ~.: (그들이) ~라고 그러네. imaginative: 창의적인, 상상력이 풍부한

13 ④번과 ⑤번은 강조 용법으로 생략할 수 있다.

14 ① My grandmother lives there by herself. ③ Which do you like better, tea or coffee? ④ George himself made the cake for his girlfriend. ⑤ Why don't you introduce yourself?.

15 ③번은 재귀 용법으로 쓰인 재귀대명사이고, 나머지는 모두 강조 용법의 재귀대명사이다.

16 (1), (3) 주어와 목적어가 동일할 경우 재귀대명사를 써야 한다.

17 (1) for oneself: 혼자 힘으로 (2) 강조 용법으로 쓰인 재귀대명사로 행위자 바로 뒤나 문장의 끝에 쓰여 행위자를 강조하며 생략할 수 있다. graduate from: 졸업하다 (3) Avatar와 Alita 중에서 선택하는 것이므로 which를 써야 한다.

18 (1) 주어와 목적어가 동일한 경우 재귀대명사를 써야 한다. (2) of the three로 한정되고 있으므로 which가 적절하다.

19 by oneself: 혼자서 pull out ~: ~을 꺼내다 / '동사+부사'로 된 경우 it, them 따위의 인칭대명사 목적어는 반드시 동사와 부사 사이에 위치해야 함에도 주의한다.

20 (1) 명령문의 주어는 you이므로 주어와 목적어의 관계가 동일하므로 재귀대명사를 써야 한다. (2) tennis or baseball이라고 한정된 대상 중에서 묻고 있으므로 which가 적절하다. (3) 주

어를 강조하는 강조 용법으로 쓰인 재귀대명사로 주어가 He이므로 himself가 적절하다. (4) for oneself: 혼자 힘으로, by oneself: 혼자서

21 '활동'을 가리킨다.

22 have fun = have a good time = enjoy oneself: 즐기다, ③ 놀리다

23 take a chance = take a risk: 잘 되든 안 되든 해보다, 모험을 하다

24 ③ 위 글은 '4가지 색깔별 성격 유형'에 관한 글이다.

25 주황색 줄에 더 많은 동그라미 표시가 있는데, 보기 ④번은 초록색 줄의 성격에 해당한다.

26 ③ 황금색 유형이 왜 분명한 규칙이 제시된 경우에 가장 잘 일하는지는 대답할 수 없다. ① A wonderful energizer. ② Gold. ④ I'm a great listener. ⑤ Yes.

27 ⓐ와 ①번은 단계, ② 걸음을 옮기다, ③ (죽 이어진 계단의 한) 단[계단], ④ 내딛다, (발을) 디디다, ⑤ 방법, 조치

28 모든 사람들은 '특별한' 색깔을 지니고 있기 때문에, 스스로에게 귀를 기울이고, 스스로에 관하여 '특별한' 것들을 발견하며, 그것들을 최대한 활용해 보면 어떨까요?

29 don't를 보충하면 된다.

30 글쓴이는 '돈키호테형'이라고 말해진다.

단원별 예상문제 p.46~49

01 (s)etting 02 ④ 03 (f)ollow, (O)rganize, (P)lease / (1) please (2) follow (3) organize

04 (1) inventor (2) (p)ersonality (3) result (4) season (5) (u)nique (6) stage

05 Which sleeping position do you prefer?

06 healthy → unhealthy 07 ④ 08 ③

09 ④ 10 They will eat some pancakes at a new snack shop. 11 ① 12 flavor

13 ② 14 ④ 15 ⑤

16 performance → personality 17 ②, ⑤

18 ①, ④ 19 The personality test

20 (1) 나는 뛰어난 조직가이다.
  (2) 나는 충직하고 조심스럽다.
  (3) 나는 분명한 규칙이 제시된 경우에 가장 잘 일한다.

21 ① 22 ④ 23 a problem solver

24 ②

01 setting: 환경, 장소, 배경

02 ④ chance: 가능성; 기회 ④에서는 '기회'의 의미로 사용되었다./ 나는 전에 그의 음악을 들을 기회가 있었어.

03 (1) please: 기쁘게 하다, 어떤 사람을 행복하고 만족스럽게 만들다 / 우리는 모든 사람들을 기쁘게 할 수 없다. (2) follow: 따

르다, 누군가가 당신에게 조언해 준 것을 하다 / 너는 그의 조언을 따라야 한다. (3) organize: 조직하다, 활동 또는 행사를 준비하거나 정리하다 / 폴더를 사용하여 메시지를 정리할 수 있다.

04 (1) inventor: 발명가 (2) personality: 성격, 개성 (3) result: 결과 (4) season: 계절 (5) unique: 독특한, 하나뿐인 (6) stage: 무대

05 which: 어느 position: 위치, 자리, 자세 prefer: 선호하다

06 '수면 과학자들은 우리가 나쁜 자세로 잠을 자면 건강해진다.'고 한다는 말은 내용상 어색하다. unhealthy: 건강하지 못한

07 ④ What is ~ like?: ~는 어때? / 성격을 묻는 표현이므로 좋아하는 것을 말하는 것은 어울리지 않는다.

08 ⓐ In which position ⓑ What are ⓒ say that they ⓓ How good ⓔ say that it's

09 would like to 동사원형: ~하고 싶다

10 will: ~할 것이다 pancake: 팬케이크 snack shop: 간식 가게

11 Why don't we ~?: ~하는 게 어때?

12 flavor: 맛

13 ① Jane knows herself. ③ Socrates, do you know yourself? ④ Andy finished the difficult project himself. ⑤ He went there by himself. 주어와 목적어의 관계가 동일할 경우 재귀대명사를 써야 한다. by oneself: 혼자서

14 ④ of these questions로 한정되고 있으므로 Which가 적절하다.

15 ⓐ with people: 사람들과 '함께', ⓑ with directions: 지침을 '가지고'

16 만일 당신이 누구인지 혹은 어떤 유형의 사람인지 알고 싶다면 당신은 흥미로운 '성격' 검사를 해볼 수 있다. performance: 수행, 공연, 연주회

17 ⓐ와 ①, ③, ④는 명사적 용법, ② 부사적 용법(목적), ⑤ 형용사적 용법

18 Why don't you 동사원형? = How about ~ing? = What about ~ing?: ~ 하는 게 어때?

19 '성격 검사'를 가리킨다.

20 성격 검사에서 말한 것을 쓰면 된다.

21 ① '어떤 과목을 더 열심히 공부해야 할까?'라고 물었을 뿐이다. ② 뛰어난 조직가 유형이다. ③ 충직하고 조심스러운 성격이다. ④ 분명한 규칙이 제시된 경우에 가장 잘 일한다. ⑤ 자신의 장점을 최대한 활용하고 싶어 한다.

22 위 글은 각 색깔의 유형에 속하는 사람의 구체적인 특징을 보다 상세히 설명하는 글이므로, 제목으로는 '색깔별로 내가 누군지 알아맞혀봐!'가 적절하다.

23 초록색 유형인 사람은 '문제 해결자'이다.

24 ② 기술과 용기를 가치 있게 여기는 사람은 '주황색' 유형의 사람이다.

01 (1) Yes, they do. → Yes, they are.
   (2) deliciously → delicious
   (3) What flavor → Which flavor

02 Which cake do you like most

03 I like the chocolate cake most.

04 (1) It is true that nature itself is a teacher.
   (2) One can use Taekwondo to defend oneself.
   (3) Which book did he read, this black one or that red one?
   (4) What color do you want to paint it?
   (5) Come in and make yourself(또는 yourselves) at home.

05 (1) Van Gogh는 자기 자신을 그렸다. (자화상을 그렸다)
   (2) Van Gogh는 그를 그렸다.
   (1) 그림을 그린 대상이 자기 자신임.
   (2) 그림을 그린 대상이 자신이 아닌 다른 남자임.

06 personality

07 (1) 사람들과 함께 일하기 (2) 새로운 친구를 사귀기
   (3) 다른 사람들을 즐겁게 해 주기
   (4) 새로운 패턴을 찾기 (5) 운동 경기를 하기

08 (A) blue (B) a, great, listener

09 (A) witty (B) faithful

10 I work best in game settings.

01 (1) 'Are they ~?'로 질문하고 있으므로 'Yes, they are.'나 'No, they aren't.'가 어울린다. (2) look+형용사: ~하게 보이다 (3) 선택할 수 있는 아이스크림이 주어졌기 때문에 What이 아닌 Which를 사용해야 한다.

02 which ~: 어느, 어떤 most: 가장

03 like: 좋아하다 most: 가장 chocolate: 초콜릿

04 (1) 자연 그 자체는 nature itself로 쓴다. (2) One이 주어로 쓰였으므로 defend의 목적어로 oneself를 쓴다. (3) 둘 중에서 선택해야 하므로 which를 써야 한다. (4) 한정된 것이 아닐 경우 what을 쓴다. (5) make oneself at home: 편히 하다

05 주어와 목적어의 관계가 동일할 경우 재귀대명사를 써야 한다.

06 성격, 인격 / 너의 전체 성격과 본성

07 '2, 9, 11, 12, 16번에 동그라미 표시를 했다.

08 '푸른색' 줄에 더 많은 동그라미 표시가 있기 때문에 이 사람은 '대단한 경청자'이고 집단과 더불어 가장 잘 일한다.

09 (A) 형용사가 보어로 와야 하므로 witty가 적절하다. wit: 기지, 재치, witty: 재치 있는, (B) 형용사가 보어로 와야 하므로 faithful이 적절하다. faith: 충실, 신의, faithful: 충실한

|모범답안|

01 Which, do, you, prefer, green, tea, cake, carrot, cake / green, tea, cake, to, carrot, cake

02 (1) I felt myself comfortable.

(2) She introduced herself to us.

(3) I myself walked the dog.

(4) He made spaghetti himself.

03 (A) subjects　(B) personality　(C) an, excellent organizer　(D) with, clear, rules　(E) strong, points

01 'Which ~ do you prefer?'는 주어진 대상 가운데 어떤 것을 더 좋아하는지를 묻는 표현이다. prefer A to B: A를 B보다 선호하다 green tea: 녹차 carrot: 당근

01 (i)nstructions　02 by myself

03 (1) make　(2) plan　(3) ask

04 (1) (t)ype　(2) (s)tomach　05 ③

06 What type of person do you want to be?

07 energetic　08 (A) How　(B) What type　(C) What (D) Which　09 ⑤　10 ⑤

11 In which position do you sleep?

12 stomach　13 ③　14 (1) herself　(2) himself

(3) itself　15 ②　16 ④

17 (1) We should love ourselves.

(2) Don't have the whole pizza on the table by yourself.

(3) If I don't finish this work by tomorrow, I myself will be angry.

(4) You must expect great things of yourself before you can do them.

18 ④　19 is　20 to plan → planning

21 ③　22 (A) green　(B) on your own

23 ⑤　24 ②　25 ①

01 direction: (복수형으로 사용되는 경우) 지시, 명령

02 on one's own: 혼자서, 단독으로 by oneself: 홀로, 혼자서

03 (1) make the most of ~: ~을 최대한 이용하다 (2) plan ~ out: ~을 생각해 내다, 안을 세우다, 기획하다 (3) ask 사람 for advice: 조언[충고]을 구하다

04 (1) type: 유형 (3) stomach: 위(장)

05 ③의 영영풀이는 lively(생기 넘치는)에 대한 것이다. caring: 배려하는, 보살피는 kind, helpful and sympathetic towards other people 다른 사람에게 친절하고, 도움을 주고, 공감을 나타내는 ① activity: 활동 / 사람들이 하는 것; 당신이 즐기기 때문에 하는 어떤 것 ② stage: 무대 / 공연장의 배우나 음악가가 공연하는 부분 ④ personality: 성격, 개성 / 어떤 사람의 특성, 특히 다른 사람들을 대할 때 그들이 행동하는 방식 ⑤ tradition: 전통 / 매우 오래된 관습이나 믿음

06 type: 유형 want to be: ~이 되기를 원하다

07 energetic: 활동적인

08 (A) How did you like ~?: ~이 어땠어? (B) What type: 어떤 유형 type: 유형 (C) What is ~ like?: ~는 어때? (D) Which ~: 어떤 ~

09 learn about: ~에 대해 배우다 be good at: ~을 잘하다

10 make: [사람이] (발달·성장해서) ~이 되다

11 position: 위치, 자리, 자세

12 stomach: 위(장) / 음식이 섭취된 후 몸에서 사용되기 위해 분해되는 몸 안의 주머니 같은 기관

13 ③ 주어와 목적어의 관계가 동일하므로 재귀대명사로 써야 한다. We can express ourselves through our fashion.

14 (1) by oneself: 혼자서 (2) 혼자서 차에 있었다고 했으므로 주어와 목적어의 관계가 동일하므로 재귀대명사를 써야 한다. (3) of itself: 저절로

15 ②번은 강조 용법으로 쓰인 재귀대명사이고 나머지는 모두 재귀 용법의 재귀대명사이다.

16 blue or green이라고 나와 있으므로 한정된 것 중에서 선택할 때 쓰이는 Which가 적절하다.

17 (1) 주어와 목적어가 동일하므로 재귀대명사가 적절하다. (2) by oneself: 혼자서 (3) 주어를 강조하는 강조 용법으로 쓰인 재귀대명사로 주어가 I이므로 myself가 적절하다. (4) 주어와 목적어가 동일하므로 재귀대명사를 써야 한다.

18 이 글은 나는 누구인가, 나는 어떤 유형의 사람인가를 알기 위한 흥미로운 성격 검사에 대한 글이므로, 제목으로는 '나는 어떤 유형의 사람인가?'가 적절하다.

19 here는 말하는 사람 또는 글을 쓰는 사람이 상대방의 주의를 끌기 위한 표현으로, '여기에' 정도의 뜻을 지닌다. "Here we have ~"는 "Here is/are ~"로 바꾸어 쓸 수 있다.

20 enjoy와 at의 목적어에 해당하므로 동명사로 쓰는 것이 적절하다.

21 재치 있고 생기 있으며, 게임 환경에서 가장 잘 일하는 사람은 '활력소 (역할을 하는 사람)'이라고 하는 것이 적절하다. ① 소비자, ② 조력자, ④ 말썽꾼, ⑤ 멘토(경험 없는 사람에게 오랜 기간에 걸쳐 조언과 도움을 베풀어 주는 유경험자, 선배)

22 당신의 색깔이 '초록색'이라면, 당신은 호기심 많은 사색가입니다. 당신은 멋지고 조용하며, '혼자서 (일할 때)' 가장 잘 일합니다.

23 ⓑ와 ⑤번은 (자격, 기능 등이) …로(서), ① …만큼 ~한, ② …하는 동안에, ③ …이기 때문에, ④ …하다시피[…이듯이]

24 ⓐ questions about ~: ~에 대한 질문들, ⓑ make the most of = make the best of: ~을 최대한 이용하다

25 ① '어떤 방과 후 활동에 가입해야 할까?'라고 물었을 뿐이다. ② An excellent organizer. ③ No. ④ The writer works best with clear rules. ⑤The writer knows that he or she can do really well this year.

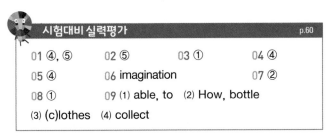

Old Things, New Art

01 ④, ⑤	02 ⑤	03 ①	04 ④
05 ④	06 imagination		07 ②
08 ①	09 (1) able, to (2) How, bottle		
(3) (c)lothes (4) collect			

01 ①~③은 '쓰레기'의 의미를 지닌다. object: 물건, bit: 작은 조각

02 green: 환경 보호의, 친환경적인 go green: 친환경적이 되다 ① 유명한 ② 재활용된 ③ 소중한, 귀중한 ④ 저장된 ⑤ 환경 친화적인

03 mess: (지저분하고) 엉망인 상태 clean up: 치우다, 청소하다 ② 어려움 ③ 매트리스 ④ 실 ⑤ 부품, 부분, 일부

04 used: 중고의 second-hand: 중고의

05 famous: 유명한 well-known: 유명한

06 imagine: 상상하다 imagination: 상상력, 상상 / 그는 예술 작품을 창조하기 위해 상상력을 발휘했다

07 agree with: ~에 동의하다 / 죄송합니다만, 저는 당신의 의견에 동의하지 않습니다.

08 hurry: 서두르다, 급히 하다 / 서두를 필요 없어. 천천히 해.

09 (1) be able to 동사원형: ~할 수 있다 (2) how: 어떻게 bottle: 병 (3) clothes: 옷 (4) collect: 모으다, 수집하다

01 disagree   02 (1) reuse   (2) worried
03 make   04 part   05 to
06 (1) (r)ubbish   (2) (w)rapped
06 (1) All they want is a little bit of bread.
   (2) The man covered the table with a cloth.
   (3) His handlebars broke during a bicycle race.
   (4) Junk artists turn trash into beautiful shapes.
   (5) I nailed the sign to the wall.

01 주어진 단어는 반의어 관계이다. agree: 동의하다 disagree: 동의하지 않다

02 (1) reuse: 재사용하다 (2) be worried about: ~에 대해 걱정하다

03 make: 만들다 make use of: ~을 이용하다 / · 그들은 우리가 쓰레기를 덜 만들어야 한다고 말한다. · 너는 영어로 말할 수 있는 모든 기회를 이용해야 한다.

04 part: 부품, 부분 / · 그들은 엔진을 만들기 위해 그 부품들이 필요하다. · 이것은 이 영화에서 가장 재미있는 부분이다.

05 forget to 동사형: ~할 것을 잊다 be able to 동사원형: ~할 수 있다 / · 나는 카메라 가지고 오는 걸 잊었다. · 너는 그 노래를 부를 수 있니?

06 (1) trash: 쓰레기 rubbish: 쓰레기 (2) pack: 포장하다 wrap: (포장지 등으로) 싸다

07 (1) bit: 작은 조각 (2) cloth: 옷감, 천 (3) handlebar: (흔히 복수형으로 쓰여) 핸들 (4) junk: 폐물, 고물 turn A into B: A를 B로 바꾸다 (5) nail: 못으로 박다; 못

[교과서]
Conversation

1 I'm, worried, about
2 I'm worried I didn't do well on the English test.
3 I agree with you.   4 telling, me
5 You can say that again.

교과서 대화문 익히기

1 F   2 T   3 T   4 T   5 F   6 T

교과서 확인학습   · p.66~67

Listen & Speak 1 Get Ready
1 What's / about

Listen & Speak 1 A
1 What's / worried about, presentation / Don't, do
2 forgot to / worried about forgetting
3 unhappy / I'm worried / Don't worry, pass

Listen & Speak 1 B
1 I'm worried about, waste / reuse / can reuse bottles
2 worried about / too, should reuse / idea, reuse, as

green / say

1 mess / clean, up, keep, clean / can say
2 Hurry, going to / I think we should / agree
3 wearing / is / shouldn't wear / agree

poster for, contest / is / like, More, Less, Where, get, idea / got, from / uses / does, worried about, have to / can say that

look / I'm worried, speech / Don't, such / worried / Don't be, fine

---

시험대비 기본평가   p.68

01 ①   02 ④

03 I'm worried about the test.   04 ③, ⑤

01 be worried about: ~에 대해 걱정하다

02 pass the test: 시험에 합격하다 You will pass 다음에 the test가 생략되어 있다

03 be worried about: ~에 대해 걱정하다 test: 시험

04 ①, ②, ④는 상대방의 의견에 동의하는 표현이고, ③, ⑤는 상대방의 의견에 동의하지 않을 때 사용하는 표현이다.

시험대비 실력평가   p.69~70

01 ④   02 ③, ⑤   03 ④
04 You can say that again.   05 ⑤   06 ④
07 ②   08 ①   09 ⑤   10 job
11 (B) → (C) → (A)   12 ②   13 ④

01 be worried about: ~에 대해 걱정하다 concerned: 걱정하는, 염려하는 be worried about과 바꾸어 쓸 수 있는 표현에는 be anxious about, be concerned about이 있다.

02 ③과 ⑤는 걱정하는 상대방을 안심시키기 위한 표현이다. Don't worry too much.: 너무 걱정하지 마. Everything will be okay.: 모든 것이 다 잘 될 거야.

03 thrown-away: 버려진

04 'You can say that again.'은 상대방의 말에 동의하는 표현으로, '동감이다' 또는 '정말 그렇다'라는 뜻을 나타낸다.

05 ⑤번 뒤에 나온 문장의 it이 the waste problem을 의미하므로, 주어진 문장은 'We have to do something about it.(우리는 그것에 대해 무언가를 해야만 해.)' 앞에 들어가는 것이 적절하다. '출발해.'라는 의미이다.

---

06 ① 세호는 나라가 만든 구호를 좋아한다. ② 나라는 쓰레기 문제에 대해 걱정하고 있다. ③ 세호는 쓰레기 문제에 대한 나라의 의견에 대해 동의한다. ④ 미술 대회를 위한 포스터를 만든 사람은 나라이다. ⑤ 폐품 예술은 버려진 물건들을 사용한다.

07 ② bringing → to bring. forget은 목적어가 동명사일 때와 to부정사일 때 그 의미가 달라진다. forget to부정사: ~할 것을 잊다 forget 동명사: ~한 것을 잊다. 내용상 책을 가져온 것을 잊는 것이 아니라, 책을 가져올 것을 잊었다는 것이므로 to부정사를 사용해야 한다.

08 (A)에는 상대방의 걱정에 대해 물어보는 표현이 들어가야 적절하다. 'What's wrong with you?', 'What's the matter?', 'Is there anything wrong?', 'What happened?' 등이 상대방의 걱정에 대해 물어보는 표현이다. How was your presentation?: 너의 발표는 어땠니?

09 be worried about: ~에 대해 걱정하다

10 do a good job: 잘하다

11 쓰레기 문제에 대해 걱정하고 있다는 말에, (B) 동의를 하며, 사용했던 것들을 재사용해야 한다고 하자 (C) 그 의견에 동의하며, 오래된 잡지를 포장지로 재사용하는 것을 제안하자 (A) 좋은 생각이라고 말한다.

12 ② '여름 방학은 지금보다 더 길어져야 한다.'는 말에, '나의 의견으로는 그것(여름 방학이 길어져야 한다는 것)이 좋지 않다.'고 말하면서, 상대방의 의견에 동의를 한다는 말은 어색하다.

13 (A)에는 쓰레기 문제에 대해 걱정하고 있는 상대방에 동의를 하고 일상용품을 재사용해야 한다는 의견을 내는 것이 어울린다. (B)는 재사용에 대한 의견에 동의를 하고, 재사용의 구체적인 예인 병을 꽃병으로 재사용할 수 있다는 말을 하는 것이 적절하다.

서술형 시험대비   p.71

01 Many people are worried about too much trash.
02 more → less   03 forgetting
04 Let's clean up it. → Let's clean it up.
05 happy → unhappy
06 We can reuse spoons as hangers.
07 (B) → (C) → (D) → (A)   08 (C) → (A) → (B)

01 be worried about: ~에 대해 걱정하다 too much: 너무 많은 trash: 쓰레기

02 많은 사람들이 너무나 많은 쓰레기에 대해 걱정하고 있으므로, 쓰레기를 덜 만들어야 한다고 말하는 것이 적절하다.

03 be worried about: ~에 대해 걱정하다 about은 전치사이므로 뒤에 명사나 동명사가 와야 한다.

04 'clean up'은 이어동사인데, 이어동사는 '동사+부사(on, off, up, over 등)'로 이루어져 있다. '동사+부사+목적어'의 어순이

나 '동사+목적어+부사'의 어순 둘 다 가능하다. 하지만 목적어 자리에 it, them 따위의 인칭대명사가 올 때는 반드시 '동사+목적어+부사'의 어순으로 써준다.

05 시험을 걱정하고 있는데 행복해 보이는 것은 내용상 적절하지 않다.

06 can: ~할 수 있다 reuse: 재사용하다 as: ~으로 hanger: 옷걸이

07 (B) 상대방이 긴장한 것처럼 보인다는 말에 (C) 웅변대회에 대해 걱정하고 있다고 대답한다. (D) 걱정하지 말라고 격려해주자 (A) 격려에 고마워하지만, 걱정은 된다고 대답하자, 긴장하지 말고, 잘 할 것이라고 격려를 다시 한다.

08 (C) Tom이 또 늦는지 묻는 질문에 (A) 그렇다고 답하고 (B) 모임에 늦지 말아야 한다고 말하자 그 말에 동의한다.

교과서 Grammar

핵심 Check p.72~73

1 (1) was, built (2) was, made, for
2 (1) not, only (2) from, people

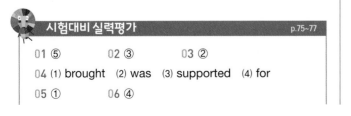
시험대비 기본평가 p.74

01 ⑤   02 ④   03 ③
04 (1) written (2) cruel (3) were
05 were → was

01 옷이 팔리는 것이므로 수동태가 적절하다. Some nice dresses are sold at the store.

02 by the prince로 보아 파티에 초대받았다는 것이 적절하다.

03 not only A but also B: A뿐만 아니라 B도

04 (1) 수동태는 'be동사+pp'의 형태이다. (2) 'not only A but also B' 구문에서 A와 B는 문법적으로 같은 성격의 것이어야 한다. (3) 수동태에서 be 동사의 수는 주어에 일치시킨다.

05 'not only A but also B'가 주어로 쓰일 경우 B에 수를 일치시킨다. 'A뿐만 아니라 B도'라는 의미로 인해 복수라고 생각하지 않도록 주의한다.

시험대비 실력평가 p.75~77

01 ⑤   02 ③   03 ②
04 (1) brought (2) was (3) supported (4) for
05 ①   06 ④

07 (1) Bulguksa was built in 528.
   (2) *Sunflowers* was painted by Vincent van Gogh.
   (3) Katherine is not only smart but also kind.

08 ②   09 was, created, was, titled, was, made

10 ④   11 Was your wallet found by John?

12 (1) Sam not only understood it but also remembered it.
   (2) He plays not only soccer but also baseball.

13 (1) He was respected by lots of people.
   (2) The children appeared in the park.
   (3) This question was asked of all the students by the teacher.
   (4) The furniture was made of oak tree.
   (5) Butterflies were seen to fly from flower to flower.
   (6) The voices of people in the next room can be heard.

14 ③   15 ②   16 ⑤

01 'not only A but also B'가 주어로 쓰일 경우 B에 수를 일치시킨다. Not only old things but also his imagination was used by him to create this sculpture in 1942.

02 ① The desk was made by my elder brother last weekend. ② Thomas Edison invented the light bulb in 1879. ④ These boxes were sent to her by Tom. ⑤ The question was asked of the teacher by students.

03 ② 'not only A but also B'에서 A와 B는 문법적으로 동등한 구조로 연결되어야 한다.

04 (1) 외제품이 무엇을 가져오는 것이 아니라 가져와지는 것이므로 수동태, (2) 건물이 건축되는 것이므로 수동태, (3) by many people로 보아 수동태가 적절하다. (4) 4형식에서 buy는 직접목적어를 주어로 한 수동태에서 간접목적어 앞에 전치사 for를 써야 한다.

05 not only A but (also) B = not only A but B as well = not simply[merely, just] A but (also) B = B as well as A

06 ① The houses were destroyed. ② His room was cleaned by his mom. ③ The photo was taken by Sean. ④ The police caught the thief. ⑤ The door was painted blue.

07 (1) 불국사가 무엇을 지을 수 있는 것이 아니라 지어지는 것이므로 수동태가 적절하다. (2) 그림이 그려지는 것이므로 수동태로 써야 한다. (3) only와 also가 있으므로 'not only A but also B(A뿐만 아니라 B도) 구문을 이용한다.

08 B as well as A = not only A but (also) B = not simply[merely, just] A but (also) B = not only A but B as well

13

09 이 작품은 Su Blackwell에 의해 만들어졌다. 그것은 '보물섬 (Treasure Island)'이라는 제목이 붙여졌고 2013년에 제작되었다.

10 ④번에서 has a nice car의 has가 빠져야 한다. 'not only A but also B'에서 A와 B는 문법적으로 동등한 구조로 연결되어야 한다.

11 지갑이 발견된 것이므로 수동태로 쓴다. 과거시제이므로 'was+pp' 형태에서 의문문이므로 was를 맨앞으로 보낸다.

12 'not only A but also B' 구문에서 A와 B는 문법적으로 같은 성격의 것이어야 한다는 것에 유의한다.

13 (1) lots of people이 목적어가 아니라 행위의 주체이므로 by가 앞에 있어야 한다. (2) appear는 자동사이므로 수동태로 쓰이지 않는다. (3) 직접목적어를 주어로 한 수동태에서 ask는 간접목적어 앞에 of를 쓴다. (4) be made of: ~로 만들어지다(물리적 변화: 재료의 형태나 성질 등이 남아 있는 것) be made from: ~로 만들어지다(화학적 변화: 형태나 성질 등이 완전히 바뀌는 것). (5) 목적격보어가 원형부정사인 경우, 수동태 문장에서는 to부정사로 바뀐다. (6) 사람들의 목소리가 들리는 것이므로 수동태로 써야 하며 조동사가 있는 문장의 수동태는 '조동사+be+p.p.' 형식을 갖는다.

14 첫 문장은 앞에 not only가 나오므로 but also나 but이 적절하고, 두 번째 문장은 예술이 무엇을 만드는 것이 아니라 만들어지는 것이므로 수동태로 쓰인 be made가 적절하다.

15 「This rule applies to parents as well as children. = This rule applies to not only children but (also) parents. ③번의 경우 to parents에서 to가 있으면 문법적이 구조가 다르기 때문에 삭제해야 한다.

16 be filled with: : ~로 가득 차다. 나머지는 전치사 by를 쓴다.

서술형 시험대비
p.78~79

01 (1) was invented (2) was painted (3) was heard

02 (1) The birthday party was cancelled due to the bad weather.
(2) David Edgar created this artwork, Fish Lamp.
또는 This artwork, *Fish Lamp*, was created by David Edgar.
(3) *Dakgalbi* was cooked for Angie by me.
(4) I was surprised at the speed.
(5) It was made to teach people a foreign language.
(6) A letter was written to Cecil by Edan.

03 (1) Sumi is a good dancer as well as a good singer.
(2) I watched *Frozen* as well as Avatar.
(3) We smile with our eyes as well as with our mouths.
(4) I drank some juice as well as ate a hamburger.
(5) Her students as well as the teacher were excited to see the films.

04 (1) A healthy diet is important for children as well as adults.
(2) The woman is not only beautiful but also intelligent.
(3) Alex as well as you is responsible for it.
(4) By whom was the radio invented?
(5) The problem will be solved soon.

05 was, created, was, titled, were, used

06 (1) Some presents were given to her mom by Hannah. Her mom was given some presents by Hannah.
(2) In some areas, the shells of sea snails were used as money for a long time (by people).
(3) He was heard to sing by me while he was doing the dishes.
(4) A storybook was read to her daughter by Anna every night.
(5) Dorothy was satisfied with the services at the restaurant.
(6) The work will be finished by tomorrow (by us).

07 (1) Mathematics has beauty as well as truth.
(2) She wanted to be a singer as well as taught how to sing to students.
(3) Andrew as well as I wants to play basketball.

01 (1) 한글이 만들어진 것이므로 수동태 (2) The Kiss가 그려진 것이므로 수동태 (3) 큰 소리가 들리는 것이므로 수동태가 적절하다.

02 (1) The birthday party가 무엇을 취소하는 것이 아니므로 진행형이 아닌 수동태 'be+과거분사'가 적절하다. (2) David Edgar를 주어로 하면 능동태가, This artwork, Fish Lamp를 주어로 하면 수동태가 적절하다. (3) 직접목적어를 주어로 한 수동태에서 cook은 간접목적어 앞에 for를 쓴다. (4) be surprised at: ~에 놀라다 (5) 목적격보어가 원형부정사인 경우, 수동태 문장에서는 to부정사로 바뀐다. (6) write는 직접목적어를 주어로 하는 수동태만 가능하다.

03 (1)~(4) not only A but (also) B = B as well as A 여기서 A와 B는 문법적으로 같은 성격의 것이어야 한다는 것에 주의한다. (5) 'not only A but also B'나 B as well as A가 주어로 쓰일 경우 B에 수를 일치시킨다.

04 (1) B as well as A: A뿐만 아니라 B도 (2) not only A but also B: A뿐만 아니라 B도 (3) B as well as A가 주어로 쓰일 경우 B에 수를 일치시킨다. (4) 의문문이므로 By whom을 문두에 쓴다. 의문문의 수동태는 능동태의 의문문을 평서문으로

바꾼 후 이것을 수동태로 고치고, 다시 의문문으로 바꾸면 쉽다.
(5) 조동사가 있는 문장의 수동태는 '조동사+be+p.p.' 형식을
갖는다.

05 이 작품은 Louise Baldwin에 의해 만들어졌다. 이것은 '수요일
(Wednesday)'이라는 제목이 붙여졌고 재활용된 재료들이 이용
되었다.

06 (1) 직접목적어를 주어로 한 수동태에서 give는 간접목적어 앞
에 전치사 to를 쓴다. (2) 능동태에서 목적어인 the shells of
sea snails를 수동태에서 주어로 쓴다. people은 흔히 생략된
다. (3) 지각동사 hear의 목적격보어로 원형부정사가 쓰인 경우
수동태 문장에서는 to부정사로 바뀐다. (4) read는 직접목적어
를 주어로 하는 수동태만 가능하다. (5) be satisfied with: ~에
만족하다 (6) 조동사가 있는 문장의 수동태는 '조동사+be+p.p.'
형식을 갖는다.

07 'not only A but (also) B = not only A but B as well =
B as well as A: A뿐만 아니라 B도. 'not only A but also B'
나 B as well as A가 주어로 쓰일 경우 B에 수를 일치시킨다.

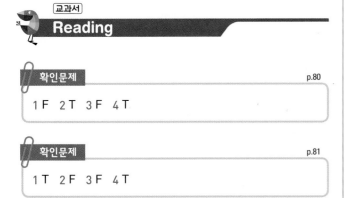

Reading

확인문제 p.80

1 F 2 T 3 F 4 T

확인문제 p.81

1 T 2 F 3 F 4 T

교과서 확인학습 A p.82~83

01 Old, New   02 be, made, out, of
03 are, often, made, from, such, as   04 Junk
05 How, like   06 was, created   07 to, make
08 During, there, were, not
09 stop, creating, picked, up
10 not, only, but, also, to, create   11 Thrown-away
12 was, created, by
13 thrown-away, objects   14 are, good, for
15 pieces, of, paper, bits, of, wood
16 glued, nailed, to   17 moved, to
18 take, out, of, looked, like
19 What, old, things   20 What, new,
artwork   21 something, new
22 trash, another's, treasure

교과서 확인학습 B p.84~85

1 Old Things, New Art
2 Art can be made out of all kinds of old things around us.
3 Famous sculptures and pictures are often made from everyday things such as cans, bottles, and bits of paper.
4 Bicycle Junk and *Bull's Head*
5 How do you like this artwork?
6 It was created by Pablo Picasso.
7 He used a bicycle seat and handlebars to make this sculpture!
8 During World War II, there were not a lot of useful things for art.
9 But Picasso couldn't stop creating artwork, so he picked up junk such as old bicycles and mattress springs.
10 He used not only old things but also his imagination to create this sculpture in 1942.
11 Thrown-away Things and New Art
12 This artwork was created by Kurt Schwitters.
13 He used thrown-away objects to make artwork.
14 He often said, "Old things are good for art."
15 Schwitters walked the streets and collected not only pieces of paper but also bits of wood.
16 He glued and nailed them to a board, and created a new style of art, Rubbish.
17 In 1937, he moved to Norway.
18 He was able to take his famous work out of Germany because it looked like rubbish.
19 What old things do you have around you?
20 What new artwork can you make out of them?
21 Use your imagination and create something new.
22 One person's trash is another's treasure!

시험대비 실력평가 p.86~89

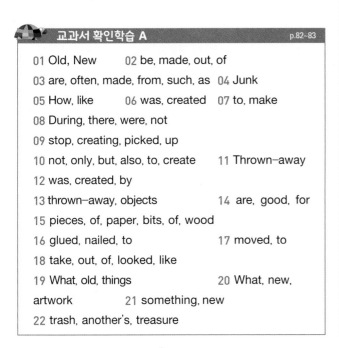

01 ④   02 ③, ⑤   03 ②
04 Thrown-away objects were used to make artwork by him.
05 ④   06 ③   07 his famous work
08 One person's trash is another's treasure!
09 ④   10 ②   11 ③   12 ③
13 ③   14 (1) stopped → couldn't stop
(2) because → (al)though   15 ①, ⑤
16 (1) pieces of paper   (2) bits of wood   17 ②
18 an old → a new   19 ④   20 ①

01 ④는 Bull's Head가 아니라 작품의 재료로 쓸 수 있는 '고물'을 지칭한다.

02 ⓐ와 ③, ⑤는 부사적 용법, ① 형용사적 용법, ②, ④ 명사적 용법

03 유명한 조각품들과 그림들은 종종 깡통, 병 및 종잇조각과 같은 '일상' 용품으로 만들어진다. everyday: 일상적인, every day: 매일

04 thrown-away objects를 주어로 해서 바꾸면 된다.

05 ⓑ 오래된 것들은 예술에 '좋다'라고 해야 하므로 for가 적절하다. be good for: ~에 좋다, be good at: ~을 잘하다, ⓒ 그것들을 '판자에' 풀이나 못으로 붙였다고 해야 하므로 to가 적절하다.

06 이 글은 Schwitters가 오래된 것들을 사용하여 미술 작품을 만든 것에 관한 글이다.

07 '그의 유명한 작품'을 가리킨다.

08 another's: 다른 사람의

09 Schwitters가 오래된 것들로 얼마나 많은 작품을 만들었는지는 대답할 수 없다. ① He moved to Norway in 1937. ② Because it looked like rubbish. ③ No. ⑤ You need to use your imagination.

10 ⓐ와 ②번은 특색, 특징, ① (~의) 특징을 이루다(동사), ③ (신문·잡지 등의) 기사, 특집 기사, ④ 주연하다(동사), ⑤ (배우를) 주연[출연]시키다

11 ③번 다음 문장의 We에 주목한다. 주어진 문장의 Minho, Changsu, and Nami를 가리키므로 ③번이 적절하다.

12 ③ '플라스틱 병의 입구를 막아야 한다.'는 설명은 없다.

13 위 글은 '미술은 우리 주변의 모든 오래된 것들로 만들어질 수 있다'는 내용의 글이므로, 제목으로는 '우리 주변의 오래된 것들로 만들어진 미술'이 적절하다.

14 제2차 세계 대전 중에는 미술을 위해 쓸 수 있는 것들이 많지 '않았지만' Picasso는 '작품 창작을 멈출 수 없었다.'

15 not only[merely, simply, just] A but (also) B = B as well as A: A뿐만 아니라 B도

16 '종잇조각'과 '나무 조각'을 가리킨다.

17 목적을 나타내는 부사적 용법의 to부정사는 in order to, so as to, in order that 주어 can[may], so that 주어 can[may]를 사용하여 바꿔 쓸 수 있다.

18 Rubbish라는 '새로운' 방식의 예술을 창조했다고 하는 것이 문맥상 적절하다.

19 위 글은 한 사람의 쓰레기가 다른 사람의 보물이라는 내용의 글이므로, 제목으로는 '가치 없게 여겨지는가? 아니, 그것은 가치

있다!'가 적절하다.

20 ⓐ와 ①번: ~와 같은(전치사), ②, ③, ⑤ ~을 좋아하다(동사), ④ 비슷한(형용사)

21 -thing으로 끝나는 부정대명사는 형용사가 뒤에서 수식한다.

22 몇몇 사람들은 플라스틱 병을 '쓰레기'라고 여겼지만, David Edgar는 그것을 자신의 '미술 작품'을 만들기 위한 소중한 재료로 여겼다.

24 (1) '쓰던' 것을 모아라. (2) '종잇조각'을 판자에 풀로 붙여라. (3) '나무 조각'을 판자에 못질해라.

🦉 서술형 시험대비

01 문장 끝의 around us를 참조하여, We를 주어로 해서 바꾸면 된다.

02 (A) 일상 용품으로 '만들어 진다'고 해야 하므로 from이 적절하다. be made from: ~으로 만들어지다, be made by: ~에 의해 만들어지다, (B) 이 작품은 '어떻습니까?'라고 해야 하므로 How가 적절하다. How do you like ~?: ~은 어떻습니까?, ~이 마음에 드십니까? (C) 뒤에 기간을 나타내는 명사(World War II)가 나오므로, During이 적절하다. during+기간을 나타내는 명사, while+주어+동사

03 Picasso가 Bull's Head를 만들기 위해 사용한 오래된 것들은 '자전거 좌석'과 '핸들'이다.

04 not only A but also B = B as well as A: A뿐만 아니라 B도

05 '종잇조각'과 '나무 조각'을 가리킨다.

06 'of'를 보충하면 된다. 동격인 a new style of art와 Rubbish 사이에 콤마를 찍는다.

07 ⓐ Schwitters가 종잇조각과 나무 조각을 판자에 풀이나 못으로 붙여 만든 새로운 방식의 예술을 일컫는 말이다.

08 한 사람이 '가치 없다'고 여기는 어떤 것이 다른 사람에 의해서는

'가치 있게' 여겨질 수도 있다.

09 How do you like ~?: ~은 어떻습니까?, ~이 마음에 드십니까?

10 로마 숫자를 포함하고 있는 단어를 영어로 읽을 때 '단어+기수' 또는 'the+서수+단어'로 읽는다. 단, Elizabeth II는 Elizabeth the second로 읽는다.

11 주어가 복수(a lot of useful things)이므로 were가 적절하다.

13 '버려진 물건들'이 사용되었다.

14 종이를 셀 때는 pieces나 sheets를 쓸 수 있다.

15 두 번째 단락의 내용을 쓰면 된다.

영역별 핵심문제
p.93~97

01 (c)apable 02 ④ 03 ①, ⑤ 04 ③

05 ② 06 ③ 07 at → about

08 ② 09 I'm really worried about forgetting things. 10 ③ 11 ④ 12 up

13 ⑤ 14 ③ 15 ④ 16 ②

17 was, created, was, titled, was, made

18 (1) She was not invited to the party.

(2) America was discovered by Columbus.

(3) A dictionary was bought for her daughter by Mariel.

(4) She plays not only tennis but also golf.

(5) He is a poet as well as a scholar.

(6) It not only tastes good but is full of nutrients as well.

19 (1) He can not only read English but also speak it.

(2) Amy as well as I likes to enjoy a cup of coffee after dinner.

20 (1) I took my famous artwork out of Germany.

(2) J. K. Rowling wrote Harry Potter.

(3) They[People] built the Eiffel Tower in 1889.

(4) What new artwork can be made out of old things by you?

(5) Not only a plastic bottle but also his imagination was used to make this artwork by him.

21 ④ 22 junk 23 ③ 24 ②

25 ④ 26 (A) because (B) like (C) What

27 ⑤ 28 ② 29 (1) as, well, as

(2) as, well 30 Fish Lamp

01 주어진 단어는 동의어 관계이다. rubbish: 쓰레기 trash: 쓰레기 able: ~할 수 있는, 유능한 capable: 유능한

02 glue: 접착제; 접착제로 붙이다

03 sort, type, kind는 모두 '종류'의 의미를 가진다.

04 board: 판자 / 나무나 플라스틱의 조각으로 평평하고 얇은 직사각형 모양의 조각 ① 병 ② 쓰레기 ④ 동전 ⑤ 접시

05 (A) 무슨 소음인지 물어보는 질문에 (D) 저쪽에 있는 어린 소년들이라고 대답한다. (B) 이어서 공원에서 시끄럽게 굴면 안 된다고 자신의 생각을 말하며, 상대방은 어떻게 생각하는지 묻자 (C) 그 어린 소년들이 그저 즐거운 시간을 갖고 있다고 대답한다.

06 ③ 동의하는 표현은 'You can say that again.'이다. 의자에 대해 말하지 말라고 하며, 그 의자가 마음에 든다는 문장은 어울리지 않는다.

07 be worried about: ~에 대해 걱정하다

08 남자아이가 여자아이의 책을 안 가져와서 미안해하는 상황이다.

09 be worried about: ~에 대해 걱정하다 really: 정말로

10 ① 남호는 여자아이의 책을 빌렸다. ② 남호는 여자에게 미안함을 느낀다. ③ 남호가 여자아이의 책을 가져오지 않은 것은 이번이 처음이다. ④ 남호는 여자아이에게 빌린 책을 가져오는 것을 잊었다. ⑤ 남호는 종종 일들을 잊어버린다.

11 ① 정돈(된 상태) ② 어려움 ③ 문제 ④ (지저분하고) 엉망인 상태 ⑤ 환경 보호의, 친환경적인

12 clean up: 치우다, 청소하다

13 not only A but also B에서 also는 생략할 수 있다. sculptor: 조각가

14 write는 직접목적어를 주어로 하는 수동태만 가능하다. A long e-mail was written to Harold by Jessy.로 쓸 수 있다.

15 ④ be covered with: ~로 덮여 있다. 나머지는 전치사 by를 쓴다.

16 not only A but also B: A뿐만 아니라 B도

17 이 작품은 Kyle Bean에 의해 만들어졌다. 이것은 '무엇이 먼저인가(What Came First)'라는 제목이 붙여졌고 계란 껍데기로 제작되었다.

18 (1)~(3) 수동태인 'be동사+pp'의 형태로 쓴다. buy는 직접목적어를 주어로 하는 수동태만 가능하며 간접목적어 앞에 전치사 for를 써야 한다. (4) not only A but also B: A뿐만 아니라 B도 (5) B as well as A: A뿐만 아니라 B도 (6) not only A but B as well: A뿐만 아니라 B도. 여기서 A와 B는 문법적으로 같은 성격의 것이어야 하므로 tastes good과 is full of nutrients로 써야 한다는 것에 주의한다. scholar: 학자 nutrient: 영양분, be full of = be filled with: ~로 가득 차다

19 (1) 'not only A but (also) B'에서 A와 B는 문법적으로 같은 성격의 것이어야 하므로 not only에 이어지는 read English처럼 but also 다음에도 '동사+목적어'의 형태인 speak it이 되어야 한다. (2) 'not only A but also B'나 B as well as A가 주어로 쓰일 경우 B에 수를 일치시킨다.

21 이 글은 '미술은 우리 주변의 모든 오래된 것들로 만들어질 수 있다'는 내용의 글이므로, 주제로는 '오래된 것들로 만들어진 미

술 작품'이 적절하다.

22 junk: 쓸모없는 물건, 폐물 / 가치가 거의 없고 당신이 더 이상 원치 않는 오래된 중고 물품들

23 ⓑ와 ①, ⑤는 부사적 용법, ② 형용사적 용법 ③과 ④ 명사적 용법

24 ⓐ와 ②번은 물건들, ① 목적, 목표, ③ (연구 등의) 대상, 목적, ④ 목적어, ⑤ (사고·감정·행동 등의) 대상, the objects of consideration: 고려의 대상이 되는 것들

25 ④ '상자'가 아니라 '판자'에 붙였다.

26 (A) 뒤에 '주어+동사'가 있으므로 because가 적절하다. because+절, because of+구, (B) 쓰레기처럼 '보였기' 때문이라고 해야 하므로 like가 적절하다. look at: ~을 보다, look like: ~처럼 보이다, (C) '어떤' 새로운 작품을 만들 수 있느냐고 해야 하므로 What이 적절하다.

27 ⓐ out of Germany: 독일 밖으로, ⓑ make out of ~: ~으로 만들다

28 당신의 상상력을 이용하여 주변의 오래된 것들을 새로운 것으로 창작하라고 하고 있으므로, 필자는 '한 사람의 쓰레기가 다른 사람의 보물이라고' 주장한다고 할 수 있다.

29 not only A but also B = B as well as A = not only A but B as well: A뿐만 아니라 B도

30 'Fish Lamp'를 가리킨다.

단원별 예상문제　　　　　p.98~101

01 ③　　　　02 also　　　　03 use
04 (h)andlebar　　　　　05 ②
06 Reuse More, Waste Less!　　　07 contest
08 the waste problem　　09 ②　　10 ④
11 They shouldn't make noise in the park. 12 having
13 (1) Kurt Schwitters created this artwork.
　　(2) A new style of art, Rubbish, was created by him.
　　(3) This flower is fragrant as well as pretty.
14 ④　　　15 ④　　　16 ②, ③
17 (1) He used not only old things but also his imagination to create this sculpture in 1942.
　　(2) He used his imagination as well as old things to create this sculpture in 1942.
　　(3) He used not only old things but his imagination as well to create this sculpture in 1942.
18 collecting → collected　　19 Rubbish　20 ⑤
21 If　　　　22 ④
23 wonderful → like rubbish[trash] 또는 valueless
24 ①, ④　　　25 ①

01 used: 중고의

02 also: 또한 / 그것은 힘든 일이지만 또한 재미도 있다. not only A but also B: A 뿐만 아니라 B도 / 그의 직업은 재미있을 뿐 아니라 보수도 매우 좋다.

03 use: 사용하다 / 몇몇 미술가는 미술 작품을 만들기 위해 오래된 컴퓨터 부품을 사용한다. make use of: ~을 이용하다 / 온라인 신문을 이용하는 건 어때?

04 handlebar: (흔히 복수형으로 쓰여) 핸들 / 조종을 위한 손잡이가 달린 곡선의 금속 막대기

05 주어진 문장은 "어디서 저런 아이디어를 얻었니?"이다. 어디서 아이디어를 얻었는지에 대한 정보가 대답으로 나와야 하므로 ② 가 적절하다.

06 reuse: 재사용하다 waste: 낭비하다 more: 더 많이 less: 더 적게

07 contest: 대회, 시합 / 특별히 선정된 심판들의 모임에 의해 판정되는 경쟁

08 나라는 쓰레기 문제에 대해 걱정하고 그것(쓰레기 문제)에 대해 무언가를 해야만 한다고 생각하고 있다.

09 ⓐ nervous ⓑ about ⓒ too much ⓓ such ⓔ fine

10 What do you think?: 넌 어떻게 생각하니?

11 should: ~해야 한다 make noise: 시끄럽게 떠들다, 소란을 피우다

12 have a good time: 즐거운 시간을 보내다

13 (1), (2) 수동태는 능동태로, 능동태는 수동태로 바꾼다. (3) not only A but also B = B as well as A

14 ① This book was written by a famous writer. ② He was heard to open the door. ③ Lots of Christmas presents were given to the children. ⑤ An e-mail was written to Jack by Amanda yesterday.

15 모든 오래된 것들로 '만들어질 수 있다'고 해야 하므로 out of가 적절하다. out of: (재료) ~으로, be made out of: ~으로 만들어지다

16 ⓑ와 ②, ③번은 동명사, 나머지는 다 현재분사

17 not only A but also B = B as well as A = not only A but B as well: A뿐만 아니라 B도

18 walked와 병렬구문을 이루도록 과거시제로 고치는 것이 적절하다.

19 Schwitters는 작품을 만들기 위해 버려진 물건들을 사용했고, 거리를 걸으면서 모은 종잇조각과 나무 조각들을 판자에 풀이나 못으로 붙여 새로운 방식의 예술을 창조했기 때문에 Rubbish가 적절하다. rubbish: 쓰레기

20 ⑤ Schwitters가 왜 새로운 방식의 미술을 창조했는지는 대답할 수 없다. ① No, he didn't. ② He often said, "Old things are good for art." ③ He collected not only pieces of paper but also bits of wood. ④ He glued and

nailed them to a board.

21 '명령문, and ~' 구문은 'If'를 사용하여 바꿔 쓸 수 있다.

22 ④ '화려한 천'은 재료에 해당하지 않는다.

23 1937년 그는 노르웨이로 이주했을 때, 그의 유명한 작품이 '쓰레기'처럼(가치 없게) 보였기 때문에 그는 그것을 독일에서 가져갈 수 있었다.

24 ⓐ '한 사람의 쓰레기'에 해당하는 것: ①, ④

25 ① 종잇조각뿐만 아니라 나무 조각도 '모았다.'

서술형 실전문제   p.102~103

01 We shouldn't wear slippers in the school garden.

02 I'm with you on that. / You can say that again. / I agree with you.

03 I don't think so. → I agree with you. 또는 You can say that again.

04 (1) They[People] built the Great Wall of China about 2,200 years ago.
  (2) Picasso created many great sculptures.
  (3) The song is sung very beautifully by her.
  (4) *Harry Potter* was read to her daughter by Melanie.
  (5) The house was covered with snow.
  (6) The game was put off because of the rain (by them).

05 (1) This dress is not only cheap but also beautiful.
  (2) Willy not only writes but also speaks French well.

06 (1) Schwitters collected bits of wood as well as pieces of paper.
  (2) The artist used his imagination as well as toilet paper rolls to make this artwork.
  (3) Aaron is lazy as well as poor.

07 every day → everyday

08 What do you think of this artwork?

09 (A) useful, things   (B) stop, creating

10 created → was created

11 (A) thrown-away   (B) collected

12 Old things are good for art.

01 should: ~해야 한다 wear: 입다, 신다 garden: 정원

02 상대방의 말이나 의견에 전적으로 동의할 때, 'You can say that again.', 'I agree (with you).', 'I'm with you on that.' 등을 사용할 수 있다.

03 첫 번째 여자아이는 공원에서 떠드는 아이들에 대해 즐거운 시간을 갖고 있으므로 시끄럽게 구는 것에 대해 나쁘게 생각하고 있지 않다. 두 번째 여자아이 역시 작은 소음은 문제가 안 된다

고 말하고 있으므로, 두 여자아이들의 생각이 같기 때문에 동의하는 말이 나와야 한다.

04 (1) 일반인 주어는 수동태에서 종종 생략된다. (2) 'by 목적격'을 주어로 하여 과거시제로 쓴다. (3) 능동태의 목적어를 주어로 하고 주어를 'by+목적격'으로 고쳐 쓴다. (4) read는 직접목적어를 주어로 한 수동태만 가능하다. (5) be covered with: ~로 덮여 있다 (6) put off는 하나의 동사처럼 취급되므로 수동태로 바꿔어도 off를 빠뜨리면 안 된다.

05 not only A but also B: A뿐만 아니라 B도

06 not only A but (also) B = not only A but B as well = B as well as A: A뿐만 아니라 B도

07 유명한 조각품들과 그림들은 종종 깡통, 병 및 종잇조각과 같은 '일상용품'으로 만들어진다고 해야 하므로 'everyday'로 고치는 것이 적절하다. everyday: 일상적인, every day: 매일

08 How do you like ~?: ~은 어떻습니까?, ~이 마음에 드십니까? What do you think of ~?: ~을 어떻게 생각합니까?, ~이 마음에 드십니까?

09 제2차 세계 대전중에는 미술을 위해 '쓸 수 있는 것들'이 많지 않았지만 Picasso는 작품 '창작을 멈출 수' 없었다.

10 이 작품은 Kurt Schwitters에 의해 '창작되었다'고 해야 하므로 수동태로 고치는 것이 적절하다.

11 (A) '버려진' 물건들을 사용했다고 해야 하므로 thrown-away가 적절하다. (B) 종잇조각뿐만 아니라 나무 조각도 '모았다'고 해야 하므로 collected가 적절하다. correct: 바로잡다, 정정하다

12 be good for: ~에 좋다

창의사고력 서술형 문제   p.104

|모범답안|

01 late / are, late, for, school / worried, about / Don't, worry

02 (1) The movie was produced in 2012.
  (2) The song is sung by us.
  (3) Pablo Picasso was laughed at because of his special way of painting.
  (4) Paper is made from wood.
  (5) The artwork was created by my sister.

03 (A) was created, (B) not only, (C) but also, (D) trash, (E) treasure

01 be late for: ~에 늦다 be worried about: ~에 대해 걱정하다

단원별 모의고사   p.105~108

01 (h)urry   02 ③

03 (1) seat   (2) object   (3) part   (4) slogan

04 (1) (m)ess (2) (p)atches (3) sculptures
    (4) treasure (5) (u)pset

05 (1) There is nothing to worry about.
    (2) Wrap all the glasses in newspaper.
    (3) She is holding an object in her hands.

06 problem   07 (A) reuse   (B) used

08 (C) more   (D) Why   09 worried   10 ④

11 Waste   12 ①

13 ⓐ for ⓑ from ⓒ about ⓓ about   14 slogan

15 I not only read the book but also wrote an essay
    about it.

16 (1) Who is going to create the artwork?
    (2) About 4.7 million Korean people watched
        Zootopia.
    (3) A bowl of chicken soup was made for Tom by
        Matilda.
    (4) Many of his discoveries were laughed at at
        first (by people).

17 ⑤

18 (1) I as well as my sisters am learning English.
    (2) Chris likes not only playing the piano but also
        playing the guitar. 또는 Chris likes playing not
        only the piano but also the guitar.
    (3) The bulgogi was made last night.
    (4) Wasn't the house painted by Dan?

19 like   20 Pablo Picasso created it.

21 to create → creating   22 ②

23 ③번, it → them   24 ②, ⑤

25 old things (around you)   26 rubbish

---

01 rush: 돌진하다, 서두르다 hurry: 서두르다, 급히 하다

02 such: 너무나 ~한 'such+a+형용사+명사'의 어순이다.

03 (1) seat: 좌석, 안장 (2) object: 물건 (3) part: 부품, 부분, 일부 (4) slogan: 구호, 슬로건

04 (1) mess: (지저분하고) 엉망인 상태 (2) patch: 부분, 조각 (3) sculpture: 조각상 (4) treasure: 보물 (5) upset: 속상하게 만들다

05 (1) worry: 걱정하다 (2) wrap: (포장지 등으로) 싸다 (3) object: 물건

06 problem: 문제 / 사람들에게 어려움을 일으키는 상황

07 reuse: 재사용하다 used: 중고의

08 I couldn't agree more: 전적으로 동감이야. Why don't we ~?: ~하는 게 어떨까?

09 worried: 걱정하는

10 여자아이가 민호를 격려하고 있다.

11 waste: 쓰레기, 낭비하다 (A)에서는 동사, 'I'm worried about the waste problem.'에서는 명사로 사용하였다.

12 have to: ~해야 한다 You can say that again: 동감이다, 정말 그렇다.

13 ⓐ ~을 위한 ⓑ ~로부터 ⓒ be worried about: ~에 대해 걱정하다 ⓓ ~에 대해

14 slogan: 구호, 슬로건 / 광고 메시지를 표현하는 짧은 어구

15 not only A but also B : A뿐만 아니라 B도

16 (1) 의문문의 수동태를 능동태로 바꾸려면 먼저 의문문을 평서문으로 바꾼 후 이것을 능동태로 고치고, 다시 의문문으로 바꾸면 쉽다. (2) 'by 목적격'을 주어로 하여 과거시제로 쓴다. (3) make는 직접목적어를 주어로 하는 수동태만 가능하며 간접목적어 앞에 전치사 for를 쓴다. (4) laugh at은 하나의 동사처럼 취급되므로 수동태로 바뀌어도 at을 빠뜨리면 안 된다.

17 not only A but also B = B as well as A

18 (1) B as well as A가 주어로 쓰일 경우 B에 수를 일치시킨다. (2) not only A but also B 구문에서 A와 B는 문법적으로 같은 성격의 것이어야 한다. (3) 주어가 불고기이므로 수동태가 적절하다. (4) 수동태의 의문문은 'be+pp'의 be 동사를 문두로 보낸다.

19 such as = like: 예를 들어 (~와 같은)

20 Pablo Picasso를 주어로 해서 바꾸면 된다.

21 stop ~ing: ~하기를 그만두다, stop+to부정사: ~하기 위하여 멈추다

22 이 글은 Schwitters가 버려진 물건들을 사용하여 Rubbish라는 새로운 방식의 예술을 만든 것에 관한 글이므로, 제목으로는 '버려진 것들과 새로운 예술'이 적절하다.

23 '종잇조각'과 '나무 조각'을 가리키는 것이기 때문에, them이라고 해야 적절하다.

24 쓰레기처럼 보였기 때문에, 즉 '가치 없게' 보였기 때문에, 그는 그의 유명한 작품을 독일에서 가져갈 수 있었다. ③ priceless: 대단히 귀중한, ④ precious: 소중한

25 (당신 주변에 있는) '오래된 것들'을 가리킨다.

26 trash = rubbish: 쓰레기

Go, Team!

시험대비 실력평가
p.112

01 ①	02 ④	03 ②	04 ⑤
05 ②	06 ④		

07 (1) denied   (2) important   (3) penalty, kick
   (4) looking, forward, to   (5) (p)opular

01 보기, ① as는 접속사로 '~와 같이, ~한 대로'의 의미이다. ② (접) ~할 때 ③ (전) ~로서 ④ (접) ~이기 때문에 ⑤ (전) ~로서 be known as: ~로 알려지다

02 chance: 기회

03 hang: 매달리다

04 save: 아끼다, 절약하다

05 select: 선발[선정/선택]하다 / 우리는 다음 매니저를 자격을 갖춘 지원자들 중에서 선발할 것입니다. pick: 뽑다, 선발하다 qualified applicant: 자격을 갖춘 지원자

06 cut down: 절약하다 / 그런 방법으로 너는 비용을 줄일 수 있을 것이다. save: 아끼다, 절약하다

07 (1) deny: 부인하다 (2) important: 중요한 (3) penalty kick: 페널티 킥 (4) look forward to (동)명사: ~을 기대하다, ~을 고대하다 (5) popular: 인기 있는, 유명한

서술형 시험대비
p.113

01 (1) speaker   02 made, a, basket
03 (1) penalty kick   (2) opening   (3) coach   (4) list
04 for   05 like   06 (t)ie   07 (g)uess
08 (1) The man denied the rumor about him.
   (2) He is in the junior soccer club.
   (3) I don't care whether she comes or not.
   (4) He scored on a penalty kick.

01 kick: 발길질, 차기, 발로 차다 kicker: (축구에서 공을) 차는 사람 speak: 말하다 speaker: 연사, 연설가

02 make a basket: 농구 경기에서 득점하다

03 (1) penalty kick: 페널티 킥 (2) opening: 기회, 자리 (3) coach: 코치, 감독 (4) list: 목록, 리스트

04 look for: ~을 바라다[기대하다] be ready for (동)명사: ~할 준비가 되다 / • 많은 사람들은 지금 변화를 기대한다. • 나는 내일 시험에 대한 준비가 되어 있다고 생각하지 않는다.

05 feel like+(동)명사: ~하고 싶다 like: ~처럼/ • 정말 더 이상 일하고 싶지 않아요. • 나는 저렇게 춤을 출 수 있다.

06 tie: 동점; 동점을 이루다 / 같은 수의 점수를 갖다

07 guess: 추측하다 / 모든 사실에 대한 확신이 없이 무언가에 대해 답을 하거나 판단을 하려고 노력하다

08 (1) deny: 부인하다 (2) junior: (스포츠에서) 주니어의; (스포츠 팀의) 주니어 선수 (3) whether ~ or not: ~이든 아니든 (4) penalty kick: 페널티 킥

교과서
Conversation

핵심 Check
p.114~115

1 looking, to, trip   2 (B) → (C) → (A)
3 It's significant to use public transportation.
  I want to stress that we use public transportation.
4 It's important to be on time.

교과서 대화문 익히기

Check(√) True or False
p.116

1 F   2 T   3 T   4 T   5 T   6 F

교과서 확인학습
p.118~119

Listen & Speak 1 Get Ready
visiting us / forward to seeing

Listen & Speak 1 A
1 know, are going to go to / I'm, forward
2 coming / are, looking forward to seeing / believe
3 are going to have, next / finally, am, winning

Listen & Speak 1 B
1 is coming, can't wait / looking, doing / looking / dance
2 I can't wait / What are you looking forward to doing / looking forward, running, three-legged

Listen & Speak 2 Get Ready
it's, call

Listen & Talk 2 A
1 want to be, like / it's important to use
2 ready to go / safety, It's, wear
3 What, doing / turn off, It's, to save energy

시험대비 기본평가　p.120

01 ③　　02 seeing　　03 ②　　04 ⑤

01 어떤 일에 있어서 중요한 사항, 항목 및 정보 등을 나타낼 때 'It's important to+동사원형 ~.'을 사용한다.

02 'I'm looking forward to 동명사 ~.: 나는 ~하는 것을 고대하고 있다.

03 (B) 야구 시합 준비가 되었느냐는 질문에 (A) 준비되었다고 대답하며, 시합에서 이기기를 고대하 고 있다고 말한다. (D) 상대방도 그렇다고 말하고, 시합에서 이기려면 무엇을 해야 할지 질문을 하 고 (C) 공을 세게 치는 것이 중요하다고 대답한다.

04 be looking forward to 동명사: ~하는 것을 고대하고 있다

시험대비 실력평가　p.121~122

01 ②　　　　02 ④　　　　03 what　　04 to

05 He looks forward to going to Jeju (for his school trip.) / He looks forward to his school trip.

06 to go　　07 ④　　08 ①　　09 ④

10 ③　　11 ⑤　　12 ②

13 ⑤ I can believe it! → I can't believe it!

01 be looking forward to 동명사: ~하기를 고대하고 있다

02 남호에게 페널티 킥을 차야 한다고 말하는 준하에게 남호는 거절하며 준하가 페널티 킥 전담이라는 사실을 언급한다. (C) 준하는 남호가 올 스타 팀에 선발될 기회를 바라고 있는 점을 들어 페널티 킥을 차야 한다고 설득한다. (B) 남호는 맞지만 시합을 이기는 것이 중요하고 준하 가 공을 가장 잘 차는 선수라고 언급한다. (A) 결국 준하가 페널티 킥을 차고 점수를 얻는다. (D) 준하가 멋진 슛을 한 것에 감탄한다.

03 You know what?: 너 그거 아니? / 상대방의 주의를 끌 때 'You know what?'을 쓸 수 있다.

04 go to 장소: ~에 가다 be looking forward to 명사[대명사]: ~을 고대하고 있다

05 남자아이는 학교 여행으로 제주도에 가는 것을 고대하고 있 다.

06 be ready to 동사원형: ~할 준비가 되다

07 safety: 안전

08 be ready for: ~의 준비가 되다

09 ④ 공을 빠르게 패스하는 것이 중요해.

10 ③ 무엇을 고대하는지 묻는 질문에 '나도 그래.'는 어울리지 않는다.

11 ⑤ turn on → turn off 에너지를 절약하는 것이 중요하다고 말하는 것과 불을 켜는 것은 어울리지 않는다.

12 공기가 좋지 않은 상황에 마스크를 쓰는 게 중요하 다고 말하는 것이 내용상 어울린다. ① 공기에 습기 가 많다. ② 공기가 깨끗하지 않다. ③ 공기가 온화하 다. ④ 공기가 건조하다. ⑤ 공기가 매우 희박하다.

13 I can't believe it!: 믿을 수 없는 일이야! / 어떤 상황에 대 하여 놀람을 표현할 때 사용한다.

서술형 시험대비　p.123

01 (1) are going having → are going to have

　(2) looking forward to win → ooking forward to winning

02 It's important to saving energy. → It's important to save energy.

03 I want to stress that you must call 119 first.

04 (A) to be (B) to do

05 it's important to use English every day

06 (B) → (C) → (A)　　07 (C) → (A) → (D) → (B)

01 be going to 동사원형: ~할 것이다 be looking forward to 동명사: ~하기를 고대하고 있다

02 어떤 일에 있어서 중요한 사항, 항목 및 정보 등을 나타낼 때 'It's important to+동사원형 ~.'을 사용한다. 여기서 It은 가주 어이고, to 이하의 부분은 진주어이다.

03 어떤 일에 있어서 중요한 사항, 항목 및 정보 등을 나타낼 때 'It's important to+동사원형 ~.'를 사용하며 'I want to stress that 주어+동사 ~.'와 바꿔 쓸 수 있다.

04 want는 목적어로 to부정사를 취한다. need to 동사원형: ~할 필요가 있다

05 It's important to+동사원형 ~: ~하는 것은 중요하다

06 (B) 학교 체육대회를 기대하고 있다는 말에 (C) 상대방도 그 렇다고 얘기한다. 이어서 무엇을 하기를 고대하는지 묻자 (A) 퍼레이드에 참여하기를 고대하고 있다고 대답한다.

07 (C) 주말에 로봇 축제가 있다고 말하자 (A) 상대방도 알고 있다고 말하면서 그 로봇 축제를 고대하고 있다고 말한다. (D) 처음 말한 화자 역시 그 축제를 고대하고 있으며, 함께 같이 가자고 제안하고 (B) 제안에 좋다고 대답한다.

교과서
Grammar

핵심 Check　p.124~125

1 (1) safe to wear　(2) to choose　(3) of you to go

2 (1) enough time　(2) warm enough　(3) far enough

　(4) wide enough

01 (1) exercise → to exercise   (2) enough warm →
    warm enough   (3) attending → attend
    (4) enough close → close enough
02 (1) clean enough   (2) to listen carefully   (3) cute
    enough   (4) for us   (5) of him
03 (1) It is dangerous to use your phone while
     walking.
    (2) It is wrong for you to tell a lie to me.
    (3) The bike is cheap enough for you to buy.
    (4) Is the content familiar enough?

01 (1), (3) 가주어 it과 진주어 to를 쓰는 것이 옳다. 혹은 동명사
   로 써도 무방하다. (2), (4) cool과 close는 모두 형용사이므로
   enough가 뒤에서 수식한다.
02 (1), (3) enough가 형용사를 수식하는 경우 '형용사+enough'
   의 어순으로 쓰인다. (2) 가주어가 쓰이고 있으므로 진주어로 to
   부정사를 써야 한다. (4), (5) to부정사의 의미상 주어는 'for+
   목적격'을 쓰지만, 사람의 태도나 성격에 관한 형용사가 올 경
   우 'of+목적격'을 쓴다.
03 (1), (2) 가주어 it과 진주어 to부정사를 이용하여 문장을 만
   든다. (3), (4) enough가 형용사를 수식하는 경우 '형용사
   +enough'의 어순으로 쓰인다.

01 ③   02 ④   03 ③
04 It is interesting to talk about the future.
05 ③   06 ⑤   07 ③
08 It is important to do our best.   09 ⑤
10 ① experienced enough ② to ask
11 is not warm enough outside.   12 ④
13 ②   14 cool enough   15 ⑤
16 This car is not fast enough for racing.
17 ③   18 ④   19 thick enough
20 ④   21 ④   22 ②   23 ④
24 It is easy to make the soup.

01 모두 형식 주어로 쓰인 it이지만 ③번은 인칭대명사 it으로 '그
   것'이라고 해석한다.
02 내용상 loud가 쓰이는 것이 옳으며, loud는 형용사이므로
   enough가 뒤에서 꾸며준다. loud: (소리가) 큰
03 에너지를 갖는 것을 주어로 쓰고 가주어 It을 사용하여 'It ~ to
   부정사' 구문을 이용한다. energy는 명사이므로 enough가 앞
   에서 수식하도록 하는 ③번이 적절하다.
04 '미래에 관하여 이야기하는 것'이 주어이므로 진주어로 to talk
   about the future를 쓰는 것이 옳다.
05 ⓐ to believe로 진주어 ⓒ enough가 형용사를 수식할 때에는
   뒤에서 수식한다. ⓓ 의미상의 주어로 'for+목적격'이 쓰이고 있

으므로 진주어로는 to부정사를 쓰는 것이 옳다.
06 '형용사/부사+enough' 어순이다.
07 진주어는 'to+동사원형' 형태이다.
08 '최선을 다하는 것'이므로 to부정사를 이용하여 주어를 쓴다.
09 모두 가주어 It을 쓰지만 ⑤번에는 Speaking 혹은 To speak
   가 쓰인다.
10 ① experienced는 과거분사로 be 동사의 보어 역할을 하는 형
   용사로 쓰였다. 따라서 enough의 수식을 뒤에서 받는다. ② 가
   주어 it이 쓰이고 있으므로 진주어 to부정사를 써야 한다.
11 여기에서 쓰인 it은 날짜, 날씨, 거리, 명암 등을 표현하는 비인
   칭 주어 It이다. warm은 형용사이므로 enough의 수식을 뒤
   에서 받는다.
12 hard는 부사이므로 enough의 수식을 뒤에서 받는다.
13 주어진 문장에서 쓰인 It은 가주어 it이다. 따라서 ②번이 옳다.
14 답변으로 미루어보아 충분히 식지 않았다고 말했음을 알 수 있다.
15 모두 to부정사의 부사적 용법으로 쓰였으나 ⑤번은 진주어로
   명사적 용법으로 쓰인 to부정사이다.
16 fast는 형용사이므로 enough의 수식을 뒤에서 받는다.
17 ③ handsome은 형용사이므로 enough가 뒤에서 수식한다.
18 ④ enough는 형용사를 뒤에서 수식한다.
19 답변으로 미루어보아 충분히 두꺼운지 묻는 말이 들어가는 것이
   옳다.
20 talented는 형용사로 enough의 수식을 뒤에서 받는 것이 옳다.
21 모두 '아기를 돌보는 것은 쉽지 않다'라는 문장이지만 ④번은
   '아기를 돌보지 않는 것은 쉽다'라는 의미이다.
22 enough가 부사로 쓰일 때 형용사나 부사를 뒤에서 수식하는
   것에 유의한다.
23 fast는 형용사와 부사의 형태가 같으므로 run fast enough라
   고 쓰는 것이 옳다.
24 '그 수프를 만드는 것'이므로 to make the soup라고 쓰는 것이
   옳다.

01 read this book is interesting / is interesting to
    read this book.
02 (1) sweet enough   (2) warm enough
    (3) close enough   (4) short enough
    (5) long enough
03 big[large] enough
04 to work with you again
05 close enough to hear
06 It is necessary to finish the work by tomorrow.
07 to fly a kite , enough wind
08 It is not easy to understand other people.
09 this lake clean enough   10 to read , time to read
11 It was natural to accept her apology.
12 big enough
13 It is dangerous to play with a knife.

14 It's because I am not tired enough.

15 it is not long enough. 16 to change the plan

17 (1) It is dangerous to run near a pool.

(2) It is important to go there in time.

(3) The bath is not warm enough.

01 It은 가주어이다.

02 '형용사/부사+enough' 어순에 유의한다.

03 답변으로 미루어보아 방이 충분히 큰지를 물었고, 다소 작다 고 대답한 것임을 알 수 있다.

04 to부정사 진주어를 이용하여 답을 쓸 수 있다.

05 그가 하고 있는 말을 들을 수 있을 만큼 충분히 가까이 있었 다는 의미이다.

06 '그 일을 내일까지 끝내는 것'이므로 to finish the work by tomorrow라고 문장을 만든다.

07 A: 연을 날리고 싶어. B: 내 생각에 오늘 연을 날리는 것은 불가능해. 네가 연을 날리고 싶다면, 바람이 충분히 불어야 해. 하지만 오늘은 바람이 충분히 없어.

08 '다른 사람을 이해하는 것'이라고 하였으므로 to understand other people을 주어로 쓰는 것이 옳다.

09 답변으로 미루어 보아 호수가 수영하기에 충분히 깨끗한지 를 물었음을 알 수 있다.

10 '신문을 읽는 것'이 주어이므로 to read a newspaper를 주어로 쓴다.

11 '그녀의 사과를 받아주는 것'이므로 to accept her apology라고 쓰는 것이 옳다.

12 스웨터가 충분히 크지 않기 때문에 더 큰 것으로 바꾸어야 한다는 의미가 된다.

13 그것을 내려놔! 칼을 가지고 노는 것은 위험해.

14 tired는 형용사로 쓰인 과거분사이다. 따라서 enough가 뒤에서 수식한다.

15 다소 짧다는 것은 충분히 길지 않다는 의미이다.

17 (1) '수영장 근처에서 뛰는 것'이 주어이므로 'to run near a pool'이라고 쓰는 것이 옳다. (2) '그곳에 제시간에 가는 것'이 주어이므로 'to go there in t ime'을 진주어로 쓴다. in time: 제 때에, 제시간에 (3) bath: 욕조, 욕조 속의 물

Reading

확인문제	p.132

1 T 2 T 3 F 4 T

확인문제	p.133

1 T 2 F 3 T 4 F 5 F

01 over   02 it, were

03 While, were, in, handed, a, card

04 a, list, of, on 05 As, you, all, know, an, opening

06 Why, don't, you, pick   07 Check

08 looked, at, saw

09 sighed, put, next, to

10 deny, that, good, enough

11 collected, every, card   12 were, high

13 wanted, to, be

14 looked, up, a, tie, between   15 leaped

16 was, surprised, that

17 wonderful, enough, hard, to, pick

18 have, to, pick   19 walked, over

20 such, a, good, shot

21 the, most, baskets   22 does

23 whether, there's, a, player, or, not

24 to, play, for 25 Don't, when, see, one

26 walked, out, of   27 felt like, giving

28 Then, saw 29 Suddenly, sorry, for

30 don't, care, for,   31 smiled, what

32 was, surprised, did   33 do, your, best

34 played, for, won

35 Congratulations

1 The game was over.

2 The junior team won it, and all the players were happy.

3 While they were in the locker room, the coach handed every boy a card.

4 It had a list of the players on the junior team.

5 "As you all know, we have an opening for a player on the senior team," said the coach.

6 "Why don't you pick a player for the team?

7 Check one name on the list."

8 Scottie looked at the list and saw his name.

9 Then he sighed and put a check next to Michael's name.

10 He couldn't deny that Michael was good enough for the senior team.

11 The coach collected every card from the boys.

12 Everyone's hopes were high.

13 They all wanted to be on the senior team.

14 The coach looked up and said, "Well, it's a tie between Michael and Scottie."

15 Scottie's heart leaped.

16 He was surprised that he was tied with Michael.

17 "Well," said the coach, "both are wonderful enough for the senior team, and it's hard to pick just one player.

18 But I have to, so I'll pick Scottie."
19 Then the coach walked over to Scottie and said, "Congratulations!"
20 "Thank you, but Michael is such a good shot.
21 He makes the most baskets," said Scottie.
22 "Of course, he does," said the coach.
23 "But he shoots whether there's a player in a better position or not.
24 It's important to play for the team!
25 Don't worry. I know a good player when I see one."
26 Scottie walked out of the room.
27 He felt like giving a loud and happy shout.
28 Then he saw Michael.
29 Suddenly Scottie felt sorry for him.
30 "I guess you don't care, but I picked you for the senior team," said Scottie.
31 Michael smiled. "You know what? I picked YOU."
32 Scottie was surprised. "You did?"
33 "Yeah. You always do your best, and you're a team player.
34 Today you played for the team, and we won the game.
35 Congratulations!"

시험대비 실력평가
p.138~141

| 01 ③ | 02 pick | 03 ⑤ | 04 ③ |
| 05 ④ | 06 ⑤ | | |

07 It was not easy to pick just one player. 08 ②
09 picked me   10 ④   11 ②
12 ④   13 Michael was good enough for the senior team 14 As you all know 또는 As all of you know   15 ①   16 ③
17 The coach handed a card to every boy in the locker room. 18 ②   19 ③   20 He felt surprised.   21 to be on the senior team
22 Scottie and Michael   23 ③   24 ⑤
25 Because both were wonderful enough for the senior team.   26 You always do your best.
27 plays for the team   28 ⑤

01 빈칸 (A)에는 While이 들어간다. 따라서 ③번이 답이다. ① Because ② As soon as 혹은 When ④ if ⑤ or
02 그룹 중에서 선택하거나 고르는 것은 pick이다.
03 명단에 몇 개의 이름이 있었는지는 글에 나와 있지 않다.
04 such의 어순은 'such+a(n)+형용사+명사'이다.
05 (B)는 가주어 it이다. 따라서 ④번이 옳다.
06 중요한 것은 팀을 위해 경기하는 것이라고 하였다.
07 '단 한 명의 선수를 선정하는 것'이 주어이므로 to pick just one player로 쓰는 것이 옳다.

08 ②번 다음 문장의 him이 가리키는 것이 Michael이다.
09 "네가 나를 뽑았다고?"라는 의미이다.
10 위 글을 읽고 Michael이 무엇을 잘하는지는 알 수 없다.
11 (A)에는 with가 들어간다. be satisfied with: ~에 만족하다 ① of ③ on[off] ④ up ⑤ of
12 두 사람이 동점을 얻었다고 하였다. 따라서 Scottie는 Michael과 똑같은 표를 얻었다고 말하는 것이 옳다.
13 Michael이 시니어 팀에 충분히 훌륭하다고 생각해서 그를 뽑았다고 하였다.
14 as: ~이다시피, ~이듯이
15 (A) 절을 이끄는 접속사 while, (B) A card를 지칭하므로 단수를 받는 인칭대명사 It, (C) Why don't you+동사원형 ~?
16 ⓐ, ⓒ, ⓓ가 글의 내용과 일치한다.
17 로커룸에서 소년들에게 카드 한 장씩을 건네주었다고 하였다.
18 next to는 '~ 옆에'라는 의미이다.
19 모든 선수들은 시니어 팀에 들어가기를 원했다고 하였으므로 ③번은 글의 내용과 일치하지 않는다.
20 Michael과 동점이라는 말에 Scottie는 놀랐다고 하였다.
21 시니어 팀에 들어가는 것이 모든 선수들이 원하는 것이라고 하였다.
22 Scottie와 Michael 두 사람을 의미한다.
23 한 명의 선수를 골라야 하므로 Scottie를 고르겠다는 의미이다. 결과를 이끄는 접속사 so가 옳다.
24 Michael이 몇 점의 득점을 했는지는 알 수 없다.
25 두 선수 모두 시니어 팀에 들어가기에 충분히 훌륭하기 때문에 한 명을 선정하는 것이 어렵다고 하였다.
26 빈도부사 always는 일반 동사 앞에 위치하는 것에 유의하여 답을 쓴다.
27 팀플레이어란 팀을 위해서 경기하는 사람이다.
28 크고 기쁜 소리를 지르고 싶은 마음 → Michael을 보고 미안함을 느낌 → Michael이 자신을 골랐다는 사실을 알고 놀람

서술형 시험대비
p.142~143

01 The junior team won the game.
02 the coach handed a card to every boy.
03 There was a list of players on the junior team on the card.
04 pick a player, checking
05 to be on the senior team
06 It is a tie between Michael and Scottie.
07 he was tied with Michael.   08 leap
09 I have to pick just one player
10 whether there's a player in a better position or not
11 He thinks that it is important to play for the team.
12 the senior team   13 felt sorry for him
14 Scottie plays for the team.
15 It is important to make the most baskets.
16 passing and shooting   17 good teamwork

01 게임 결과를 묻는 문제이다. 주니어 팀이 경기에서 승리했다고 하였다.
02 hand는 4형식 동사이다. 3형식으로 전환할 경우 간접목적어 앞에 전치사 to를 붙인다.
03 카드에는 주니어 팀에 있는 모든 선수들의 명단이 있었다.
04 코치는 명단에서 하나의 이름에 체크 표시함으로써 시니어 팀을 위한 선수 한 명을 뽑으라고 제안했다.
05 모든 선수들의 바람은 시니어 팀에 들어가는 것이다.
06 두 사람이 동점이라는 의미이다.
07 Scottie가 놀란 이유는 자신이 Michael과 동점이 되어서라고 하였다.
08 빠르게 혹은 갑자기 움직이거나 행동하는 것은 leap이다.
09 단 한 명의 선수를 뽑는 것이 어렵지만 해야만 한다는 의미이다.
11 코치는 팀을 위해서 경기하는 것이 중요하다고 생각한다.
12 Scottie는 Michael을 시니어 팀에 가도록 뽑았음에도 불구하고 자신이 뽑힌 상황이다.
13 Michael을 본 Scottie는 갑자기 그에게 미안한 감정이 들었다고 하였다. as soon as: ~하자마자
14 Scottie가 a team player라고 하였다.
15 가주어와 진주어를 활용하여 문장을 만들 수 있다.
16 practice는 동명사를 목적어로 취하는 동사이다.
17 좋은 팀워크가 없으면 시합에서 이길 수 없다는 것이 글의 흐름상 옳다.

영역별 핵심문제

p.145~149

01 ② 02 forward, to, three-legged
03 You can communicate with many people at the same time. 04 ④ 05 ② 06 (A) like (B) What 07 you use English every day
08 ⑤ 09 ④ 10 ④ 11 ②
12 You are looking forward to winning this match, aren't you? 13 ④ 14 (A) Are you ready for the three-legged race? (B) What should we do to win it? 15 ③ to get → get, ⑤ enough clean → clean enough 16 ④ 17 ⑤ 18 It is not a good idea to stay up all night. 19 ③
20 ⑤ 21 ②, ⑤ 22 am passionate enough 23 ② 24 ③
25 This safety belt is strong enough. 26 ③
27 good enough to have a conversation 28 ⑤
29 ④ 30 ⑤ every boys → every boy
31 both are wonderful enough for the senior team
32 ⑤ 33 It is hard to say that Michael is a team player. 34 It is also important to have good teamwork. 35 ④

01 ② quite: 아주, 매우 / 이 작은 마을은 매우 가난하고 많은 문제들을 갖고 있다. ① 그는 매우 빠르게 걷는다. ③ 뉴욕에 가본 적이 있나요? ④ 그들은 똑같이 생겼다. ⑤ 이 공을 네가 할 수 있는 만큼 세게 차라.
02 be looking forward to 동명사: ~하기를 고대하고 있다 three-legged race: 2인 3각 경주
03 at the same time: 동시에
04 pass: 건네다, 넘겨주다 hand: 건네주다
05 shoot: 슛을 쏘다 / 골대 안으로 공을 차거나 때리거나 던지려고 하다
06 (A) like: (전) ~처럼 (B) 어떤 목표나 하고 싶은 일을 달성하기 위해서 무엇을 해야 할지 물을 때 'What do I need to do?'를 사용한다.
07 강조하는 표현에는 'It's important to 동사원형 ~.', ' It's important that 주어+동사 ~.'
08 로봇 축제에 같이 가는 것을 제안하고, 'Sounds great!(좋아!)'로 제안을 수락한다.
09 ④ 로봇 축제는 다음 주말이 아니라 이번 주말에 열린다. ① 남자아이는 여자아이와 같이 로봇 축제에 가기를 원한다. ② 여자아이는 로봇 축제를 고대하고 있다. ③ 여자아이는 로봇 축제에 갈 것이다. ⑤ 남자아이는 로봇 축제에 대한 어떤 것을 보고 있다.
10 ⓐ coming to ⓑ they are ⓒ looking forward to ⓓ too ⓔ can't believe
11 ⓐ going ⓑ joining ⓒ looking ⓓ to win ⓔ to jump.
12 be looking forward to 동명사: ~하기를 고대하고 있다 win: 이기다, 승리하다
13 ⓓ saves your energy → save your energy.
14 (A) be ready for 동명사: ~의 준비가 되다 three-legged race: 이인삼각 경주 (B) should: ~해야 한다 win: 이기다
15 ③ let+목적어+목적격보어(동사원형): 목적어가 ~하도록 하게 하다[시키다] ⑤ 형용사+enough: 충분히 ~한
16 big은 형용사이므로 enough가 뒤에서 수식한다.
17 모두 to get이 들어가지만 ⑤번에는 전치사 of의 목적어로 동명사 getting이 쓰인다.
18 '밤을 새는 것'이므로 'to stay up all night'을 주어로 쓴다.
19 '네가 힘이 없지만 이 노트북은 네가 들고 다닐 수 있을 정도로 충분히 가볍다'는 의미이다. light는 형용사이므로 enough가 뒤에서 수식하고, 의미상의 주어 'for+목적격'이 쓰이고 있으므로 진주어는 to부정사를 쓰는 것이 옳다.
20 enough가 부사로 쓰일 때 형용사, 부사, 동사를 뒤에서 수식한다. 따라서 practice enough라고 쓰는 것이 옳다.
21 주어진 문장의 It은 가주어로 쓰였다. 따라서 ②, ⑤번이 답이다. ① 비인칭 주어, ③, ④ 특정한 명사를 가리키는 인칭대명사
22 passionate은 형용사이므로 enough의 수식을 뒤에서 받는다.
23 주어진 말을 영어로 쓰면 'It is interesting enough to ride a horse.'이다.
24 'for+목적격'은 to부정사의 의미상의 주어이다. '그가 많은 사람들 앞에서 말하는 것은 쉽다'는 의미이므로 진주어로 to부정사를 쓰는 것이 옳다.
25 strong은 형용사이므로 enough가 뒤에서 수식한다.
26 진주어로 쓰일 수 있는 것은 to부정사이다.

27 대화를 나눌 만큼 충분히 영어를 잘하는지 묻는 말이다. good 는 형용사이므로 enough가 뒤에서 수식하는 것이 옳다.

28 [D] 로커 룸에 있을 때 코치가 카드를 줌 → [B] 카드(It)에는 선수들의 이름이 있음 → [C] 시니어 팀에 들어갈 선수를 선수들이 뽑게 함 → [A] Scottie는 Michael의 이름 옆에 체크 표시를 함

29 ④ 주니어 팀에 있는 선수들의 명단이 카드에 있었다.

30 every 뒤에는 단수명사가 온다.

31 두 사람 모두 시니어 팀에 들어가기에 훌륭하다는 의미이다. wonderful은 형용사이므로 enough의 수식을 뒤에서 받는 것에 유의하여 답을 쓴다.

32 Michael이 Scottie에 대해서 어떻게 생각하는지 글에 나와 있지 않다.

33 코치의 말에 따르면 Michael은 팀플레이어라고 말하기 힘들다. that을 생략해도 무방하다.

34 'Having[To have] good teamwork is also important.'라고 써도 무방하다.

12 '너에게 전화하는 것'이므로 'to call you'를 진주어로 쓸 수 있다.

13 '물 없이 살아가는 것'이 주어이므로 to live without water라고 쓰는 것이 옳다. impossible: 불가능한

14 게임에서 이길 만큼 잘하지는 않았다는 의미이다. well은 부사이므로 enough의 수식을 뒤에서 받는다.

15 '단단한'이란 의미의 hard는 형용사이므로 enough의 수식을 뒤에서 받는다.

16 사다리가 충분히 높다고 쓸 수 있다.

17 '그곳에 도착하는 것'이 주어이므로 to get there를 진주어로 쓴다.

18 모두 Scottie를 지칭하는 말이지만 ⑤번은 코치를 지칭하는 말이다.

19 put a check 체크하다

20 (A)와 ①, ②, ④, ⑤는 진주어로 쓰인 to부정사이다. ③은 목적격보어로 쓰인 것이다.

21 코치의 반응으로 보아 Michael이 가장 많은 득점을 했다는 것을 알고 있다.

22 이 두 선수들을 생각할 때면 내 심장이 뛴다. Michael은 정말 좋은 골잡이였다. 그가 위대한 선수였다는 것은 누구도 부인할 수 없다.

23 [C]방에서 나와 Michael을 봄 → [B]미안한 마음이 들어 자신이 Michael을 뽑았음을 말하자 Michael은 Scottie를 뽑았음을 말함 → [A]이 사실에 Scottie는 놀람.

24 놀라움을 느낀 것이므로 surprised라고 쓰는 것이 옳다.

25 그는 Scottie를 뽑았다고 하였다.

26 이유를 나타내는 접속사가 알맞다.

27 그들이 얼마나 오랫동안 연습하는지는 알 수 없다.

단원별 예상문제 p.150~153

01 ⑤ 02 enough 03 (l)eap
04 ① 05 (A) stay (B) save (C) pull
06 shout 07 ④ 08 looking 09 ①
10 It's more important to win it, and I'll go for it.
11 ④ 12 It was hard to call you. Because I am not brave enough. 13 ②, ④ 14 ④
15 ② 16 This ladder is tall enough.
17 It is impossible to get there on time. 18 ⑤
19 ① 20 ③ 21 ⑤
22 (A) leaps (B) such a good shot (C) deny
23 [C]–[A]–[B] 24 ③
25 He picked Scottie. 26 ①, ⑤ 27 ⑤

01 call: 전화하다

02 형용사+enough: 충분히 ~한 / 시험을 준비하기 위해 충분한 시간을 보내지 않았다. 소녀는 그 문제를 해결할 정도로 충분히 현명했다.

03 leap: 뛰다, 빠르게 또는 갑작스럽게 움직이거나 행동하다

04 팀으로 하는 경기이며, 힘을 아끼는 것과 줄을 동시에 당기는 것과 관련된 경기는 줄다리기이다.

05 stay: 유지하다 save: 아끼다, 절약하다 pull: 당기다

06 shout: 소리 지르다 / 큰 소리의 부름 또는 고함

07 quite: 아주, 매우

08 look for: ~을 바라다[기대하다] be looking forward to 동명사: ~하기를 고대하고 있다

09 score: 득점하다

10 It's important to+동사원형 ~: ~하는 것은 중요하다 win: 이기다

11 cute은 형용사이므로 enough의 수식을 뒤에서 받는다.

서술형 실전문제 p.154~155

01 we are going to have an English speech contest next Friday.
02 I want to win a prize
03 ready to → ready for / to hitting → to hit
04 hard enough
05 It is important to warm up before swimming.
06 comfortable enough
07 It takes a lot of time to speak English fluently enough.
08 It is difficult to compare the two.
09 But he shoots whether there's a player in a better position or not. 10 a (good) player
11 He felt like giving a loud and happy shout.
12 Michael picked him (for the senior team).
13 It was my duty to pick just one player.
14 play for the team, make the most baskets

01 be going to 동사원형: ~할 것이다 contest: 대회

02 'I'm looking forward to 동명사 ~.'와 'I want to 동사원형 ~.'은 바람을 나타내는 표현들이다.

03 be ready for: ~의 준비가 되다 be ready to 동사원형: ~할 준

27

비가 되다 It's important to+동사원형 ~: ~하는 것은 중요하다

04 '열심히 일하다'는 work hard이며 enough가 부사로 hard를 수식할 경우 뒤에서 수식한다.

05 가주어 it과 진주어 to부정사를 이용하여 문장을 쓸 수 있다.

06 comfortable은 형용사이므로 enough가 뒤에서 수식한다.

07 fluently는 부사이므로 fluently enough라고 쓰는 것에 유의한다.

08 '그 둘을 비교하는 것'이 주어이므로 'to compare the two'를 쓰는 것이 옳다.

09 '~이든 아니든'이라는 의미로 whether가 쓰이는 것이 옳다.

10 선수를 가리키는 말이다.

11 feel like Ving: ~하고 싶은 기분이다

12 Michael이 Scottie를 뽑았다는 사실을 알고 놀랐다고 하였다.

13 to부정사가 진주어이다.

14 to부정사 진주어가 more ~ than으로 연결되어 있다.

창의사고력 서술형 문제
p.156

|모범답안|

01 looking forward to, birthday / are you going to / will, go to a musical with

02 (1) It is a good idea to play for a team.
(2) It is important to pass the ball to the better player.
(3) It is rude to violate rules.
(4) It is necessary to cooperate with your fellow players.
(5) It is essential to do fair play.

03 (1) The pants are big enough for you to wear.
(2) The car is not large enough.
(3) We always have enough room for everybody.
(4) There are enough flowers to decorate the wedding room.
(5) The boy is confident enough to say his opinion out loud.

01 be looking forward to: ~을 고대하고 있다 be going to 동사원형: ~할 것이다

단원별 모의고사
p.157~160

01 (g)uess   02 (C)ongratulations
03 (1) leap   (2) tie   (3) kick   (4) believe
04 (1) rope   (2) quickly   (3) (q)uite   (4) safety
05 ⑤   06 I'm looking forward to taking part in the parade.   07 ②   08 ②
09 (A) winning (B) kicker   10 ④
11 ② the air is clean today. → the air is not clean today.   12 ③I'm looking forward it! → I'm looking forward to it!   13 ③   14 ⑤
15 ④   16 It is necessary to wear a swimming cap.   17 to build a new airport   18 ②

19 ⑤   20 ③   21 ⑤
22 He gave a card to every boy.
23 I was tied with Michael   24 ④
25 This room is wonderful enough for both of you.

01 주어진 단어는 동의어 관계이다. chance: 기회 opportunity: 기회 guess: 추측하다 infer: 추측하다

02 Congratulations!: 축하합니다!

03 (1) leap: 뛰다, 빠르게 움직이다 / 물고기가 물 밖으로 뛰어올랐다. (2) tie: 동점; 동점을 이루다 / 축구 경기는 무승부로 끝났다. (3) kick: 발길질, 차기; 발로 차다 / 아이는 공을 세게 찼다. (4) believe: 믿다 / 나는 그의 말을 믿을 수 없다.

04 (1) rope: 줄, 로프 (2) quickly: 빨리, 빠르게 (3) quite: 아주, 매우 (4) safety: 안전

05 Same here.: 나도 그래.

06 take part in: ~에 참여[참가]하다 look forward to (동)명사: ~을 기대하다, ~을 고대하다

07 ⓐ ready for ⓑ Yes, I am ⓒ to winning ⓓ to win ⓔ It's

08 준하가 남호에게 페널티 킥을 차야 한다고 하는 말에 남호가 하는 말이다.

09 be looking forward to 동명사: ~하는 것을 고대하고 있다 win: 이기다 kick: 발길질, 차기; 발로 차다 kicker: (축구에서 공을) 차는 사람

10 ④ 지금 경기의 점수는 언급되어 있지 않았다. ① 누가 공을 더 잘 차는가? ② 누가 페널티 킥 전담인가? ③ 누가 올스타 팀에 선발될 기회를 바라고 있는가? ⑤ 그들은 어디에 있는가?

11 공기가 좋은데 마스크를 가져다주는 것은 어색하다.

12 be looking forward to 명사: ~을 고대하고 있다

13 smart는 형용사이므로 enough의 수식을 뒤에서 받는다.

14 모두 to make가 쓰이지만 ⑤번에는 making이 쓰인다. keep Ving: 계속해서 V하다

15 easy는 형용사이므로 enough의 수식을 뒤에서 받는다. 따라서 easy enough to read라고 쓰는 것이 옳다.

16 a swimming cap: 수영 모자

17 새로운 공항을 짓는 것을 어떻게 생각하느냐는 질문이므로 to build a new airport라고 쓰는 것이 옳다.

18 주어진 문장의 It이 가리키는 것은 코치가 나누어준 카드이다.

19 ⑤ 코치가 누구를 뽑았는지는 위 글을 읽고 답할 수 없다.

20 (A)는 완전한 문장을 이끄는 명사절 접속사이다. 따라서 불완전한 문장을 이끄는 ③번이 관계대명사로 (A)와 쓰임이 다르다.

21 among은 일반적으로 셋 이상의 것 중에서 선택할 때 쓰는 전치사이다. 둘 사이의 선택은 between이 옳다.

22 코치가 선수들에게 준 것은 카드이다.

23 자신이 Michael과 동점이라는 사실을 들은 것은 놀라움을 주었다는 의미이다.

24 크고 기쁜 소리를 지르고 싶은 마음이었다고 하였으므로 ④번이 옳다.

25 wonderful이 형용사이므로 enough의 수식을 뒤에서 받는 것에 유의한다.

교과서 파헤치기

Lesson
1

01 과학자	02 지시, 명령	03 무대
04 예술가, 미술가	05 충직한, 충성스러운, 신의가 있는	
06 계절	07 친근한	08 정직한
09 배려하는, 보살피는		10 맛
11 패턴, 정형화된 양식		12 기대하다
13 제공하다	14 장난기 많은	15 생각이 깊은
16 선호하다	17 발명가	18 재치 있는
19 가장 나쁜	20 조직하다, 정리 정돈하다	
21 결과	22 수다스러운	23 맛있는
24 행, 선	25 전통	
26 창의적인, 상상력이 풍부한		27 호기심 많은
28 활동적인	29 성격, 개성	30 가능성, 기회
31 해결하다	32 생기 넘치는	33 건강하지 못한
34 신중한	35 ~을 최대한 활용하다	
36 ~을 생각해 내다, 안을 세우다		37 혼자서, 단독으로
38 ~을 잘하다	39 ~하고 싶다	40 ~이 어땠어?
41 ~하는 게 어때?	42 ~에게 조언[충고]을 구하다	
43 ~는 어때?		

01 careful	02 energetic	03 stomach
04 energize	05 flavor	06 follow
07 position	08 tradition	09 chance
10 imaginative	11 curious	12 lively
13 unhealthy	14 active	15 please
16 engineer	17 unique	18 personality
19 energizer	20 activity	21 solve
22 type	23 friendly	24 talkative
25 worst	26 caring	27 faithful
28 witty	29 thoughtful	30 organize
31 serve	32 expect	33 result
34 playful	35 Why don't we ~?	
36 look at	37 would like to+동사원형	
38 on one's own	39 be going to+동사원형	
40 ask ~ for advice		41 what kind of ~
42 be good at	43 What is ~ like?	

1 lively, 생기 넘치는   2 tradition, 전통

3 caring, 배려하는, 보살피는   4 follow, 따르다

5 activity, 활동   6 please, 기쁘게 하다   7 chance, 기회

8 prefer, 선호하다   9 solve, 해결하다

10 personality, 성격, 개성   11 stage, 무대

12 organize, 조직하다, 정리 정돈하다

13 pattern, 패턴, 정형화된 양식

14 engineer, 기술자   15 faithful, 충직한, 충성스러운

16 stomach, 위(장)

Listen & Speak 1 A

1 I'm / too, don't we go / idea, open / say that, seves special, on Sunday

2 Are there, this weekend / say that there's / on Saturday / What kind of / say that it's really exciting

Listen & Speak 1 B

1 the result / got / What, like / say, is thoughtful

2 What, result / I got / What is like / They say that, imaginative

Listen & Speak 2 A

1 Look at / look yummy / Which, do you like / like, most

2 Are, flavors / they, look delicious / Which flavor, prefer / prefer, flavor

Listen & Speak 2 B

1 Which season, prefer / What, like / say that, quiet and thoughtful / am, I'm not

2 Which season do you prefer / prefer, like / faithful and honest / I am, I'm not

Communication

How did, like / really fun, about myself / What type of / da-Vinci-type / sounds, are, good at / say that, people, inventors / Which one, prefer / not sure, I'm going to ask, for, advice

Real-Life Task

In which position / in, position / What, like / say that, warm and friendly / How good, health / the best position

Listen & Speak 1 A

1 G: I'm hungry.

   B: Me, too. Why don't we go to Sweet Snack?

G: That's a good idea. But is it open today?

B: Yes, it is. They say that it serves special pancakes on Sunday.

2 G: Are there any good programs this weekend?

B: Well, they say that there's a special dance show at the Youth Center on Saturday.

G: What kind of dance show is it?

B: It's an Indian dance show. People say that it's really exciting.

Listen & Speak 1 B

1 A: What was the result?

B: I got Hamlet.

A: What is a Hamlet–type person like?

B: They say that a Hamlet–type person is thoughtful.

2 A: What was the result?

B: I got da Vinci.

A: What is a da–Vinci–type person like?

B: They say that a da–Vinci–type person is imaginative.

Listen & Speak 2 A

1 G: Look at the cakes!

B: They look yummy.

G: Which cake do you like most?

B: I like the chocolate cake most.

2 B: Are they new ice cream flavors?

G: Yes, they are. They look delicious.

B: Which flavor do you prefer?

G: I prefer the strawberry flavor.

Listen & Speak 2 B

1 A: Which season do you prefer?

B: I prefer summer. What are summer people like?

A: They say that summer people are quiet and thoughtful. Are you?

B: Yes, I am. / No, I'm not.

2 A: Which season do you prefer?

B: I prefer winter. What are winter people like?

A: They say that winter people are faithful and honest. Are you?

B: Yes, I am. / No, I'm not.

Communication

Nara: How did you like the test?

Seho: It was really fun. I learned a lot about myself.

Nara: What type of person are you?

Seho: I'm a da–Vinci–type person.

Nara: That sounds cool. What are da–Vinci people good at?

Seho: They say that da–Vinci people make good

inventors and artists.

Nara: Which one do you prefer?

Seho: I'm not sure. I'm going to ask my teacher for some advice.

Real-Life Task

A: In which position do you sleep?

B: I sleep in the back position.

A: What are back sleepers like?

B: People say that they are warm and friendly.

A: How good is that position for your health?

B: Scientists say that it's the best position for sleeping.

본문 TEST Step 1   p.09~10

01 What, Your Color   02 Who am

03 What type, person

04 Do, these questions

05 Here, interesting personality

06 Which activities, ones, at

07 enjoy, good at 08 free, having, with

09 taking chances, following

10 working, own, writing

11 learning, following, rules

12 making, planning, out

13 pleasing, finding, patterns

14 stage, with directions   15 solving, playing

16 your color   17 Circle, from, with, most

18 What type of   19 more circles, line, energizer

20 witty, lively, in, settings

21 gold line, excellent organizer

22 faithful, careful, work, rules

23 Knowing yourself, wisdom

24 circles, line, great listener

25 warm, caring, in groups

26 on, green, curious thinker

27 cool, work, own

28 type, how much, like

29 Take, as, step, true

30 unique, special

31 Why don't, make, most

본문 TEST Step 2   p.11~12

01 What, Your Color   02 Who am

03 What type of   04 these questions

05 an interesting personality test

06 Which activities, which ones are, good at

07 good at 08 free, having fun, working with

09 taking chances, following

10 on my own, writing

11 learning, things, following, rules

12 making new friends, planning, out

13 pleasing, new patterns

14 on stage, with directions 15 solving, playing

16 your color 17 Circle, from, with, most circles

18 What type of person

19 orange line, wonderful energizer

20 witty, lively, work best in

21 more circles, excellent organizer

22 faithful, careful, best with

23 Knowing yourself, wisdom

24 blue line, great listener

25 caring, in groups 26 curious thinker

27 cool, work best on your own

28 type, how much

29 Take, as, try to find

30 unique, had, special

31 Why don't you, make the most of

---

21 황금색 줄에 더 많은 동그라미 표시가 있다면, 당신은 뛰어난 조직가입니다.

22 당신은 충직하고 조심스러우며, 분명한 규칙이 제시된 경우에 가장 잘 일합니다.

23 스스로를 아는 것은 모든 지혜의 시작이다. – 아리스토텔레스

24 푸른색 줄에 더 많은 동그라미 표시가 있다면, 당신은 대단한 경청자입니다.

25 당신은 따뜻하고 남을 잘 돌보며, 집단과 더불어 가장 잘 일합니다.

26 초록색 줄에 더 많은 동그라미 표시가 있다면, 당신은 호기심 많은 사색가입니다.

27 당신은 멋지고 조용하며, 혼자서 (일할 때) 가장 잘 일합니다.

28 당신의 유형은 무엇이며, 그것을 얼마나 좋아합니까?

29 이 성격 검사를 첫 단계로 삼아서, 당신의 진정한 색깔을 찾아보려고 노력하세요.

30 모든 사람들은 독특하고 특별한 색깔을 지니고 있습니다.

31 스스로에게 귀를 기울이고, 스스로에 관하여 특별한 것들을 발견하며, 그것들을 최대한 이용해 보면 어떨까요?

본문 TEST Step 3
p.13~14

1 당신의 색깔은 무엇입니까?

2 나는 누구인가?

3 나는 어떤 유형의 사람인가?

4 이런 질문들을 가지고 있나요?

5 여기에 당신을 위한 흥미로운 성격 검사가 있습니다.

6 [Step1] 당신은 어떤 활동을 즐겨 합니까, 그리고 어떤 활동을 잘하나요?

7 나는 ~을 즐긴다/나는 ~을 잘한다

8 1. 자유로우며 재미있게 놀기 2. 사람들과 함께 일하기

9 3. 운(運)에 맡기고 해 보기 4. 전통을 따르기

10 5. 혼자서 일하기 6. 이야기 쓰기

11 7. 새로운 것 배우기 8. 규칙을 따르기

12 9. 새로운 친구를 사귀기 10. 계획을 세우기

13 11. 다른 사람을 즐겁게 해 주기 12. 새로운 패턴을 찾기

14 13. 무대에 서기 14. 지시를 받고 일하기

15 15. 수수께끼 풀기 16. 운동 경기를 하기

16 [Step2] 당신의 색깔은 무엇입니까?

17 Step 1에서 고른 숫자에 동그라미 표시를 하고, 가장 많은 동그라미 표시가 있는 줄을 찾으세요.

18 [Step3] 당신은 어떤 유형의 사람입니까?

19 주황색 줄에 더 많은 동그라미 표시가 있다면, 당신은 놀라운 활력을 주는 사람입니다.

20 당신은 재치 있고 생기 있으며, 게임 환경에서 가장 잘 일합니다.

본문 TEST Step 4- Step 5
p.15~18

1 What Is Your Color?

2 Who am I?

3 What type of person am I?

4 Do you have these questions?

5 Here we have an interesting personality test for you.

6 Step 1 Which activities do you enjoy, and which ones are you good at?

7 I enjoy … / I'm good at …

8 1. being free and having fun. 2. working with people.

9 3. taking chances. 4. following traditions.

10 5. working on my own. 6. writing stories.

11 7. learning new things. 8. following the rules.

12 9. making new friends. 10. planning things out.

13 11. pleasing others. 12. finding new patterns.

14 13. being on stage. 14. working with directions.

15 15. solving puzzles. 16. playing sports.

16 Step 2 What is your color?

17 Circle the numbers from Step 1, and find the line with the most circles.

18 Step 3 What type of person are you?

19 If you have more circles on the orange line, you are a wonderful energizer.

20 You are witty and lively, and you work best in game settings.

21 If you have more circles on the gold line, you are an excellent organizer.

22 You are faithful and careful, and you work best with clear rules.

23 Knowing yourself is the beginning of all wisdom. – Aristotle

24 If you have more circles on the blue line, you are a great listener.

25 You are warm and caring, and you work best in groups.

26 If you have more circles on the green line, you are a curious thinker.

27 You are cool and quiet, and you work best on your own.

28 What is your type, and how much do you like it?

29 Take this personality test as a first step and try to find your true color.

30 Everyone is unique and has a special color.

31 Why don't you listen to yourself, find special things about yourself, and make the most of them?

2. I'm a fall person, and I'm a stomach sleeper.

3. They say that I'm a Don-Quixote-type person.

4. I'm going to put an art board on the classroom wall.

5. Why don't you show your dreams, plans, and ideas on the board?

Look and Write

1. Which subjects can I do well in? Which clubs should I join?

2. I have a lot of questions about school life.

3. The personality test says that I am a curious thinker.

4. It also says that I am cool and quiet and I work best on my own.

5. I am going to start from my strong points.

6. I want to make the most of them.

7. I know that I can do really well this year.

Language Detective

1. I went to Mina's birthday party.

2. I met her parents and introduced myself to them.

3. They welcomed me and said, "Would you please help yourself to the food?"

4. It was a great party, and my friends and I enjoyed a lot.

구석구석지문 TEST Step 1   p.19

Communication Step B

1. My color

2. fall person, stomach sleeper

3. They say that, type

4. I'm going to put

5. Why don't you show

Look and Write

1. Which, do well in, Which, should I

2. a lot of

3. personality test, that

4. also says, best on my own

5. going to start, strong points

6. to make, most of

7. that, this year

Language Detective

1. went to

2. met, introduced myself

3. welcomed me, help yourself to

4. great party, a lot

구석구석지문 TEST Step 2   p.20

Communication Step B

1. My color is orange.

11 problem, 문제　12 reuse, 재사용하다

13 slogan, 구호, 슬로건　14 another, 다른, 또 하나의

15 nail, 못으로 박다　16 collect, 모으다, 수집하다

단어 TEST Step 1　　　　　　　　p.21

01 유명한	02 쓰레기	03 못으로 박다; 못
04 옷감, 천	05 구호, 슬로건	06 모으다, 수집하다
07 버려진	08 속상하게 만들다	09 핸들
10 예술 작품	11 중고의	
12 서두르다, 급히 하다		13 상상력, 상상
14 나무, 목재	15 걱정하다	16 보물
17 (포장지 등으로) 싸다		18 흔히
19 부분, 조각	20 문제	21 더 적은
22 좌석, 안장	23 물건	24 여성
25 쓰레기	26 조각품	27 세트
28 그러한	29 쓸모 있는, 유용한	30 폐물, 고물
31 재사용하다	32 실; (실 등을) 꿰다	33 쓰레기; 낭비하다
34 창작하다	35 ~할 수 있다	36 서두르다
37 ~에 늦다	38 A뿐만 아니라 B도	
39 ~을 이용하다	40 ~에 대해 걱정하다	
41 다소, 약간	42 줍다, 얻다	43 ~처럼 보이다

단어 TEST Step 2　　　　　　　　p.22

01 board	02 mess	03 button
04 pass	05 create	06 treasure
07 glue	08 cloth	09 another
10 worry	11 wood	12 bit
13 junk	14 imagination	15 clothes
16 slipper	17 reuse	18 able
19 thrown-away	20 used	21 nail
22 mattress	23 part	24 quilt
25 agree	26 waste	27 piece
28 thread	29 collect	30 artwork
31 sculpture	32 wrap	33 useful
34 famous	35 a bit	36 pick up
37 be worried about		38 agree with
39 make use of	40 clean up	41 be late for
42 hurry up	43 make noise	

단어 TEST Step 3　　　　　　　　p.23

1 used, 중고의　2 pass, 합격하다, 통과하다

3 artwork, 예술 작품　4 less, 더 적은　5 create, 창작하다

6 board, 판자　7 contest, 대회, 시합　8 rubbish, 쓰레기

9 glue, 접착제로 붙이다　10 junk, 폐물, 고물

대화문 TEST Step 1　　　　　　　　p.24~25

Listen & Speak 1 Get Ready

What's / worried about, sick

Listen & Speak 1 A

1 What's / worried about, presentation / Don't worry, do

2 forgot to bring / not again / worried about forgetting

3 look unhappy / I'm worried about / Don't worry, will pass

Listen & Speak 1 B

1 I'm worried about, waste / should reuse / can reuse bottles as

2 worried about, waste problem / too, should reuse / idea, reuse, as wrapping paper

Listen & Speak 2 Get Ready

green / can say, again

Listen & Speak 2 A

1 Look at, mess / clean, up, keep, clean / can say that again

2 Hurry up, going to / I think we should / don't agree

3 wearing, isn't he / is / shouldn't wear slippers / agree

Conversation

poster for, contest / is / like, More, Less, Where, get, idea / got, from junk art / uses, doesn't it / does, worried about, have to do something / can say that

Check My Progress

look, What's wrong / I'm worried about, speech / Don't worry, such / feel worried / Don't be nervous, fine

대화문 TEST Step 2　　　　　　　　p.26~27

Listen & Speak 1 Get Ready

B: What's wrong?

G: I'm worried about my dog. He is very sick.

Listen & Speak 1 A

1 G: What's wrong, Seho?

　B: I'm worried about my science presentation.

　G: Don't worry too much. You'll do a good job.

2 B: Oops. I forgot to bring your book.

G: No, not again, Namho!

B: I'm sorry. I'm really worried about forgetting things.

3 B: You look unhappy, Sumi.

G: I'm worried about the test.

B: Don't worry too much. You will pass.

Listen & Speak 1 B

1 A: I'm worried about the waste problem.

B: Me, too. We should reuse everyday things

A: That's a good idea. We can reuse bottles as flower vases.

2 A: I'm worried about the waste problem.

B: Me, too. We should reuse everyday things.

A: That's a good idea. We can reuse old paper as wrapping paper.

Listen & Speak 2 Get Ready

B: We should go green.

G: You can say that again.

Listen & Speak 2 A

1 G: Look at this mess!

B: Let's clean it up. We should keep our classroom clean.

G: You can say that again.

2 G: Hurry up! We're going to be late.

B: I think we should have longer lunch breaks.

G: Well, I don't agree.

3 B: He's wearing his slippers, isn't he?

G: Yes, he is.

B: We shouldn't wear slippers in the school garden.

G: I agree.

Conversation

Seho: Is this your poster for the art contest, Nara?

Nara: Yes, it is, Seho.

Seho: I like your slogan, "Reuse More, Waste Less!" Where did you get that idea?

Nara: I got it from junk art.

Seho: Junk art uses thrown-away things, doesn't it?

Nara: Yes, it does. I'm worried about the waste problem. We have to do something about it.

Seho: You can say that again.

Check My Progress

G: You look nervous, Minho. What's wrong?

B: I'm worried about the speech contest.

G: Don't worry too much. You're such a good speaker.

B: Thank you, but I feel worried.

G: Don't be nervous. You'll do fine.

B: Thanks.

본문 TEST Step 1 — p.28~29

01 Old, New
02 made out, kinds, around
03 made, such as, bits
04 Junk, *Head*
05 How, like, artwork
06 was created by
07 used, seat, to make
08 During, there, useful
09 creating, picked up, such
10 not only, but also
11 Thrown-away, New
12 was created by
13 thrown-away objects, artwork
14 often, things, good
15 not, pieces, also bits
16 glued, nailed, created, style
17 In, moved to
18 able, out, looked like
19 What, things, around
20 What, artwork, out of
21 imagination, something new
22 One, trash, another's

본문 TEST Step 2 — p.30~31

01 Old, New Art
02 be made out of, around us
03 are often made, from, such as, bits of paper
04 Junk
05 How, like
06 was created by
07 used, seat, to make
08 During, there were not, useful things
09 couldn't stop creating, picked up, such as
10 not only, but also, to create
11 Thrown-away, New Art
12 was created by
13 thrown-away objects to make
14 are good for
15 collected, pieces of paper, bits of wood
16 glued, nailed, to, style of art
17 moved to
18 was able to take, out of, looked like
19 What old things, around
20 What new artwork
21 create something new
22 trash, another's treasure

본문 TEST Step 3 — p.32~33

1 낡은 것들, 새로운 예술

2 예술은 우리 주변의 모든 오래된 것들로 만들어질 수 있습니다.

3 유명한 조각품들과 그림들은 종종 깡통, 병 및 종잇조각과 같은 일상 용품으로 만들어집니다.

4 자전거 고물과 *Bull 's Head*

5 이 작품은 어떻습니까?

6 그것은 Pablo Picasso에 의해 만들어졌습니다.

7 그는 이 조각 작품을 만들기 위해 자전거 좌석과 핸들을 사용했습니다!

8 제2차 세계 대전 중에는 예술을 위해 쓸 수 있는 것들이 많지 않았습니다.

9 그러나 Picasso는 작품 창작을 멈출 수 없어서, 오래된 자전거나 매트리스 스프링과 같은 고물을 주웠습니다.

10 그는 오래된 것들뿐만 아니라 그의 상상력도 사용하여 1942년에 이 조각품을 창작하였습니다.

11 버려진 것들과 새로운 예술

12 이 작품은 Kurt Schwitters에 의해 창작되었습니다.

13 그는 작품을 만들기 위해 버려진 물건들을 사용합니다.

14 그는 종종 "오래된 것들은 예술에 좋다"고 말했습니다.

15 Schwitters는 거리를 걸으면서 종잇조각뿐만 아니라 나무 조각도 모았습니다.

16 그는 그것들을 판자에 풀이나 못으로 붙여, Rubbish라는 새로운 방식의 예술을 창조했습니다.

17 1937년 그는 노르웨이로 이주했습니다.

18 쓰레기처럼 보였기 때문에 그는 그의 유명한 작품을 독일에서 가져갈 수 있었습니다.

19 당신 주변에 어떠한 오래된 것들이 있습니까?

20 당신은 그것들로 어떤 새로운 작품을 만들 수 있습니까?

21 당신의 상상력을 이용하여 새로운 것을 창작하십시오.

22 한 사람의 쓰레기가 다른 사람의 보물입니다!

본문 TEST Step 4-Step 5 　　　　　　　　p.34~37

1 Old Things, New Art

2 Art can be made out of all kinds of old things around us.

3 Famous sculptures and pictures are often made from everyday things　such as cans, bottles, and bits of paper.

4 Bicycle Junk and *Bull's Head*

5 How do you like this artwork?

6 It was created by Pablo Picasso.

7 He used a bicycle seat and handlebars to make this sculpture!

8 During World War II, there were not a lot of useful things for art.

9 But Picasso couldn't stop creating artwork, so he picked up junk such as old bicycles and mattress springs.

10 He used not only old things but also his imagination to create this sculpture in 1942.

11 Thrown-away Things and New Art

---

12 This artwork was created by Kurt Schwitters.

13 He used thrown-away objects to make artwork.

14 He often said, "Old things are good for art."

15 Schwitters walked the streets and collected not only pieces of paper but also bits of wood.

16 He glued and nailed them to a board, and created a new style of art, Rubbish.

17 In 1937, he moved to Norway.

18 He was able to take his famous work out of Germany because it looked like rubbish.

19 What old things do you have around you?

20 What new artwork can you make out of them?

21 Use your imagination and create something new.

22 One person's trash is another's treasure!

구석구석지문 TEST Step 1 　　　　　　　　p.38

Let's Write Step 1

1. artwork

2. was created by

3. not only, but also, to make

4. trash, another's treasure

Project Across Subjects Step 3

1. Artwork

2. used, plastic, white, colored paper

3. Special Feature, swim around

4. artwork, called

5. was created by, of

6. used

7. Give, water, put, in

8. swim around

Check My Progress 4

1. cloth to make, such as

2. thread, to make, patchwork quilts

3. Making, at all

4. to make, wrapping cloth

5. around, old cloth, useful things

구석구석지문 TEST Step 2 　　　　　　　　p.39

Let's Write Step 1

1. This artwork is *Bull's Head*.

2. It was created by Pablo Picasso.

3. He used not only old bicycle parts but also his imagination to make this artwork.

4. One person's trash is another's treasure.

Project Across Subjects Step 3

1. Artwork: Color Fish

2. We used: a plastic bottle, a big white button, a small black button, and colored paper

3. Special Feature: Give the fish some water, and it will swim around.

4. This is our artwork. It is called Color Fish .

5. It was created by the three of us: Minho, Changsu, and Nami. 6

6. We used a plastic bottle, a big white button, a small black button, and colored paper.

7. Give the fish some water, and put it in the pool.

8. The colorful fish will swim around.

Check My Progress 4

1. Seminole Indians in the U.S. use old cloth to make clothes such as skirt.

2. People in Bangladesh use thread and old cloth to make flowery patchwork quilts.

3. 1. Making beautiful artwork is not easy at all.

4. 2. Indians love to make skirts and wrapping cloth.

5. 3. People around the world use old cloth to make useful things.

단어 TEST Step 1   p.40

01 인기 있는, 유명한	02 축하
03 어느 때고, 한 번이라도	04 당기다
05 슛을 쏘다 06 안전	07 먼저, 우선
08 ~이든 아니든 09 같은, 동일한	10 중요한
11 득점하다, 득점 12 믿다	13 아주, 매우
14 팀워크, 협력 15 가슴, 심장	16 슛을 쏘는 사람
17 2인 3각 경주 18 뛰다, 빠르게 움직이다	
19 (축구에서 공을) 차는 사람	20 위치
21 코치, 감독 22 건네주다	23 동점 동점을 이루다
24 매달리다 25 아끼다, 절약하다	26 기회, 자리, 개막식
27 소리 지르다 28 뽑다, 선발하다	29 추측하다
30 빨리, 빠르게 31 기회	32 한숨 쉬다
33 ~하는 동안 34 줄, 로프	35 ~에 참여[참가]하다
36 ~하는 것은 중요하다	37 ~할 준비가 되다
38 동시에 39 ~할 준비가 되다	
40 농구 경기에서 득점하다	
41 ~을 기대하다, ~을 고대하다	42 ~이든 아니든
43 ~을 바라다[기대하다]	

단어 TEST Step 2   p.41

01 basket	02 deny	03 coach
04 senior	05 guess	06 hand
07 shout	08 position	09 hang
10 junior	11 kick	12 whether
13 hard	14 teamwork	15 quite
16 call	17 while	18 shoot
19 chance	20 believe	21 leap
22 safety	23 rope	24 save
25 opening	26 list	27 pull
28 locker room	29 tie	30 heart
31 shot	32 penalty kick	33 important
34 score	35 at the same time	
36 do one's best	37 take part in	38 whether ~ or not
39 turn off	40 feel like + 동명사	41 be ready for
42 next to	43 make a basket	

단어 TEST Step 3   p.42

1 shout, 외침, 고함   2 opening, 기회, 자리

3 shot, 슛을 쏘는 사람   4 hand, 건네주다   5 chance, 기회

6 score, 득점하다 7 tie, 동점을 이루다 8 sigh, 한숨 쉬다
9 coach, 코치, 감독 10 deny, 부인하다
11 shoot, 슛을 쏘다 12 hang, 매달리다
13 leap, 뛰다, 빠르게 움직이다 14 pick, 뽑다, 선발하다
15 save, 아끼다, 절약하다 16 guess, 추측하다

대화문 TEST Step 1   p.43~44

Listen & Speak 1 Get Ready
visiting us / looking forward to seeing

Listen & Speak 1 A
1 know what, are going to go to / I'm, looking forward to
2 Are, coming to / are, looking forward to seeing / too, can't believe
3 are going to have, next / finally having, am, winning a prize

Listen & Speak 1 B
1 is coming, can't wait / Same, looking, doing / looking, doing, dance
2 I can't wait, What are you looking forward to doing / looking forward, running, three–legged

Listen & Speak 2 Get Ready
it's, to call

Listen & Speak 2 A
1 want to be, like, need to / it's important to use
2 ready to go / safety, It's, to wear
3 What, doing / Let me turn off, It's, to save energy

Listen & Talk 2 B
1 Are, ready for / am, I'm looking, winning / should, win / It's important to hit, hard
2 Are you ready / looking forward to winning / What should we do / It's important to pass

Real-Life Task
What, going to join / looking forward to joining, How about / also looking forward, What should we do to win / it's, to jump, at the same time

대화문 TEST Step 2   p.45~46

Listen & Speak 1 Get Ready
W: Grandpa is visiting us this Friday.
G: Great! I'm looking forward to seeing him!

Listen & Speak 1 A
1 G: You know what, Minho? We are going to go to Jeju for our school trip.

2 B: Are the N–Boys coming to the school festival, Jimin?
   G: Yes, they are. I'm really looking forward to seeing them!
   B: Me, too. I can't believe it
3 B: Sumi, we are going to have an English speech contest next Friday.
   G: Wow, we are finally having it. I am looking forward to winning a prize!

Listen & Speak 1 B
1 A: School Sports Day is coming soon! I can't wait.
   B: Same here. What are you looking forward to doing?
   A: I'm looking forward to doing a group dance.
2 A: School Sports Day is coming soon! I can't wait.
   B: Same here. What are you looking forward to doing?
   A: I'm looking forward to running in the three–legged race.

Listen & Speak 2 Get Ready
M: When there's a fire, it's important to call 119 first.

Listen & Speak 2 A
1 B: I want to be a good English speaker like you. What do I need to do?
   G: Well, it's important to use English every day.
2 B: I am ready to go bike riding.
   G: Wait, safety first. It's important to wear gloves.
3 B: What are you still doing in the classroom? Hurry up!
   G: Just a minute. Let me turn off the lights. It's important to save energy.

Listen & Talk 2 B
1 A: Are you ready for the baseball game?
   B: Yes, I am. I'm looking forward to winning it.
   A: Me, too. What should we do to win it?
   B: It's important to hit the ball hard.
2 A: Are you ready for the soccer match?
   B: Yes, I am. I'm looking forward to winning it.
   A: Me, too. What should we do to win it?
   B: It's important to pass the ball quickly.

Real-Life Task
A: What team sport are you going to join on School Sports Day?
B: I'm looking forward to joining the group jump rope game. How about you?
A: I'm also looking forward to it. What should we do to win the game?
B: I think it's important to jump together at the same time.

01 game, over   02 junior, won, were

03 While, were, handed every   04 list of, on

05 As, all know, opening

06 Why don't, pick   07 Check, on

08 looked at, saw

09 sighed, put, next to

10 deny that, good enough

11 collected every, from

12 Everyone's, were high   13 all wanted to

14 looked up, tie between   15 heart leaped

16 was surprised, tied

17 both, enough, hard, pick   18 have to, pick

19 Then, walked over

20 but, such a, shot

21 makes, most baskets   22 Of, does

23 whether there's, or not

24 important to play

25 Don't, when, see   26 walked out of

27 like, loud, shout   28 Then, saw

29 Suddenly, sorry for

30 don't care, picked, for

31 smiled, what, picked

32 was surprised, did   33 always do, best

34 played for, won

01 was over   02 won, were

03 While, were in, handed every, a card

04 a list of, on

05 As you all know, an opening, senior

06 Why don't you pick

07 Check, on the list

08 looked at, saw

09 sighed, put, next to

10 couldn't deny that, good enough

11 collected every card from

12 Everyone's, were high   13 wanted to be

14 looked up, a tie between   15 heart leaped

16 was surprised that, tied

17 wonderful enough, hard to pick

18 have to, so, pick   19 walked over

20 such a good shot

21 makes the most baskets

22 Of course, does

23 shoots whether there's a player, or not

24 It's to play for

25 Don't worry, when, see, one   26 walked out of

27 felt like giving, loud   28 Then, saw

29 Suddenly, felt sorry for

30 don't care, picked, for

31 smiled, what, picked

32 was surprised, did

33 always do your best

34 played for, won, Congratulations

1 경기는 끝났다.

2 주니어 팀은 경기에서 승리했고, 모든 선수들이 행복했다.

3 그들이 로커 룸에 있는 동안, 코치가 모든 소년들에게 카드 한 장씩을 건네주었다.

4 그 카드는 주니어 팀의 모든 선수들의 명단을 담고 있었다.

5 "모두 알고 있듯이, 우리는 시니어 팀에 한 자리가 비어 있어." 코치가 말했다.

6 "여러분들이 시니어 팀에 들어갈 선수를 뽑아 보는 것이 어떨까?

7 명단 위의 이름 하나에 체크 표시를 해 주게."

8 Scottie는 명단을 보았고 자신의 이름을 보았다.

9 그러고는 한숨을 쉰 후 Michael의 이름 옆에 체크 표시를 하였다.

10 그는 Michael이 시니어 팀에 충분히 훌륭하다는 것을 부인할 수 없었다.

11 코치가 소년들로부터 모든 카드를 거두었다.

12 모든 선수들의 바람은 높았다.

13 그들은 모두 시니어 팀에 들어가기를 원했다.

14 코치가 올려다보고 말했다. "흠, Michael과 Scottie가 동점이구나."

15 Scottie의 심장이 뛰었다.

16 그는 자기가 Michael과 동점이 되어서 놀라웠다.

17 "흠." 코치가 말했다. "둘 다 시니어 팀에 들어가기에 충분히 훌륭하고, 단 한 명의 선수를 선정하는 것은 어려운 일이야.

18 그러나 나는 선정해야 하기에, Scottie를 뽑겠어."

19 그리고 코치가 Scottie에게 걸어와서 말했다. "축하해!"

20 "감사합니다. 그러나 Michael은 훌륭한 골잡이에요.

21 Michael이 득점을 가장 많이 하고 있어요." Scottie가 말했다.

22 "물론, Michael이 그렇지." 코치가 말했다.

23 "그러나 Michael은 더 나은 위치에 선수가 있든 없든, 슛을 쏴.

24 팀을 위해 경기하는 것이 중요해!

25 걱정 마. 나는 보면 좋은 선수인지 안단다."

26 Scottie는 방에서 걸어 나갔다.

27 그는 크고 기쁜 소리를 지르고 싶은 마음이었다.

28 그때 그는 Michael을 보았다.

29 갑자기 Scottie는 그에게 미안한 감정이 들었다.

30 "나는 네가 신경 쓰지 않으리라고 추측하지만, 시니어 팀에 너를 뽑았어."라고 Scottie가 말했다.

31 Michael이 미소 지었다. "너 그거 아니? 나도 너를 뽑았어."

32 Scottie가 놀랐다. "네가 그랬어?"

33 "응. 너는 항상 최선을 다 해, 그리고 너는 팀플레이어야.

34 오늘 너는 팀을 위해 경기했고, 우리는 게임에서 이겼는걸.

35 축하해!"

26 Scottie walked out of the room.

27 He felt like giving a loud and happy shout.

28 Then he saw Michael.

29 Suddenly Scottie felt sorry for him.

30 "I guess you don't care, but I picked you for the senior team," said Scottie.

31 Michael smiled. "You know what? I picked YOU."

32 Scottie was surprised. "You did?"

33 "Yeah. You always do your best, and you're a team player.

34 Today you played for the team, and we won the game. Congratulations!"

1 The game was over..

2 The junior team won it, and all the players were happy.

3 While they were in the locker room, the coach handed every boy a card.

4 It had a list of the players on the junior team.

5 "As you all know, we have an opening for a player on the senior team," said the coach.

6 "Why don't you pick a player for the team?

7 Check one name on the list."

8 Scottie looked at the list and saw his name.

9 Then he sighed and put a check next to Michael's name.

10 He couldn't deny that Michael was good enough for the senior team.

11 The coach collected every card from the boys.

12 Everyone's hopes were high.

13 They all wanted to be on the senior team.

14 The coach looked up and said, "Well, it's a tie between Michael and Scottie."

15 Scottie's heart leaped.

16 He was surprised that he was tied with Michael.

17 "Well," said the coach, "both are wonderful enough for the senior team, and it's hard to pick just one player.

18 But I have to, so I'll pick Scottie."

19 Then the coach walked over to Scottie and said, "Congratulations!"

20 "Thank you, but Michael is such a good shot.

21 He makes the most baskets," said Scottie.

22 "Of course, he does," said the coach.

23 "But he shoots whether there's a player in a better position or not.

24 It's important to play for the team!

25 Don't worry. I know a good player when I see one."

After I Read B

1. Congratulations

2. am sure that, do well

3. Good for

4. a lot, do my best

5. wonderful enough

6. feel, down, keep going

7. work harder

Before I Read

1. leaps, think about

2. such, good shot

3. No one, deny

4. lots of, because, a lot

Let's Write

1. everyone

2. after school

3. practice, shooting because, to pass

4. It, to have

5. Without, it's, to win

6. want to be

7. join us, enjoy

After I Read B

1. Coach: Congratulations!

2. I am sure that you will do well on the senior team.

3. Good for you!

4. Scottie: Thanks a lot ! I'll do my best!

5. Coach: I know that you are wonderful enough.

6. Don't feel so down, and keep going!

39

7. Michael: Thank you so much! I'll work harder.

Before I Read

1. My heart leaps when I think about these two players.
2. Michael was such a good shot.
3. No one can deny that he was a great player.
4. Michael could make lots of baskets because Scottie helped him a lot.

Let's Write

1. Hello, everyone,
2. We play soccer after school.
3. We practice passing and shooting because it is important to pass and shoot well in soccer.
4. It is also important to have good teamwork.
5. Without good teamwork, it's hard to win the match.
6. Do you want to be a team player?
7. Come, join us and enjoy team play.

적중100

영어 기출 문제집

정답 및 해설

능률 | 양현권

Middle School 2-1

중간고사 완벽대비

적중 100

영어 기출 문제집

중 2

능률 | 양현권

Best Collection

내용문의 중등영어발전소 적중 100 편집부 TEL 070-4416-3636

값 16,000원

9 791133 718580

53370

ISBN 979-11-337-1858-0